P9-APA-813

Macromedia®

Dreamweaver® 4

Illustrated Introductory

Sherry Bishop

COURSE TECHNOLOGY
THOMSON LEARNING™

Australia • Canada • Mexico • Singapore • Spain • United Kingdom • United States

Macromedia® Dreamweaver® 4—Illustrated Introductory

by Sherry Bishop

Managing Editor:
Nicole Jones Pinard

Product Manager:
Rebecca Berardy

Associate Product Manager:
Emeline Elliot

Editorial Assistant:
Christina Garrett

Production Editor:
Danielle Power

Developmental Editor:
Ann Fisher

Composition House:
GEX Publishing Services

QA Manuscript Reviewer:
John Freitas, Jeff Schwartz, Ashlee Welz

Text Designer:
Joseph Lee, Black Fish Design

Cover Designer:
Doug Goodman, Doug Goodman Designs

COPYRIGHT © 2002 Course Technology, a division of Thomson Learning, Inc. Thomson Learning™ is a trademark used herein under license.

Printed in the United States of America

3 4 5 6 7 8 9 BM 04 03 02

For more information, contact Course Technology, 25 Thomson Place, Boston, Massachusetts, 02210.

Or find us on the World Wide Web at: www.course.com

ALL RIGHTS RESERVED. No part of this work covered by the copyright hereon may be reproduced or used in any form or by any means—graphic, electronic, or mechanical, including photocopying, recording, taping, Web distribution, or information storage and retrieval systems—without the written permission of the publisher.

Some of the product names and company names used in this book have been used for identification purposes only and may be trademarks or registered trademarks of their respective manufacturers.

Macromedia Copyright Notice:
Copyright © [1997-2001]. Macromedia, Inc., 600 Townsend Street, San Francisco, CA 94103 USA. All rights reserved.

Macromedia Trademark Notice:
Macromedia and Dreamweaver 4 are trademarks or registered trademarks of Macromedia, Inc. in the United States and/or other countries.

For permission to use material from this text or product, contact us by
Tel (800) 730-2214
Fax (800) 730-2215
www.thomsonrights.com

Disclaimer
Course Technology reserves the right to revise this publication and make changes from time to time in its content without notice.

ISBN 0-619-01819-4

Exciting New Products

Try out Illustrated's New Product Line: Multimedia Tools

Multimedia tools teach students how to create text, graphics, video, animations, and sound, all of which can be incorporated for use in printed materials, Web pages, CD-ROMs, and multimedia presentations.

New Titles

- Adobe Photoshop 6.0—Illustrated Introductory (0-619-04595-7)
- Adobe Illustrator 9.0—Illustrated Introductory (0-619-01750-3)
- Macromedia Director 8 Shockwave Studio—Illustrated Introductory (0-619-01772-4)
- Macromedia Dreamweaver 4—Illustrated Introductory (0-619-01819-4)
- Macromedia Dreamweaver 4—Illustrated Brief (0-619-05724-6)
- Macromedia Director 8 Shockwave Studio—Illustrated Complete (0-619-05658-4)
- Multimedia Concepts—Illustrated Introductory (0-619-01765-1)
- Macromedia Shockwave 8—Illustrated Essentials (0-619-05656-8)
- Macromedia Fireworks 4—Illustrated Essentials (0-619-05657-6)

Check Out Multimedia Concepts

Multimedia Concepts—Illustrated Introductory, by James E. Shuman, is the quick and visual way to learn cutting-edge multimedia concepts. This book studies the growth of multimedia, has an Internet focus in every unit, includes coverage of computer hardware requirements, and teaches students the principles of multimedia design. This book has two hands-on units: Incorporating Multimedia into a Web site and Creating a Multimedia Application Using Macromedia® Director® 8.

This text is organized into eight units. In these units students learn how to plan and create a Web site; plan Web page layout and set Web page properties; format text; create and apply cascading style sheets; create and manage Web site links; format and create tables; and create frames and layers. This CD also includes a time-limited trial version of Macromedia® Director® 8 to give students the tools they need to practice creating multimedia movies.

Enhance any Illustrated Text with these Exciting Products

Course Technology offers a continuum of solutions to meet your online learning needs. Three Distance Learning solutions enhance your classroom experience: MyCourse.com (hosted by Course Technology), Blackboard, and WebCT.

MyCourse.com is an easily customizable online syllabus and course enhancement tool. This tool adds value to your class by offering brand new content designed to reinforce what you are already teaching. MyCourse.com even allows you to add your own content, hyperlinks, and assignments.

WebCT and Blackboard are course management tools that deliver online content for eighty-five Course Technology titles. This growing list of titles enables instructors the ability to edit and add to any content made available through WebCT and Blackboard. In addition, you can choose what students access. The site is hosted on your school campus, allowing complete control over the information. WebCT and Blackboard offer their own internal communication system, including internal e-mail, Bulletin Boards, and Chat rooms. For more information please contact your Course Technology sales representative.

Create Your Ideal Course Package with CourseKits™

If one book doesn't offer all the coverage you need, create a course package that does. With Course Technology's CourseKits—our mix-and-match approach to selecting texts—you have the freedom to combine products from more than one series. When you choose any two or more Course Technology products for one course, we'll discount the price and package them together so your students can pick up one convenient bundle at the bookstore.

Preface

Welcome to *Macromedia Dreamweaver 4—Illustrated Introductory*. This highly visual book offers users a hands-on introduction to Macromedia® Dreamweaver® 4 and also serves as an excellent reference for future use.

This book is a member of Illustrated's **Multimedia Tools** series. These books teach students how to create text, graphics, video, animations, and sound for use in print publications, CD-ROM products, and Web-based applications. Check out books on Photoshop, Illustrator, and Multimedia Concepts for more multimedia curriculum.

▶ Organization and Coverage

This text is organized into eight units. In these units students learn how to plan and create a Web site; plan Web page layout and set page properties; format text; create and apply cascading style sheets; use and manage graphics; create and manage Web site links; format and create tables; and work with frames.

▶ About this Approach

What makes the Illustrated approach so effective at teaching software skills? It's quite simple. Each skill is presented on two facing pages, with the step-by-step instructions on the left page, and large screen illustrations on the right. Students can focus on a single skill without having to turn the page. This unique design makes information extremely accessible and easy to absorb, and provides a great reference for after the course is over. This hands-on approach also makes it ideal for both self-paced or instructor-led classes.

Each lesson, or "information display," contains the following elements:

Each 2-page spread focuses on a single skill.

Clear step-by-step directions explain how to complete the specific task, with what students are to type in green. When students follow the numbered steps, they quickly learn how each procedure is performed and what the results will be.

Concise text that introduces the basic principles discussed in the lesson. Procedures are easier to learn when concepts fit into a framework.

Dreamweaver 4

Adding New Pages to a Web Site

Web sites may be as small as one page or contain hundreds of pages. New pages are named and added to the Web site folder structure in the root folder, and then content, such as text and graphics, is added to them. It is better to add as many pages as you think you will need in the beginning, rather than wait until you are ready to design them. This will enable you to set up the navigation structure of the Web site, and view how each page is linked to others. When you are satisfied with the overall structure, you can then create the content for the pages. After consulting your storyboard, you create new Web pages to add to the TripSmart Web site. You create new pages called products, services, packages, newsletter, clothing, and accessories, and place them in the root folder.

Steps

1. Click the **Show Site icon** on the status bar to open the Site window
   You create new pages for a Web site using the Site window.
2. Click the **plus sign** to the left of the assets folder to open the folder and view its contents
   The tripsmart.gif file is in the assets folder, as shown in Figure B-13.
3. Click **File** on the menu bar, then click **New File**, type **products.htm** in the filename text box to replace untitled.htm, then press **[Enter]**
   The products page is added to the Web site.
4. Repeat Step 3 to add the five more blank pages to the TripSmart Web site, and name the new files **services.htm**, **packages.htm**, **newsletter.htm**, **clothing.htm**, and **accessories.htm**
   The new pages are listed in the tripsmart root folder, as shown in Figure B-14.

QuickTip
If you create a new file in the Site window, you must type the filename extension (.htm or .html) manually.

1. Click the **Show Site icon** on the status bar to open the Site window
   You create new pages for a Web site using the Site window.
2. Click ▶ to the left of the assets folder to open the folder and view its contents
   The tripsmart.gif file is in the assets folder, as shown in Figure B-13.
3. Click **Site** on the menu bar, point to **Site Files View**, then click **New File**, type **products.htm** in the filename text box to replace untitled.html, then press **[return]**
   The products page is added to the Web site.
4. Repeat Step 3 to add the five more blank pages to the TripSmart Web site, and name the new files **services.htm**, **packages.htm**, **newsletter.htm**, **clothing.htm**, and **accessories.htm**
   The new pages are listed in the tripsmart root folder, as shown in Figure B-14.

Navigation structure
When creating a Web site, an important consideration is how your viewers will navigate, or move from page to page within the site. The navigation structure includes links that can be displayed as tabulated text, tables, graphics, or an image map. The navigation structure, whether text, buttons, or icons, should have a consistent look among all pages in the site. Otherwise, the viewer may become confused or lost within the site. Every page should have a link back to the home page. It's also a good idea to include back and forward links to take the viewer to the previous or next page in the site, instead of relying on the viewer to use the Back button on the browser toolbar.

▶ DREAMWEAVER B-12 CREATING A WEB SITE

Hints as well as trouble-shooting advice, right where you need it – next to the step itself.

Design Matters help students apply smart design principles to their Web sites. Each Design Matters deals exclusively with design considerations for Web pages or Web sites, such as ease of use, navigation, and appeal.

Additional Features

The two-page lesson format featured in this book provides the new user with a powerful learning experience. Additionally, this book contains the following features:

- **Trial Software**
  At the back of this book, you will find a CD-ROM containing a trial version of Macromedia® Dreamweaver® 4 for both Macintosh and Windows operating systems. Students can use this software to gain additional practice away from the classroom. *Note:* The trial software will cease operating after 30 days. Check the Read Me on the CD-ROM for more information.
- **Dual Platform**
  The text in this book can be completed on either a Macintosh or Windows operating system. (Mac) and (Win) is included next to any step where differences occur, and Mac and Win icons also split lessons when more explanation is needed for both platforms.
- **Real-World Case**
  The case study used throughout the textbook, a fictitious company called TripSmart, is designed to be "real-world" in nature and introduces the kinds of activities that students will encounter when working with Dreamweaver. With a real-world case, the process of solving problems will be more meaningful to students.
- **End-of-Unit Material**
  Each unit concludes with a Concepts Review that tests students' understanding of what they learned in the unit. The Concepts Review is followed by a Skills Review, which provides students with additional hands-on practice of the skills. The Skills Review is followed by Independent Challenges, which pose case problems for students to solve. At least one independent challenge in each unit, the E-Quest, asks students to use the World Wide Web to find information to complete a project or to research topics related to the unit. A Design Quest is the fifth independent challenge in the unit. It directs students to Web sites and asks them to evaluate effective design elements from each site. The Visual Workshop follows the Independent Challenges and helps students develop critical thinking skills. Students are shown completed Web pages or screens and are asked to recreate them from scratch.

Every lesson features large-size, full-color representations of what the students' screen should look like after completing the numbered steps.

FIGURE B-13: Site window showing the tripsmart.gif in the assets folder

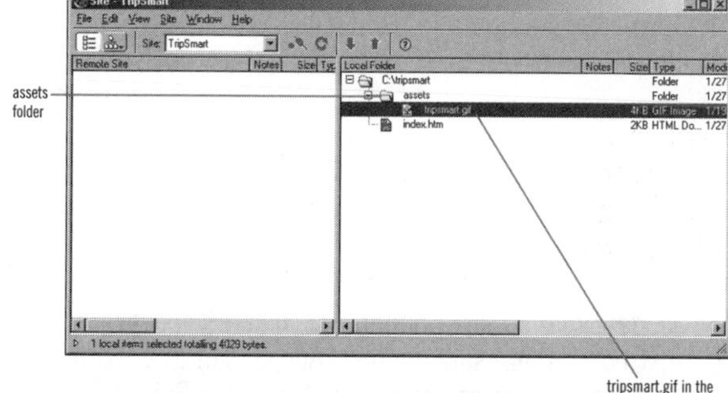

assets folder

tripsmart.gif in the assets folder

FIGURE B-14: New pages added to the TripSmart Web site

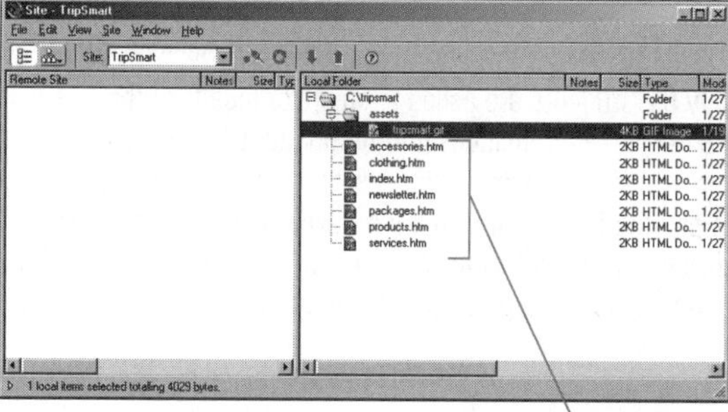

New pages added to the tripsmart root folder (the order of your pages may differ)

Dreamweaver 4

CLUES TO USE

Using the Site window for file management

Using the Site window, you can add, delete, move, or rename files and folders in a Web site. It is very important that you perform these file maintenance tasks in the Site window rather than in Windows Explorer (Win) or at the Finder level (Mac). If you make changes to the Web site folder structure outside of the Site window, Dreamweaver will not recognize these changes. You use Windows Explorer (Win) or the Finder (Mac) to create the original root folder or to move or copy the root folder of a Web site to another location. If you move or copy the root folder to a new location, you will have to define the Web site again in Dreamweaver, as you did in the lesson on defining a Web site.

CREATING A WEB SITE DREAMWEAVER B-13

The page numbers are designed like a road map. B indicates the fourth unit and 13 indicates the page within the unit.

Instructor's Resource Kit

The Instructor's Resource Kit is Course Technology's way of putting the resources and information needed to teach and learn effectively into your hands. With an integrated array of teaching and learning tools that offers you and your students a broad range of technology-based instructional options, we believe this kit represents the highest quality and most cutting edge resources available to instructors today. Many of these resources are available at **www.course.com**. The resources available with this book are:

ExamView This textbook is accompanied by ExamView, a powerful testing software package that allows instructors to create and administer printed, computer (LAN-based), and Internet exams. ExamView includes hundreds of questions that correspond to the topics covered in this text, enabling students to generate detailed study guides that include page references for further review. The computer-based and Internet testing components allow students to take exams at their computers, and also save the instructor time by grading each exam automatically.

Instructor's Manual Available as an electronic file, the Instructor's Manual is quality-assurance tested and includes unit overviews, detailed lecture topics for each unit with teaching tips, an Upgrader's Guide, solutions to all lessons and end-of-unit material, and extra Independent Challenges. The Instructor's Manual is available on the Instructor's Resource Kit CD-ROM or you can download it from **www.course.com**.

Course Faculty Online Companion You can browse this textbook's password-protected site to obtain the Instructor's Manual, Solution Files, Project Files, and any updates to the text. Contact your Customer Service Representative for the site address and password.

Project Files Project Files contain all of the data that students will use to complete the lessons and end-of-unit material. A Readme file includes instructions for using the files. Adopters of this text are granted the right to install the Project Files on any standalone computer or network. The Project Files are available on the Instructor's Resource Kit CD-ROM, the Review Pack, and can also be downloaded from **www.course.com**.

Solution Files Solution Files contain every file students are asked to create or modify in the lessons and end of-unit material. A Help file on the Instructor's Resource Kit includes information for using the Solution Files.

Figure Files The figures in the text are provided on the Instructor's Resourse Kit CD to help you illustrate key topics or concepts. You can create traditional overhead transparencies by printing the figure files. Or you can create electronic slide shows by using the figures in a presentation program such as PowerPoint.

Author's Vision

There are few fields of study more creative or stimulating than multimedia and Web design. It has been a joy to write a textbook about Dreamweaver, the Web designer's dream program. If this is your first experience with Dreamweaver, you are in for the ride of your life. I have never worked with such an exciting program.

My goals for writing this book were similar to my goals as a classroom teacher. I hoped to create a book that:

- Stimulates the senses and stretches the mind
- Transfers my excitement for Dreamweaver
- Incorporates basic design principles
- Makes learning fun
- Creates a desire to experiment and learn more

ACKNOWLEDGMENTS

There is not enough available space to thank the many individuals who have guided and encouraged me. The Illustrated Team is the best. I owe much to Nicole Pinard for offering me this project and helping me believe in myself. Rebecca Berardy was my constant encourager and problem solver. I will miss my daily talks and e-mails with an amazing editor, Ann Fisher. John Freitas, Jeff Schwartz, and Ashlee Welz patiently tested each file and offered insightful suggestions for improvement. Danielle Power, the Production Editor, guided the pages throughout the production process. My heartfelt thanks go to each of you and to everyone behind the scenes that I did not have the pleasure of "meeting."

Two key players were Dr. Virginia Brouch and Jeff Diamond, the textbook reviewers, whose expertise immeasurably raised the quality of this book. My heartfelt thanks are offered to both of them.

Lastly, I want to thank my family and friends, all of whom have encouraged me along the way. You will meet them, as they are sprinkled like angels throughout these pages. Special thanks go to my husband, Don, who ate more cereal the last four months than he has during most of his adult life—he never complained once.

Brief Contents

Contents

Contents

Contents

Read This Before You Begin

Project Files

To complete the lessons and end-of-unit material in this book, you need to obtain the necessary project files. Please refer to the directions on the front cover for various methods to obtain these files. Once obtained, select where to store the files, such as the hard drive, a network server, or a Zip drive. The instructions in the lessons will refer to "the drive and folder where your Project Files are stored" when referring to both the Project Files for the book and the Web files you create during the lessons and end-of-unit material.

When opening a file from the Projects Files folder to import into a Web site, it is necessary to check all internal links, including those to graphic images, and remove all absolute path references. For example: if a page with the TripSmart logo is opened and saved in the TripSmart Web site:

1. Click the image on the page to select it.
2. Use the Property Inspector to check the Src text box.
3. The Src text box should read assets/tripsmart.gif.
4. If the Src text box has a longer path the extra characters should be removed.

   Example: file:/d:/project_files/Unit_H/assets/tripsmart.gif should be changed to assets/tripsmart.gif
5. Save the file with the same name, overwriting the original file.

Dreamweaver for Windows and Macintosh

This book is written for the Windows version and the Macintosh version of Macromedia Dreamweaver 4. Both versions of the software are virtually the same, but there are a few platform differences. When there are differences between the two versions of the software, steps written specifically for the Windows version end with the notation (Win) and steps for the Macintosh version end with the notation (Mac). In instances when the lessons are split between the two operating systems, a line divides the page and is accompanied by Mac and Win icons.

Creating Web sites that have not been built through previous consecutive units (Windows)

If you begin an assignment that requires a Web site that you did not create or maintain before this unit, you will need to perform the following steps:

1. Copy the solution files folder from the preceding unit for the Web site you wish to create onto the hard drive, Zip drive, or a high-density floppy disk. For example, if you are working on Unit E, you will need the solution files folder from Unit D. Your instructor will furnish this folder to you.
2. Start Dreamweaver and show the Site window by clicking the Show Site icon on the Launcher bar or status bar.
3. Click Site on the menu bar, then click Define Sites.
4. Click New to display the Site Definition for Unnamed Site 1 dialog box.
5. Type the name you want to use for your Web site in the Site Name text box. Spaces and upper case letters are allowed in the Site name.
6. Click the Browse for File icon (folder) next to the Local Root Folder text box.
7. Click the drive and folder where your solution files folder is placed to locate the local root folder. The local root folder contains the name of the Web site you are working on. For example, the local root folder for the TripSmart Web site is called tripsmart.
8. Double-click the local root folder, click Select, then click OK to close the Site Definition for Unnamed Site 1 dialog box.
9. A dialog box appears stating that the "Initial site cache will now be created. This scans the files in your site and starts tracking links as you change them." Click OK to accept this message.
10. Click Done to close the Define Sites dialog box.

11. Click index.htm in the Local Folder list of the Site window to select it.
12. Click Site on the menu bar, then click Set as Home Page.

Creating Web sites that have not been built through previous consecutive units (Macintosh)

If you begin an assignment that requires a Web site that you did not create or maintain before this unit, you will need to perform the following steps:

1. Copy the solution files folder from the preceding unit for the Web site you wish to create onto the hard drive, Zip drive, or a high-density floppy disk. For example, if you are working on Unit E, you will need the solution files folder from Unit D. Your instructor will furnish this folder to you.
2. Start Dreamweaver and show the Site window by clicking the Show Site icon on the Launcher bar or status bar.
3. Click Site on the menu bar, then click Define Sites.
4. Click New to display the Site Definition for Unnamed Site 1 dialog box.
5. Type the name you want to use for your Web site in the Site Name text box. Spaces and upper case letters are allowed in the Site name.
6. Click the Browse for File icon (folder) next to the Local Root Folder text box,
7. Click the drive and folder where your solution files folder is placed to locate the local root folder. The local root folder contains the name of the Web site you are working on. For example, the local root folder for the TripSmart Web site is called tripsmart.
8. Click the local root folder, click Choose, then click OK to close the Site Definition for Unnamed Site 1 dialog box.
9. A dialog box appears stating that the "Initial site cache will now be created. This scans the files in your site and starts tracking links as you change them." Click OK to accept this message.
10. Click Done to close the Define Sites dialog box.
11. Click index.htm in the Local Folder list of the Site window to select it.
12. Click Site on the menu bar, point to Site Map View, then click Set as Home Page.

Free 30-day Trial Software

Included on a CD with this book is the Macromedia® Dreamweaver® 4 30-day Trial Software. The trial software is for your use away from the classroom, and it should not be used in a classroom lab because it will expire after 30 days. Please check the CD for more information.

Installation instructions for the CD-ROM are included below.

Windows. Insert the CD in the CD-ROM drive, open Windows Explorer, select the CD-ROM drive, double-click the Dreamweaver4 TBYB.exe in the right pane of Windows Explorer, then follow the on-screen instructions to complete the installation.

Macintosh. Insert the CD in the CD-ROM drive, double-click the CD icon titled Dreamweaver4TBYB.sea, then follow the on-screen instructions to complete the installation.

Browsers

We recommend using Microsoft Internet Explorer 5.5 or higher or Netscape Navigator 4.7 or higher for browser output.

The Internet as a learning tool

This book uses the Internet to provide real-life examples in the lessons and end of unit exercises. Because the Internet is constantly changing to display current information, some of the links used and described in the book may be deleted or modified before the book is even published. If this happens, searching the referenced Web sites will usually locate similar information in a slightly modified form. In some cases, entire Web sites may move. Technical problems with Web servers may also prevent access to Web sites or Web pages temporarily. Patience, critical thinking skills, and creativity are necessary whenever the Internet is being used in the classroom.

Getting Started with Macromedia Dreamweaver 4

Objectives

- Define Web design software
- Start Dreamweaver 4
- View the Dreamweaver work area
- Open a Web page and insert an image
- Save a Web page
- Get Help
- View a Web page in a browser window
- Close a Web page and exit Dreamweaver

Dreamweaver is a Web design program used to create multimedia-rich Web pages and Web sites. Dreamweaver's easy-to-use dialog boxes, panels, and tools let you create sophisticated features such as animations and interactive forms. Dreamweaver integrates seamlessly with other text editors so you don't have to be concerned with conflicting HTML code. In this unit, you will learn to start Dreamweaver and examine the work area. Next, you will open a Web page, save a Web page, and learn how to use Dreamweaver's Help feature. Finally, you will close a Web page and exit Dreamweaver. You have recently been hired as an intern at TripSmart, a full-service travel outfitter that specializes in travel products and services. You have been assigned to the Web development team to work on the company's Web site. You begin by familiarizing yourself with Dreamweaver, the Web design software of choice for TripSmart.

Dreamweaver 4

Defining Web Design Software

Dreamweaver is a Web design program. A **Web design program** allows you to create dynamic interactive Web pages incorporating many types of components, such as text, images, hyperlinks, animation, sounds, and video. You can create some components for your Web page in Dreamweaver, or you can import them from other software programs. Dreamweaver files are saved with the .htm extension (Win) or the .html extension (Mac), indicating that Dreamweaver files are HTML documents. **HTML** is the acronym for Hypertext Markup Language, the language used to create Web pages. You begin your first day as an intern by learning about some of Dreamweaver's basic features:

Using Dreamweaver you can:

- **Create new Web pages or new Web sites**

  Dreamweaver lets you create new Web pages or new Web sites, depending on your project needs. You can also import Web pages created in other programs to edit them in Dreamweaver or to incorporate them into an existing Web site.

- **Add text, images, tables, and multimedia files**

  You can add text, images, tables, and multimedia files to a Dreamweaver Web page by using the Objects panel. The **Objects panel** contains icons for creating or inserting many types of objects, such as tables, images, forms, frames, and layers. Using the Objects panel, you can also insert elements made with other Macromedia software programs, including Fireworks, Flash, and Shockwave.

- **Use organizational tools**

  Design Notes is a feature that allows you to record notes to yourself and to other team members concerning the details of the project you are working on. Using Design Notes is a handy way to remind yourself of tasks that need to be completed for a Web site. Design Notes are not part of the HTML source code that can be viewed by others. **Check In/Check Out** is another organizational feature that keeps track of which files in the Web site are currently "checked out" by other team members.

QuickTip

Information in the Property Inspector changes to reflect the options available for the type of object that is currently selected.

- **Use the Property Inspector to add and manage hyperlinks**

  Hyperlinks, also known as links, are graphics or text on a Web page that, when clicked, take you to another location on the page, another Web page in the same Web site, or to a Web page in a different Web site. Dreamweaver makes adding and editing your links easy through the use of the Property Inspector. The **Property Inspector** is a panel that displays the properties of the currently selected object on the page. Figure A-1 shows a Web page open in Dreamweaver. The properties of the highlighted text can be seen in the Property Inspector.

- **Use Roundtrip HTML**

  Roundtrip HTML means that HTML files created in other programs, such as Microsoft FrontPage, can be opened in Dreamweaver without Dreamweaver adding additional coding, such as meta tags or spaces. Conversely, you can open and edit a file created in Dreamweaver in other Web design software programs such as Microsoft FrontPage. You can be confident that your HTML code will be able to "travel" between programs without coding problems. Pages being edited in Dreamweaver are displayed as **WYSIWYG**, which stands for "What You See Is What You Get." As you design a Web page in Dreamweaver, you are seeing the page exactly as it will appear in a browser window. A **browser**, such as Microsoft Internet Explorer or Netscape Navigator, is software that is used to display Web pages in a Web site.

- **Manage Web sites**

  The site-management feature of Dreamweaver lets you manage the pages within a Web site, ensuring that all links work properly. As a Web site grows quickly with the addition of new pages, this becomes a very important feature. An example of a site-management tool is the **Site Map**, a graphical representation of how the pages relate to each other within a Web site.

FIGURE A-1: Web page open in Dreamweaver

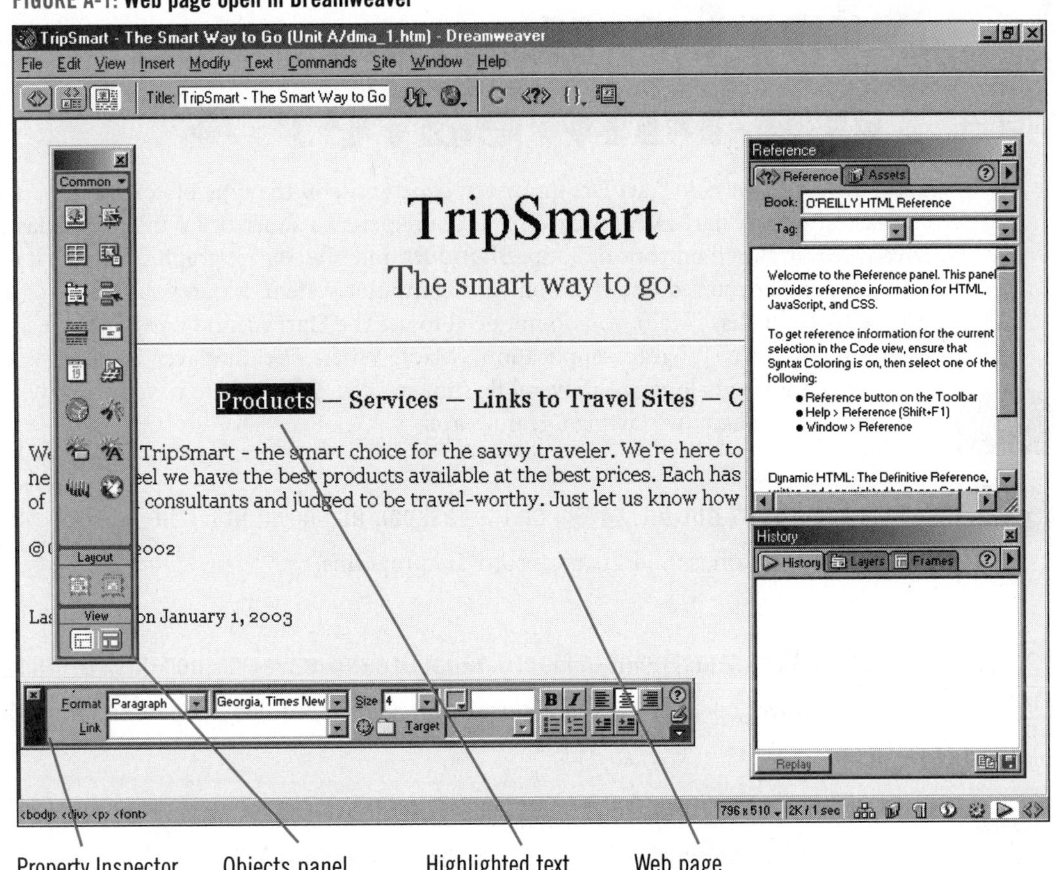

Dreamweaver 4

Cleaning up HTML

Dreamweaver comes with two features for "cleaning up" HTML code. **Clean up HTML** and **Clean up Word HTML** (for files created in Microsoft Word) can be used to remove undesirable or unnecessary code, such as proprietary remarks or extra spaces. Unnecessary coding is considered sloppy and uses valuable memory. A good goal to have when writing HTML is to use the smallest amount of code possible. This ensures smaller file sizes, which download faster than larger ones.

Dreamweaver 4

Starting Dreamweaver 4

There are many ways to start Dreamweaver, depending on the type of computer you are using. The fastest way to start Dreamweaver is to double-click a shortcut (Win) or an alias (Mac) for Dreamweaver placed on your desktop. **Shortcuts** and **aliases** are graphic icons that represent a software program stored elsewhere on your computer system. When you double-click a shortcut (Win) or an alias (Mac), you do not need to use the Start menu (Win) or open a lot of windows to find your program application (Mac). When Dreamweaver is open, a document window is displayed along with several floating panels. You have been given your first assignment and begin by starting Dreamweaver.

1. Click the **Start button** on the taskbar, as shown in Figure A-2

   The Start button is used to access software programs.

Trouble?

Your Start menu may list different programs than those shown in Figure A-2.

2. Point to **Programs**, point to **Macromedia Dreamweaver 4**, then click **Dreamweaver 4**

   Dreamweaver opens, and a blank document, named Untitled-1, opens in the work area.

1. Double-click the **hard drive icon**, as shown in Figure A-3

   The hard drive icon is in the upper-right corner of the desktop.

Trouble?

Your Dreamweaver folder may be in another folder called Applications. See your instructor or technical support person if you have trouble locating Dreamweaver.

2. Double-click the **Macromedia Dreamweaver 4 folder**

   The Macromedia Dreamweaver folder contains the Dreamweaver 4 program icon.

3. Double-click the **Dreamweaver 4 program icon**

   Dreamweaver opens, and a blank document, named Untitled-1, opens in the work area.

FIGURE A-2: Starting Dreamweaver 4 (Windows)

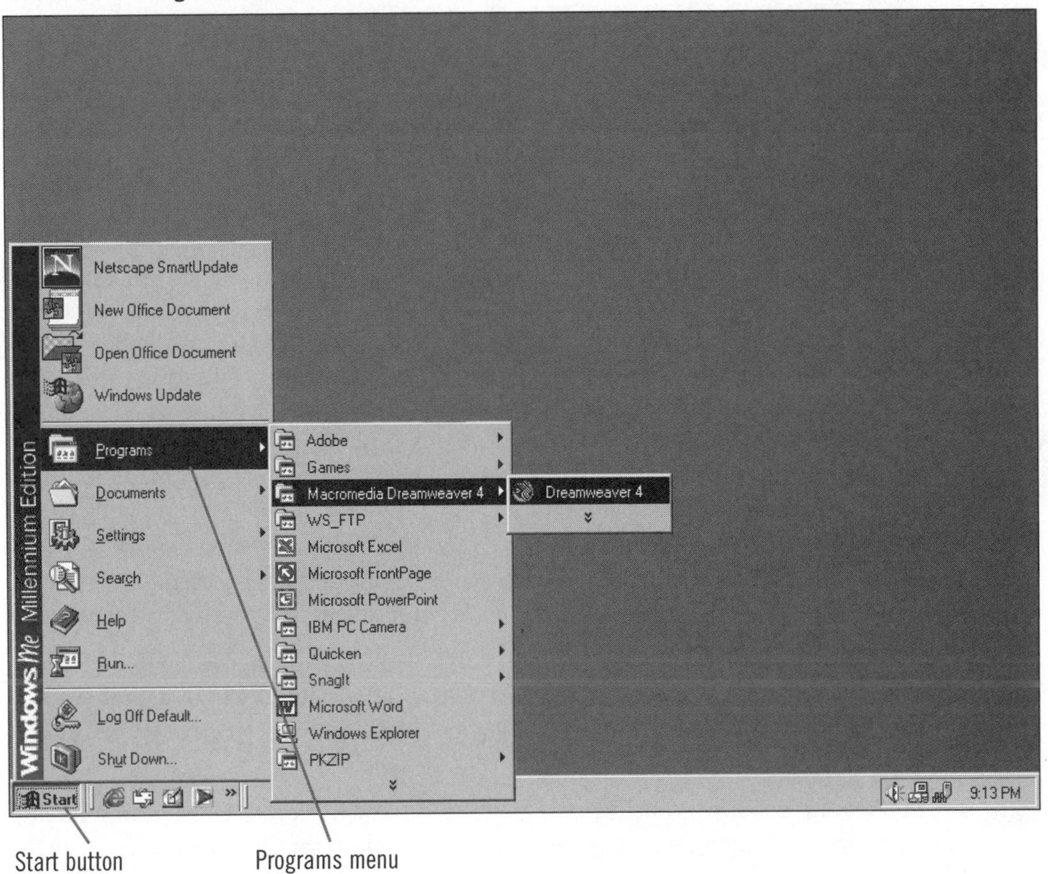

FIGURE A-3: Starting Dreamweaver 4 (Macintosh)

Dreamweaver 4

Dreamweaver 4

Viewing the Dreamweaver Work Area

The **work area** is made up of the document window, the menu bar, the toolbar, inspectors, and panels. The work area is the white area in the program window where Web pages are created and edited. **Inspectors** are floating palettes that display the properties of the currently selected object. Inspectors allow you to view an object's properties and make formatting changes quickly and easily, without having to access menus. **Panels** are also floating palettes, containing icons for activating Dreamweaver features and commands. You spend some time familiarizing yourself with the Dreamweaver work area. Use Figure A-4 to find the following elements.

Details

- The **title bar** displays the name of the program (Dreamweaver), the name of the file, and the title of the open page enclosed in parentheses. The title bar also includes buttons for closing, minimizing, and resizing the window in the upper-left or upper-right corner, depending on which type of computer you are using.
- The **menu bar**, located at the top of the document window, lists the names of the menus that contain Dreamweaver commands. Many menu items can be accessed by using shortcut keys or by clicking corresponding icons on the various panels.
- The **toolbar** contains icons for changing the current work mode of Dreamweaver, previewing Web pages, debugging Web pages, and accessing options for file management. The toolbar icons are listed in Table A-1.
- The **Objects panel** contains icons that allow you to insert objects, such as images, tables, and horizontal rules. When you insert an object, a dialog box will open, giving you a choice of parameters about the object being inserted. You can also insert an object by dragging an icon from the Objects panel to the document window.
- The **Property Inspector** displays the properties of the selected object on a Web page. You can change an object's properties using the text boxes, drop-down menus, and icons on the Property Inspector. The contents of the Property Inspector vary according to the object currently selected.
- The **Launcher bar** contains icons that open Dreamweaver panels, inspectors, and windows. It is normally displayed on the right end of the **status bar**, but can also be displayed as a separate panel. The status bar is displayed at the bottom of the Dreamweaver window. The left end of the status bar displays the HTML tags being used at the current insertion point.
- **Panels**, such as the Frames, Layers, and Timelines panels, are accessed through the Window menu. Panels can be **docked** if desired, meaning that they can be grouped with other panels. Docking panels keeps your work area less cluttered. When two or more panels are docked, you can access the panel you want by clicking its name tab.

Trouble?

If you do not see the toolbar, click View on the menu bar, then click Toolbar.

FIGURE A-4: The Dreamweaver work area

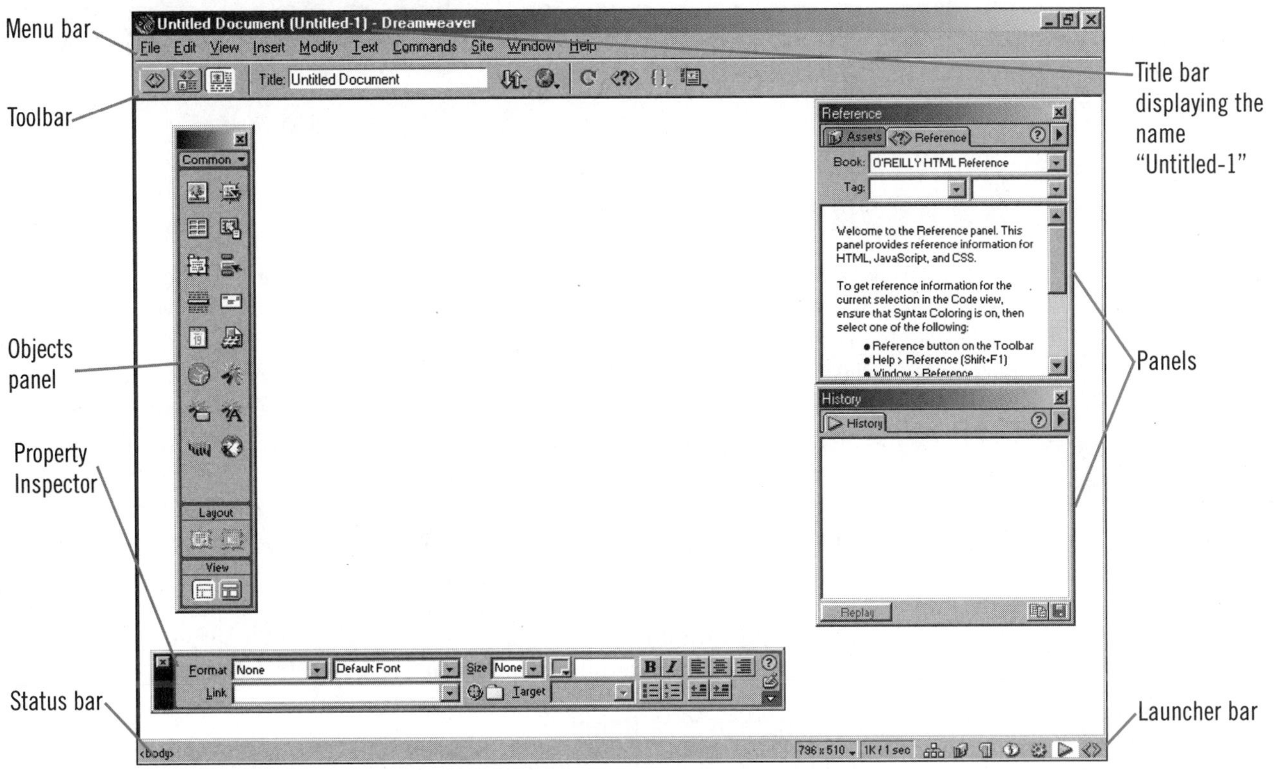

TABLE A-1: Toolbar icons

icon	name	function
	Show Code View	Displays only the Code View in the Document window
	Show Design View	Displays only the Design View in the Document window
	Show Code and Design Views	Displays both the Code and Design Views
	File Management	Displays file management options
	Preview/Debug in Browser	Activates the browser for viewing the page
	Refresh Design View	Will force the browser to reread the page to view changes made in editing
	Reference	Activates the Reference panel
	View Options	Activates the Options menu
	Code Navigation	Allows you to navigate through the source code

Dreamweaver views

Dreamweaver has three working views. Design View shows a full-screen layout and is primarily used when designing and creating a Web page. Code View shows a full screen with the HTML code for the page and is used whenever it is desirable to read or directly edit the code. Code and Design View is a combination of the Code View and the Design View. This view is the most helpful for debugging or correcting errors on the page, because you can see both views simultaneously.

Dreamweaver 4

Opening a Web Page and Inserting an Image

After opening Dreamweaver, you can create a new Web site, create a new Web page, or open an existing Web site or Web page. The first Web page that is displayed when a Web site is accessed is referred to as the home page. The **home page** sets the look and feel of the Web site and contains a navigation structure that directs the viewer to the rest of the pages in the Web site. Images can be easily inserted into new or existing pages by using the Insert menu or the Objects panel. The Design department has designed a new logo for TripSmart. You open the TripSmart home page and insert the new logo for everyone to view.

Steps

1. Click **File** on the menu **bar**, then click **Open**
   The Open dialog box opens. See Figure A-5 (Win) or A-6 (Mac).
2. Click the **Look in list arrow** (Win) or (Mac), double-click the drive and folder where your Project Files are stored, then double-click the **Unit A folder**
3. Click **dma_1.htm**, then click **Open**
   The document called dma_1.htm opens in the work area.
4. With the insertion point at the top of the page, Click **Insert** on the menu bar, click **Image**, double-click the **assets** folder to open it, click **tripsmart.gif**, then click **Select** (Win) or **Open** (Mac)
   The TripSmart logo appears at the top-left corner of the Web page.

QuickTip

You can also double-click a file to open it or click File on the menu bar, then click one of the recent files listed at the bottom of the menu.

FIGURE A-5: Open dialog box (Windows)

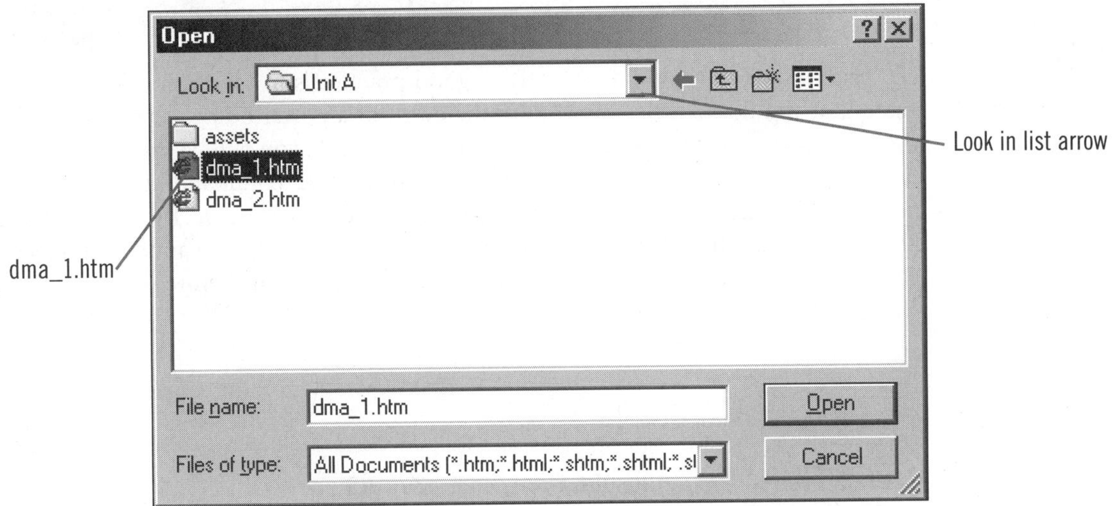

FIGURE A-6: Open dialog box (Macintosh)

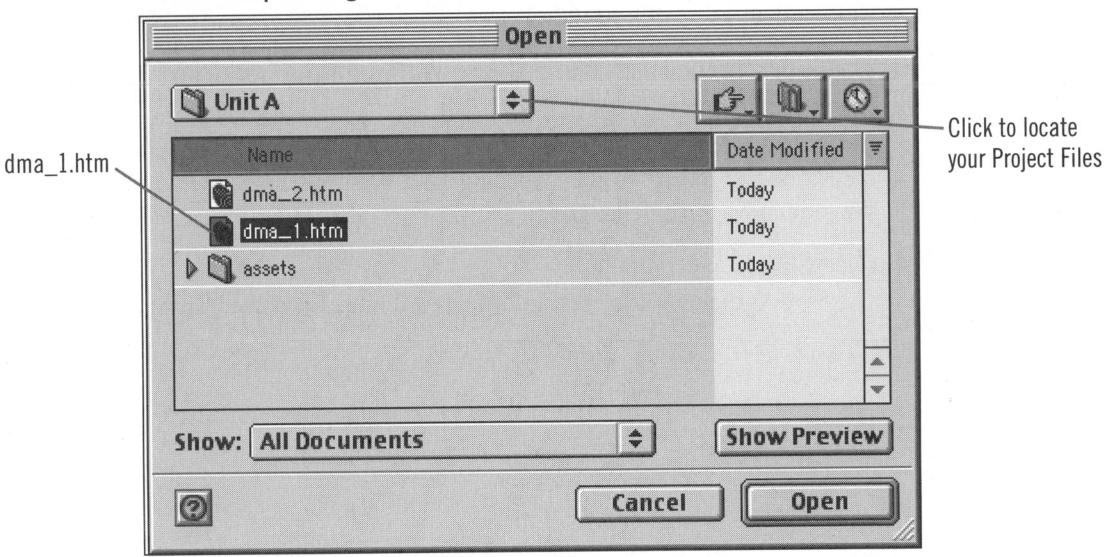

Docked panels

If a panel blocks part of your work area, you can move it to a different area on the screen by dragging the panel title bar. The panel title bar is the blue area (Win) or the dotted gray area (Mac) at the top or on the left side of each panel. You can also group panels together by docking them to each other. To dock a panel, drag the panel tab you want to dock directly on top of the panel that you want to dock it to. To activate a docked panel, simply click its name tab. To undock a panel, drag its name tab away from the panel it is grouped to. The Launcher, Property Inspector, and Site window cannot be docked.

FIGURE A-7: Docked panels

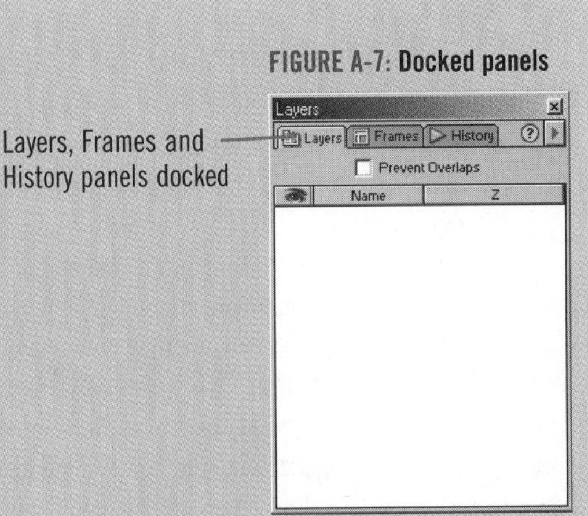

Saving a Web Page

It is wise to save your work frequently. A good practice is to save every five or ten minutes to insure that you do not lose any work in the event of a power outage or computer problem. To save your work, you use the Save command. In this book, you will be instructed to use the Save As command after you open each Project File. The Save As command duplicates the open document and requires you to give the new document a different name. By duplicating the Project Files, you will be able to repeat an exercise or start a lesson over again if you make a mistake. You decide to save your Web page with a unique name before you continue working.

1. Click **File** on the menu bar, then click **Save As**
   The Save As dialog box opens.
2. Click the **Save in list arrow** (Win) or [icon] (Mac), then click the drive and folder where your Project Files are stored
3. Type **index** in the File name text box (Win) or in the Name text box (Mac) to name the file, as shown in Figures A-8 and A-9
   If you are working on a Macintosh computer, .html is the default extension that is placed in the Name text box. If you are working on a Windows computer, .htm is the default extension added when you click Save.
4. Click **Save**
   The Save As dialog box closes, and the new document name appears in the title bar.

QuickTip

If a filename already appears in the File name text box (Win) or the Name text box (Mac), highlight the existing filename then type a new name to replace the current one.

Choosing filenames

When you choose a name for a Web file, you should use a descriptive name that reflects the contents of the file. For example, if the page is about a company's products, it could be named "*products*". You will also need to follow some general rules for naming Web pages. For example, the **home page**, or the page that first opens when you go to a Web site, should be named **index**. This is a basic naming convention. Most file servers look for the file named index to use as the initial page for a Web site. Files are saved with the default filename extension of **.htm** (Win) and **.html** (Mac or UNIX). Do not use spaces, special characters, or punctuation in Web page filenames or the names of any graphics that will be inserted in your Web site. Spaces in filenames can cause errors when a browser attempts to read a file, and they may cause your graphics to load incorrectly. Another rule is not to use a number for the first character of a filename. **To ensure that everything will load properly on all platforms, including UNIX, assume the filenames are case-sensitive and use lowercase characters.**

FIGURE A-8: **Save As dialog box (Windows)**

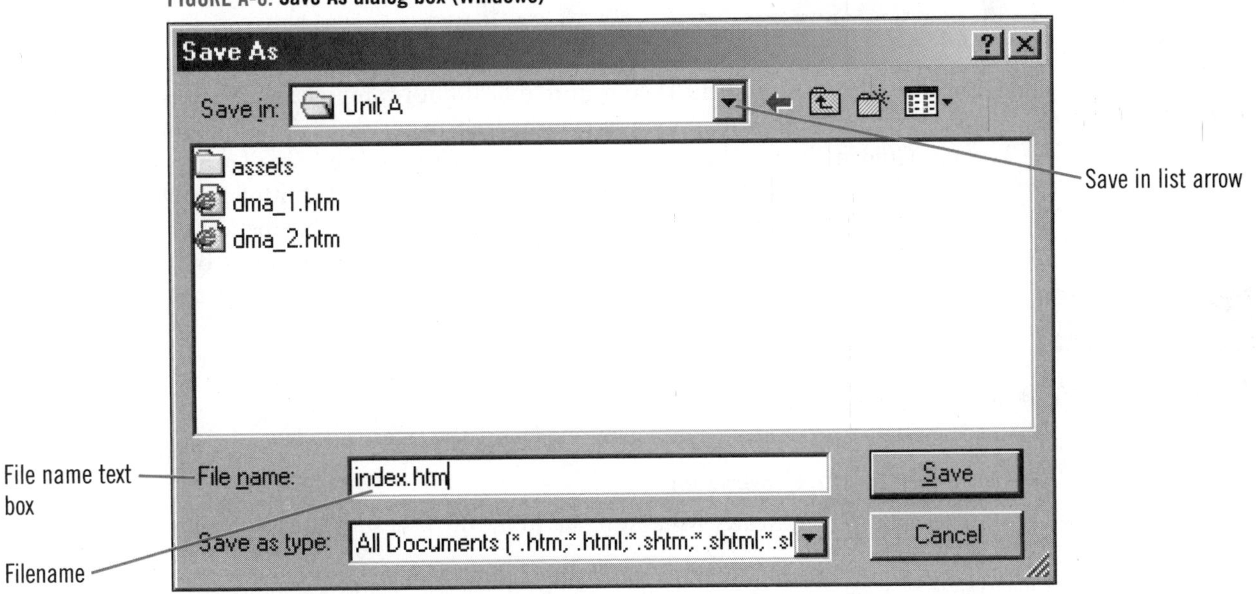

FIGURE A-9: **Save As dialog box (Macintosh)**

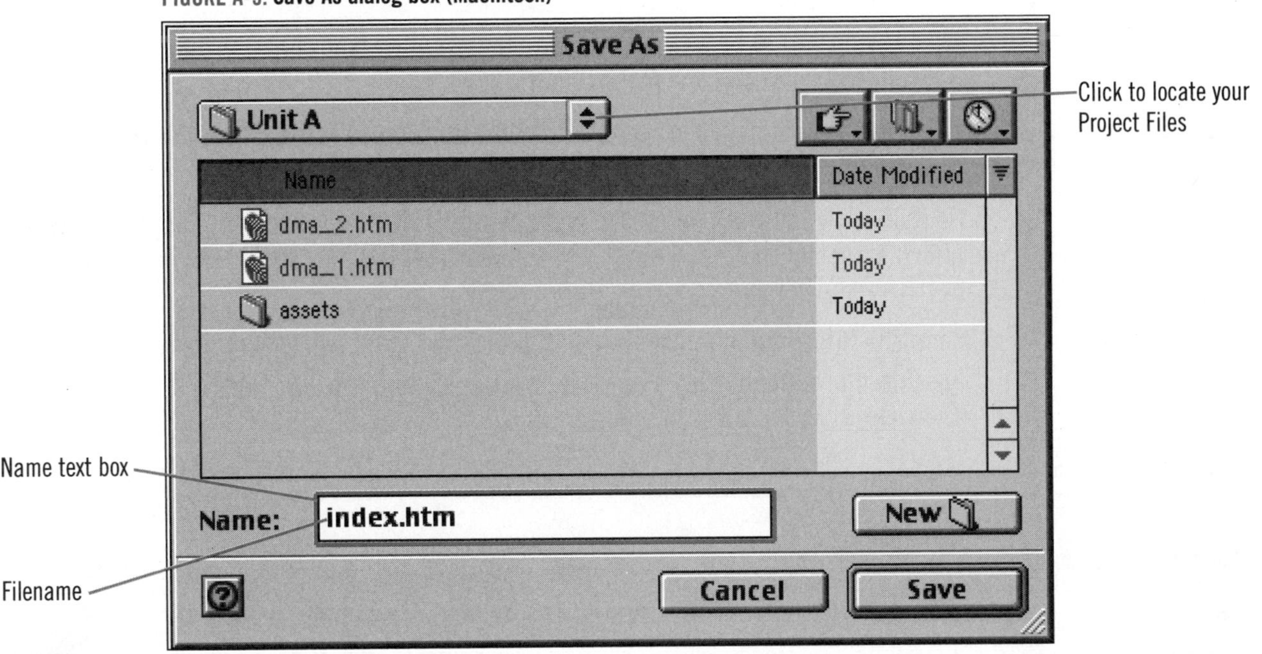

CLUES TO USE

Choosing filename extensions

When you save a Dreamweaver document for the first time, you are prompted to give the document a new name in the Save As dialog box. The extension .htm or .html is automatically added to the document's name. If you are working on a Windows computer, the default filename extension is .htm. If you are working on a Macintosh computer, the default is .html. You can choose which filename extension you want added to your document names, by clicking Edit on the menu bar, clicking Preferences, then changing the current extension in the text box next to Add Extension when Saving in the General category of the Preferences dialog box. Preferences are settings that you can modify to customize your working environment in Dreamweaver. You can also remove the checkmark in the Add Extension when Saving check box to ensure that no filename extension is used. In a team environment, designers may be using both Windows and Macintosh computers when working on the same Web site. You can eliminate many file management problems by choosing one filename extension for all Dreamweaver pages.

Dreamweaver 4

Getting Help

Dreamweaver has an excellent Help feature that is both comprehensive and easy to use. When questions or problems arise, you can access the Help menu, which includes Using Dreamweaver, Lessons, Guided Tour, and Dreamweaver Support Center. The Using Dreamweaver Help window includes Contents, Index, and Search buttons. The **Contents** button lists Dreamweaver topics by category. You can click **Index** to choose topics listed in alphabetical order or **Search** to enter a keyword to activate a search for a topic. The Help files open in a browser window. See Table A-2 for a list of Dreamweaver Help features. You decide to access the Help feature to learn more about Dreamweaver.

Steps

Trouble?

If Dreamweaver locks up after you click Help, you may not have browser software installed on your computer, or Dreamweaver may not be able to find it. See your instructor or technical support person for help.

1. Click **Help** on the menu bar
   The Help menu appears, displaying the Help categories. See Figure A-10.
2. Click **Using Dreamweaver**
   The Using Dreamweaver window opens in the browser software installed on your computer.
3. Click the **Search button** in the Using Dreamweaver window
   The Search dialog box opens. You can enter one word or several words joined by plus signs in the Search dialog box.
4. Type **saving** in the Search text box, then click the **List Topics button**
   A list of topics about saving appears in the window below. Note the number of topics listed.
5. Type **saving + files** in the Search text box, then press **[Enter]** (Win) or **[return]** (Mac)
   Note the number of topics listed this time, as shown in Figure A-11.
6. Double-click **Creating, opening, and saving HTML documents – Using Dreamweaver**
   Information on creating, opening, and saving HTML documents appears in the main frame, or right frame, of the browser, as shown in Figure A-12.
7. Scan the information, close the Search window, then close the Help window by clicking **File** on the menu bar, then clicking **Close** (Win) or **Quit** (Mac)
   The Help window closes, and you return to the Dreamweaver work area.

TABLE A-2: Dreamweaver Help features

item	description
Using Dreamweaver	Traditional Contents, Index, and Search displayed in the primary browser window
Reference	Activates context-sensitive CSS, HTML, and JavaScript coding Help
What's New	Describes the new features of Dreamweaver 4
Guided Tour	Six animated explanations on basic Dreamweaver 4 topics
Lessons	Seven step-by-step interactive tutorials on how to use some Dreamweaver 4 features
Dreamweaver Exchange	Connects to Macromedia's Online Resource Center for downloads and product information
Manage Extensions	Activates the Dreamweaver Extension Manager
Dreamweaver Support Center	Connects to Macromedia's Dreamweaver Support Center with an abundance of information and downloads
Macromedia Online Forums	Connects to Macromedia's Online Forum for Dreamweaver and the opportunity to share information and ideas
Extending Dreamweaver	Activates online information on Extending Dreamweaver
Creating and Submitting Extensions	Information on how to create and submit new extensions

FIGURE A-10: **Help menu**

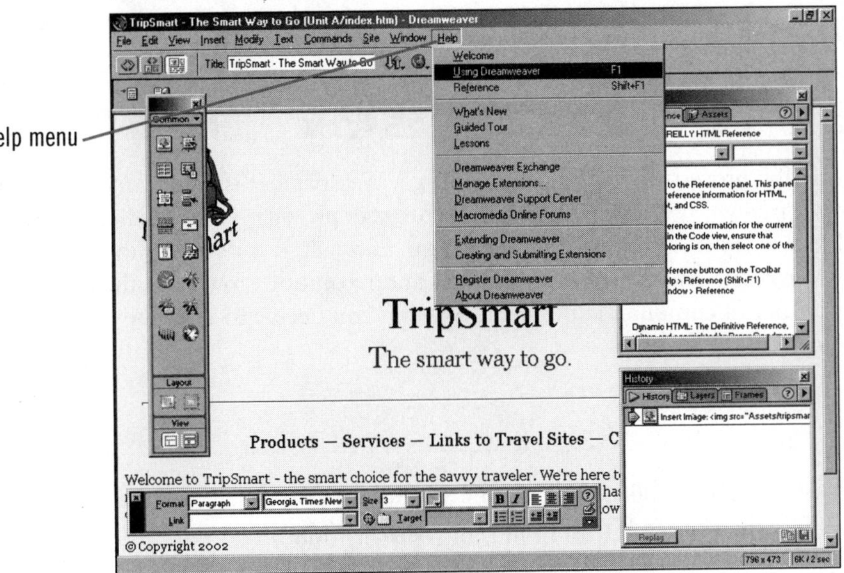

FIGURE A-11: **Search dialog box**

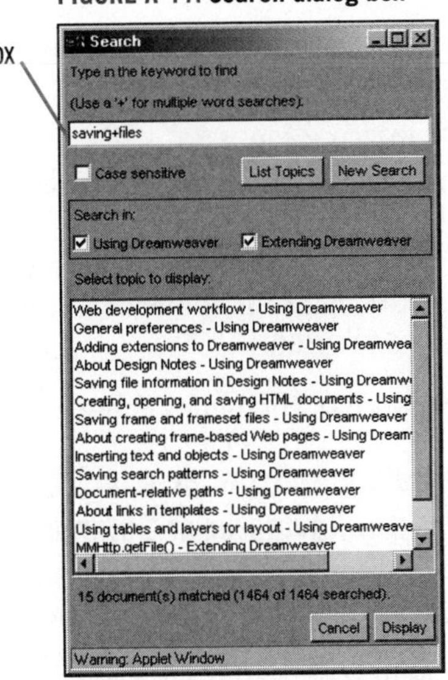

FIGURE A-12: **Using Dreamweaver Help window**

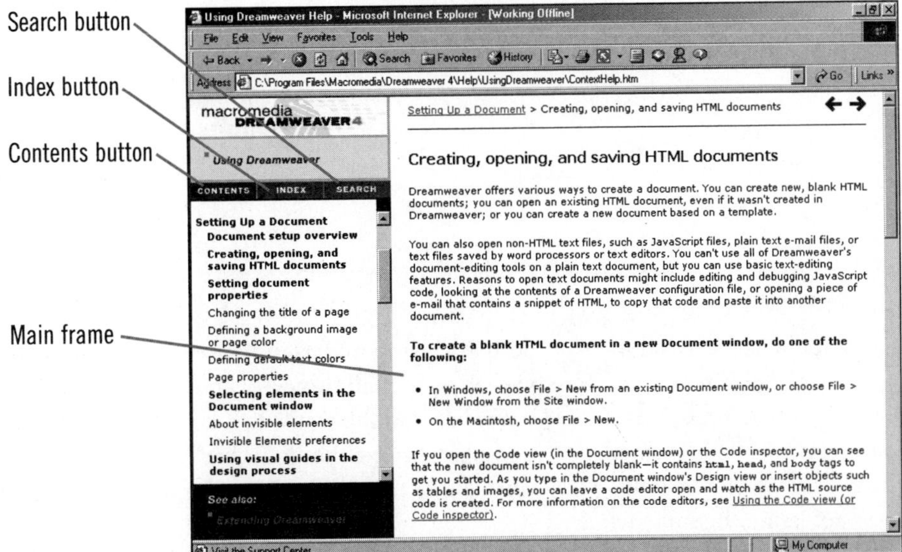

Dreamweaver 4

Viewing a Web Page in a Browser Window

During the process of creating and editing a Web page, it is helpful to view the page in a Web browser frequently. Viewing the page in a browser provides visual feedback of what the page will look like when it is published on the Internet. In fact, it is desirable to view the page using different browsers and different screen sizes and resolutions to ensure the best view of your page on all types of computer equipment. You decide to view the TripSmart home page in your default browser.

Steps

Trouble?
You may need to use the scroll to find Last updated on January 1, 2003.

1. Place the insertion point at the end of the sentence **Last updated on January 1, 2003**, then press **[Enter]** (Win) or **[return]** (Mac)
2. Type your name
   Your name appears under the last updated statement.

Trouble?
The first set of numbers that appears as the new window size may vary if you have resized your window.

3. Click the **Window Size pop-up menu**, as shown in Figure A-13, then click **760 × 420 (800 × 600, maximized)**
   The screen size is set to 760 × 420.
   See Table A-3 for more window size options. When you choose your screen size, it is important to consider the equipment your audience is using. Although the most common screen size that designers use today is 800 × 600, a large number of viewers still view at 640 × 480. If you want to make sure that your audience will not have to scroll to see your entire page, set your screen size to 640 × 480.
4. Click **File** on the menu bar, then click **Save**
5. Click the **Preview/Debug in Browser icon**, then click **Preview in iexplore** (Win) or **Preview in Netscape Navigator** or **Communicator** (Mac)
   The browser window opens and the page is displayed, as shown in Figure A-14. You may have a different default browser on your computer. If you do, select it instead.

QuickTip
There is not a printing option in Dreamweaver. You can, however, print a Web page from your browser window.

6. Click **File** on the menu bar, then click **Print**
   The Web page is printed.

Window screen sizes

One concern every designer should address is how Web pages will look on monitors of different sizes and with different screen resolution settings. It is important to check the appearance of your Web page using several different screen sizes. With the wide variety of computer systems accessing the Internet, designers need to design their pages so they can be viewed well in all browsers and screen sizes. To set the screen size on the status bar, click the Window Size pop-up menu on the status bar, then choose the setting you want to use. See Table A-3 for window size options.

FIGURE A-13: Window Size pop-up menu

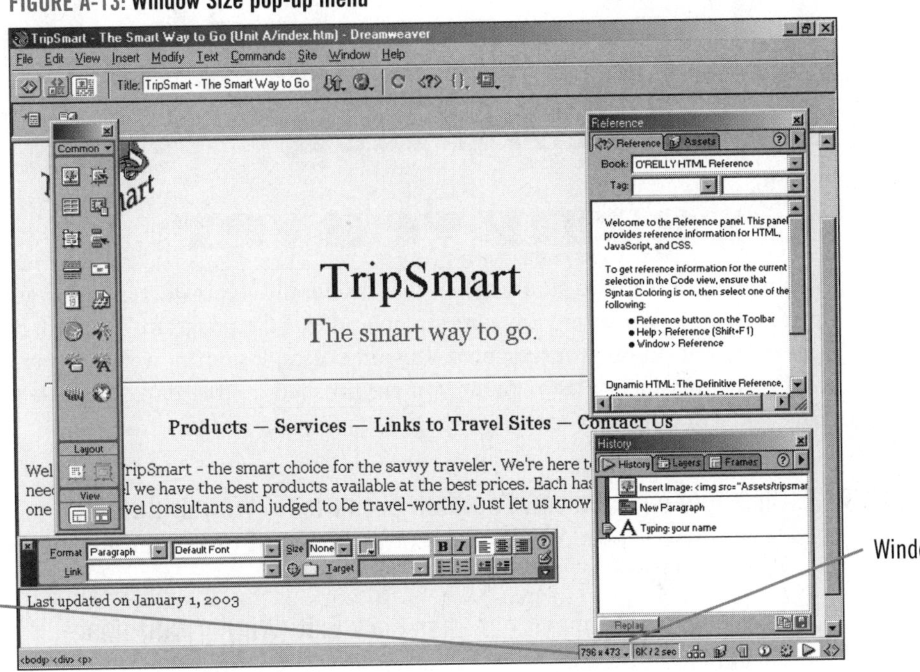

These numbers may vary if you have resized your window

Window Size menu

FIGURE A-14: Preview in browser

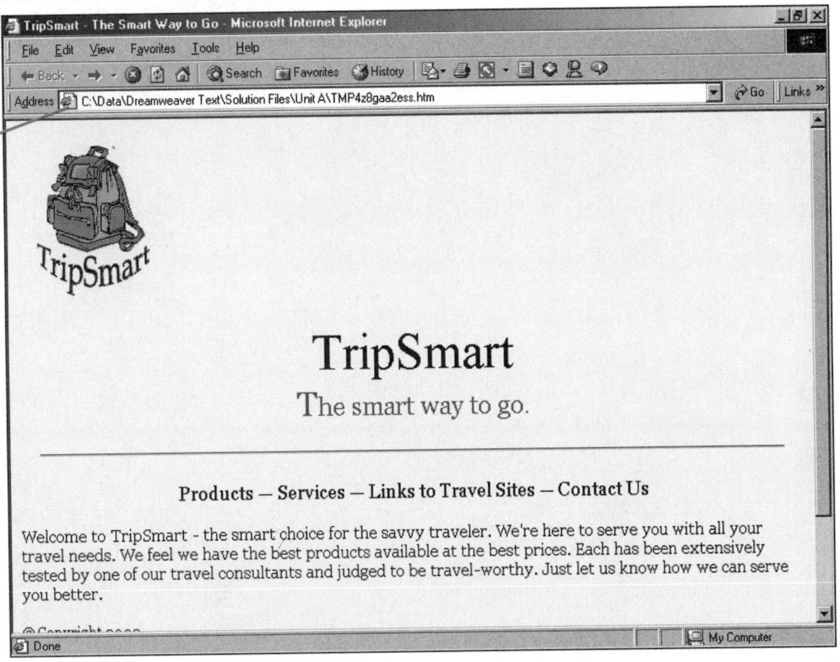

The filename in the address box uses a temporary filename for previewing

TABLE A-3: Window Size options

window size	monitor size
592W	
536 × 196	640 × 480, default
600 × 300	640 × 480, maximized
760 × 420	800 × 600, maximized
795 × 470	832 × 624, maximized
955 × 600	1024 × 768, maximized
544 × 378	Web TV

Dreamweaver 4

Closing a Web Page and Exiting Dreamweaver

When you are ready to stop working with a file in Dreamweaver, it is a good idea to close the current page or pages you are working on and exit the program. This will hopefully prevent the loss of data if power is interrupted. In some cases, loss of power can corrupt an open file and render it unusable. Since you are finished for the day, you close the TripSmart home page and exit Dreamweaver.

Steps

Trouble?

You may need to click the Dreamweaver title bar to activate Dreamweaver.

1. Click **File** on the menu bar, then click **Close** (Win) or **Quit** (Mac)
   The browser closes. You should see your finished project in the Dreamweaver window, as shown in Figure A-15.
2. Click **File** on the menu bar, then click **Exit** (Win) or **Quit** (Mac)
   Dreamweaver closes.

CLUES TO USE

Closing Dreamweaver files

During the process of opening Dreamweaver and working with Web sites and files, a blank, untitled page may open that you never use. When you exit Dreamweaver, you will be prompted to save any files that you have not saved. It is OK to close this document without saving it. If you like to avoid having unnecessary open windows, close the untitled document when it opens, rather than waiting until you exit Dreamweaver.

FIGURE A-15: The finished project

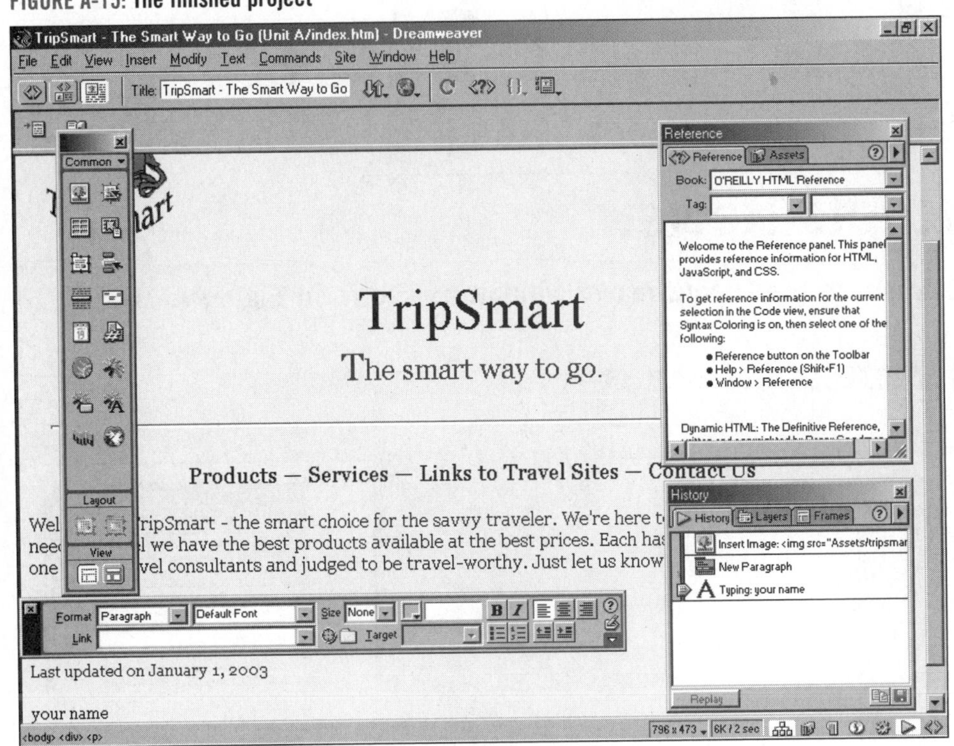

CLUES TO USE

Dreamweaver on-line support

Macromedia has an extensive amount of help information on their Web site. The Dreamweaver Support Center is one example, and is listed as an option in the Help menu. When this option is clicked, Dreamweaver will activate your Internet browser and connect to the Macromedia Web site at *www.macromedia.com/support/dreamweaver/contents.html.*

Practice

Concepts Review

Label each element in the Dreamweaver window as shown in Figure A-16.

FIGURE A-16

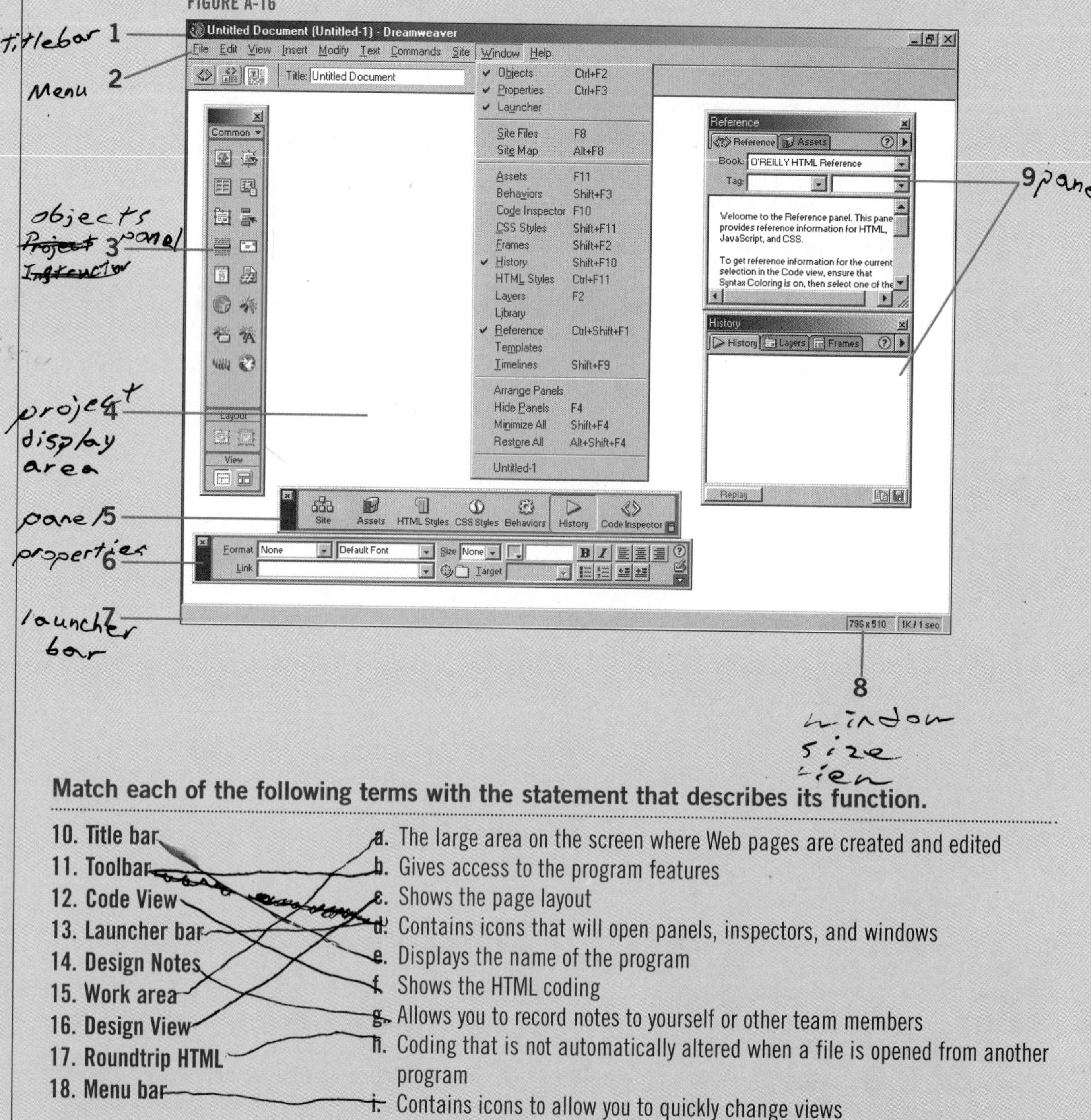

Match each of the following terms with the statement that describes its function.

10. Title bar
11. Toolbar
12. Code View
13. Launcher bar
14. Design Notes
15. Work area
16. Design View
17. Roundtrip HTML
18. Menu bar

a. The large area on the screen where Web pages are created and edited
b. Gives access to the program features
c. Shows the page layout
d. Contains icons that will open panels, inspectors, and windows
e. Displays the name of the program
f. Shows the HTML coding
g. Allows you to record notes to yourself or other team members
h. Coding that is not automatically altered when a file is opened from another program
i. Contains icons to allow you to quickly change views

Select the best answer from the following list of choices.

19. Dreamweaver allows you to use features such as animations and interactive forms through easy-to-use:

a. Windows.
b. Panels.
c. Tools.
d. All of the above.

20. Dreamweaver is a(n):

a. Graphics program.
b. Animation program.
c. Web design program.
d. Drawing program.

21. WYSIWYG is the acronym for:

a. What You Show Is What You Get.
b. What You See Is What You Get.
c. Why You See It Where You Go.
d. None of the above.

22. The tool that allows you to show the properties of the various page elements is called the:

a. Tool Inspector.
b. Element Inspector.
c. Objects panel.
d. Property Inspector.

23. The Dreamweaver feature that shows how the pages in a Web site relate to each other is called the:

a. Site Inspector.
b. Site panel.
c. Site Map.
d. Site view.

24. The view that is primarily used when designing and creating a Web page is:

a. Code View.
b. Design View.
c. A combination of both Code and Design View.
d. All of the above.

► Skills Review

1. Define Web design software.

a. Write a short paragraph describing at least three features of Dreamweaver, using scrap paper or your word processing software.

b. Add your name to the top of the page.

2. Start Dreamweaver 4.

a. Start Dreamweaver.

b. List the panels that are currently displayed on the screen.

c. Using the Window menu, show the History panel and the Reference panel, if necessary.

d. Dock the History panel to the Reference panel.

e. Undock them.

3. View the Dreamweaver work area.

a. Locate the title bar.

b. Locate the menu bar.

c. Locate the toolbar.

d. Locate the Objects panel.

e. Locate the Property Inspector.

f. Locate the Launcher bar.

4. Open a Web page and insert an image

a. Open dma_2.htm from the drive and folder where your Project Files are stored in the Unit A folder.

b. With the insertion point at the top of the page, click Insert on the menu bar, click Image, double-click the assets folder, click blooms_logo.gif, then click Select.

5. Save a Web page.

a. Save the page as *blooms.htm* in the drive and folder where your Project Files are stored.

6. Get Help.

a. Click Help on the menu bar.

b. Click Using Dreamweaver.

c. Find information on using the Assets panel.

d. Select a topic and double-click the topic name to open it.

e. Close the Search window, if necessary, and click the right side of the window to select the article.

f. Print the information.

g. Close the Help window.

7. **View a Web page in a browser window.**
   a. Note the view that is currently set in Dreamweaver.
   b. Change the window size to a different setting.
   c. Click the Preview/Debug in Browser icon, then click Preview in iexplore (Win) or Preview in Netscape Navigator or Communicator (Mac).
   d. Close the browser window.

8. **Close a Web page and exit Dreamweaver.**
   a. Close the page.
   b. Exit (Win) or Quit (Mac) Dreamweaver.

► Independent Challenge 1

Dreamweaver has a Help feature called Guided Tour, which teaches you how to use Dreamweaver, using movies of Dreamweaver tasks being performed. Figure A-17 shows a clip from the Guided Tour about working with text.

a. Start Dreamweaver.
b. Click Help on the menu bar, then click Guided Tour.
c. Click Getting started.
d. Follow the directions on the screen and click the movie icons to view the movies.
e. Close the Help window when you are done.

FIGURE A-17

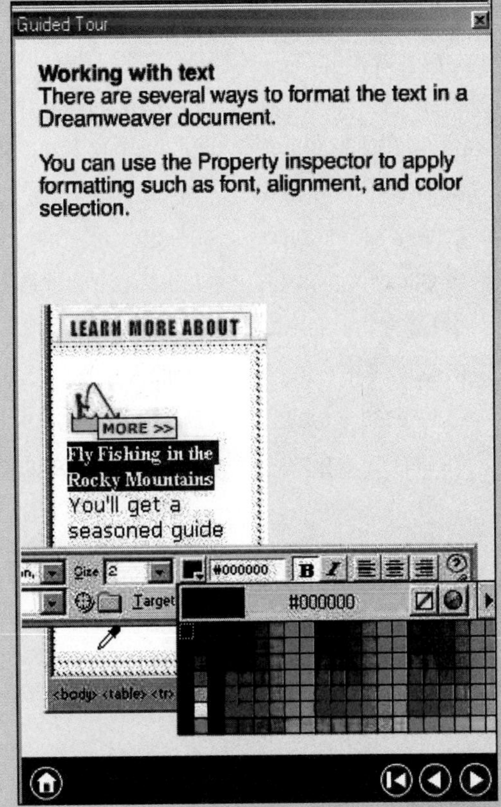

▶ Independent Challenge 2

When you work in Dreamweaver, it is very important to organize your panels so that you have a good view of the work area and are not distracted by panels that are in your way or that you are not currently using. You can dock panels to each other to save room in your work area.

a. Start Dreamweaver.

b. Click Help on the menu bar, then click Using Dreamweaver.

c. Locate information explaining how to dock floating panels.

d. Select a topic and double-click the topic name to open it.

e. Close the Search window, if necessary, and click the right side of the window to select the article.

f. Print the information.

g. Close the your browser.

▶ Independent Challenge 3

The Dreamweaver Support Center provides answers to common questions and suggestions for troubleshooting problems that arise when using Dreamweaver. The Support Center may help you find information you need, and save you from having to place a telephone call to technical support.

a. Start Dreamweaver.

b. Verify that you have an active Internet connection.

c. Click Help on the menu bar, then click Dreamweaver Support Center.

d. Click the Getting Stared link.

e. Click the Common Questions link.

f. Choose a topic under the TechNotes heading.

g. Choose a question that interests you and read the response.

h. Print the page.

Independent Challenge 4

The Macromedia Web site has a feature called Showcase. Showcase includes links to Web sites that were created using Macromedia software, such as Dreamweaver, Flash, and Fireworks. The Showcase feature includes the Site of the Day and Weekly Features. The Weekly Features links provide information about the company being showcased, the challenge that was presented to the design team, the solution, and the resulting benefits to the company.

a. Connect to the Internet and go to Macromedia at *www.macromedia.com.*

b. Click the Showcase link, then click one of the companies listed under Weekly Features.

c. Read the information about the company, and print the page from the browser window.

d. Close your browser window.

e. Using a word-processing program or scrap paper, write a short summary (two paragraphs) of the Web site you visited, then list three things that you learned about the Macromedia software used to create the site. For example: "I learned that Flash animation files can be inserted into Dreamweaver."

► Visual Workshop

Open Dreamweaver and use the Windows menu to open the panels and windows as shown in Figure A-18. If necessary, drag the panels into the position on the screen shown in Figure A-18. Exit (Win) or Quit (Mac) Dreamweaver.

FIGURE A-18

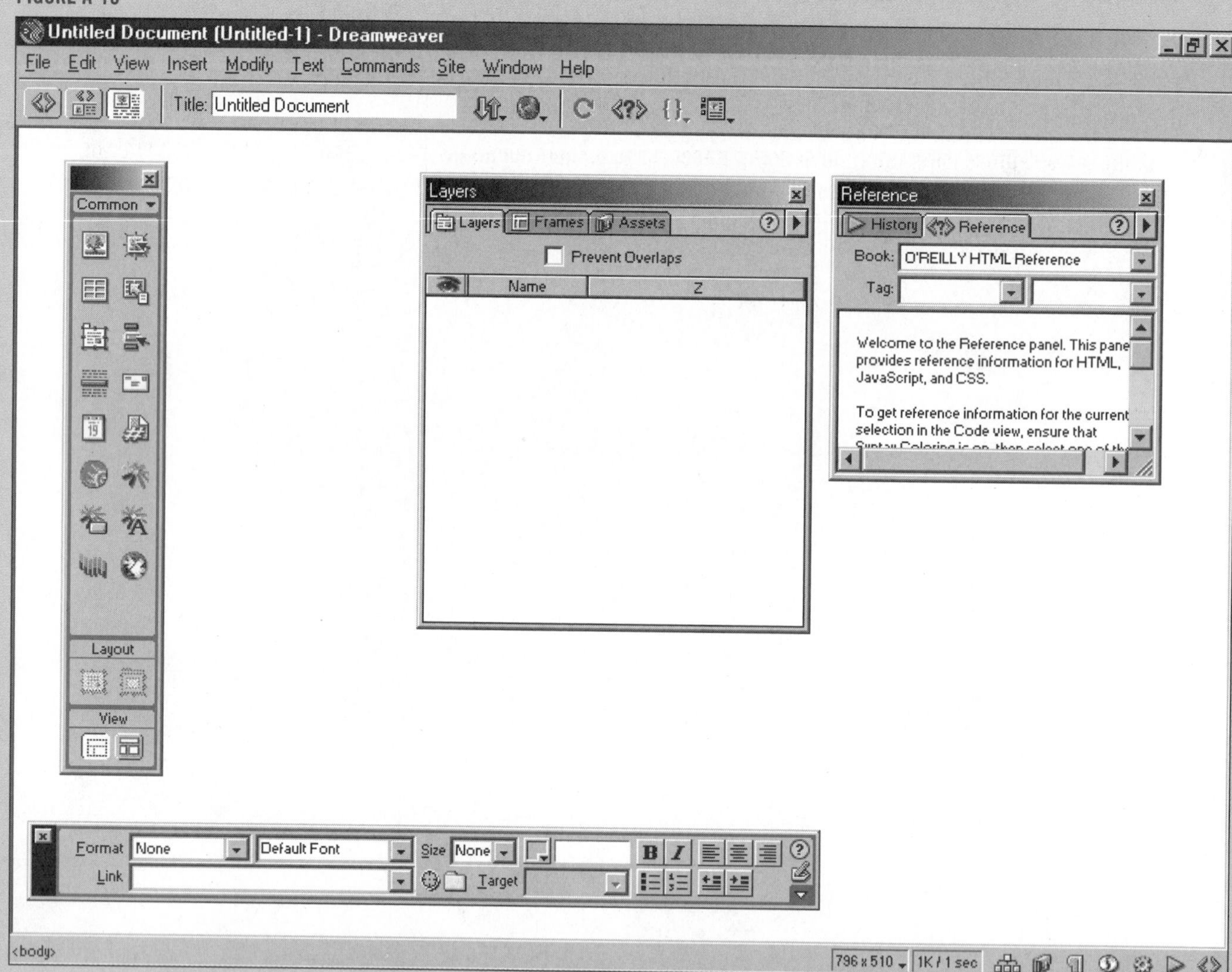

Creating a Web Site

Objectives

- Plan a Web site
- Create a folder for Web site management
- Define a Web site
- Add a folder to a Web site
- Set the home page
- Add new pages to a Web site
- Use Design Notes
- Set up Web server access
- Create and view a Site Map
- Modify pages from the Site window

A **Web site** is a group of related Web pages that are linked together and share a common interface and design. A Web site can also be referred to as a Web, or a site. Creating a Web site requires a lot of thought and careful planning. The process of developing a Web site is a continuous one. Even when a Web site is considered done, Web designers look for ways to improve it, and frequently need to update it with new information. Dreamweaver has many tools to help you manage your Web site during all development phases. In this unit, you will use these tools to plan and design a new Web site. You will also learn how to maintain your Web site using the site management features in Dreamweaver. The owners of TripSmart meet with you to discuss their ideas for a new and improved Web site. You assure them that you can create a great Web site for TripSmart, using Dreamweaver.

Dreamweaver 4

Planning a Web Site

Planning is an *essential* part of creating a Web site. Other projects may have a short planning stage, but planning a Web site extends into the publishing stages of the site. Figure B-1 illustrates the steps involved in Web site planning. As you create, test, and modify Web pages, you will most likely run into areas that need troubleshooting. This is especially true when you test your Web site on different types of computers. Part of your plan needs to encompass how to handle problems that may arise in any stage of the creation process. Careful planning of your Web site may prevent unnecessary mistakes that would be costly and time-consuming to fix later on. After consulting with the lead member of the Web development team, you find that there are several key steps in planning and creating a Web site. You review the steps below before you start working in Dreamweaver.

Details

- **Research**
  The research phase of planning a Web site consists of creating a checklist of questions about the site, and finding the answers to them before you begin. For example, "What are the company's or client's goals for the Web site? What software will be required to construct the site? Who will create the animation for the site?" The more questions that you can answer about the site, the more prepared you will be when you begin the development phase. In addition to a checklist, you may want to create a timeline and a budget for the Web site.
- **Create a storyboard**
  A **storyboard** is a small sketch that represents every page in a Web site. Like a flowchart, a storyboard shows the relationship of each page to the other pages in the Web site. Storyboards, like the one shown in Figure B-2, are very helpful when planning a Web site because they allow you to visualize how each page in the site is linked to others.
- **Create a folder hierarchy**
  Before you create your Web site, you should create a folder hierarchy for all of the elements that will be used in the Web site. Start out by creating a folder for the Web site with a descriptive name such as the name of the company. Then create a subfolder called **assets** in which you store all of the files that are not Web pages, such as images and video clips. An organized folder system will make it easy for you to find files quickly when you are in the development and editing stages of your Web site.
- **Collect the page content and create the Web pages**
  This is the fun part. After studying your storyboard, you need to gather the files that will be used to create the pages, such as text, graphics, buttons, video, and animation. Some of these elements will come from other software programs, and some will be created in Dreamweaver. For example, text can be created in a word-processing program and inserted into Dreamweaver, or it can be created and formatted in Dreamweaver.
- **Test the pages**
  It is important to test your Web pages using different browser software. The two most common browsers are Microsoft Internet Explorer and Netscape Navigator. You should also test your Web site using different versions of each browser, a variety of screen resolutions, and modem speeds. More people are using cable modems or DSL (Digital Subscriber Line); however, some still use slower dial up modems. Testing is a continuous process, so you should allocate plenty of time for it as you plan a Web site.
- **Modify the pages**
  After you create a Web site, you'll find that you need to keep making changes to it, especially when information in the site needs to be updated. Each time you modify something about a Web site, it is wise to test the site again.
- **Publish the site**
  The process of **publishing** a Web site means that you are making it available for viewing on the Internet. A Web site is published to a **Web server**, a computer that is connected to the Internet with an **IP (Internet Protocol) address**. Until a Web site is published, it cannot be viewed without access to the storage device that contains the Web site.

QuickTip

A storyboard can be easily created on a computer using a software program such as Paint, Paintshop Pro, Macromedia Freehand, or Macromedia Fireworks. You may find it easier to make changes to a storyboard created on a computer than on one created on paper.

FIGURE B-1: Steps in Web site planning

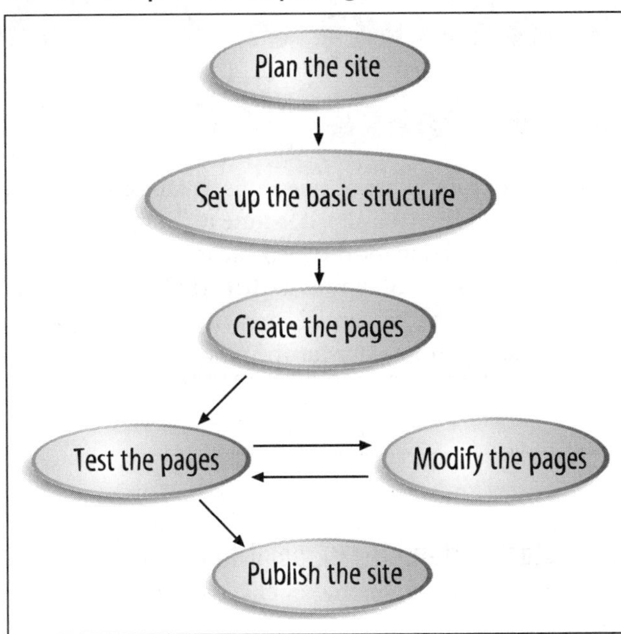

FIGURE B-2: TripSmart Web site plan

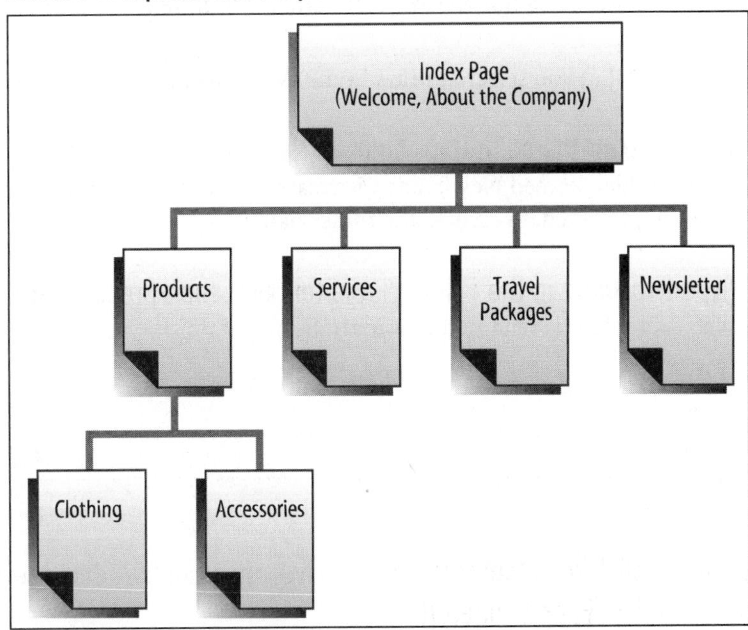

IP addresses and domain names

To access a Web site over the Internet, it must be published to a Web server with a permanent IP address. An **IP address** is an assigned series of numbers, separated by periods, that designate an address on the Internet. To access a Web page, you can enter either an IP address or a domain name in the address box of your browser window. A **domain name** is expressed in letters instead of numbers, and it usually reflects the name of the business represented by the Web site. An example would be the Macromedia Web site. The domain name is www.macromedia.com, but the IP address would read something like 123.456.789.123. Because domain names use descriptive text instead of numbers, they are much easier to remember. Compare an IP address to your Social Security number and a domain name to your name. Both your Social Security number and your name are used to refer to you as a person, but your name is much easier for your friends and family to use than your Social Security number.

Dreamweaver 4

Creating a Folder for Web Site Management

After composing your checklist of questions, creating storyboards, and gathering the files and resources you need for the Web site, it is time to set up the folder structure for the Web site. The first folder you should create for the Web site is called a root folder. A **root folder** is a folder on your hard drive, zip disk, or floppy disk that will hold all the files and folders for the Web site. You should avoid using spaces, special characters, or uppercase characters in your folder names. You create the root folder for the new TripSmart Web site, and name it tripsmart.

WIN

Trouble?

You may find Windows Explorer in Accessories, rather than Programs.

1. Click the **Start button**, point to **Programs**, then click **Windows Explorer**
   The Windows Explorer window opens and displays the drives, folders, and files on your computer.
2. Click the **Address list arrow**, then click the drive and folder where your Project Files are stored
   The drive that you select appears in the Windows Explorer Address box.
3. Click **File** on the menu bar, point to **New**, then click **Folder**
   A new folder, named New Folder, is created. You can type directly over New Folder while it is still highlighted, to change the folder name.
4. Type **tripsmart** in the Folder Name text box, then press **[Enter]**
   The root folder is renamed tripsmart. See Figure B-3.

Trouble?

If you cannot rename the folder, right-click the folder name, New Folder, click Rename, type tripsmart, then press [Enter].

MAC

1. Double-click the **Macintosh hard drive**, then double-click the folder where you store your Project Files to open it
2. Click **File** on the menu bar, then click **New Folder**
   A new folder, named untitled folder, appears. You can type directly over untitled folder while it is still highlighted, to change the folder name.
3. Type **tripsmart**, then press **[return]** to rename the folder
   The root folder is renamed tripsmart. See Figure B-4.

Trouble?

If you cannot rename the folder, click the folder name, untitled folder, to highlight it, type tripsmart, then press [return].

FIGURE B-3: Creating a root folder using Windows Explorer

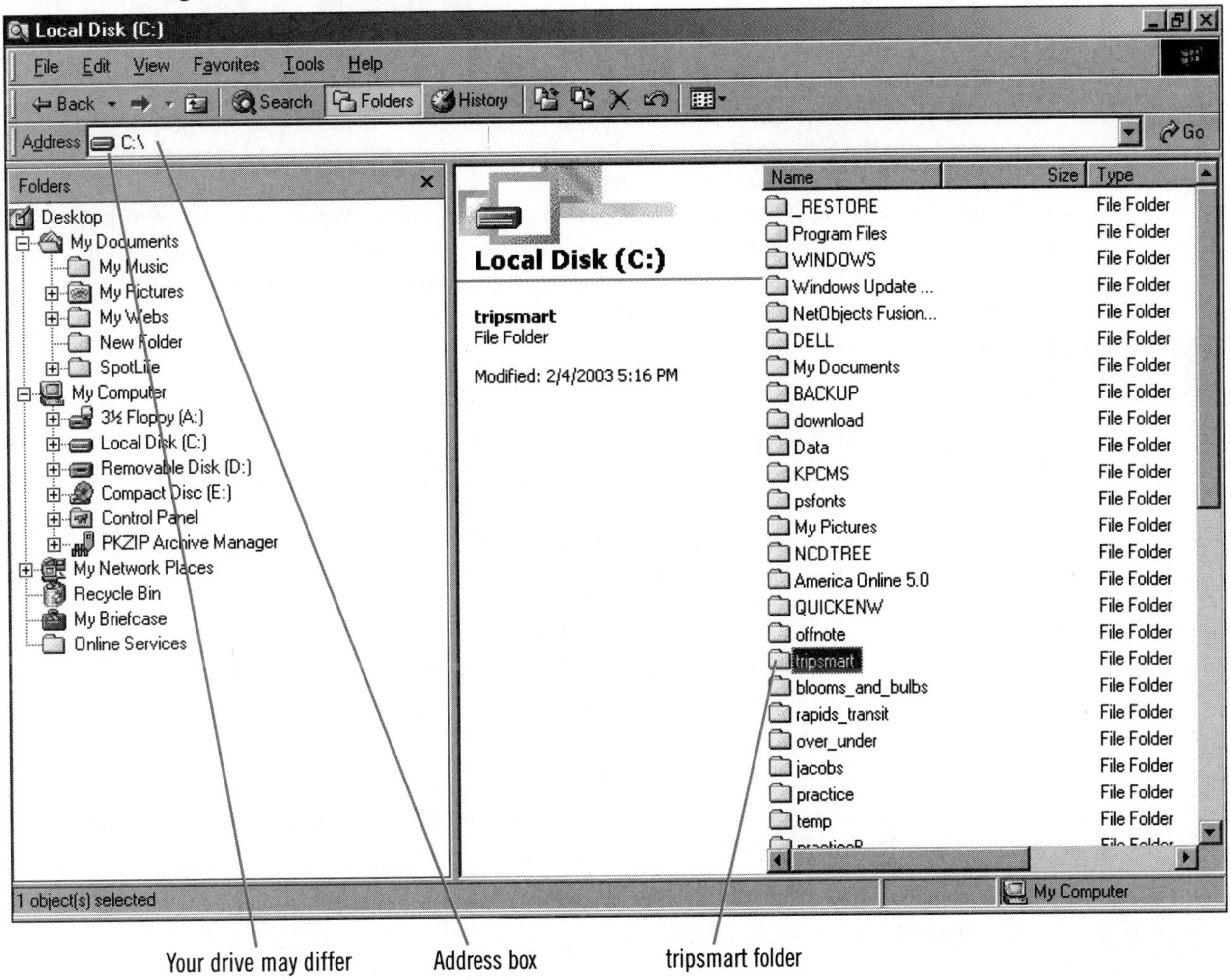

Your drive may differ
Address box
tripsmart folder

FIGURE B-4: Creating a root folder on a Macintosh

Type over the highlighted folder name to rename it

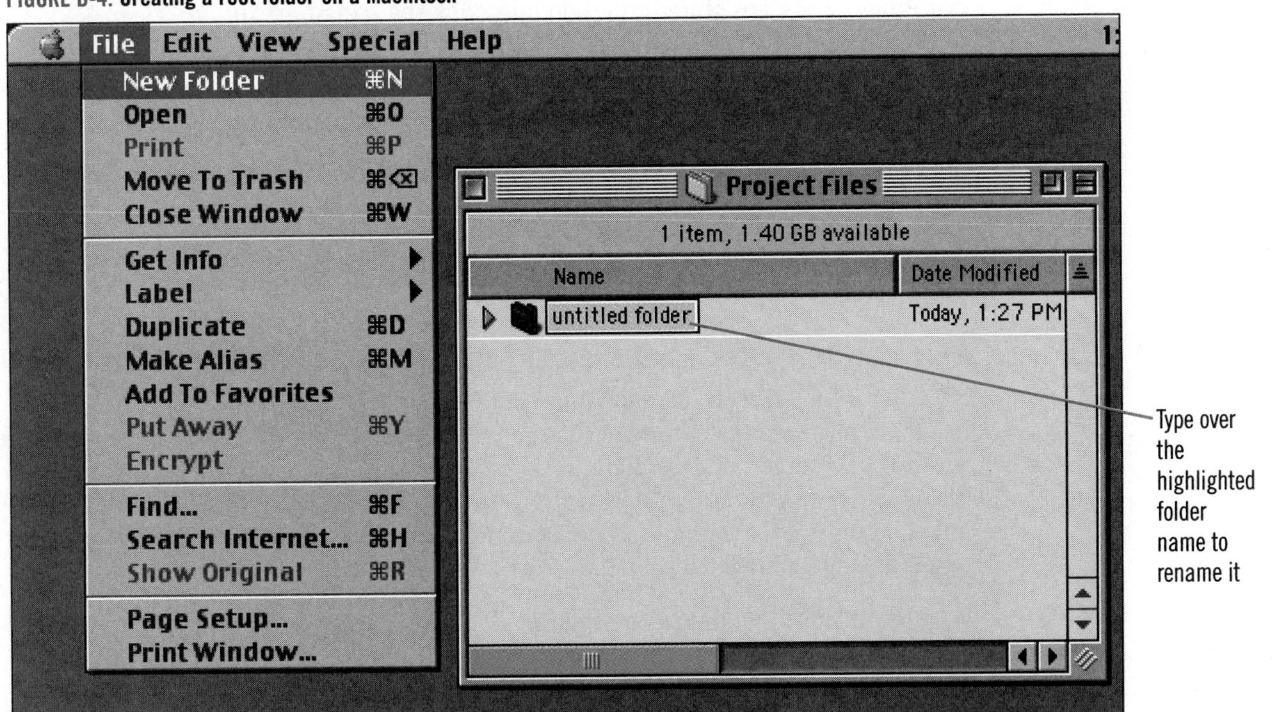

Dreamweaver 4

Defining a Web Site

After you create a root folder, you need to define your Web site. When you **define** a Web site, you are actually creating a mirror image, or copy, of the root folder. This duplicate folder is copied into the **Site window**, a window where Dreamweaver stores and manages your files and folders. Using the Site window to manage your files ensures that the site links work correctly when the Web site is published. If you plan to publish your Web site to a different location, or remote server, you will transfer your files using the FTP (File Transfer Protocol) capability in the Site window. **FTP** is the process of uploading and downloading files to and from a remote site. You define the TripSmart Web site.

Steps

1. **Start Dreamweaver**
   A new Dreamweaver document named Untitled Document opens.
   (Mac) If a message window appears stating that the local root folder, Lesson Files, does not exist, and asking you to choose a new local root folder from the Define Sites dialog, click Cancel.

2. **Click Site on the menu bar, then click Define Sites**
   The Define Sites dialog box opens. It lists all of the current sites and allows you to add new sites or delete existing sites.

3. **Click New to define a new site**
   The Site Definition for Unnamed Site 1 window opens, as shown in Figure B-5.
   The Site Definition dialog box is used to define the settings in Dreamweaver that will be applied to this Web site.

> **QuickTip**
> It is acceptable to use uppercase letters in the site name, because it is not the name of a folder or file.

4. **Type TripSmart in the Site Name text box**
   The Web site name is TripSmart.

5. **Click the folder icon next to the Local Root Folder text box, click the Select list arrow (Win) or ⬍ (Mac) from the Choose Local Folder dialog box, click the drive and folder where your Project Files are stored, then double-click the tripsmart folder**
   The local root folder, tripsmart, is designated as the location for the Web site files and folders. See Figure B-6.

6. **Click Select (Win) or Choose (Mac)**
   The Local Root Folder text box in the Site Definition dialog box displays your selected drive followed by \tripsmart\ (Win) or :tripsmart (Mac), as shown in Figure B-7.
   (Mac) If the Choose button is unavailable, you may have clicked the Open button before clicking the Choose button. If this happens, click ⬍, click the drive and folder containing the tripsmart folder, click the tripsmart folder, then click Choose.

7. **Verify that the Refresh Local File List Automatically and the Enable Cache check boxes are both checked, as shown in Figure B-7, then click OK**
   Enable Cache means that you want the computer system to use temporary memory on the hard drive, or **cache**, while you are working. The Enable Cache option improves the processing speed of your site management tasks. The Refresh Local File List Automatically option means that the computer system automatically reflects changes made in your file listings. A message appears telling you that the initial site cache will now be created.

8. **Click OK to close the message window**
   The Define Sites window opens, showing the new TripSmart site in the list of sites.

9. **Click Done to close the Define Sites dialog box**
   The Site window for TripSmart opens. Your screen should resemble Figure B-8.

FIGURE B-5: The Site Definition for Unnamed Site 1 window

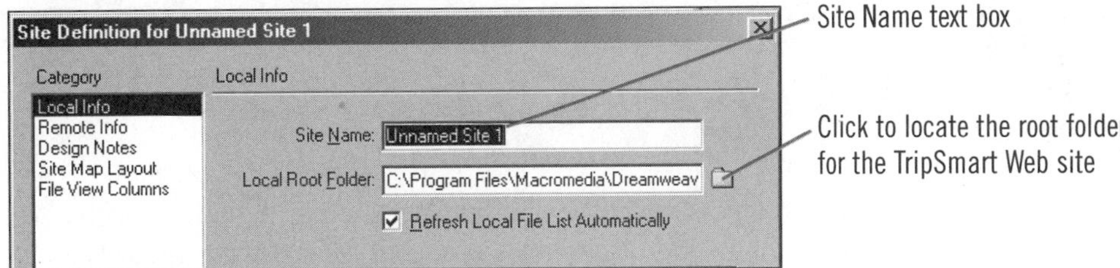

FIGURE B-6: Choose Local Folder dialog box

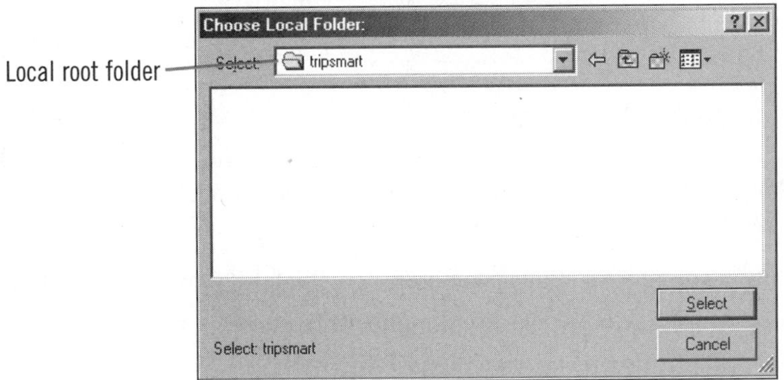

FIGURE B-7: Site Definition dialog box

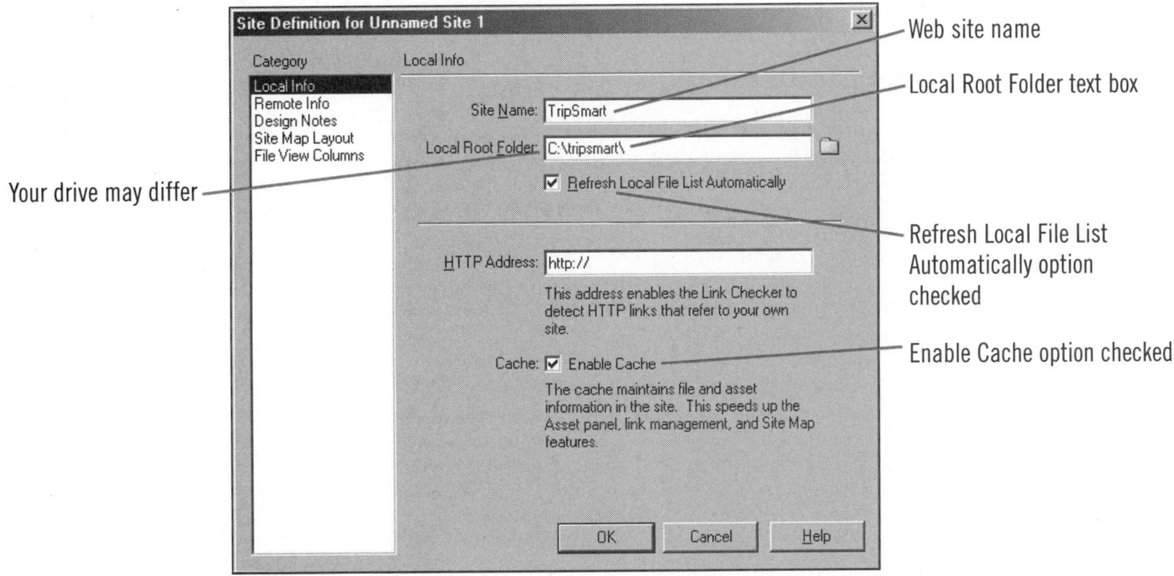

FIGURE B-8: Site window for TripSmart

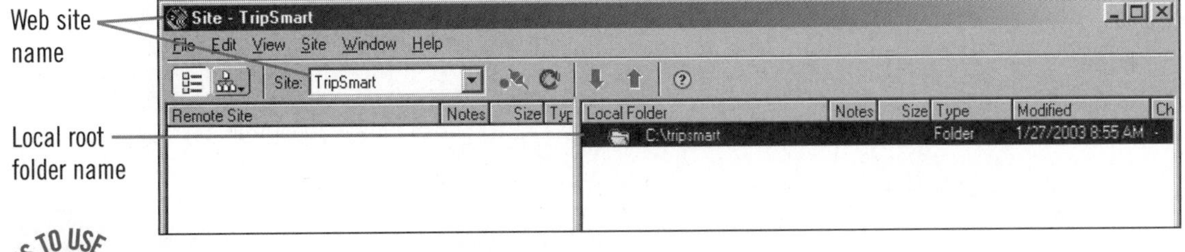

CLUES TO USE

Using the Define Sites dialog box

The Define Sites dialog box shows you a list of all of the Web sites on your computer. Using this dialog box, you can add, edit, duplicate, or remove Web sites. To access the Define Sites dialog box, click Site on the menu bar, then click Define Sites.

Dreamweaver 4

Dreamweaver 4

Adding a Folder to a Web Site

After defining your Web site, you need to create folders for the Web site. Creating a folder called **assets** is a good beginning. Complex Web sites with many types of multimedia files or text files may have subfolders under the assets folder to use for organizing purposes. For example, you might have folders for text files, graphic files, sound files, or video clips. You create a folder called assets for the TripSmart Web site.

Steps 1 2 3 4

1. **Make sure that the Site window is still open**
   You can open the Site window by clicking Window on the menu bar, then clicking Site Files, by clicking the Show Site icon on the Launcher bar or the status bar, or by pressing [F8] on the keyboard.

2. **(Win) If you are using a Windows computer, Click File on the menu bar, then click New Folder or (Mac) if you are using a Macintosh computer, press and hold [control], click the tripsmart folder, then click New Folder**
   A new untitled folder appears, however, if you are using a Macintosh, you may not see the new folder if the tripsmart folder is closed.

3. **(Win) If you are using a Windows computer, type assets in the folder text box, then press [Enter] or (Mac) If you are using a Macintosh computer, click the triangle ▶ to the left of the tripsmart folder to open it, if necessary, click untitled on the new folder, type assets as the folder name, then press [return]**
   See Figure B-9. You will use the assets folder to store graphics and other elements used in the Web site.

Trouble?

You will not see the new folder until you expand the tripsmart folder by clicking the triangle ▶ to the left of the tripsmart folder (Mac).

FIGURE B-9: TripSmart Site window with assets folder created (Windows and Macintosh)

Windows

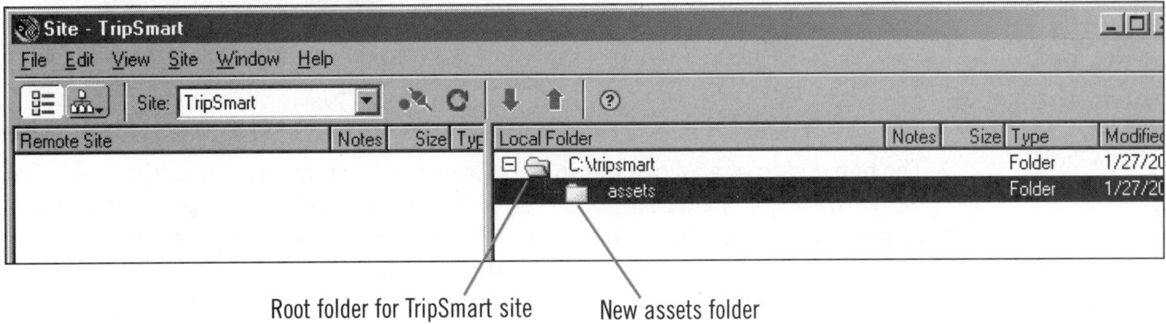

Macintosh

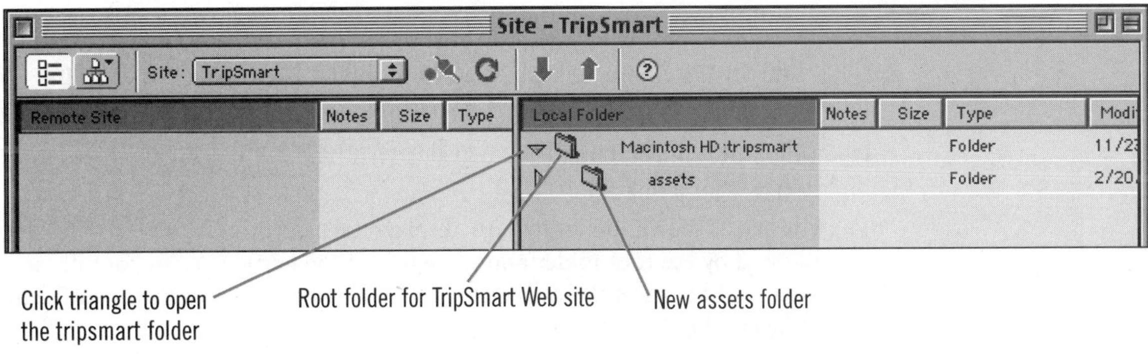

Design Matters

Choosing a primary browser

Microsoft Internet Explorer and Netscape Navigator (or Communicator) are popular browsers used for viewing Web pages. As with all software, the companies that make these browsers, Microsoft and Netscape, introduce new versions of the software frequently. It is critical to view your Web page in several different browsers and browser versions to make sure your Web site looks the way you want it to and functions correctly with all possible browsers. For instance, older versions of browsers may not display frames properly. You would want to be aware of this problem before you published your Web site. As a Web designer, you should download at least two browser versions that are available from the Microsoft Web site (*www.microsoft.com*) and the Netscape Web site (*www.netscape.com*). When you click the Preview/Debug in Browser icon on the toolbar, a list of each browser installed on your computer will appear. The first browser listed is called the **primary browser**. You can designate which browser should be the primary browser by clicking Edit on the menu bar, clicking Preferences, clicking Preview in Browser in the Category list, clicking the browser and version in the Browsers list, then clicking the Primary Browser check box. You can also choose a Secondary Browser from this dialog box.

Dreamweaver 4

Setting the Home Page

Steps

The home page of a Web site is the first page that a viewer sees when they visit your Web site. Most Web sites contain many other pages that all connect back to the home page. Dreamweaver uses the home page as a starting point for creating a **Site Map**, a graphical representation of the Web pages in a Web site. The home page filename is usually index.htm. You set the index page as the home page for the TripSmart Web site.

1. Make sure that the Site window is still open, then click **File** on the menu bar, click **Open**, click the drive and folder where your Project Files are stored, double-click the **Unit B folder**, then double-click **dmb_1.htm**
   The page opens in the document window in Design View. This is the page that viewers will see when they first access the TripSmart Web site.
2. Click **File** on the menu bar, click **Save As**, click the **Save in list arrow** (Win) or (Mac) to navigate to the root folder (tripsmart), double-click the **tripsmart folder**, type **index.htm** in the File name text box (Win) or Name text box (Mac) of the Save As dialog box, then click **Save**
   The title bar, as shown in Figure B-10, displays the page title, TripSmart – The Smart Way to Go, followed by the root folder and the name of the home page in parentheses. The information within the parentheses is called the **path**, or location of the open file in relation to any folders in the Web site.
3. Click the **Show Site icon** on the status bar to bring the Site window in front of the document window
   The index.htm file is in the tripsmart root folder of the TripSmart Web site. Your screen should resemble Figure B-11. You are ready to set the index page as the home page for the Web site.
4. Click **index.htm** in the Site window to select it, click **Site** on the menu bar, then click **Set As Home Page** (Win) or click **Site** on the menu bar, point to **Site Map View**, then click **Set as Home Page** (Mac)
   The index.htm file is now set as the home page for the Web site. The TripSmart logo must be copied to the assets folder.
5. Double-click **index.htm** to open it in Design View, then click the **TripSmart logo**, as shown in Figure B-12
   Selection handles appear around the image, and the Property Inspector displays the properties of the logo. The Src text box in the Property Inspector displays the current location of the TripSmart logo image.
6. Click the **folder icon** next to the Src text box on the Property Inspector, click the **Look in list arrow** (Win) or (Mac), click the drive and folder where your Project Files are stored, double-click the **Unit B folder**, double-click the **assets folder**, click **tripsmart.gif**, then click **Select** (Win) or **Open** (Mac)
   A message displays on the screen asking you if you would like to copy the graphic file to the root folder of your Web site.
7. Click **Yes**, click the **assets** folder in the Copy File As dialog box, click **Open**, then click **Save**
   The Src text box in the Property Inspector now reads assets/tripsmart.gif.

Trouble?

If you cannot see the TripSmart logo, drag any floating panels or the Site window out of the way.

FIGURE B-10: The TripSmart home page

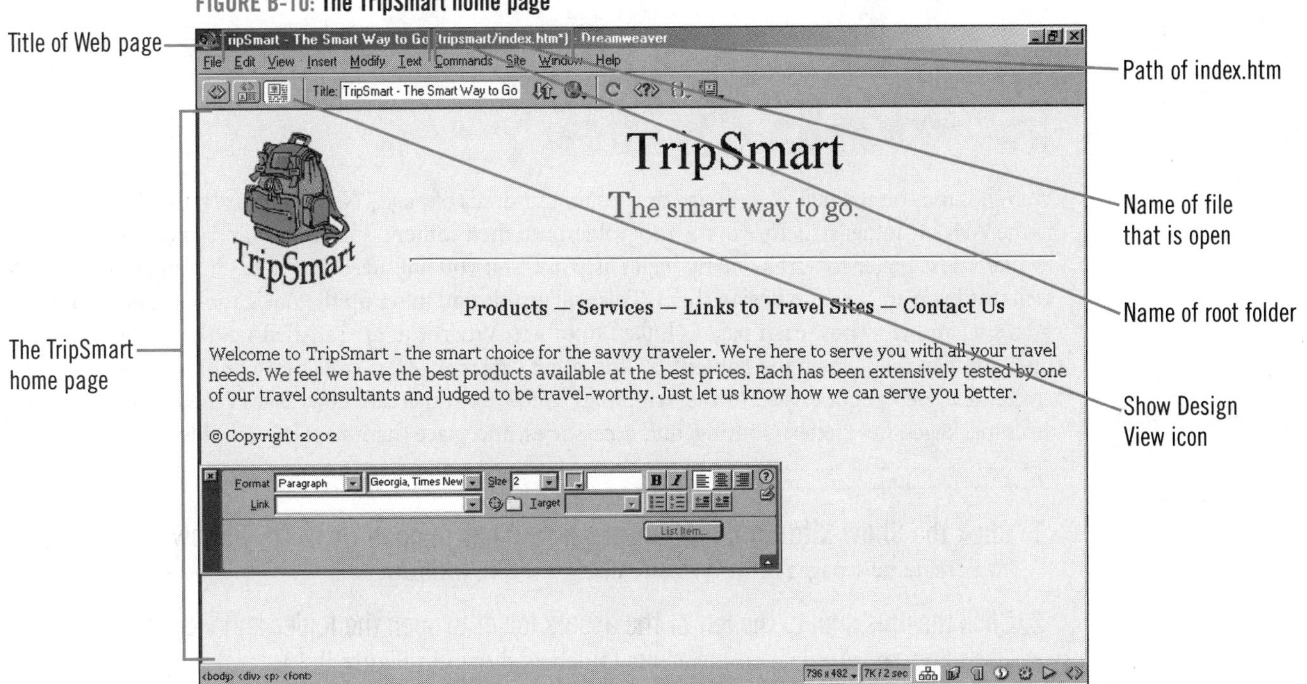

FIGURE B-11: Index.htm placed in the tripsmart root folder

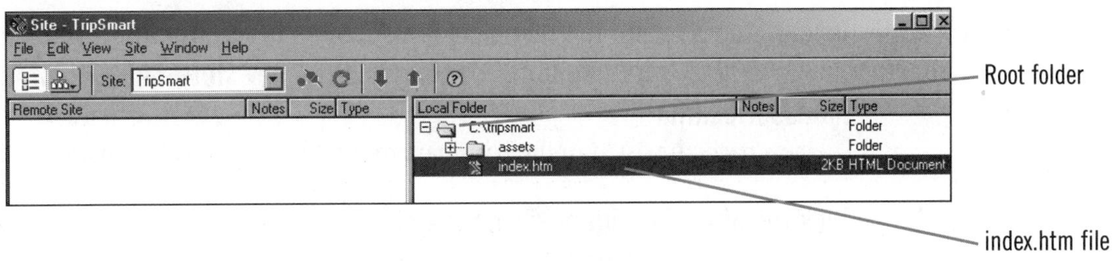

FIGURE B-12: Property Inspector showing properties of TripSmart logo

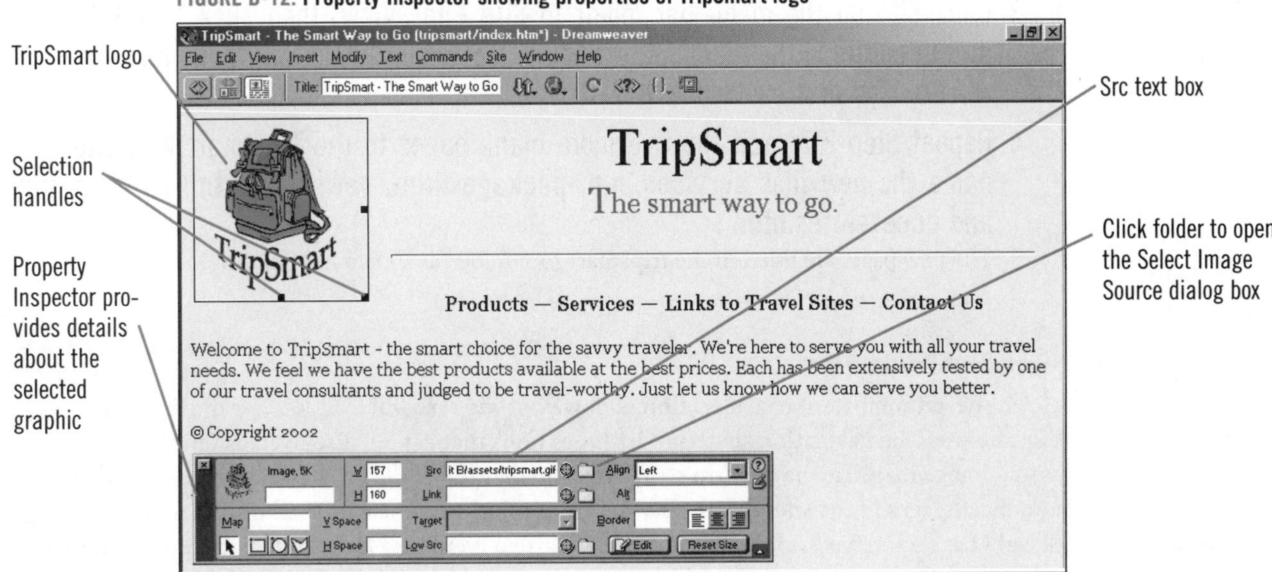

Dreamweaver 4

Dreamweaver 4

Adding New Pages to a Web Site

Web sites may be as small as one page or contain hundreds of pages. New pages are named and added to the Web site folder structure in the root folder, and then content, such as text and graphics, is added to them. It is better to add as many pages as you think you will need in the beginning, rather than wait until you are ready to design them. This will enable you to set up the navigation structure of the Web site, and view how each page is linked to others. When you are satisfied with the overall structure, you can then create the content for the pages.  After consulting your storyboard, you create new Web pages to add to the TripSmart Web site. You create new pages called products, services, packages, newsletter, clothing, and accessories, and place them in the root folder.

Steps

WIN

1. Click the **Show Site icon** on the status bar to open the Site window
   You create new pages for a Web site using the Site window.
2. Click the **plus sign** to the left of the assets folder to open the folder and view its contents
   The tripsmart.gif file is in the assets folder, as shown in Figure B-13.
3. Click **File** on the menu bar, then click **New File**, type **products.htm** in the filename text box to replace untitled.htm, then press **[Enter]**
   The products page is added to the Web site.
4. Repeat Step 3 to add the five more blank pages to the TripSmart Web site, and name the new files **services.htm**, **packages.htm**, **newsletter.htm**, **clothing.htm**, and **accessories.htm**
   The new pages are listed in the tripsmart root folder, as shown in Figure B-14.

QuickTip

If you create a new file in the Site window, you must type the filename extension (.htm or .html) manually.

MAC

1. Click the **Show Site icon** on the status bar to open the Site window
   You create new pages for a Web site using the Site window.
2. Click ▶ to the left of the assets folder to open the folder and view its contents
   The tripsmart.gif file is in the assets folder, as shown in Figure B-13.
3. Click **Site** on the menu bar, point to **Site Files View**, then click **New File**, type **products.htm** in the filename text box to replace untitled.html, then press **[return]**
   The products page is added to the Web site.
4. Repeat Step 3 to add the five more blank pages to the TripSmart Web site, and name the new files **services.htm**, **packages.htm**, **newsletter.htm**, **clothing.htm**, and **accessories.htm**
   The new pages are listed in the tripsmart root folder, as shown in Figure B-14.

Navigation structure

When creating a Web site, an important consideration is how your viewers will **navigate**, or move from page to page within the site. The navigation structure includes links that can be displayed as tabulated text, tables, graphics, or an image map. The navigation structure, whether text, buttons, or icons, should have a consistent look among all pages in the site. Otherwise, the viewer may become confused or lost within the site. Every page should have a link back to the home page. It's also a good idea to include back and forward links to take the viewer to the previous or next page in the site, instead of relying on the viewer to use the Back button on the browser toolbar.

FIGURE B-13: Site window showing the tripsmart.gif in the assets folder

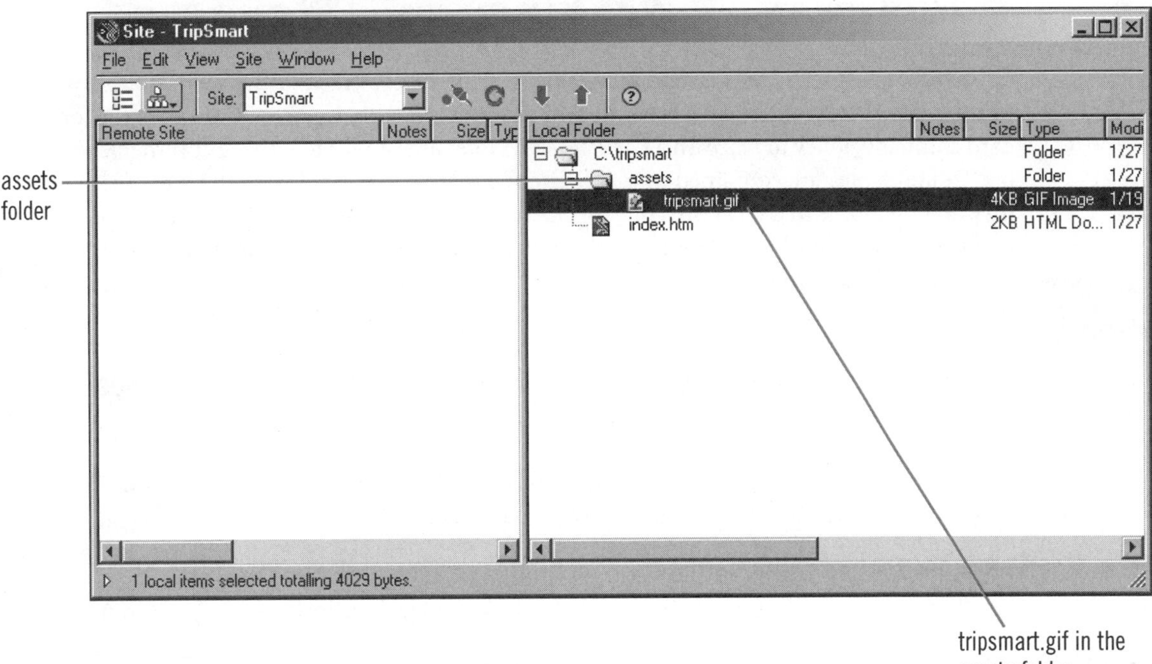

FIGURE B-14: New pages added to the TripSmart Web site

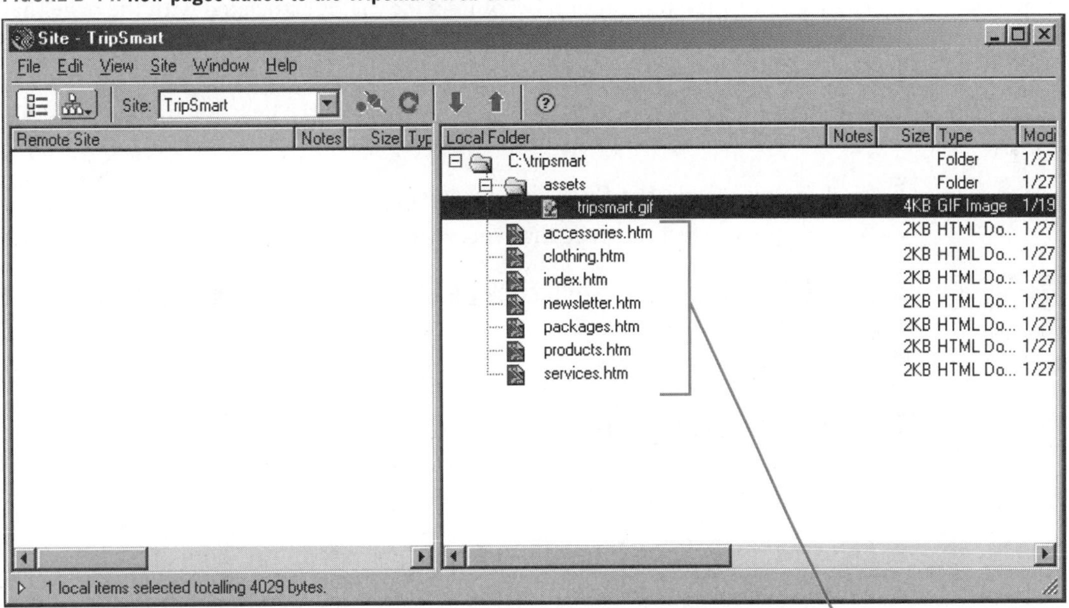

Using the Site window for file management

Using the Site window, you can add, delete, move, or rename files and folders in a Web site. It is very important that you perform these file maintenance tasks in the Site window rather than in Windows Explorer (Win) or at the Finder level (Mac). If you make changes to the Web site folder structure outside of the Site window, Dreamweaver will not recognize these changes. You use Windows Explorer (Win) or the Finder (Mac) to create the original root folder or to move or copy the root folder of a Web site to another location. If you move or copy the root folder to a new location, you will have to define the Web site again in Dreamweaver, as you did in the lesson on defining a Web site.

Dreamweaver 4

Using Design Notes

Design Notes is a Dreamweaver feature that helps you keep track of the various tasks you need to complete while working on a Web site. For example, you may need to locate a graphic or a standard company policy to place on a page. Design Notes are similar to writing comments in HTML, but Design Notes are contained in a separate file that is associated with the page file; therefore, they do not appear in the HTML code for the page. To use Design Notes, you must first make sure that the feature is enabled. Design Notes apply to the entire Web site, but are created for individual pages. You verify that the TripSmart Web site has the Design Notes option enabled, then create reminder notes to yourself in the Design Notes dialog box for the index page.

Steps

1. **Verify that you are in the Site window, click Site on the menu bar, then click Define Sites**
   The Define Sites dialog box opens.
2. **Click TripSmart in the Define Sites dialog box, if necessary, then click Edit**
   The Site Definition dialog box for TripSmart opens.
3. **Click Design Notes in the Category list, as shown in Figure B-15.**
   The options in the Site Definition dialog box change to reflect Design Notes options.
4. **Verify that there is a check mark in the Maintain Design Notes and the Upload Design Notes for Sharing check boxes, as shown in Figure B-15, click OK, then click Done**
   The Design Notes information becomes a file that is associated with the page that the notes were created for. If a page file is deleted, the associated Design Notes file will also be deleted. The Upload Design Notes for Sharing option allows the Design Notes file to be shared with other team members. If another team member opens a page file that has Design Notes, the Design Notes file associated with the page will also open.

QuickTip

Design Notes may also be used with objects, such as buttons or images on Web pages, by right-clicking (Windows) or [control]-clicking (Macintosh) the object, then clicking Design Notes.

5. **Click index.htm in the Site window to select it**
   You must first select the page that you want to create notes for.
6. **Click File on the main menu, click Design Notes, then click the Basic Info tab in the Design Notes dialog box**
   The Design Notes dialog box opens, and the Basic Information is displayed.

Trouble?

If you receive a message saying that Design Notes are disabled for this file, you probably did not select the file first. Click OK, click index.htm, and try again.

7. **Click the Status list arrow, then click draft**
   The Status list shows various stages of the page development process. You can choose the option that best describes the stage of development you are in.
8. **Click the Insert Date icon to insert the date in the Notes text box**
   It is helpful to have a record of when you created your notes.
9. **Click below the date in the Notes text box, then type**

   Ask Bob for a copy of the company history
   Choose the links for this page – add a newsletter link?
   Do we need another graphic on the page? Random travel photo?
10. **Click the Show When File Is Opened check box, as shown in Figure B-16, then click OK**
    The Design Notes dialog box closes. Notice the yellow Design Notes icon in the Notes column for the index page shown in Figure B-17. This icon indicates that there are notes attached to this file. You can double-click this icon to view the notes. Each time the index.htm file is opened in Design View, the Design Notes dialog box opens, displaying the notes associated with the open file.

QuickTip

You can also view Design Notes by clicking File on the menu bar, then clicking Design Notes, when you are in the Design View.

FIGURE B-15: Site Definition dialog box with Design Notes category selected

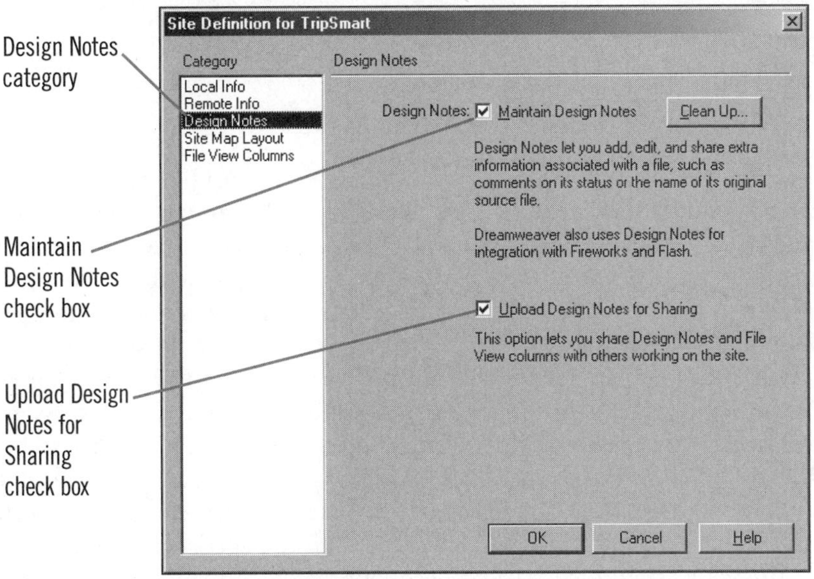

Design Notes category

Maintain Design Notes check box

Upload Design Notes for Sharing check box

Site Definition for TripSmart

Category: Local Info, Remote Info, Design Notes, Site Map Layout, File View Columns

Design Notes

Design Notes: Maintain Design Notes   Clean Up...

Design Notes let you add, edit, and share extra information associated with a file, such as comments on its status or the name of its original source file.

Dreamweaver also uses Design Notes for integration with Fireworks and Flash.

Upload Design Notes for Sharing

This option lets you share Design Notes and File View columns with others working on the site.

OK   Cancel   Help

FIGURE B-16: Design Notes dialog box

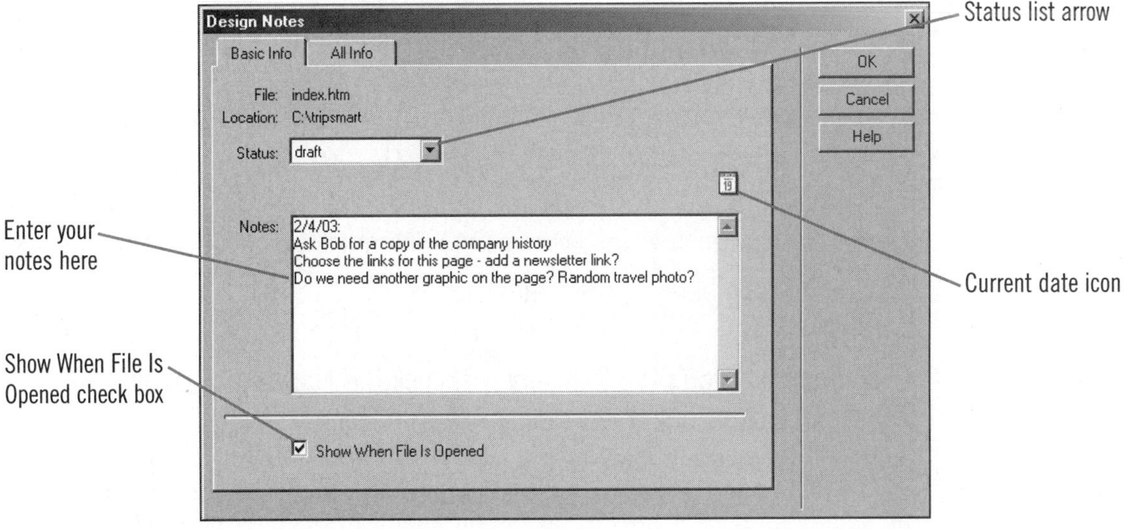

FIGURE B-17: Design Notes icon for the index.htm page

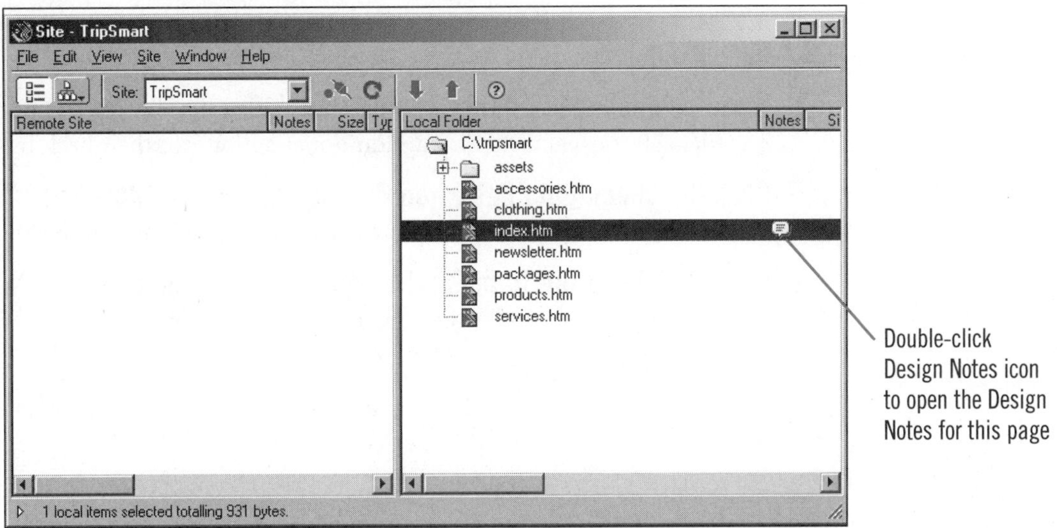

Dreamweaver 4

Dreamweaver 4

Setting Up Web Server Access

Before a Web site can be viewed on the Internet, it must be published. The process of publishing a Web site means that you are making it available for viewing on the Internet. A Web site is published to a **Web server**, a computer that is connected to the Internet with a **static** (permanent) **IP (Internet Protocol) address**. Web servers are either **local** (your computer is connected to the server) or **remote** (your computer is not connected to the server). Choosing a local or remote server is known as setting up your **web server access**. If you use a remote server, your Web files can be uploaded using **File Transfer Protocol**, or **FTP**. You use the Site Definition dialog box in Dreamweaver to set up your Web server access. As you work on individual pages in the Web site, you can deny access to them by other Web designers, using the **Check In/Check Out** feature. This also shows other team members which files are checked out and who checked them out, in case they need to locate them. When you check out a page, you ensure that no one else can edit that page until you check it back in. You can enable the Check In/Check Out feature when you choose your remote server access type in the Site Definition window. You set up remote server access for the TripSmart Web site. Since you will be working with other team members on the site, you decide to enable the Check In/Check Out feature.

Steps

1. Make sure you are in the Site window by clicking the **Show Site icon** on the status bar or the Launcher bar, if necessary
   The Show Site icon is available on both the status bar and the Launcher bar.
2. Click the **Site list arrow**, then click **Define Sites**, as shown in Figure B-18
   The Define Sites dialog box opens with the TripSmart site highlighted. You need to fill in the information for remote access, because you will be publishing your site to a remote server.
3. Click **Edit** in the Define Sites dialog box
   The Site Definition dialog box opens.
4. Click **Remote Info** in the Category list, click the **Access list arrow** (Win) or **Server Access list arrow** (Mac), then click **FTP**
   To be able to use the FTP access, you need to complete the information that Dreamweaver will use to find the FTP site and log on to it in order to publish the files. You must include the address for the FTP host, the name you will use to access the host site, and the password that was assigned when the account was created.
5. Click the **FTP Host text box**, then type **ftp.hostsite.com**
   See Figure B-19. The host is the server that will "host," or house, the Web site files so they may be accessed over the Internet through the host IP address.
6. Click the **Enable File Check In and Check Out check box** to enable this option
   The dialog box expands to display additional options for the Check In/Out feature.
7. Click the **Check Out Files when Opening check box**, unless it is already checked
   When a page is checked out, only the person who checked it out will have access to it.
8. Click the **Check Out Name text box**, type your name, then press **[Tab]**
   The [Tab] key brings you to the E-mail Address text box.
9. Type your e-mail address
   See Figure B-20. Your name and e-mail address will be displayed for team members to show who has checked out the file.
10. Click **OK**, then click **Done**
    The Site Definition and the Define Sites dialog boxes close.

FIGURE B-18: **Accessing the Define Sites dialog box using the Site list arrow**

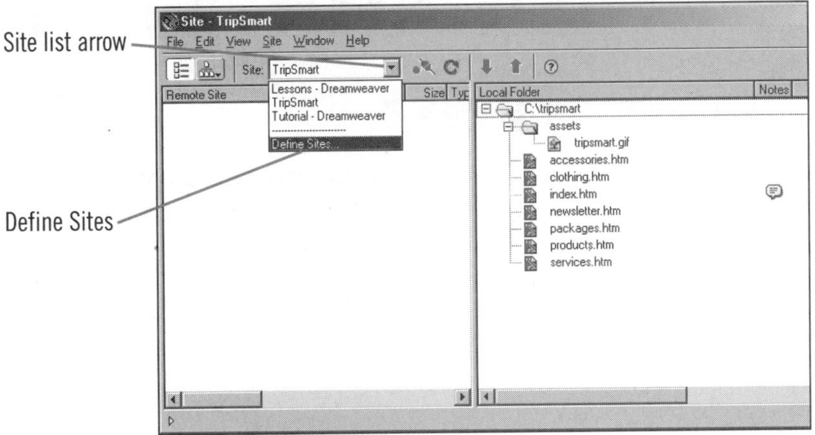

FIGURE B-19: **Choosing FTP as the type of remote access**

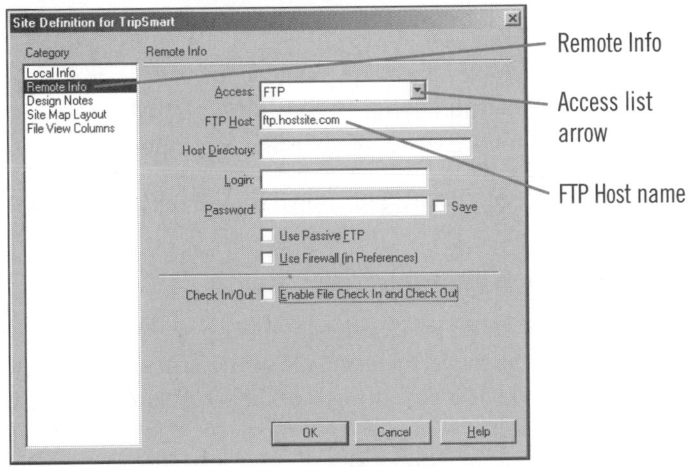

FIGURE B-20: **Remote Info Check In/Out information**

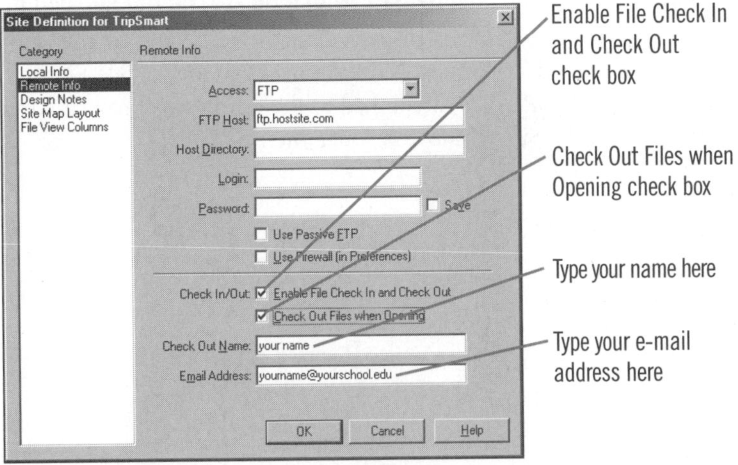

Using the Site window with a remote server

If you have set up remote server access for your Web site, you can use the Site window to connect to that server. You can also upload and download files to the server using the **Put** and **Get** icons on the toolbar. The Put icon is used to send files to the remote server, and the Get icon is used to retrieve files from the remote server. The left pane of the Site window displays the files and folders on the remote server. The right pane displays the files and folders on your computer. Dragging files from one pane to the other is another method of moving files between the remote server and the local folder.

Dreamweaver 4

Dreamweaver 4

Creating and Viewing a Site Map

As new Web pages are added to a Web site, it is easy to lose track of how they all link together. Dreamweaver has a feature called a **Site Map**, which is a graphical representation of the Web pages in the Web site. You can find out details about each page by viewing the visual clues in the Site Map. For example, the Site Map uses icons to indicate pages with broken links, e-mail links, or links to external Web sites. It also indicates which pages are currently checked out. You create a Site Map for TripSmart. The Site Map only shows the home page, since you have not linked other pages to it yet.

Steps

1. Click the **Show Site icon** if necessary to show the Site window, click the **Site list arrow**, click **Define Sites**, click **TripSmart** if necessary, then click **Edit**
   The Site Definition dialog box opens.
2. Click **Site Map Layout** in the Category list
   Options for the layout of your Site Map appear in the Site Definition dialog box.
3. Verify that index.htm is shown as the home page in the Home Page text box, as shown in Figure B-21
4. Click the **Page Titles option button**
   This option is used if you want to display the page titles instead of the filenames in the Site Map; for example, the page title of the TripSmart Web site is TripSmart – The Smart Way to Go, and the filename of the TripSmart Web site is index.htm.
5. Click **OK**, then click **Done**
   The Site Definition dialog box and the Define Sites dialog box close.
6. Press and hold the **Site Map icon** on the Site window toolbar, then click **Map and Files**
   The Site Map is displayed in the left pane of the Site window, showing the home page, named TripSmart – The Smart Way to Go. See Figure B-22. The Site Map only shows the Web pages that are linked to the home page. You can drag the border between the two panes in the Site window to resize them.

Trouble?

If the index.htm file is not shown as your home page, click the folder icon next to the Home Page text box, then double-click the index.htm filename.

QuickTip

You can click the small black triangle on the Site Map icon to choose Map Only or Map and Files. If you choose Map Only, the files and folders on the right side of the Site window disappear.

FIGURE B-21: Options for the Site Map Layout

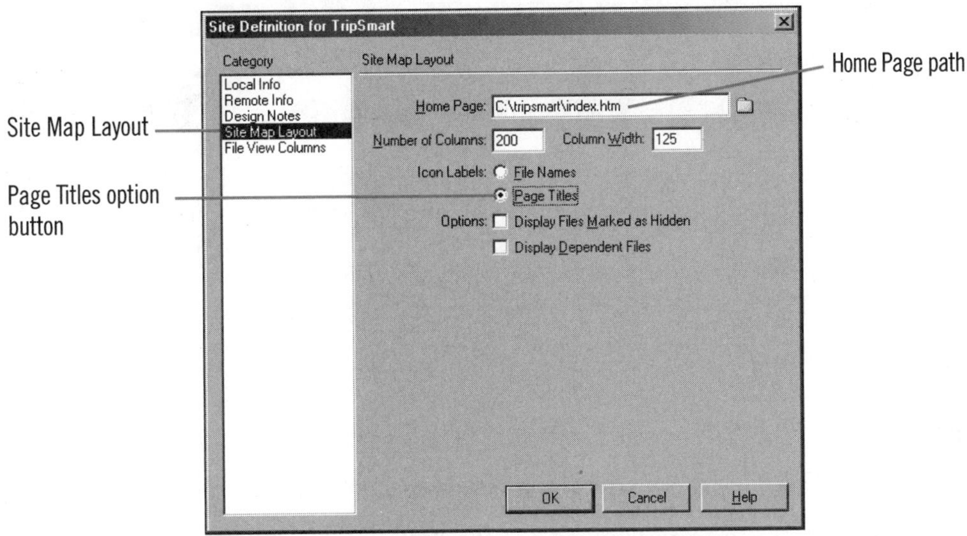

FIGURE B-22: The Site Map for TripSmart

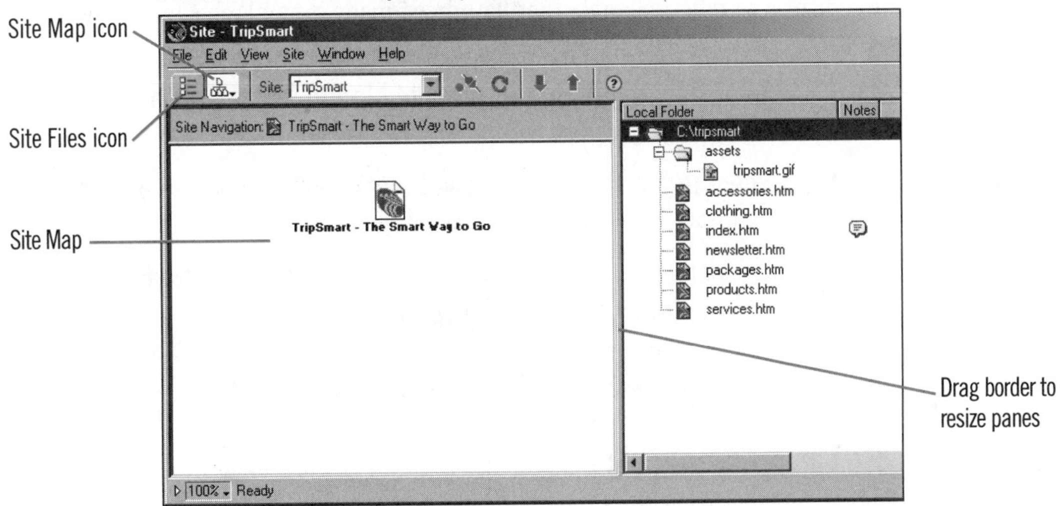

Design Matters

Using Site Map images in Web pages

Dreamweaver gives you the option of saving a Site Map for printing purposes or for viewing on a page in a Web site. It is very helpful to include a graphic of the Site Map in a Web site, to help viewers understand the navigation structure of the site. To save a Site Map, click File on the menu bar, then click Save Site Map (Win) or click Site on the menu bar, point to Site Map View, point to Save Site Map, then click save Site Map as PICT or Save Sit Map as JPEG (Mac). If you are using a Windows computer, the Save Site Map dialog box opens. You should name the Site Map in the File name text box, then save the Site Map as a BMP (bitmapped) file or as a PNG file (Portable Network Graphics file). Choose BMP if you want to print the Site Map or insert it into a page layout program or a slide show. Choose PNG if you plan on inserting the Site Map on a Web page. If you are using a Macintosh, you'll be prompted to choose Save Site Map as PICT or Save Site Map as JPEG, then the Save dialog box will appear, where you can name the saved Site Map. Choose PICT if you want to print the Site Map or insert it into a page layout program or a slide show. Choose JPEG if you plan on inserting the Site Map on a Web page. Though gaining in popularity, PNG files are not available on the Macintosh platform and are not supported by older versions of browsers. However, they are capable of showing millions of colors, are small in size, and compress well without losing image quality.

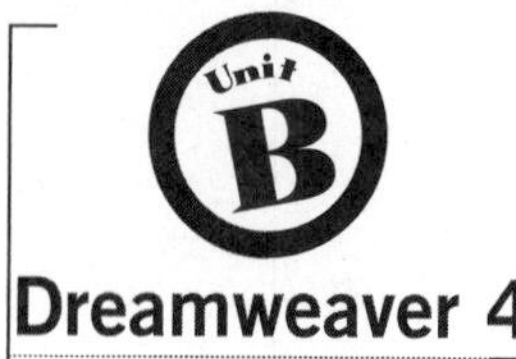

Dreamweaver 4

Modifying Pages from the Site Window

There are several tasks that are easily accomplished in the Site window. You can double-click a file in the Site window and open it in Design View for editing. You can then switch to Code View or Code and Design View, if necessary. You can also edit page titles for pages listed in the Site Map. The Site window is the safest place to rename, move, and delete pages in a Web site to ensure that the page links will remain intact. You decide to change the page title to Welcome to Tripsmart – The Smart Way to Go.

Steps

1. Make sure you are still in the Site Map view of the Site window
2. Click the **Refresh icon** to refresh the view in the Site window if necessary
   Refreshing the view means that Dreamweaver will reread the files and make adjustments in the display to reflect changes that have been made in the Web site, such as additions, deletions, or modifications in files.
3. Click the **TripSmart page icon** in the Site Map to select it, if necessary
   The page title is highlighted in blue when the page is selected.
4. Click anywhere in the TripSmart – The Smart Way to Go name on the page icon
   The cursor appears at the end of the title name.
5. Click the insertion point before the **T** in TripSmart, type **Welcome to**, press the **spacebar** once, then press **[Enter]** (Win) or **[return]** (Mac)
   Pressing [Enter] (Win) or [return] (Mac) removes the cursor and keeps the new name. The page title now reads Welcome to TripSmart – The Smart Way to Go. You have finished your Site Map for the TripSmart Web site. Your screen should resemble Figure B-23.
6. Double-click **index.html** to open the page in Design View
   Notice the new page title in the title bar.
7. Click **File** on the menu bar, then click **Save**
8. Click **File** on the menu bar, then click **Exit** (Win) or **Quit** (Mac)

Trouble?

You may have to click more than once to place the cursor in the title name.

FIGURE B-23: **The finished Site Map for the TripSmart Web site**

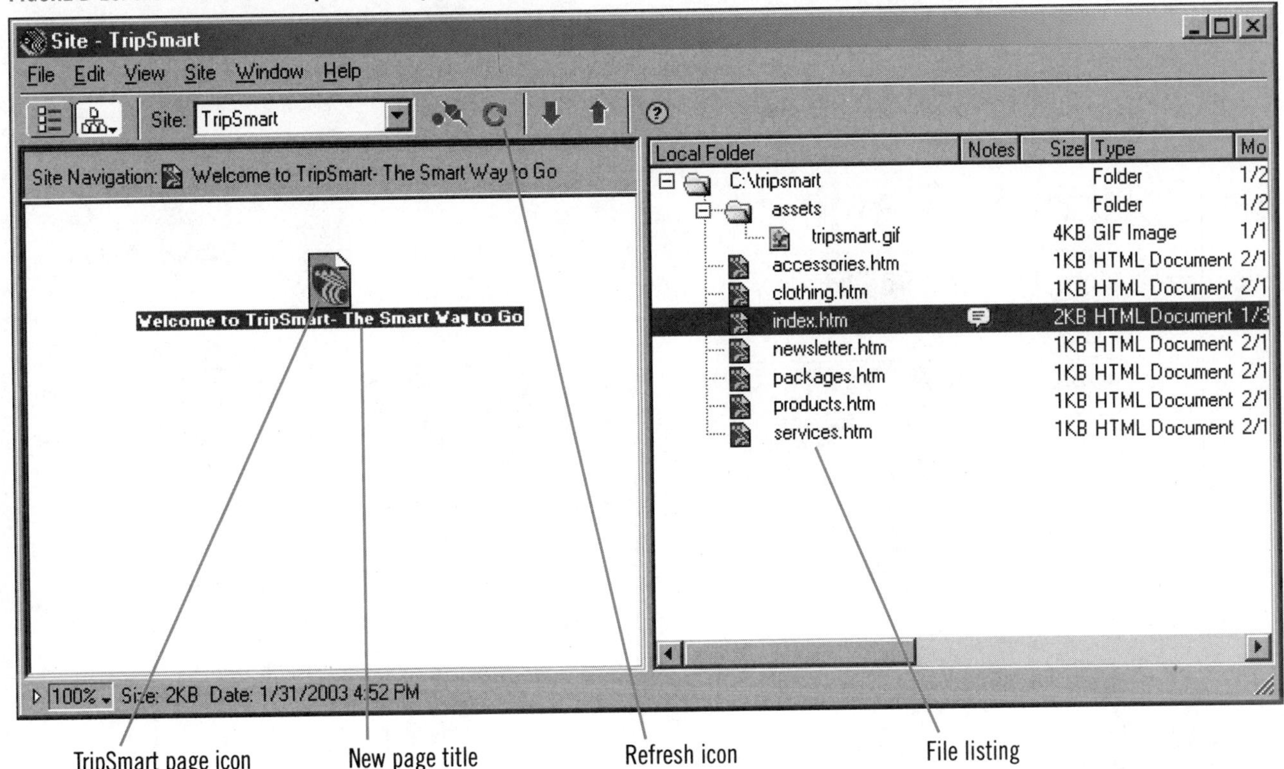

Choosing page titles

When a Web page is viewed in a browser window, its title is displayed in the browser window title bar. The page title should reflect the page content and set the tone for the page. Moreover, it is important to use words in your page title that may match keywords viewers may enter when using a search engine. Search engines compare the text in page titles to the keywords typed into the search engine. When a title bar displays "Untitled Document", the designer has neglected to give the page a title. To quickly check that you have included page titles on all of your Web pages, click the Site Map icon in the Site window, click View on the menu bar, then verify that Show Page Titles is checked (Win) or click Site on the menu bar, point to Site Map View, then click Show Page Titles (Mac).

Practice

► Concepts Review

Label each element in the Site window as shown in Figure B-24.

FIGURE B-24

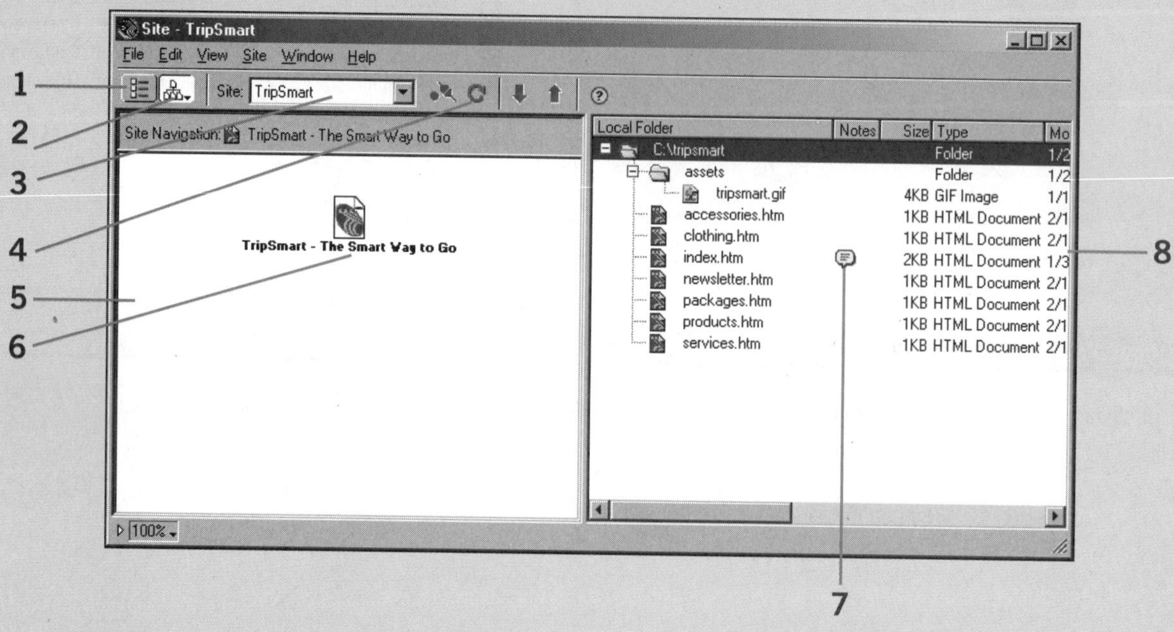

Match each of the following terms with the statement that describes its function.

9. Storyboard
10. Assets
11. IP address
12. Web server
13. FTP
14. Site cache
15. Design Notes
16. Primary browser
17. Site Map

a. An address on the Web
b. Computer connected to the Internet with an IP address
c. Temporary memory used to increase the speed of site management tasks
d. Small sketch showing the relationships among pages in a Web site
e. The first browser that is used to test Web pages being edited in Dreamweaver
f. Used to keep track of various tasks while working on the Web site
g. Folder that contains non-HTML files
h. Process of uploading and downloading files to and from a remote site
i. A diagram of the folder structure of the Web site with information about links

Select the best answer from the following list of choices.

18. A Web server that is not connected to your computer is known as a:
- **a.** Local server.
- **b.** Site server.
- **c.** Remote server.
- **d.** Design server.

19. The first step in designing a Web site should be:
- **a.** Setting up Web server access.
- **b.** Testing the pages.
- **c.** Planning the site.
- **d.** Creating the pages and developing the content.

20. Which icon do you click to refresh the Site window after changes have been made to the files in the Site window?
- **a.**
- **b.**
- **c.**
- **d.**

21. The option to show page titles instead of filenames in the Site Map is accessed through the:
- **a.** Site Definition dialog box.
- **b.** Design Notes.
- **c.** Remote Info.
- **d.** File menu.

Skills Review

1. Plan a Web site.
- **a.** Sketch a storyboard with four pages for a company called Blooms & Bulbs.
- **b.** Name the pages index, plants, events, and tips. (The plants, events, and tips pages will be links from the index page.)
- **c.** Add three pages that will link from the plants page: annuals, perennials, and water_plants.

2. Create a folder for Web site management.
- **a.** Start Dreamweaver.
- **b.** Create a new folder with the name blooms_and_bulbs.

3. Define the Web site.
- **a.** Define the site using the Site window.
- **b.** Name the site Blooms & Bulbs.
- **c.** Browse to the root folder created for the Web site in the Local Root Folder text box.
- **d.** Select Enable Cache and Refresh Local File List Automatically, if necessary, click OK, click OK again, then click Done.

4. **Add a folder to the Web site and set the home page.**
   a. Create an assets folder for the Web site, using the Site window.
   b. Open dmb_2.htm from the drive and folder where your Project Files are stored.
   c. Save the file as *index.htm* in the Blooms & Bulbs Web site.
   d. Select the logo on the page.
   f. Click the folder icon next to the Src text box on the Property Inspector, click the drive and folder where your Project Files are stored, double-click the Unit B folder, double-click the assets folder, click the blooms_logo.gif, then click Select (Win) or Open (Mac).
   g. Click Yes in the dialog box that asks you if you want to copy the file to the assets folder.
   h. Double-click the assets folder, then click Save.
   i. Return to the Site window, then set index.htm as the home page.
5. **Add new pages to a Web site.**
   a. Using the Site window, create a new page called plants.htm.
   b. Create a new page called events.htm.
   c. Create a new page called tips.htm.
   d. Create a new page called annuals.htm.
   e. Create a new page called perennials.htm.
   f. Create a new page called water_plants.htm.
6. **Use Design Notes.**
   a. Using the Site window, enable the Design Notes feature for the Blooms & Bulbs site.
   b. Open the Design Notes page for the index page.
   c. Select draft from the Status list arrow.
   d. Insert the current date in the Notes text box.
   e. In the notes text box, type **Add company history and profile**.
   f. Select the option Show When File Is Opened.
   g. Save the notes with the index page.
7. **Set up Web server access.**
   a. View the settings for Remote Info in the Site Definition dialog box.
   b. Set up the access for FTP.
   c. Use the name ftp.hostsite.com.
   d. Type your name and e-mail address in the appropriate boxes.
8. **Create a Site Map.**
   a. Create a Site Map of the Web site, using the Site Map Layout dialog box.
   b. Display the Site Map in the Site window.
   c. Save your work.
9. **Modify pages from the Site window.**
   a. Rename the page title for the index page Blooms & Bulbs - Complete Garden Center.

▶ Independent Challenge 1

Dreamweaver has a Help feature called Guided Tour, which teaches you how to use Dreamweaver, using movies of Dreamweaver tasks being performed. The Guided Tour has an excellent movie about planning your Web site.

a. Click Help on the menu bar, then click Guided Tour.
b. Click Planning your site.
c. Follow the directions on the screen and click the movie icons to view the movies.
d. Close the Help window when you are done.

▶ Independent Challenge 2

You have been hired to create a Web site for a river expedition company named Rapids Transit, located on the Buffalo River in Arkansas. In addition to renting canoes, kayaks, and rafts, they have a country store and a snack bar. River guides are available, if requested, to accompany clients on float trips. The clients range from high-school and college students to families to vacationing professionals.

a. Create a Web site plan and storyboard for this site.
b. Create a folder named rapids_transit in the drive and folder where your Project Files are stored.
c. Define the Web site with the name Rapids Transit.
d. Create an assets folder.
e. Open dmb_3.htm from the drive and folder where your Project Files are stored, then save it in the Web as *index.htm*, and set it as the home page.
f. Save the rapids_logo.gif in the assets folder.
g. Create four additional files for the pages in your plan, and name them the following: guides.htm, rentals.htm, store.htm, and snacks.htm.

Independent Challenge 3

You have been asked to design a Web site for the Over Under Dive Shop in Nevis, West Indies. This is a certified Professional Association of Diving Instructors (PADI) dive center, offering PADI certification courses. They also conduct snorkeling and dive trips to various locations around the barrier reef surrounding Nevis.

a. Create a Web site plan and storyboard for this site.

b. Create a folder for the Web site in the drive and folder where your Project Files are stored.

c. Define the Web site with the name Over Under.

d. Create an assets folder.

e. Open dmb_4.htm from the drive and folder where your Project Files are stored, then save it in the Web as *index.htm*, and set it as the home page.

f. Using the Design Notes option, make several notes to yourself on the home page, using Figure B-25 as a guide.

g. Save the over_logo.gif in the assets folder.

h. Create three new pages called diving.htm, snorkeling.htm, and padi.htm.

FIGURE B-25

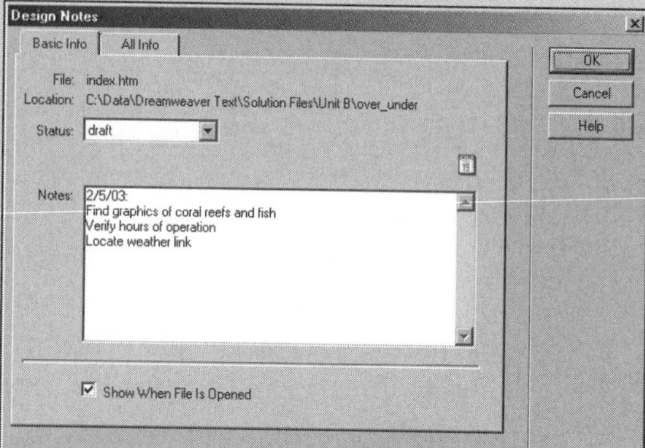

Independent Challenge 4

Your company has been selected to design a Web site for a new restaurant called Jacob's, located in the theater district in New York City. This is an upscale restaurant catering to business executives and theater patrons. They have an extensive menu including prix fixe dinners, pre-theater dinner specials, and after-theater specials. The cuisine is primarily French.

a. Create a Web site plan and storyboard for this site.

b. Create a folder for the Web site in the drive and folder where your Project Files are stored.

c. Define the Web site with the name Jacob's.

d. Create the assets folder and three new pages called after_theater.htm, pre_theater.htm, and prix_fix.htm.

e. Open dmb_5.htm from the drive and folder where your Project Files are stored, then save it as *index.htm*, and set it as the home page.

f. Save the jacobs_logo.gif in the assets folder.

g. Connect to the Internet and go to Zagat's Web site at *www.zagat.com*. Zagat's is a restaurant guide with listings of restaurants from around the world.

h. Locate some New York restaurants, and then, using a search engine such as *www.altavista.com*, search for Web sites for the restaurants you located in the Zagat guide.

i. Formulate ideas for additional pages to add to the Web site and write them down.

Independent Challenge 5

Caleb Andrew would like to buy a new car. He is considering many different makes and models, but is concentrating today on a Toyota. He is looking particularly for information on the environmental commitment of Toyotas in general and information on retail financing. Record your answers to the questions below on scrap paper or in your word-processing software.

a. Connect to the Internet and go to Toyota at *www.toyota.com.*
b. Click the Help link on the home page.
c. How has Toyota organized information to help you navigate their Web site?
d. Can you find the information that Caleb needs?
e. Did you feel that the help page was an aid in navigating the Web site?
f. Do you feel that this is a definite benefit for viewers?
g. Close your browser.

FIGURE B-26

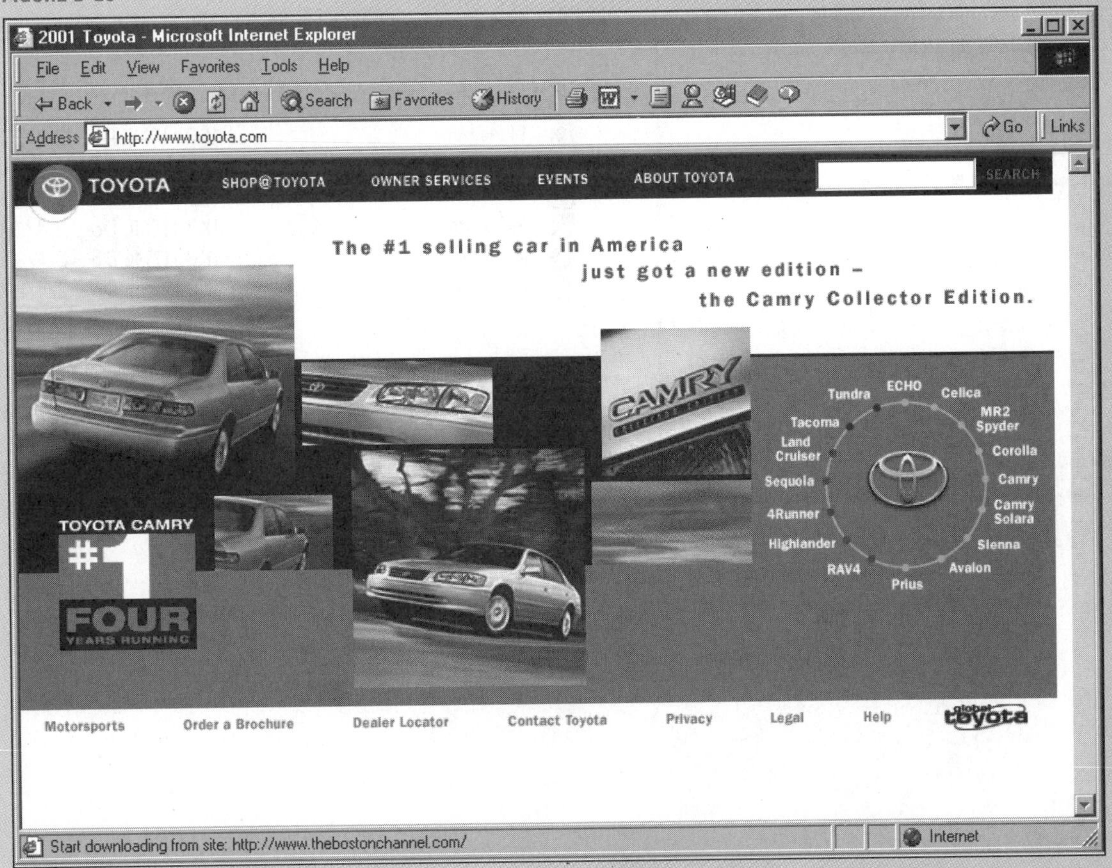

► Visual Workshop

Create the Web site pictured in Figure B-27, using the files dmb_6.htm and offnote_logo.gif, which are located in the drive and folder where your Project Files are stored.

FIGURE B-27

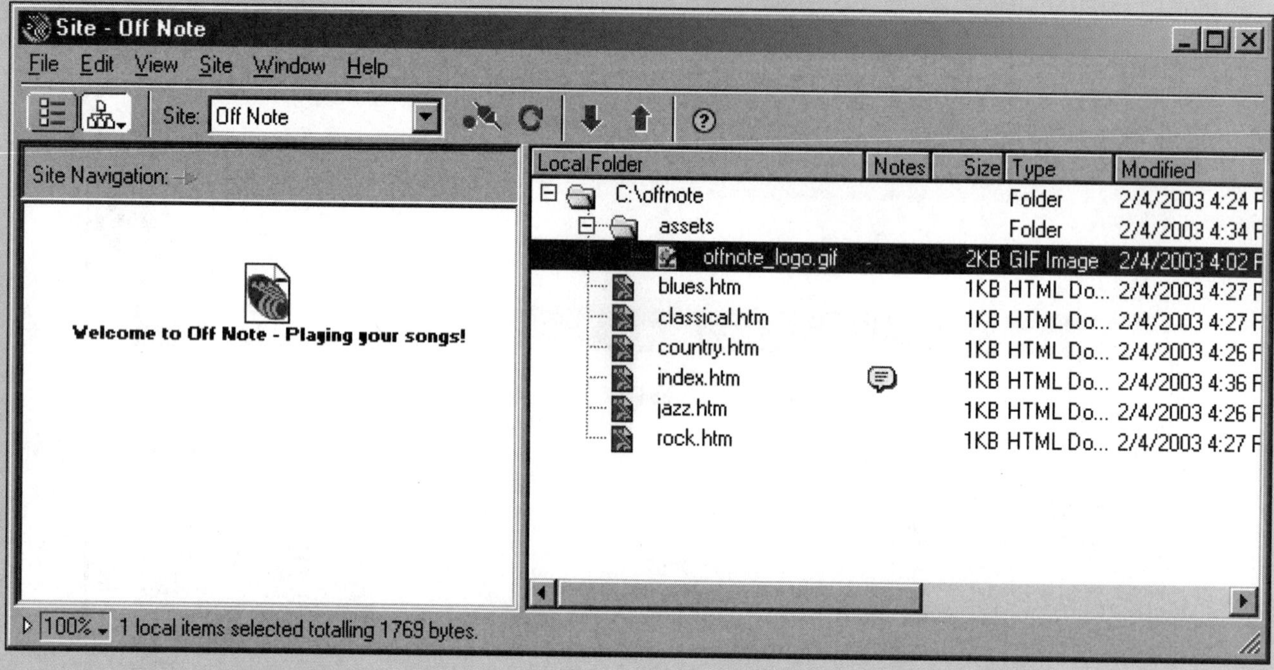

Dreamweaver 4

Developing a Web Page

Objectives

- Plan the page layout
- Create the head content
- Set Web page properties
- Create and format text
- Add links to Web pages
- Use the History panel
- View HTML code
- Test and modify Web pages

When you begin developing Web pages, you should choose the page content with the audience in mind. What is the age group of your audience? What reading level is appropriate? Should the pages be simple, containing mostly text, or rich with images and multimedia elements? In this unit, you will learn about planning a Web site, redesigning a Web page and linking it to other pages. You'll also use the History panel and the HTML Reference panel. Finally, you'll view the Code Inspector to modify some of the page code, and test the links to make sure they work. The TripSmart Web site should appeal to families, college students on a limited budget, and maturing baby boomers with leisure time and money to spend. You improve the design and content of the home page to attract this broad target audience.

Dreamweaver 4

Planning the Page Layout

When people visit your Web site, you want them to feel "at home," meaning you want them to feel as if they know their way around the pages in your site. You also want to make sure that viewers will not get "lost" in your Web site due to an inconsistency in the layout of your Web pages. When you consider the layout plan for a Web page, you need to consider all of the Web pages in the Web site. It's important that each page has a consistent look and feel. Templates can be used to maintain a common look for each page. **Templates** are Web pages that contain the basic layout for several pages in the site, such as the location of a company logo or a menu of buttons. Before you begin working on the TripSmart home page, you identify key concepts that encompass good page layout:

Details

- **Use white space effectively**
  A cluttered living room crammed with too much furniture makes it difficult to see or appreciate any of the individual pieces. The same is true of a Web page. Too many text blocks, links, and images can be distracting for viewers, and actually make them feel agitated. Consider leaving some white space on each page. **White space**, which is not necessarily white, is an area on a Web page that is not filled with text or graphics. Using white space effectively creates a harmonious balance for the page.

- **Limit multimedia elements**
  The expression "less is more" is especially true of Web pages. Too many multimedia elements, such as graphics, video clips, or sounds, may result in a page that takes too long to load. Viewers may tire of waiting for these elements to load and leave your Web site before the entire page finishes loading. Placing a multimedia element on your page without a good reason may make your Web site seem unprofessional.

- **Keep it simple**
  Often the simplest Web sites are the most appealing. The Web sites that are simple in layout and design are the easiest to create and maintain. A simple Web site that works is far superior to a complex one with errors.

- **Use an intuitive navigation structure**
  The navigation structure of a Web site should be easy to use; it can be based on text links or a combination of text and graphic links. Viewers should always know where they are in the Web site, and be able to quickly find their way back to the home page. If viewers get lost while in your Web site, they may leave the site rather than struggle to find their way around.

- **Apply a consistent theme**
  A theme can be almost anything—from the same background color on each page to common graphics, such as nautical, western, automotive, or literary buttons or icons. Common design elements, such as borders, can also be considered a theme.

- **Be conscious of accessibility issues**
  You cannot assume that your viewers all have perfect vision and hearing or full use of both hands. There are several techniques you can use to ensure that your Web site is accessible to individuals with disabilities. These techniques include using alternative text with graphic images, avoiding certain colors on Web pages, and supplying text as an alternate source for information that is presented in an audio file. You can test your Web site for accessibility before publishing it by submitting it to be tested by **Bobby**, a free service provided by **CAST**, the Center for Applied Special Technology. See Figure C-1.

FIGURE C-1: **Welcome to Bobby 3.2 CAST Web page**

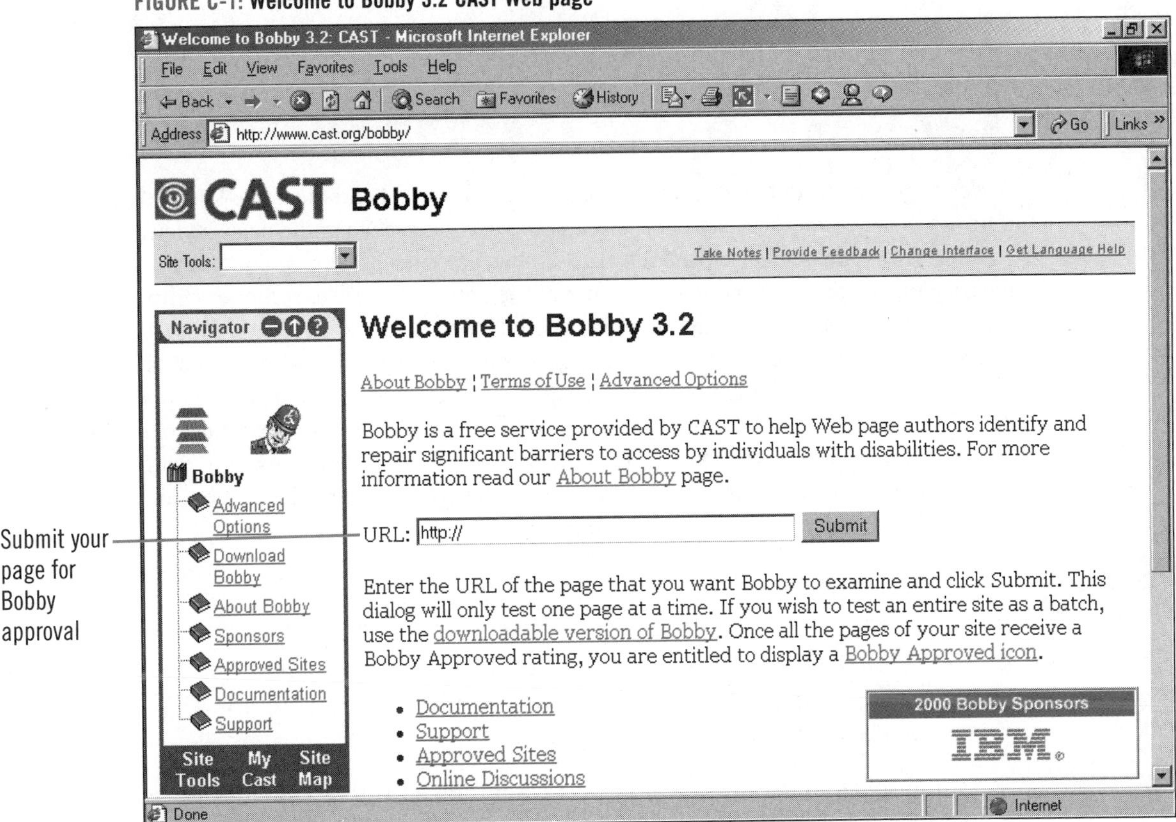

Bobby Guidelines

CAST, Center for Applied Special Technology, was founded in 1984 as an educational, non-profit organization that uses technology to expand opportunities for all people, including those with disabilities. CAST provides a free software program called Bobby that can be downloaded from their site. This program can be used to test an entire site. Individual pages, however, can be submitted for evaluation directly to Bobby through the CAST Web site. The Web site address for information about Bobby is *www.cast.org/bobby/*. The current version of Bobby supports the May 5, 1999, Web Content Accessibility Guidelines. Sites that have been approved through Bobby are entitled to display the Bobby Approved icon on their Web pages.

Dreamweaver 4

Creating the Head Content

A Web page consists of two distinct sections: the head content and the body. The **body** is the part we think of as the entire Web page, because it is the part we see when the page is viewed in a browser window. It contains the page contents, such as text, graphics, and links. The **head content** includes the page title that is displayed in the title bar of the browser, as well as some very important page elements that are not visible in the browser. These items are called meta tags. **Meta tags** are HTML codes that include information about the page, such as keywords and descriptions. **Keywords** are words that relate to the content of the Web site. Search engines find Web pages by matching the title, description, and keywords in the head content of Web pages with keywords entered in search text boxes by viewers. A **description** is a short description of the Web site. Before you work on page content for the home page, you create a good title for the page, a description, and keywords that will draw viewers to the TripSmart Web site.

Trouble?
If you click TripSmart and the Site Definition dialog box opens, click Cancel.

Trouble?
The Head Content option is not available in Code View.

QuickTip
You can also change the page title in the Title text box on the toolbar.

1. Start Dreamweaver, click the **Show Site icon** on the Launcher bar or the status bar, click the **Site list arrow** on the toolbar, then click **Tripsmart**, if necessary
   The TripSmart Web site opens.
2. Double-click **index.htm** in the Local Folder list of the Site window, click **OK** to close the Design Notes dialog box, click **View** on the menu bar, then click **Head Content**
   The head content section is displayed at the top of the TripSmart home page, as shown in Figure C-2. The head content section includes the Title icon and the Meta tag icon .
3. Click the **Objects panel list arrow**, then click **Head**
   The Objects panel displays icons representing the options available for the head content.
4. Click the **Title icon** in the head content section
   The Property Inspector displays the current title of the Web page in the Title text box, as shown in Figure C-3.
5. Click-and-drag the insertion point to highlight the title, type **TripSmart: Serving all your travel needs** in the Title text box on the Property Inspector, then press **[Enter]** (Win) or **[return]** (Mac)
   The new title replaces the old title. The new title uses the word travel, which is a word that potential TripSmart customers may use as a keyword when using a search engine.
6. Click the **Insert Keywords icon** on the Objects panel, type **travel, traveling, supplies, trips,** and **vacations** in the Insert Keywords text box, as shown in Figure C-4, then click **OK**
   The Insert Keywords icon is displayed in the head content, indicating that keywords have been created for the Web page.
7. Click the **Insert Description icon** on the Objects panel, type **TripSmart is a comprehensive travel store. We can help you plan trips, make the arrangements, and supply you with travel gear.**, then click **OK**
   See Figure C-5. The Insert Description icon is displayed in the head content, indicating that a description has been entered for the Web page.
8. Click the **Show Code View icon** on the toolbar, then click the **Show Design View icon**
   The title, keywords, and description are shown in the HTML code, as shown in Figure C-6.

FIGURE C-2: Viewing the head content

Head content

Page Title icon

Meta tag icon

Welcome to TripSmart - The Smart Way to Go (tripsmart/index.htm) - Dreamweaver

File Edit View Insert Modify Text Commands Site Window Help

Title: Welcome to TripSmart - The Smar

FIGURE C-3: Property Inspector displaying current page title

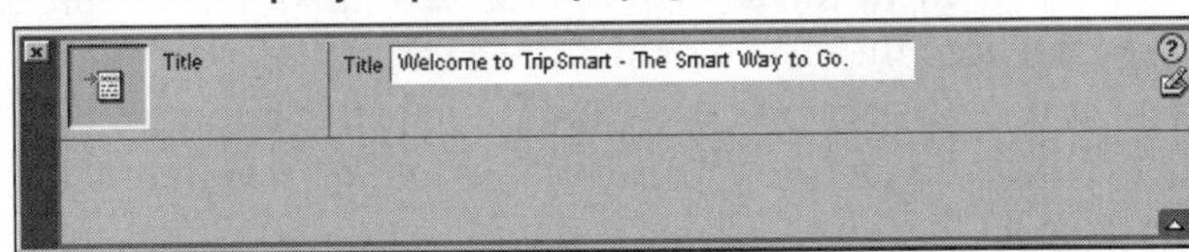

FIGURE C-4: Insert Keywords dialog box

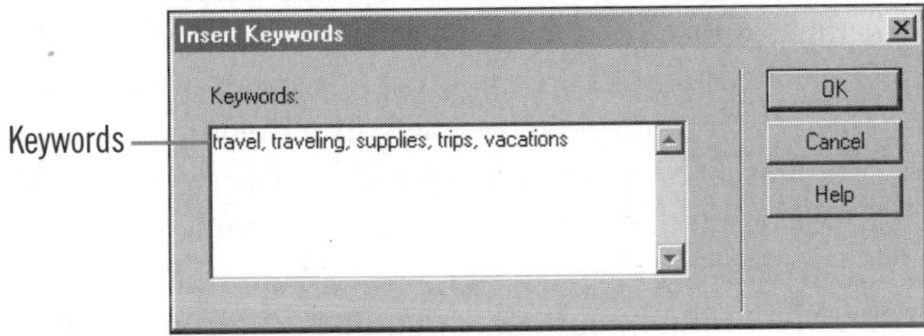

FIGURE C-5: Insert Description dialog box

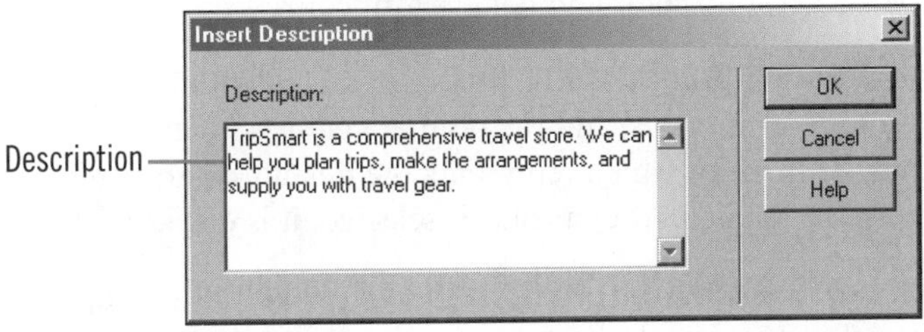

FIGURE C-6: Code View displaying head content

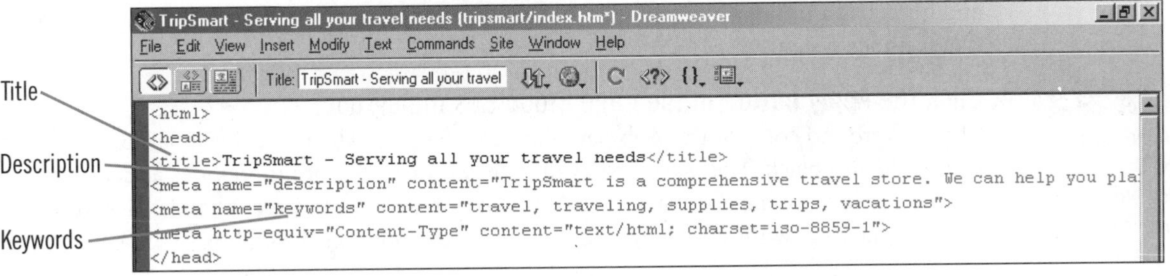

Entering titles, keywords, and descriptions

Search engines use keywords, descriptions, and titles to find pages after the user enters search terms. Therefore, it is very important to try to anticipate what your potential customers would use for search terms, and to try to include those in the keywords, description, or title. Many search engines print the page titles and descriptions when the pages are listed in the search results. Some search engines limit the number of keywords that they will index. Keep your keywords and description short and to the point, to avoid being ignored by search engines that limit the number of words you can use.

Dreamweaver 4

Setting Web Page Properties

One of the first design decisions that you should make is the background color of your Web page. The **background color** is the color that fills the entire Web page. The background color should complement the colors used for text, links, and graphics placed on the page. A strong contrast between the text color and the background color makes it easier for viewers to read the text on your Web page. You can choose a light background color and a dark text color, or a dark background color and a light text color. A white background, though not terribly exciting, is the easiest to read for most viewers, and provides good contrast in combination with dark text. The next step is to choose the default font color and default link color. The **default font color** and the **default link color** are the colors used by the browser to display text, links, and visited links. **Links** are defined as those that have not been clicked previously by the viewer. The default color for links is blue. **Visited links** are links that have been previously clicked, or visited. The default color for visited links is purple. These default settings can be changed using your browser settings; however, not all browsers recognize link color settings. You set the background color and the default font color for the TripSmart home page.

Steps

1. **Click Modify on the menu bar, then click Page Properties**
   The Page Properties dialog box opens. This dialog box is where you set page properties, such as the background color and default font color.
2. **Click the Background color box, as shown in Figure C-7**
   The color picker opens, and the pointer changes to an eyedropper. The color boxes are initially set to gray, which represents the default colors. This does not mean that the color gray will be applied. After a color is selected, it is displayed in the appropriate color box.
3. **Click the last color in the bottom row, which is white, as shown in Figure C-7**
   Each color is assigned a **hexadecimal value**, a value that represents the amount of red, green, and blue in the color. For example, white, which is made of equal parts of red, green, and blue, has a hexadecimal value of FFFFFF. F represents the number 15 in the hexadecimal number system.
4. **Click the Apply button in the Page Properties dialog box**
   The background color of the Web page changes to white. The text color is set to the default color, which is black. The black text against the white background provides a nice contrast. You decide to leave the text black. The Apply button allows you to see changes that you have made to the page without having to close the Page Properties dialog box.
5. **Click the Links color box, shown in Figure C-8, then use to select a shade of red for the color of the links on the home page**
   You decide that red would clash with the TripSmart logo, and choose the default color for links instead.
6. **Click the Links color box again, then click the Strikethrough icon**
   The color for links is set back to the default color. Your screen should resemble Figure C-8.
7. **Click OK to close the Page Properties dialog box**
   The colors for the page have been set.

Trouble?

If you don't like the color you chose in the Page Properties dialog box, click the Strikethrough icon to switch back to the default color.

FIGURE C-7: Page Properties dialog box

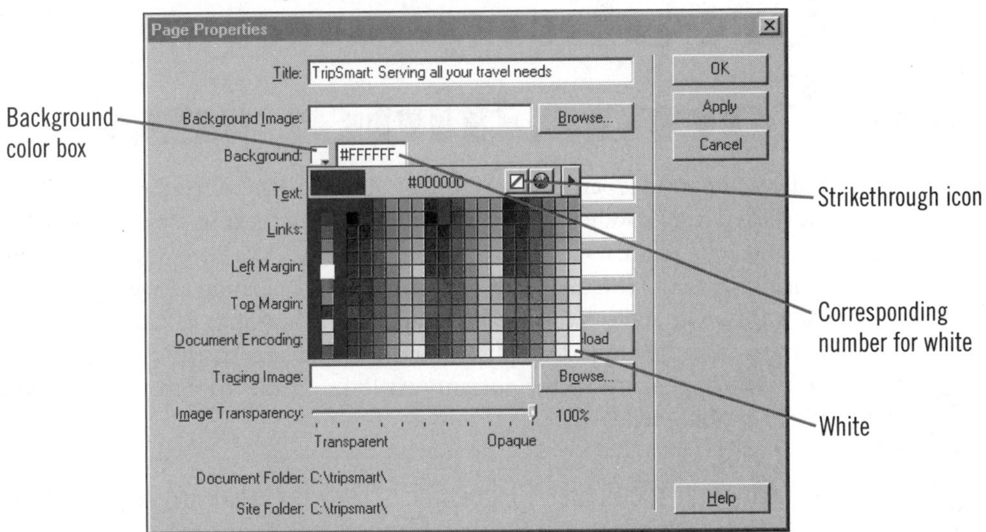

FIGURE C-8: Page Properties dialog box

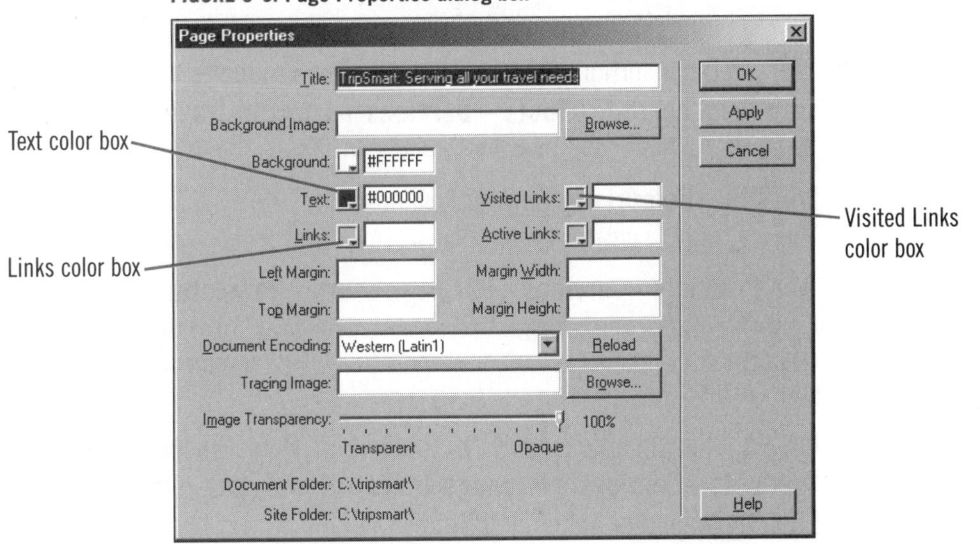

Web Safe Colors

The colors that you choose for your Web page elements should be Web safe. Web safe colors are colors that will display consistently in all browsers, and on Macintosh, Windows, and UNIX platforms. Netscape defined Web safe colors in 1994 as a set of 216 colors that are uniformly recognized by all operating systems. Before Web safe colors were established, colors were displayed differently among different platforms. If a designer chose a color, such as red, on a Windows computer, he or she could not be certain that it would look like the same shade of "red" on a Macintosh computer. Dreamweaver has two Web safe color palettes: Color Cubes and Continuous Tones. Each palette contains 216 Web safe colors. Color Cubes is the default color palette; however, you can choose another one by clicking Modify on the menu bar, clicking Page Properties, clicking the Background, Text, or Links color box, clicking the color palette list arrow, then clicking the desired color palette. Figure C-9 shows the list of color palette choices.

FIGURE C-9: Color palettes

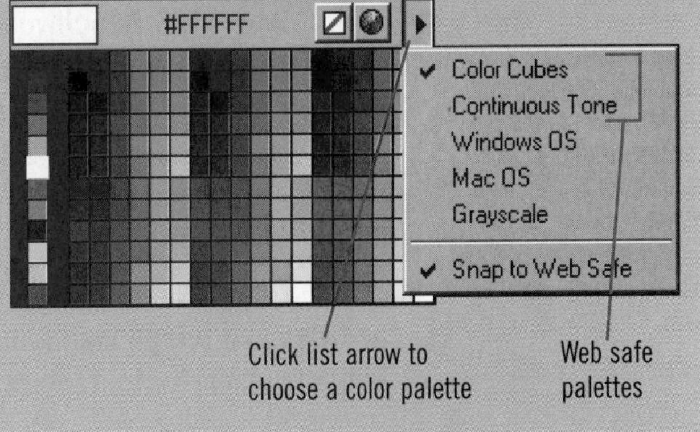

Dreamweaver 4

Dreamweaver 4

Creating and Formatting Text

Text is an important part of any Web page. Text can be created directly in Dreamweaver or copied and pasted from another document. You can format text in Dreamweaver by changing the font, size, and color of the text, just as you can in other software programs. Each time you press [Enter] (Win) or [return] (Mac) on the keyboard, you are creating a new paragraph, even if it is only a few words long. You can format paragraphs using headings. **Headings** are six different text styles that you can apply to paragraphs: Heading 1 (the largest size) through Heading 6 (the smallest size). You revise the current text links on the TripSmart home page and format them using a heading style.

Steps

Trouble?

If you do not see the Property Inspector, click Window on the menu bar, then click Properties.

1. Verify that the Property Inspector is showing, then close all other panels by clicking the **Close button** on each panel
   The Property Inspector is the only panel you need for this lesson. Closing panels that you are not using lets you see more of the page that you are working on.
2. Position the insertion point to the left of **P** in Products, as shown in Figure C-10, then drag to highlight **Products – Services – Links to Travel Sites – Contact Us**
   You must highlight text in order to delete it.
3. Press the **[Delete] key** on your keyboard
   You are ready to create new text links.
4. Type **Products** - **Services** - **Package Tours** - **Newsletter**
   Products - Services - Package Tours - and Newsletter form the page's new navigation bar. A **navigation bar** is a set of text or graphic links that viewers use to navigate to other pages in your Web site.
5. Position the insertion point to the left of **P** in Products, then drag to highlight **Products – Services – Package Tours – Newsletter**, click the **Size list arrow** on the Property Inspector, then click **None**
   The choice of None is the default text size, size 3. It also eliminates any prior formatting that has been applied to the text. Now you can apply the Heading 3 style.
6. Click the **Format list arrow** on the Property Inspector, then click **Heading 3**
   The Heading 3 format is applied to the line of text, as shown in Figure C-11.
7. Position the insertion point directly after **Just let us know how we can serve you better**, as shown in Figure C-12, press **[Enter]** (Win) or **[return]** (Mac), then type **TripSmart**

QuickTip

You can search for a word on a Web page or an entire Web site and replace it with a different word by clicking Edit on the menu bar, clicking Find and Replace, then entering text entries in the Search For and Replace With text boxes.

8. Press and hold **[Shift]**, then press **[Enter]** (Win) or **[return]** (Mac) to create a soft return, type **1106 Beechwood**, press and hold **[Shift]**, then press **[Enter]** (Win) or **[return]** (Mac), type **Fayetteville, AR 72704**, press and hold **[Shift]**, then press **[Enter]** (Win) or **[return]** (Mac), then type **(555) 433-7844**
   A **soft return** places text on separate lines without creating new paragraphs. Soft returns are useful when you want to apply the same formatting to text but place it on separate lines without starting new paragraphs. You are now ready to format the address and telephone number.
9. Position the insertion point in front of **TripSmart**, click-and-drag until the entire **address and telephone number** are highlighted, then click the **Italic icon** on the Property Inspector to italicize the text, as shown in Figure C-12

FIGURE C-10: Deleting the current navigation bar

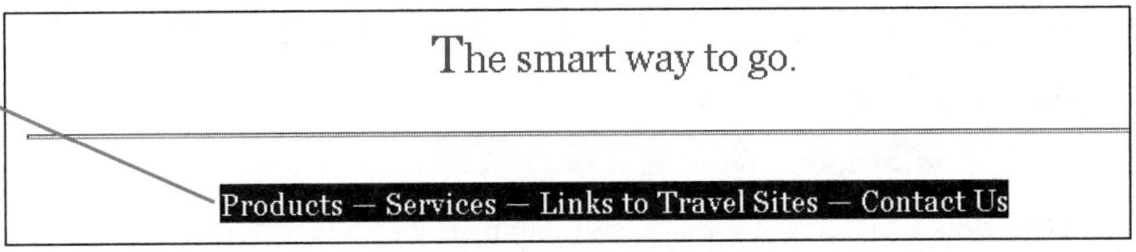

Click insertion point here, then drag to highlight the text

The smart way to go.

Products — Services — Links to Travel Sites — Contact Us

FIGURE C-11: Formatting the new navigation bar

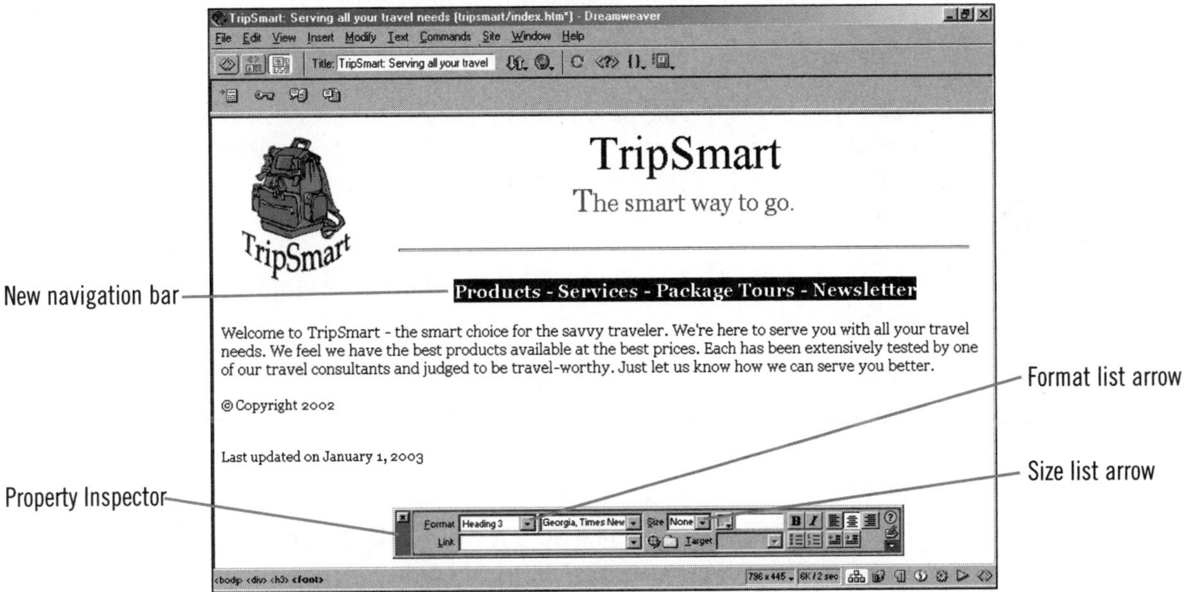

FIGURE C-12: Creating and formatting the address and telephone number

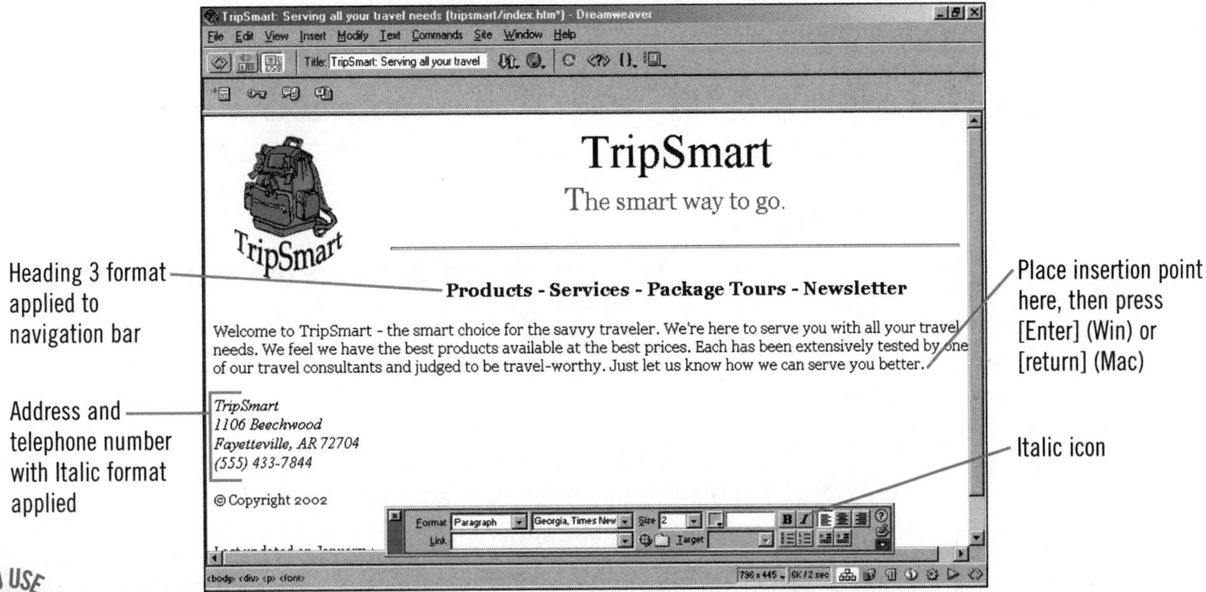

CLUES TO USE

Dreamweaver panels

Dreamweaver panels can take up a lot of space on your screen. One solution is to close them if you are not using them. However, there are many situations in which you do need several panels open at the same time. It can be frustrating to keep moving them around the screen when they are blocking your view. If your monitor is capable of displaying 1024 × 768 pixels, you will have more room on your screen for your panels and an unobstructed view of your Web page.

Dreamweaver 4

Adding Links to Web Pages

Hyperlinks, or links, are the real strength of Web pages. Links help viewers move, or navigate, through all of the pages in a Web site. Viewers are more likely to return to Web sites that have a user-friendly navigation system. Viewers also enjoy Web sites that have interesting links to other Web pages or other Web sites. When creating Web pages it is important to avoid **broken links**, links that cannot find the intended destination file for the link. You should also provide a **point of contact**, or a place on a Web page that provides viewers with a means of contacting the company if they have questions or problems. A **mailto: link**, an e-mail address for viewers to contact someone at the Web site's headquarters, is a common point of contact. You enter the links for the navigation bar for the TripSmart home page. You also create an e-mail link for viewer inquiries, which will be sent to a customer service representative at TripSmart.

Steps

1. **Double-click Products to highlight it, as shown in Figure C-13**
   You must highlight the text that you want to attach a link to.
2. **Click the Browse for File icon on the Property Inspector to browse for products.htm**
   The Select File dialog box opens, showing the tripsmart root folder for the TripSmart Web site.
3. **Click products.htm, then click Select (Win) or Open (Mac), as shown in Figure C-14**
   The Select File dialog box closes. The word Products is linked to the products.htm page in the TripSmart Web site. When the Products link is clicked in a browser window, the products.htm page will open.
4. **Click anywhere on the TripSmart home page to deselect Products**
   Notice that Products is underlined and blue, the default color for links.
5. **Repeat Steps 1–4 to create links for Services, Package Tours, and Newsletter, using services.htm, packages.htm, and newsletter.htm as the corresponding files**
   All four links are now created for the TripSmart home page. Your screen should resemble Figure C-15.
6. **Position the insertion point after the last digit in the telephone number, press and hold [Shift], then press [Enter] (Win) or [return] (Mac)**
7. **Click Window on the menu bar, then click Objects**
   The Objects panel appears.
8. **Click the Objects panel list arrow, click Common, then click the Insert Email Link icon on the Objects panel to insert an e-mail link**
   The Insert Email Link dialog box opens.
9. **Type mailbox@tripsmart.com in the Text text box, and mailbox@tripsmart.com in the E-Mail text box, as shown in Figure C-16, then click OK to close the Email Link dialog box**
   You must enter the correct e-mail address in the E-Mail text box for the link to work; however, you can use a descriptive name, such as customer service, in the Text text box.
10. **Click the Show Site icon on the status bar, then click the Site Map icon to view the Site Map**
    The Site Map shows the e-mail link and the pages that are linked to the home page.

Trouble?

When text is highlighted, you cannot see the text color.

FIGURE C-13: Highlighting Products

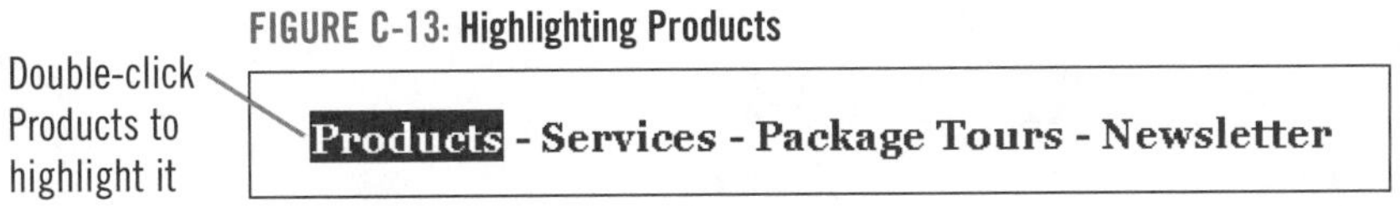

FIGURE C-14: Select File dialog box

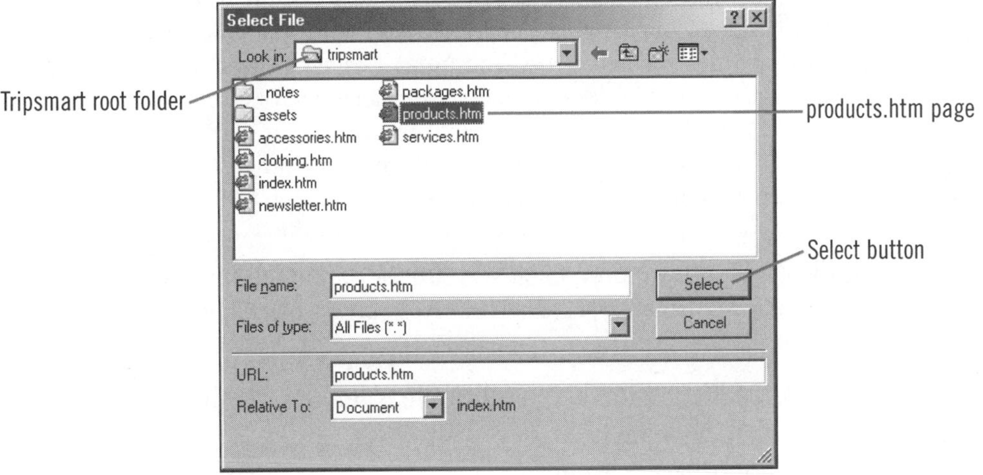

FIGURE C-15: Links added to navigation bar

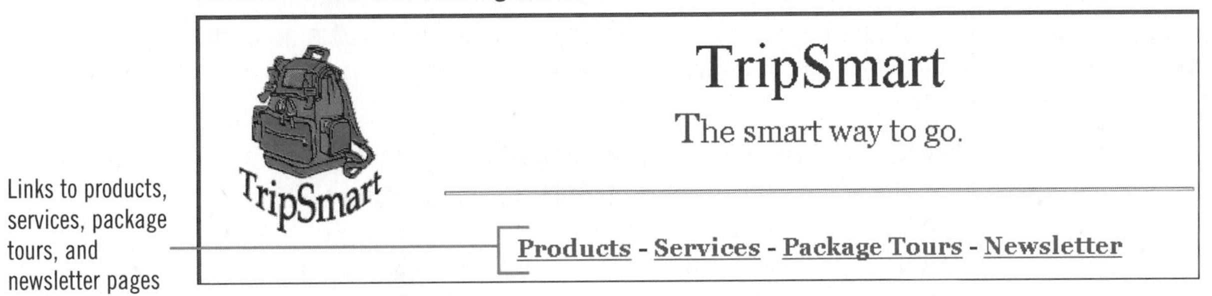

FIGURE C-16: Insert Email Link dialog box

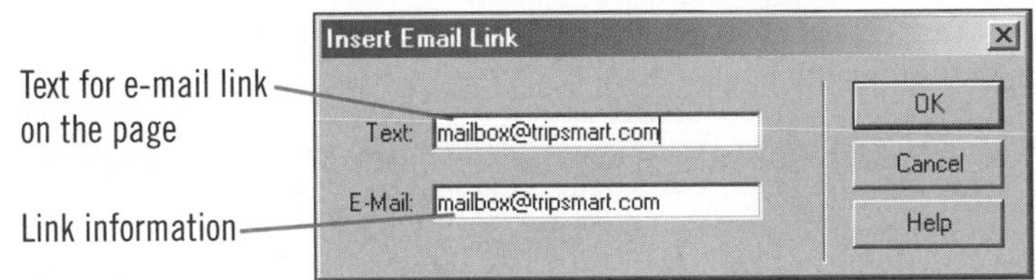

Using keyboard shortcuts

Using keyboard shortcuts, while you work in Dreamweaver, is much faster than using the mouse, especially when you need to copy and paste tedious text, such as URLs and e-mail addresses. Helpful shortcuts to remember are Select All [Control][A](Win) or [Command] [A] (Mac), Copy [Control][C] (Win) or [Command][C] (Mac), Cut [Control][X] (Win) or [Command][X] (Mac), and Paste [Control][V] (Win) or [Command][V] (Mac).

Dreamweaver 4

Using the History Panel

The **History panel** is a valuable editing tool. The History panel shows the steps that you have performed while editing and formatting a particular document in Dreamweaver. To **edit** a page means to insert, delete, or change page content by, for example, inserting a new image, adding a link, or correcting spelling errors. To **format** a page means to make adjustments in the appearance of page elements by, for example, resizing an image or changing the color of text. Formatting does not change the content of a page; it simply makes it look better. The History panel records each task that you perform and displays them in the order they were completed. You experiment with the History panel by inserting, and then formatting, a horizontal rule.

Steps

QuickTip

You can show and hide the History panel by clicking the Show History icon on the Launcher bar.

QuickTip

The default number of steps that the History panel will record is 50, unless you specify otherwise in the General Preferences dialog box. Setting this number too high requires additional memory, and may hinder the way Dreamweaver functions.

1. Close the Site window, click **Window** on the menu bar, then click **History**
   The History panel opens, and the steps you have already performed are displayed in the panel window.
2. Click the **History list arrow**, click **Clear History**, as shown in Figure C-17, then click **Yes** in the warning box
   The History panel is empty.
3. Drag the **History panel** to the top-right corner of your screen to move it out of your way
4. With the insertion point at the beginning of the first address line, click the **Insert Horizontal Rule icon** on the Objects panel to insert a horizontal rule
   A horizontal rule (also called a line) is placed on the page above the address and remains selected.
5. Click the **list arrow** next to pixels on the Property Inspector, click %, if necessary, type **90** in the W text box, then press **[Enter]** (Win) or **[return]** (Mac)
   See Figure C-18. The width of the horizontal rule is 90% of the width of the page. It is wise to set the width of a horizontal rule as a percent of the page rather than in pixels, so that it resizes itself proportionately when viewed on different-sized monitors.
6. Click the **Align list arrow** on the Property Inspector, then click **Center** to center the rule horizontally on the page
   Compare your Property Inspector settings to those shown in Figure C-18. Your horizontal rule is centered on the page.
7. Using the Property Inspector, change the width of the rule to **80%** and the alignment to **Left**
   The rule is now 80% of the width of the window and is left-aligned. You prefer the way the rule looked when it was centered, so you decide to undo the last two steps.
8. Drag the **slider** on the History panel up until it is pointing to **Set alignment: CENTER**, as shown in Figure C-19, then release the mouse button
   The bottom two steps in the History panel appear gray, indicating that these steps have been undone, and the horizontal rule returns to the centered, 90% width settings.

FIGURE C-17: **History panel**

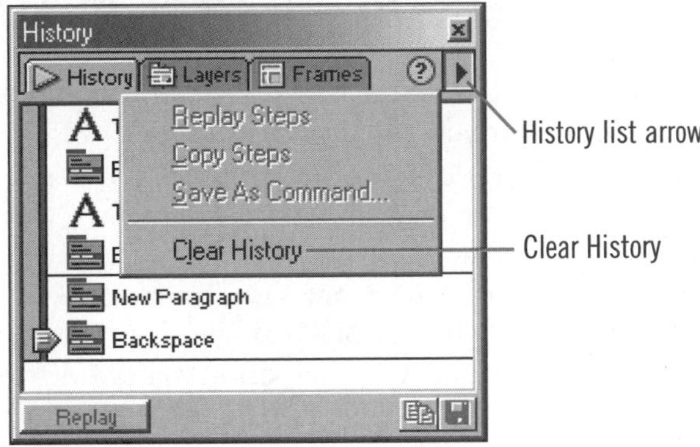

FIGURE C-18: **Property Inspector settings for rule**

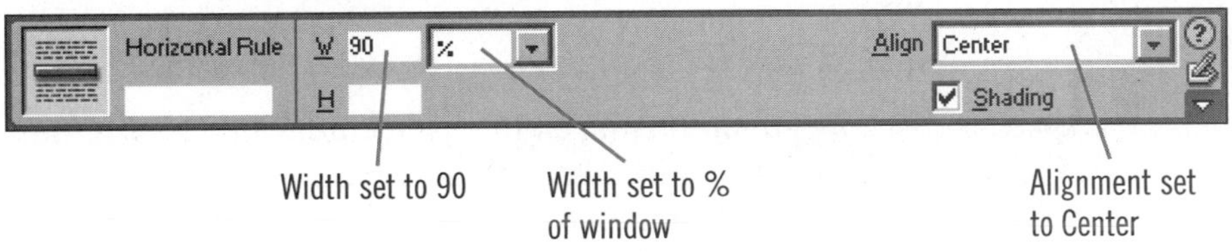

FIGURE C-19: **Undoing steps using the History panel**

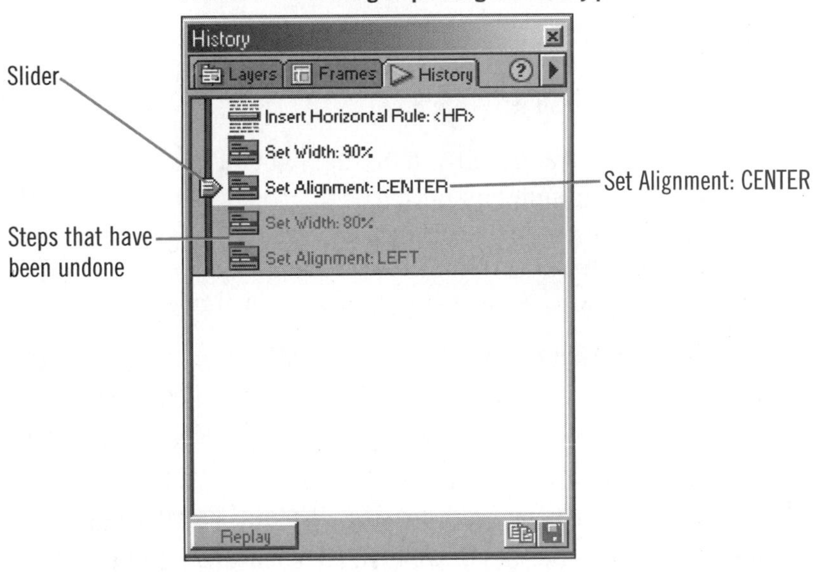

The History panel

Dragging the slider up and down in the History panel is a quick way to undo or redo steps. However, the History panel offers much more than just a quick method of undoing or redoing steps. It has the ability to "memorize" certain steps and consolidate them into one command. This is a useful feature for steps that are executed repetitively on Web pages. Some Dreamweaver features, such as Drag and Drop, cannot be recorded in the History panel, and have a red X placed next to them. The History panel does not show steps performed in the Site window.

Dreamweaver 4

Viewing HTML Code

It is often helpful to view the HTML code while editing or formatting a Web page. Some designers prefer to make changes to their pages by typing directly into the HTML code, rather than working in Design View. Features such as JavaScript functions are often added to pages by copying and pasting code into the existing page's HTML code. **JavaScript** is HTML code that adds dynamic content, such as rollovers or interactive forms, to a Web page. You can view the HTML code in Dreamweaver by using the Code View, using the Code and Design View, or opening the Code Inspector. The **Code Inspector** is basically the same as the Code View, except that it opens in a separate window. Using the Code Inspector, you can view the HTML code and the page content in two different colors, highlight HTML code that contains errors, and **debug**, or correct, HTML errors. If you are new to HTML, you can use the **HTML Reference panel** to find answers to your HTML questions. Dreamweaver also has a feature that tells you the last date that changes were made to a Web page. You view the HTML code for the home page in the Code Inspector, use the HTML Reference panel to find out how to change the color of a rule, and then insert the date on the home page.

Steps

1. **Close the History panel, then click the horizontal rule to select it, if necessary**
   The horizontal rule is now highlighted on the screen. When an object is highlighted, changes may be made to it. The Launcher bar contains icons that open various windows, including the Code Inspector window.

> **QuickTip**
> The buttons on the right end of the status bar and the Launcher bar are the same.

2. **Click the Show Code Inspector icon on the status bar**
   The Code Inspector opens. The highlighted HTML code refers to the horizontal rule on the page. You want to **wrap** the text, which means force it to appear within the width of the window.
3. **Click the View Options icon on the Code Inspector toolbar, then click Word Wrap**
   The text in the Code Inspector window appears in the width of the window, making it much easier for you to read it.
4. **Click again and verify that Highlight Invalid HTML and Syntax Coloring are checked, as shown in Figure C-20**
   If Syntax Coloring is not checked, the color of the HTML code and the text on the Web page are both black, making it harder to differentiate between the two. You are now ready to research how to change the color of the horizontal rule.
5. **Click the Reference icon on the Code Inspector toolbar, read the information in the Reference panel, as shown in Figure C-21, then close the Reference panel**
   You find out that the color of rules can only be changed using style sheets, and decide to leave the horizontal rule alone.
6. **Highlight January 1, 2003, press the [Delete] key on your keyboard, click the Insert Date icon on the Objects panel, click March 7, 1974 in the Date Format text box, click the Update Automatically on Save check box, as shown in Figure C-22, then click OK**
   March 7, 1974 is an example of a date format. The manually entered date on the page is replaced with a date that will automatically update each time the page is opened and saved. Notice that the code in the Code Inspector has changed to reflect the automatic date.
7. **Close the Code Inspector**

FIGURE C-20: Code Inspector view options

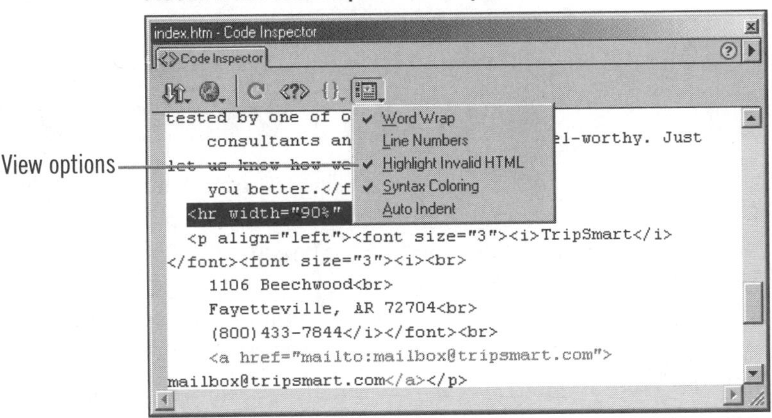

FIGURE C-21: Viewing the Reference panel

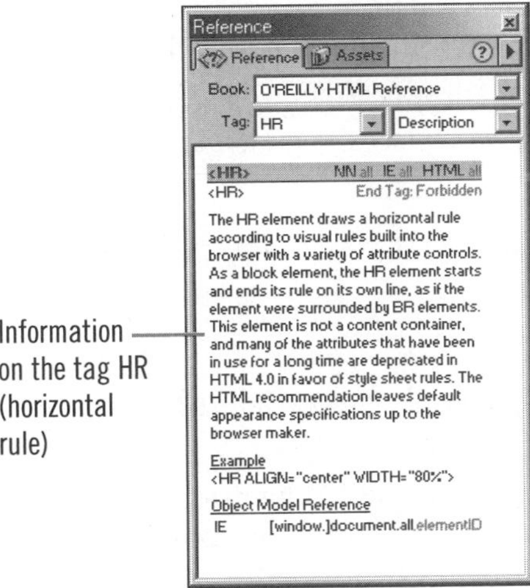

FIGURE C-22: Insert Date dialog box

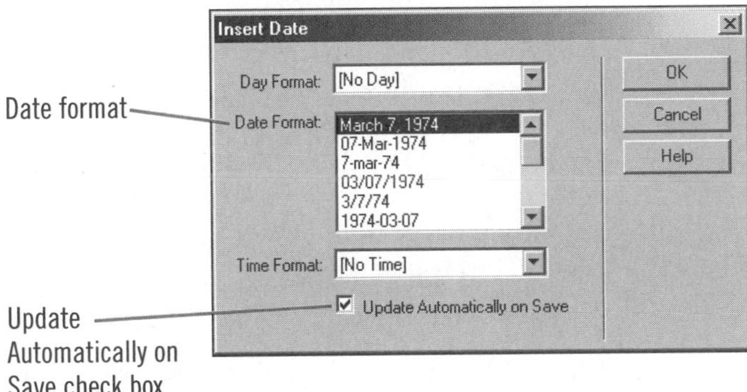

Inserting comments

A handy Dreamweaver feature is the ability to insert comments into the HTML code. Comments can provide helpful information describing portions of the coding, such as a JavaScript function. Comments can be created in any Dreamweaver view, but are only visible in the Code View or in the Code Inspector. You can create a comment by clicking the Objects panel list arrow, clicking Invisibles, clicking the Insert Comment icon, typing a comment in the Insert Comment dialog box, then clicking OK. Figure C-23 shows the Insert Comment icon on the Invisibles category of the Objects panel. Comments are not visible in browser windows.

FIGURE C-23: Invisibles category of the Objects panel

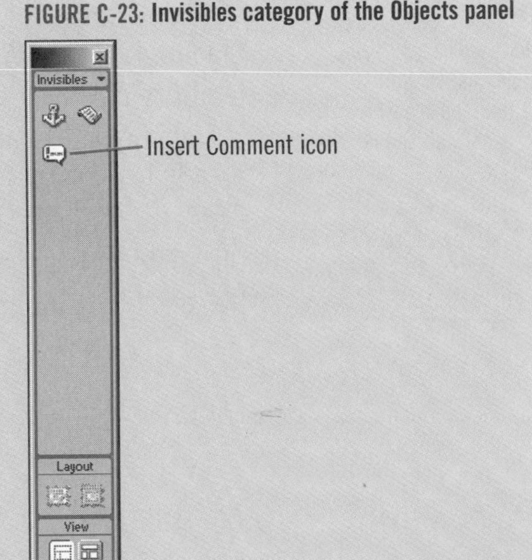

Dreamweaver 4

Testing and Modifying Web Pages

Steps

Testing Web pages is a continuous process. The best way to test a Web page is to preview it in a browser window to make sure it appears the way you expect it to. You should also check to see that your links work properly, that there are no typographical or grammatical errors, and that you have included all of the necessary information for the page. You test the TripSmart home page in Dreamweaver, preview it using the default browser, and make adjustments to the page.

1. Click the **Window Size list arrow** on the status bar, click **760 × 420 (800 × 600, Maximized)**, then view the page
   The 800 × 600 window setting is used on 15-inch monitors and some 17-inch monitors. Most consumers have at least a 15-inch monitor at their homes or offices, making this window size a good choice for a Web page.
2. Click the **Preview/Debug in Browser icon** on the toolbar, then click **Preview in iexplore** (Win) or **Preview in Netscape Communicator** or **Navigator** (Mac)
   The page opens in the browser window. You decide to replace the period after The Smart way to go with an exclamation point.
3. Close the browser, highlight the period after **The Smart way to go**, press and hold **[Shift]**, then press the **[1]** key on your keyboard
   The period is replaced with an exclamation mark.
4. Place the insertion point after **the copyright statement**, press **[Delete]** on your keyboard, press and hold **[Shift]**, then press **[Enter]** (Win) or **[return]** (Mac)
   The double space between the copyright statement and the last updated statement is replaced with a single space. Next, you change the formatting for the horizontal rule.
5. Click the **first horizontal rule** to select it, type **75** in the W text box of the Property Inspector, then press **[Enter]** (Win) or **[return]** (Mac)
   The horizontal rule is smaller and more in proportion with the bottom horizontal rule.
6. Click **File** on the menu bar, click **Save**, then click on the toolbar to view the changes
   With your finishing touches, the home page should resemble Figure C-24.
7. Click the **Products** link on the navigation bar, click the **Back button** on the Standard toolbar (Win) or the **Back button** on the Navigation toolbar (Mac) to return to the home page, then click the **Services**, **Package Tours**, and **Newsletter** links to test them also
   Each link should open a blank page in the browser, since no text or graphics have been placed on these pages yet.
8. Click **File** on the menu bar, then click **Close** (Win) or **Quit** (Mac), then click **File** on the menu bar and **Exit** (Win) or **Quit** (Mac) Dreamweaver

QuickTip

It is a good idea to make a back-up copy of the Web site fairly frequently. Save the back-up copy to a floppy disk, Zip disk, or hard drive, other than the one where the original Web site is stored.

FIGURE C-24: The finished project

TripSmart: Serving all your travel needs - Microsoft Internet Explorer - [Working Offline]

File Edit View Favorites Tools Help

Back Search Favorites History

Address C:\tripsmart\TMPdfrp2absay.htm Go Links

TripSmart

TripSmart

The smart way to go!

Products - Services - Package Tours - Newsletter

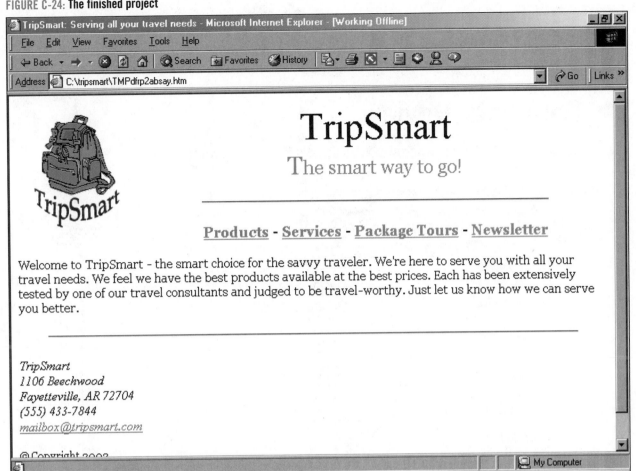

Welcome to TripSmart - the smart choice for the savvy traveler. We're here to serve you with all your travel needs. We feel we have the best products available at the best prices. Each has been extensively tested by one of our travel consultants and judged to be travel-worthy. Just let us know how we can serve you better.

TripSmart
1106 Beechwood
Fayetteville, AR 72704
(555) 433-7844
mailbox@tripsmart.com

© Copyright 2002

My Computer

Under construction

You should not publish a Web page that has a link to an unfinished page. It is frustrating to click a link to another Web page only to find an "under construction" note or graphic displayed. You want to make the best impression that you can for your viewing audience. If you cannot complete a page before publishing it, at least provide enough information on it to make it "worth the trip."

Practice

▶ Concepts Review

Label each element in the Dreamweaver window as shown in Figure C-25.

FIGURE C-25

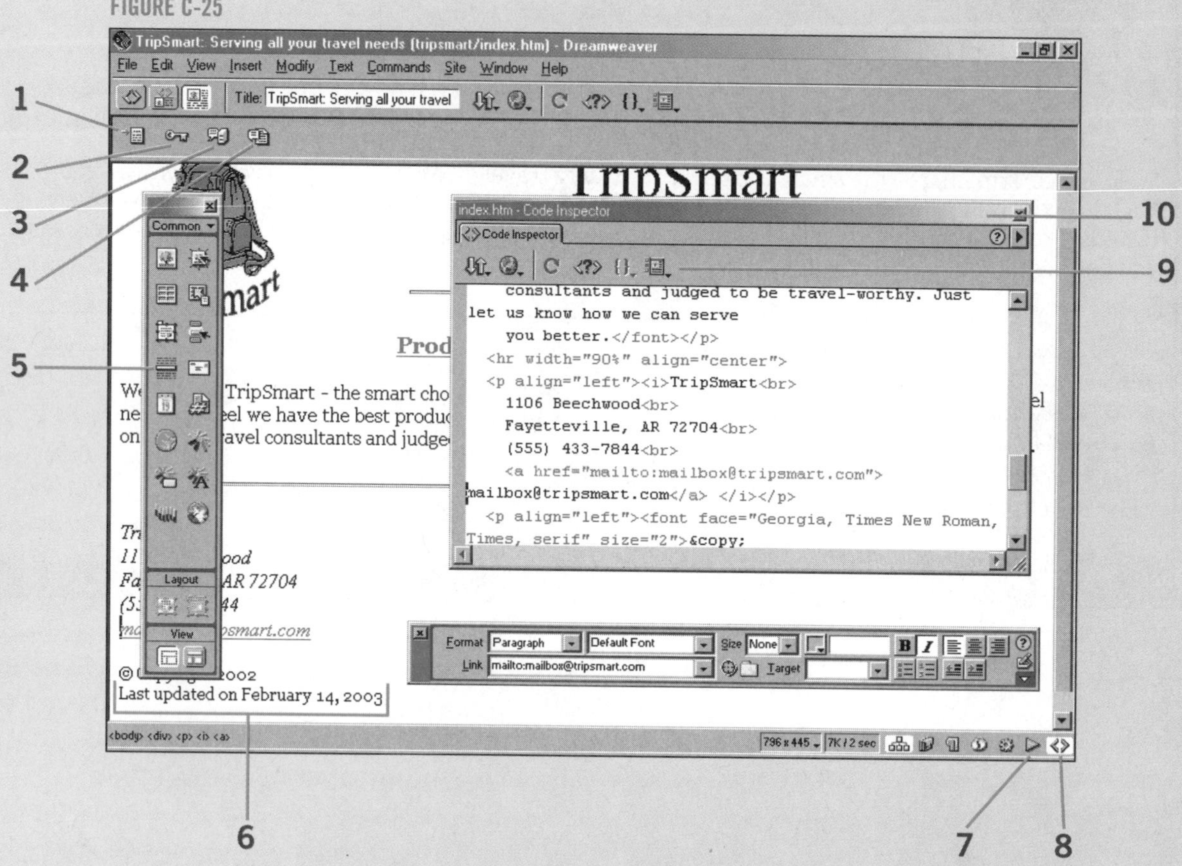

Match each of the following terms with the statement that describes its function.

11. Bobby
12. Head content
13. Body
14. Page Properties dialog box
15. Heading 1
16. Heading 6
17. Edit a page
18. Format a page

a. The part of a Web page that includes text, graphics, and links
b. A free service provided for testing the accessibility of a Web page
c. Includes the default Web page settings
d. The smallest heading style
e. Make adjustments in the appearance of page elements
f. Insert, delete, or change page content
g. The largest heading style
h. The part of a Web page that includes the page title and meta tags

Select the best answer from the following list of choices.

19. The invisible portions of a Web page can include:
- a. Keywords.
- b. Descriptions.
- c. Meta tags.
- d. All of the above

20. Links that have been previously clicked on are called:
- a. Active links.
- b. Links.
- c. Visited links.
- d. Broken links.

21. Each Web safe palette contains __________ colors.
- a. 320
- b. 216
- c. 125
- d. 250

22. The __________ is used on the History panel to undo or redo several steps.
- a. Scroll bar
- b. Pointer
- c. Slider
- d. Undo/Redo Tool

23. An example of a point of contact is a
- a. Heading.
- b. Title.
- c. Mailto: link.
- d. Keywords.

24. The Dreamweaver default color palette is the
- a. Continuous Tones palette.
- b. Color Cubes palette.
- c. Windows OS palette.
- d. Mac OS palette.

25. The Code Inspector
- a. Is the same as Code View.
- b. Opens in Design View.
- c. Opens in a separate window.
- d. Is not useful for debugging.

► Skills Review

***Important**: If you did not create the Web sites used in the following exercises in Unit B, you will need to create a root folder for each Web site and define the Web sites using files your instructor will provide. See the "Read This Before You Begin" section for more detailed instructions.*

1. **Plan the page layout.**
   a. Using a word processor or a piece of paper, list three principles of good page design, in order of most important to least important.
   b. Explain why you chose these three concepts and why you selected the order you did.
2. **Create the head content.**
   a. Start Dreamweaver.
   b. Open the Blooms&Bulbs Web site from the drive and folder where your Project Files are stored.
   c. Open the index file, close the Design Notes dialog box, and view the head content.
   d. Insert the following keywords: **garden**, **plants**, **water**, **nursery**, **flowers**, **supplies**, **landscape**, **annuals**, **perennials**, and **greenhouse**.
   e. Insert the description **Blooms&Bulbs is a premier supplier of garden plants for both professional and home gardeners**.
   f. Switch to Code View to view the HTML code for the head contents.
   g. Click the Show Design View icon.
   h. Save your work.
3. **Set Web page properties.**
   a. View the page properties.
   b. Change the background color to a color of your choice.
   c. Reset the background color to white.
   d. Save your work.
4. **Create and format text.**
   a. Place the insertion point at the beginning of the first sentence and press [Enter] (Win) or [return] (Mac).
   b. Press the up arrow on the keyboard, then type **Featured Plants**, **Upcoming Events**, and **Gardening Tips** to use as a navigation bar. Use the [Tab] key and a hyphen to separate each item from the next.
   c. Using the Property Inspector, apply the Heading 4 style to the navigation bar.
   d. Center the navigation bar.
   e. Place the insertion point at the end of the last sentence and press [Enter] (Win) or [return] (Mac).
   f. Type the following text, inserting a soft return after each line. (*Hint*: A soft return is created by pressing and holding [Shift], then pressing [Enter] (Win) or [return] (Mac).)
      Blooms&Bulbs
      Highway 7 North
      Alvin, TX 77511
      (555) 498-5033
   g. Press [Enter] (Win) or [return] (Mac), type **Last updated on**, then insert a date that will automatically update upon saving the file.
   h. Using the Property Inspector, italicize the address information.
   i. Save your work.
5. **Add links to Web pages.**
   a. Using the Property Inspector, link Featured Plants to plants.htm.
   b. Link Upcoming Events to events.htm.

c. Link Gardening Tips to tips.htm.
d. Using the Objects panel, create an e-mail link under the telephone number.
e. Type **mailbox@blooms&bulbs.com** in both the Text and the E-Mail text boxes.

6. **Use the History panel.**
   a. Clear the History panel.
   b. Using the Objects panel, insert a horizontal rule under the paragraph about Blooms&Bulbs.
   c. Using the Property Inspector, center the rule and set the width to 80% of the width of the window.
   d. Experiment with the History panel to change the settings of the horizontal rule.
   e. Set the horizontal rule width to 75% of the width of the window.
   f. Close the History panel.
   g. Save your work.
7. **View HTML code.**
   a. Using the Code Inspector, examine the code for the horizontal rule properties.
   b. Close the Code Inspector.
8. **Test and modify Web pages.**
   a. Using the Window Size pop-up menu, view the page at two different sizes.
   b. View the page in your browser.
   c. Verify that all links work correctly.
   d. Change the text Stop by and see us soon! to **We ship anywhere!**
   e. Save your work.

Important*: If you did not create the Web sites used in the following exercises in Unit B, you will need to create a root folder for each Web site and define the Web sites using files your instructor will provide. See the "Read This Before You Begin" section for more detailed instructions.*

▶ Independent Challenge 1

Dreamweaver has a Help feature called Guided Tour, which teaches you how to use Dreamweaver, using movies of Dreamweaver tasks being performed. The Guided Tour includes a movie called Designing Web pages.

a. Start Dreamweaver.
b. Click Help on the menu bar, then click Guided Tour.
c. Click Designing Web pages. The Guided Tour for Designing Web pages opens, as shown in Figure C-26.
d. Follow the directions on the screen and click the movie icon to view the movies.
e. Close the Help window when you are done by clicking the Close button.

FIGURE C-26

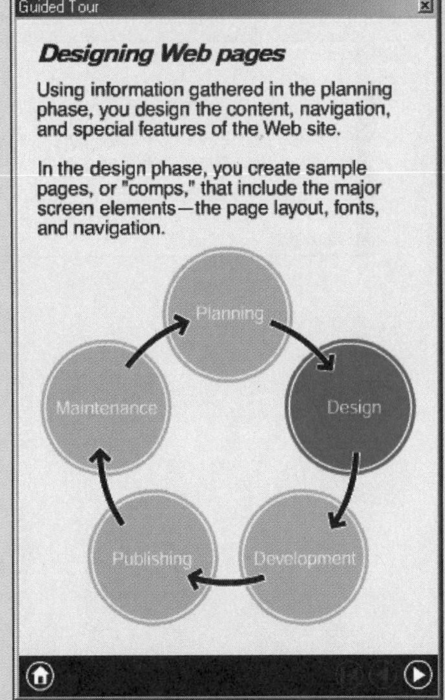

Dreamweaver 4

► Independent Challenge 2

Rapids Transit is a river expedition company located on the Buffalo River in Newton County, Arkansas. In addition to renting canoes, kayaks, and rafts, they have a country store and snack bar. River guides are available, if requested, to accompany clients on float trips. The clients range from high-school and college students to families to vacationing professionals.

a. Open the Rapids Transit Web site from the drive and folder where your Project Files are stored.
b. Open the index page in the Rapids Transit Web site.
c. Create the following keywords: **river, rafting, Buffalo, Arkansas, kayak, canoe,** and **float**.
d. Create the following description: **Rapids Transit is a river expedition company located on the Buffalo River in Arkansas**.
e. Change the page title to **Rapids Transit – Buffalo River expeditions outfitter**.
f. Create a navigation bar below the Rapids Transit logo with the following text links: **Our Guides**, **Equipment Rentals**, and **Country Store**. Place a hyphen between each text link.
g. Apply the Heading 4 style to the text links.
h. Type the following address below the paragraph about the company:
Rapids Transit
Hwy 65
Jasper, AR
(555) 222-7788
i. Italicize the address and create an e-mail link, using: **mailbox@rapidstransit.com**.
j. Add links to the entries in the navigation bar, using the files guides.htm, rentals.htm, and store.htm.
k. Change the properties of the horizontal rule to 50%, centered.
l. View the HTML code for the page, noting in particular the code for the head content, as shown in Figure C-27.
m. View the page in two different window sizes, then test the links in your browser window.

FIGURE C-27

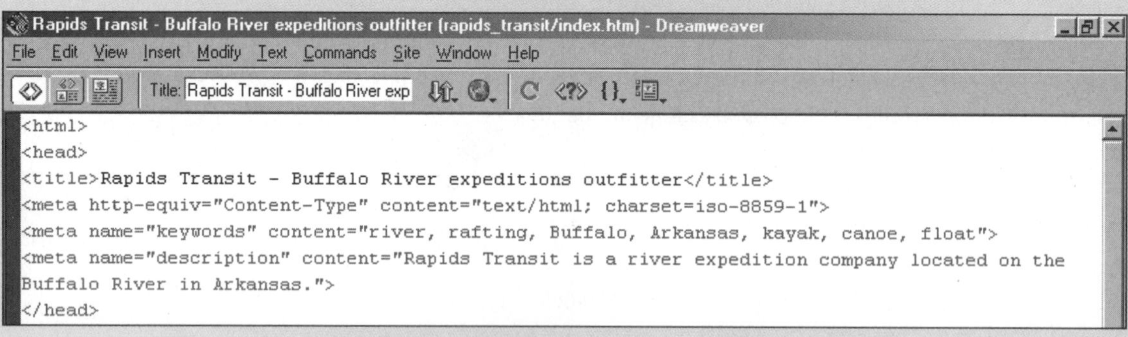

Independent Challenge 3

The Over Under Dive Shop is a dive center in Nevis, West Indies. It is a certified Professional Association of Diving Instructors (PADI) dive center offering PADI certification courses. They also conduct snorkeling and dive trips to various locations around the barrier reef surrounding Nevis.

a. Open the Over Under Web site from the drive and folder where your Project Files are stored.
b. Change the page title for the index page to a more appropriate title.
c. Create keywords for the page. See Figure C-28 for an example to get you started.
d. Create a description for the page.
e. Choose a sea green color for the background, and change the color of the text to white.
f. Create a navigation bar using the following entries: **Dive Trips**, **Snorkel Trips**, and **PADI Certifications**.
g. Link the navigation text to the appropriate pages. Make sure there is enough contrast between the links color and the background color.
h. Type the following address and phone number somewhere on the page:
   Over Under Dive Shop
   Piney Beach
   Nevis, West Indies
   (555) 255-1987
i. Create an e-mail link, using: **mailbox@overunder.com**.
j. Replace each instance of the word Padi with **PADI**.
k. View and save the Site Map in your assets folder.

FIGURE C-28

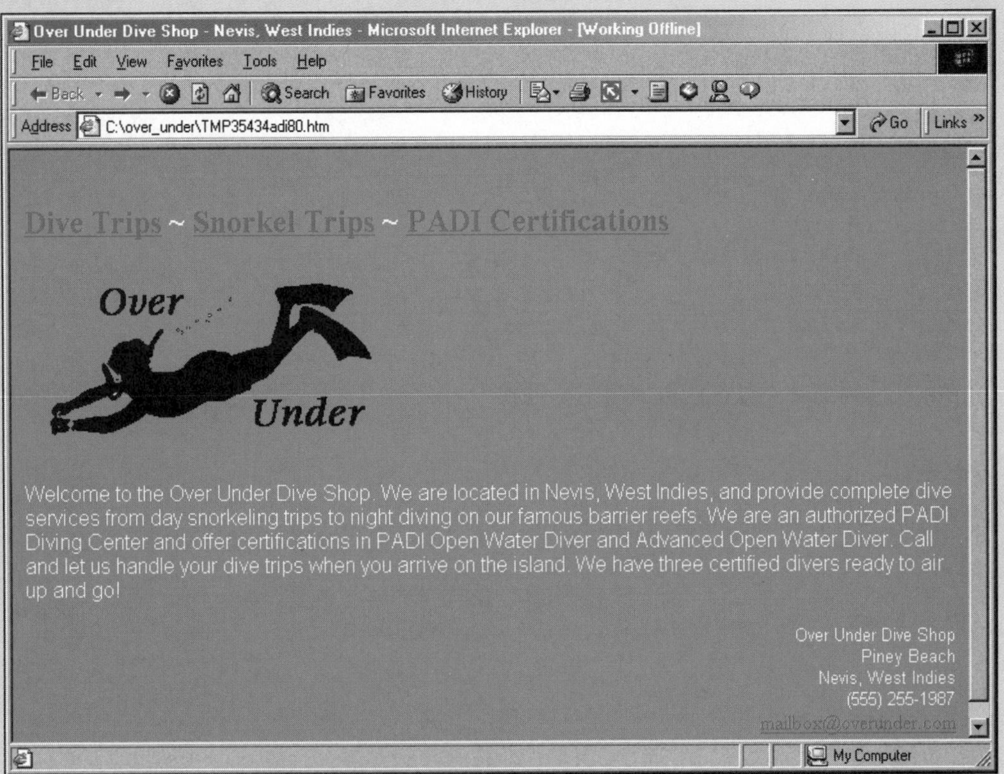

Independent Challenge 4

The World Wide Web Consortium was created in October 1994 "to lead the World Wide Web to its full potential by developing common protocols that promote its evolution and ensure its interoperability." The World Wide Web Consortium (W3C) home page includes the Web Accessibility guidelines that are used by the program called Bobby. This program can be used to evaluate entire sites or individual pages.

- **a.** Open your browser and go to the World Wide Web Consortium at *www.w3.org.*
- **b.** Click the link for Accessibility.
- **c.** Click the link for the Web Content Accessibility Guidelines.
- **d.** Using a word-processing program or a sheet of paper, list the major guideline topics covered.
- **e.** Make a checklist of the steps you would take when developing a Web site to ensure that your Web site would earn the Bobby seal of approval.

Independent Challenge 5

Angela Lou is a freelance photographer. She is searching the Internet looking for a particular type of paper to use in processing her prints. She knows that Web sites use keywords and descriptions in order to receive "hits" with search engines. She is curious as to how they work. Write your answers to the questions below on scrap paper or using your word processor.

- **a.** Connect to the Internet and go to Kodak at *www.kodak.com.*
- **b.** View the page source by clicking View on the menu bar, then clicking Source (Internet Explorer) or Page Source (Netscape Navigator or Communicator).
- **c.** Can you locate a description and keywords?
- **d.** How many keywords do you find?
- **e.** How many words are in the description?
- **f.** Are the numbers of keywords and words in the description about right, too many, or not enough?
- **g.** Go to a search engine such as Google at *www.google.com* and search for "photography" and "paper" in the search text box.
- **h.** Click the first link in the list of results and view the source code for that page. Do you see keywords and a description? Do any of them match the words you used in the search?

Visual Workshop

Jacob's is an upscale restaurant catering to business executives and theater patrons. They have an extensive menu including prix fixe dinners, pre-theater dinner specials, and after-theater specials. The cuisine is primarily French. Open the Jacob's Web site from the drive and folder where your Project Files are stored. (If you did not create this Web site in Unit B, contact your instructor for assistance.) Make the necessary modifications to the index page to duplicate Figure C-29.

FIGURE C-29

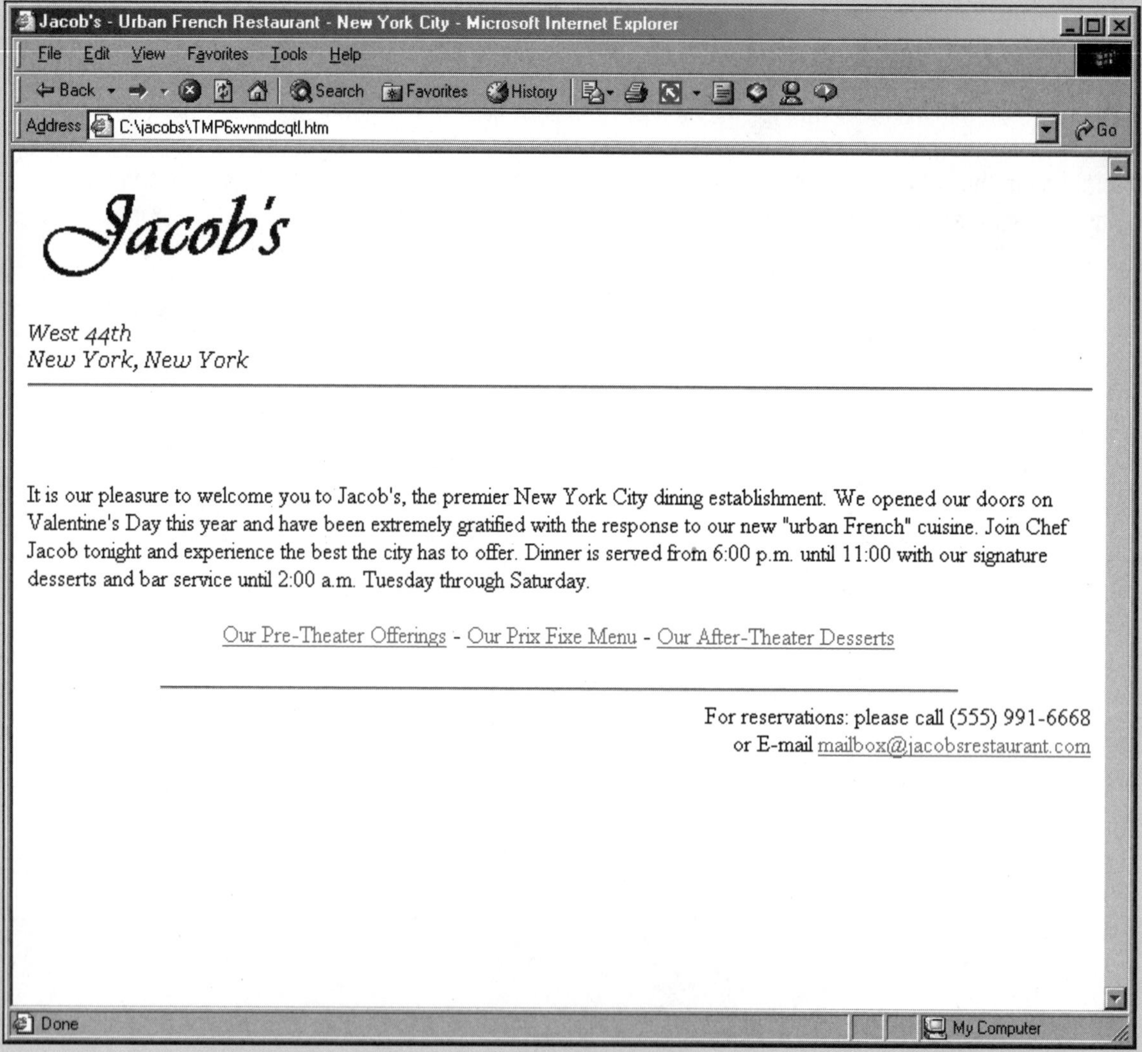

Jacob's - Urban French Restaurant - New York City - Microsoft Internet Explorer

File Edit View Favorites Tools Help

Back Search Favorites History

Address C:\jacobs\TMP6xvnmdcqtl.htm Go

Jacob's

West 44th
New York, New York

It is our pleasure to welcome you to Jacob's, the premier New York City dining establishment. We opened our doors on Valentine's Day this year and have been extremely gratified with the response to our new "urban French" cuisine. Join Chef Jacob tonight and experience the best the city has to offer. Dinner is served from 6:00 p.m. until 11:00 with our signature desserts and bar service until 2:00 a.m. Tuesday through Saturday.

Our Pre-Theater Offerings - Our Prix Fixe Menu - Our After-Theater Desserts

For reservations: please call (555) 991-6668
or E-mail mailbox@jacobsrestaurant.com

Done My Computer

Formatting Text

Objectives

- Import text
- Set text properties
- Create an unordered list
- Create an ordered list
- Edit text with Code and Design Views
- Create a Cascading Style Sheet
- Apply and edit a Cascading Style Sheet
- Insert Flash text

The majority of information on Web pages is presented in the form of text. Because text is more difficult and tiring to read on a computer screen than on a printed page, you should take steps to make the text on your Web site attractive and easy to read. Dreamweaver has many options for enhancing text, including font properties, styles that can be applied to paragraphs and lists, and Cascading Style Sheets. **Cascading Style Sheets** are used to assign common formatting specifications to page elements such as text, objects, and tables. You can also insert text created in **Flash**, a Macromedia software program used for creating animation for Web pages. TripSmart wants to add a monthly newsletter to its Web site. You have been asked to gather articles that have been written by various TripSmart departments and to place them attractively on a newsletter page.

Dreamweaver 4

Importing Text

Entering text in Dreamweaver is as easy as entering text in a word-processing program. Dreamweaver's text-editing features, listed in Table D-1, are similar to those found in word-processing programs. If you already have text that you want to place on a Dreamweaver page, you can either copy and paste it or save the text file as an HTML file, and then import it into Dreamweaver. Keep in mind that viewers must have the same fonts installed on their computers as the fonts that you apply to your text. Otherwise, the text may be displayed incorrectly. Some software programs, such as Adobe Photoshop and Adobe Illustrator, can convert text into graphics, which eliminates this problem. When text is converted to a graphic, it will retain the same appearance, even though it is no longer editable text. The Travel Services Department gives you an article with a list of items that are essential when packing for a trip. The article was created in Microsoft Word, then saved as an HTML file. You open the newsletter Web page, then import the article.

Steps

1. Open the **TripSmart Web site**, open **dmd_1.htm** from the Unit D folder where your Project Files are stored, then save it as **newsletter.htm** in the tripsmart root folder, overwriting the existing file
   Notice the "Travel Tidbits" logo at the top of the page. This is an example of text that has been converted to a graphic. This file, named masthead.jpg, must be placed in the assets folder in the tripsmart root folder.
2. Click **Travel Tidbits**, click the **Browse for File icon** next to the Src text box on the Property Inspector, click the drive and folder where your Project Files are stored, double-click the **Unit D folder**, double-click the **assets folder**, click **masthead.jpg**, then click **Select** (Win) or **Open** (Mac)
   A message appears on the screen, asking you if you would like to copy the graphic file to the root folder of your Web site. You want to copy the file to the assets folder in the tripsmart root folder.
3. Click **Yes**, double-click the **assets folder**, then click **Save** to save the file to your assets folder
   The Src text box in the Property Inspector now reads assets/masthead.jpg. You are now ready to import the Word text file into the Web site so that you can then copy the text onto the newsletter page.
4. Click **File** on the menu bar, point to **Import**, click **Import Word HTML**, click the drive and folder where your Project Files are stored, double-click the **Unit D folder**, then double-click **packing_essentials.htm**
   The Clean Up Word HTML dialog box opens, as shown in Figure D-1. This feature will delete any unnecessary HTML code from the page.
5. Make sure each check box is checked, as shown in Figure D-1, then click **OK**
   A dialog box appears, showing the Clean Up Word HTML Results, as shown in Figure D-2.
6. Click **OK**
   The imported text is placed on a new, untitled page. You need to copy and paste it on the newsletter page.
7. Click **Edit** on the menu bar, click **Select All**, click **Edit** on the menu bar, then click **Copy**
   The text is ready to be pasted on the newsletter page.
8. Click **File** on the menu bar, click **Close**, then click **No** (Win) or **Don't Save** (Mac) when you are asked if you want to save changes to the untitled document.
   The untitled document closes, and you are ready to paste the text on the newsletter.htm page.
9. Click below the **horizontal rule**, click **Edit** on the menu bar, click **Paste**, click **File** on the menu bar, then click **Save**
   The text is pasted on the newsletter page under the horizontal rule, and the changes to the page are saved.

Trouble?

Images and internal links that display a broken link or an absolute path (extra forward slashes or colons), can be fixed by selecting the graphic or the link, then clicking the Browse for File icon on the Property Inspector. Images should be saved in the assets folder overwriting the existing file, if necessary. For links, double-click the filename in the root folder, overwriting the existing file, if necessary.

Trouble?

If you do not see the newsletter.htm page, click the Show Site icon, then double-click newsletter.htm.

FIGURE D-1: **Clean Up Word HTML dialog box**

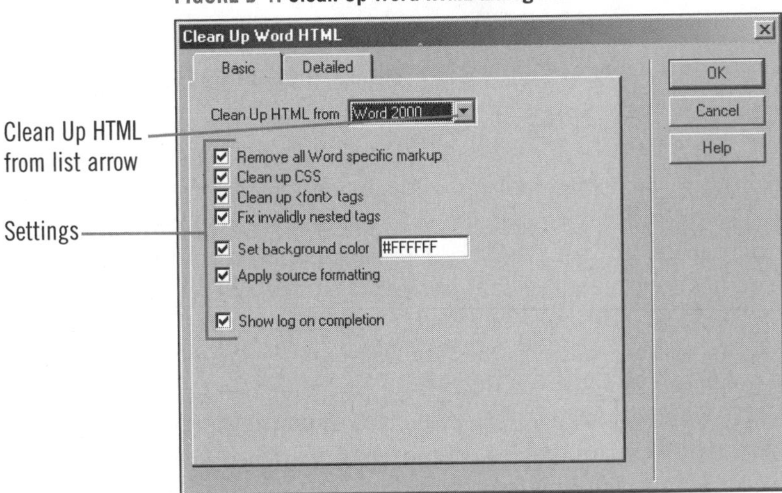

FIGURE D-2: **Clean Up Word HTML Results**

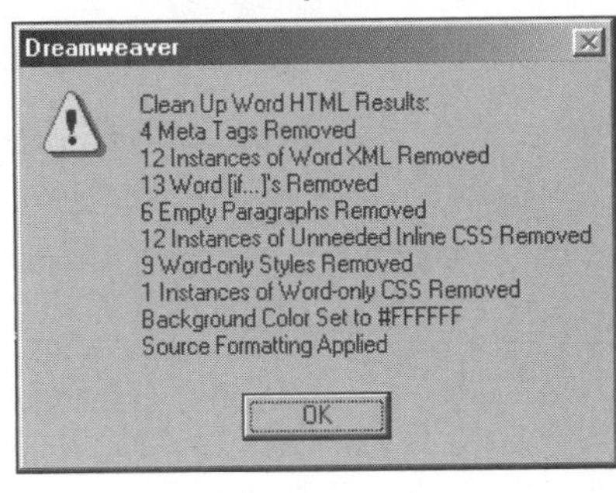

TABLE D-1: **Dreamweaver text-editing features**

feature	menu	function
Find and Replace	Edit	Finds and replaces text on the current Web page, the entire Web site, or in selected files
Outdent and Indent	Text	Indents selected text to the right or left
Paragraph Format	Text	Used to set Paragraph, H1 through H6, and preformatted text styles
Align	Text	Aligns text with the left or right margin, or centers it on the page
List	Text	Creates unordered, ordered, or definition list settings
Font	Text	Sets font groupings to be used by a browser
Style	Text	Sets various styles such as bold and italic
HTML Styles	Text	Clears and creates new HTML styles
CSS Styles	Text	Gives you the choice of creating a new CSS Style, editing an existing CSS Style, or attaching a CSS Style to a Web page
Size	Text	Sets text size from 1 to 7
Size Change	Text	Changes the font size to the next smaller or bigger font size
Color	Text	Sets text color
Check Spelling	Text	Runs a spell check on the page

Saving a Word file as HTML

When you create text in Microsoft Word that you know will eventually be used on a Web page, you should not format the text. Formatting should be applied after the text is imported into Dreamweaver. Even simple text entered in Word will have unnecessary HTML code that will be automatically removed when the file is imported into Dreamweaver. Some formatting, such as creating new paragraphs, is OK; however, you should avoid applying styles to the text or aligning it. This practice will save both time and unnecessary frustration.

Dreamweaver 4

Setting Text Properties

Once placed on a Web page, text can be manipulated in many ways to enhance the appearance of the page. Text-formatting attributes, such as paragraph formatting, heading formatting, fonts, size, color, alignment, indents, and styles are easily edited using the Property Inspector. Using fonts within the default settings is wise, because fonts set outside the default settings may not be available on all viewers' computers. Text must be selected in order to apply formatting to it. When formatting paragraphs, you can position the insertion point inside the paragraph that you want to format. Care must be taken to avoid mixing too many different fonts or formatting attributes on a Web page. This can lead to pages that are visually confusing and that may be difficult to read. Now that you have the text on the newsletter page, you decide to apply some formatting to it to improve the appearance of the page.

Steps

1. Click the insertion point anywhere within the words **Packing Essentials**
   Packing Essentials is an individual paragraph, therefore you can format it by clicking the insertion point in it instead of highlighting all of the text.
2. Click the **Format list arrow** on the Property Inspector, then click **Heading 2**, as shown in Figure D-3
   The Heading 2 style is applied to the text. You decide to set the font to the font combination Times New Roman, Times, serif. Font combinations are used so that if one font is not available, the browser will use a similar one. The browser will first look on the viewer's system for Times New Roman, then Times, then a serif font to apply to the text.
3. Select the **Packing Essentials** heading, click the **Font list arrow** on the Property Inspector, then click **Times New Roman, Times, serif**, as shown in Figure D-3
   The text is now set to these three fonts. You decide to center the heading on the page.

QuickTip

You can modify the font combinations by clicking Text on the menu bar, pointing to Font, then clicking Edit Font List.

4. Click the **Align Center icon** on the Property Inspector to center the heading
   The heading appears centered on the page. You decide to change the color of the heading to navy blue.
5. With the heading still highlighted, click the **Text Color list arrow**, then click **#000066** from the Color Picker, as shown in Figure D-4
   The Color Picker closes, and the new color is applied to the heading. You are now ready to format the rest of the text on the page. You begin by setting the font and size.
6. Click the insertion point before the **T** in **The next time you are packing**, press and hold **[Shift]**, scroll to the end of the text, click the insertion point after the end of the last sentence, then release **[Shift]**
   The entire passage of text is selected.
7. Click the **Font list arrow** on the Property Inspector, then click **Times New Roman, Times, serif**
   The font list is applied to the text selection.
8. Click the **Size list arrow** on the Property Inspector, then click **3**, as shown in Figure D-5
   Size 3 is the default size for body text.

QuickTip

When changing the size of the text, use either the Format list arrow or the Size list arrow, but not both.

9. Click anywhere on the page to deselect the text, click the **Preview/Debug in Browser icon** on the toolbar, click your browser to view the page in the browser, close the browser, then save your work

FIGURE D-3: **Property Inspector**

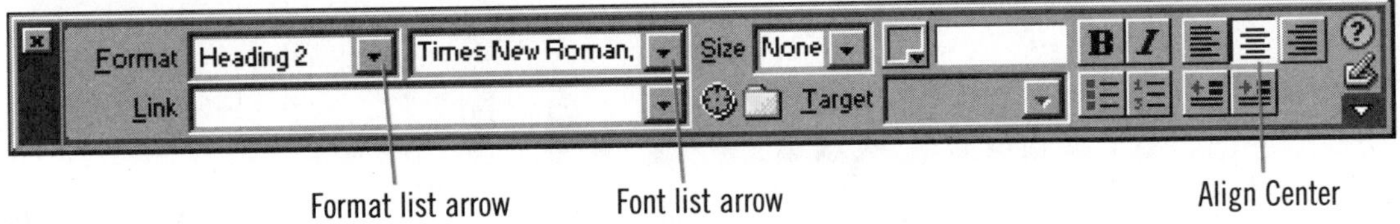

FIGURE D-4: **Color Picker**

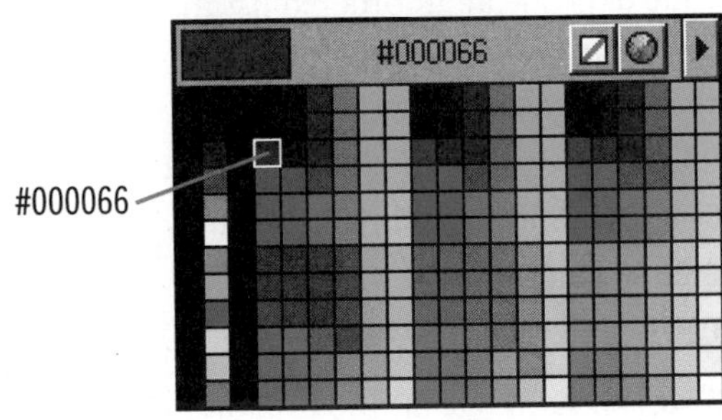

FIGURE D-5: **Property Inspector**

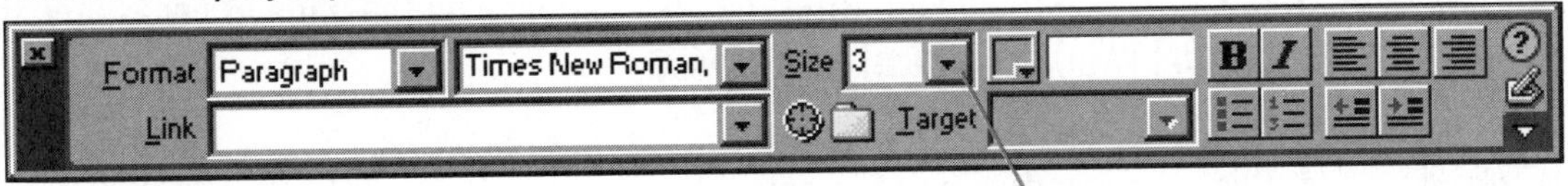

Font sizes

There are two ways to change the size of text. You can select a font size between 1 and 7, 7 being the largest, or you can change the font size relative to the default base font. The **default base font** is size 3. When you choose +1 in the size list, you are increasing the base font size from 3 to 4. If you choose –1, you are decreasing the base font size from 3 to 2. See Figure D-6. Do not confuse the font size number system with the paragraph style number system, which uses Headings from 1 to 6, with 6 being the smallest. Font sizes on Windows and Macintosh computers may differ slightly.

FIGURE D-6: **Font size menu**

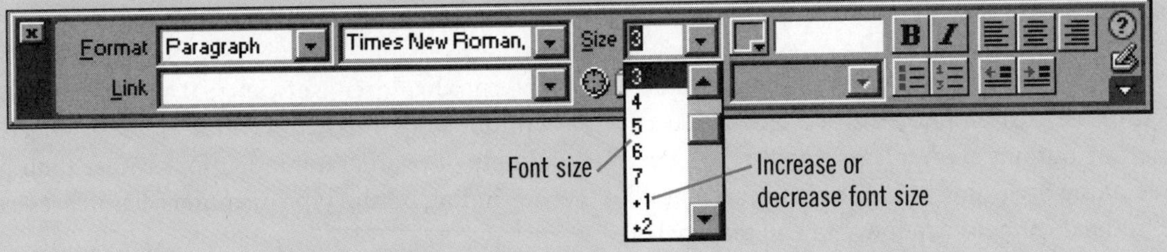

Dreamweaver 4

Creating An Unordered List

You may need to create a list of products or services on pages in your Web site. Dreamweaver provides three types of lists: unordered lists, ordered lists, and definition lists. **Unordered lists** are lists of items that do not need to be placed in a specific order. Each item is usually preceded by a **bullet**, or small raised dot or similar icon. Bullets make lists easier to read than unformatted lists. **Ordered lists** are lists of items that need to be placed in a specific order, and each item is preceded by a number. **Definition lists** consist of terms with indented descriptions or definitions. You decide to create an unordered list from the list of essential items to pack for a trip to make the list of items easier to read.

Steps

1. Click the insertion point in front of the first item, **Expandable clothesline**, scroll to the end of the page, press and hold **[Shift]**, click to the right of the last sentence on the page, then release **[Shift]**
   The ten essential packing items are selected.
2. Click the **Unordered List icon** on the Property Inspector to create an unordered list
   The list of items becomes an unordered list. If you were to continue to add to this list by placing the insertion point after the last item, then pressing [Enter] (Win) or [return] (Mac), the next line would automatically begin with a bullet.
3. Click the insertion point after the last sentence on the page, if necessary, then press **[Enter]** (Win) or **[return]** (Mac) twice
   The unordered list is closed.
4. Click the insertion point in any of the items in the unordered list, click the **arrow** in the lower-right corner of the Property Inspector to expand the Property Inspector, then click the **List Item button**
   The List Properties dialog box opens, as shown in Figure D-7.
5. Click the **Style list arrow**, click **Square**, then click **OK**
   The bullets now appear as squares rather than circles.
6. Click the insertion point before the first item in the unordered list, then click the **Show Code View icon** on the toolbar to view the code for the unordered list
   The HTML codes, or **tags**, surrounding the unordered list are <ul></ul>. Each of the items is surrounded by a <li> and </li> tag, as shown in Figure D-8. The first tag in each pair begins the code, and the last tag ends the code.
7. Click the **Show Design View icon** on the toolbar to return to Design View, click **File** on the menu bar, then click **Save**

QuickTip

Pressing [Enter] (Win) or [return] (Mac) once at the end of an unordered list creates another bulleted item. To end an unordered list, press [Enter] (Win) or [return] (Mac) twice.

Trouble?

Some browsers may not display the square bullets correctly. If not, they will default to the circular bullets.

Bulleted lists

Dreamweaver allows you to change the appearance of bullets or use custom images for bullets. These formatting options are implemented through the use of Cascading Style Sheets. These changes will not be seen in the document window, but will display in Internet Explorer. Netscape 6.0 also supports this option. Sometimes, however, it is just as effective to simply use paragraph indentions rather than bullets, depending on the type of content being presented.

FIGURE D-7: List Properties dialog box

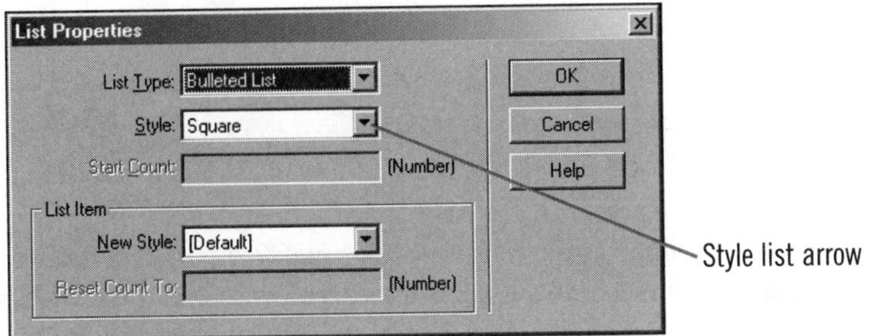

FIGURE D-8: Code View

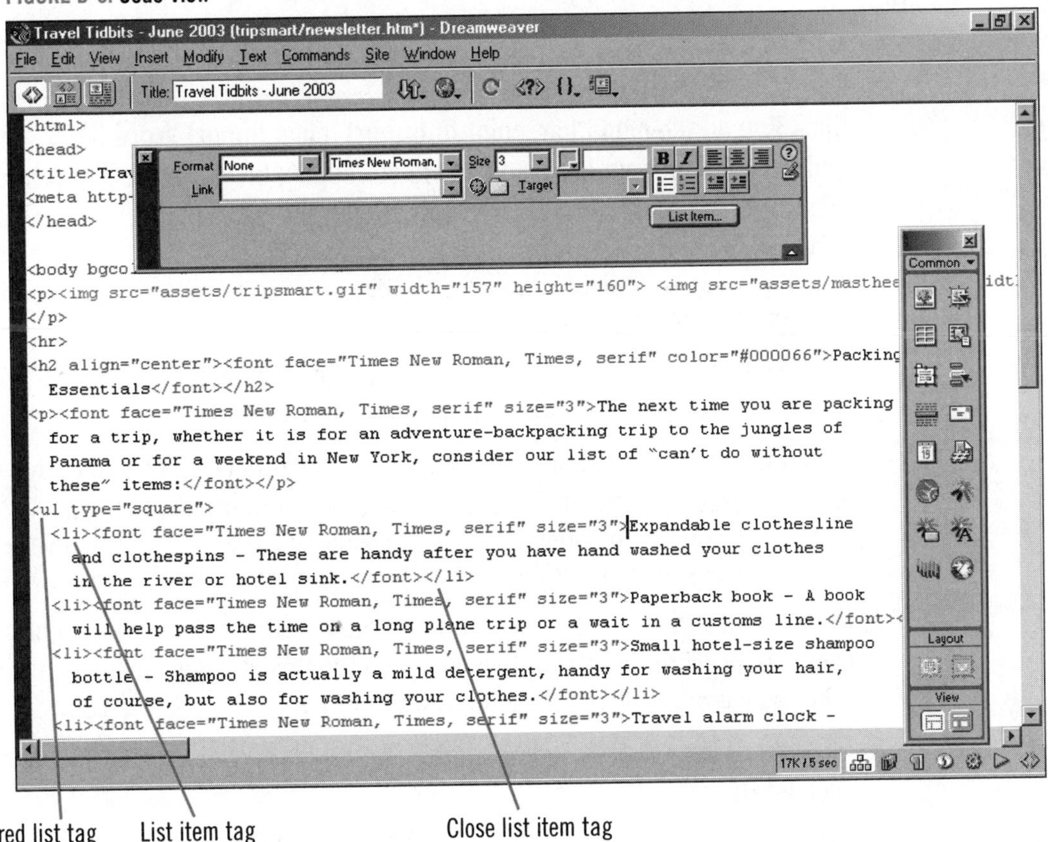

Design Matters

There are two classifications of fonts: sans-serif and serif. Sans-serif fonts are no-nonsense, block style characters. They are used frequently for headings and sub-headings in printed material. Examples of sans-serif fonts are Arial, Verdana, and Helvetica. Serif fonts are more ornate, with small extra strokes at the beginning and end of the characters. They are considered by some to be easier to read in printed material, as the extra strokes lead your eye from one character to the next. Examples of serif fonts are Times New Roman, Times, and Georgia. Many designers feel that a sans-serif font is preferable when the content of a Web site is primarily intended to be read on the screen. However, if the content is frequently printed and then read from the printed material, a serif font is preferable. A good rule of thumb is to limit each Web site to not more than three font variations. Using more than this may make your Web site look unprofessional and leans toward the "ransom note effect." The ransom note effect (a term used among Web designers) implies that fonts have been randomly used in the document without regard to style, comparing it to a ransom note where words from various sources have been cut and pasted onto a page.

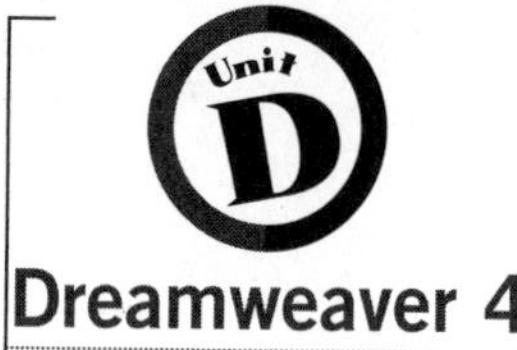

Dreamweaver 4

Creating An Ordered List

Ordered lists are lists that contain items that should be listed in a particular order, such as steps to accomplishing a task. Lists are sometimes formatted as ordered lists for emphasis. Numbers rather than bullets precede the items in ordered lists. Dreamweaver has several options for number styles, including Roman and Arabic. The Travel Services Department at TripSmart has compiled instructions for packing a suitcase for a trip. They want to include this in the newsletter. You continue to work on the newsletter page by adding a horizontal rule to divide the stories, and import the text onto the page.

Steps

QuickTip

The Clean Up Word HTML dialog box allows you to choose which version of Microsoft Word you are using.

Trouble?

If you do not see the newsletter.htm page, click the Show Site icon, then double-click newsletter.htm.

QuickTip

To end a list, click the insertion point at the end of the list, then press [Enter] (Win) or [return] (Mac) twice.

1. Click **File** on the menu bar, point to **Import**, click **Import Word HTML**, click the drive and folder where your Project Files are stored, double-click the **Unit D folder**, double-click **how_to_pack.htm**, click **OK**, then click **OK** again to close the Clean Up Word HTML Results window
   The imported text is placed on a new, untitled page in Dreamweaver. You need to copy and paste this text onto the newsletter page.
2. Click **Edit** on the menu bar, click **Select All**, click **Edit** on the menu bar, then click **Copy**
   The text is highlighted, showing that it is now selected.
3. Click **File** on the menu bar, click **Close**, then click **No** (Win) or **Don't Save** (Mac) when you are asked if you want to save changes to the untitled document
   The untitled document closes, and you are ready to paste the text onto the newsletter.htm page. The newsletter page is displayed in the document window in Design View.
4. Click the insertion point below the last line of text on the newsletter.htm page, then click the **Insert Horizontal Rule icon** on the Objects panel to insert a horizontal rule
   A horizontal rule is placed under the last line of text.
5. Click the insertion point below the **horizontal rule**, click **Edit** on the menu bar, then click **Paste**
   The text is pasted on the newsletter page under the horizontal rule.
6. Select all of the text below and including **Decide what items to take**, by clicking the insertion point before the **D** in **Decide**, pressing **[Shift]**, scrolling to the end of the page, clicking the insertion point at the end of the last sentence, then releasing **[Shift]**
   The text is selected. You are ready to format it and create an ordered list.
7. Click the **Font list arrow** on the Property Inspector, click **Times New Roman, Times, serif**, click the **Size list arrow** on the Property Inspector, then click **3**
   The font and font size are formatted to match the rest of the text on the page.
8. Click the **Ordered List icon** on the Property Inspector to create an ordered list
   The list of items becomes an ordered list, and sequential numbers precede the items.
9. Select **Steps in packing a suitcase**, click the **Bold icon** on the Property Inspector to apply bold formatting to the sentence, click the **Text Color list arrow** on the Property Inspector, click **#000066**, click once to deselect the text, click **File** on the menu bar, then click **Save**
   The sentence is now formatted as bold and navy blue, as shown in Figure D-9.

FIGURE D-9: Newsletter page

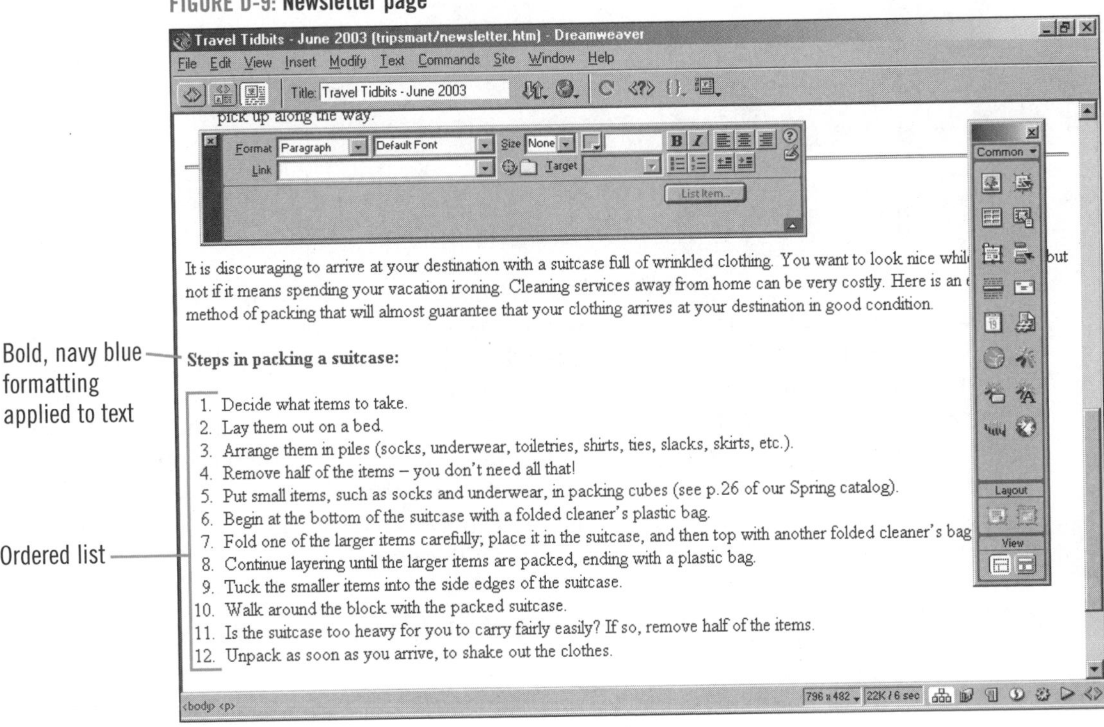

CLUES TO USE

Ordered list style options

There are several options for formatting the style of an ordered, or numbered, list. Clicking the arrow on the lower-right corner of the Property Inspector will expand the Property Inspector to display the List Item button, as shown in Figure D-10. Clicking the List Item button opens the List Properties dialog box, as shown in Figure D-11. It also gives you the option of setting two different styles by setting a start count and reset count, to define two different sets of numbers.

FIGURE D-10: Property Inspector

FIGURE D-11: List Properties dialog box

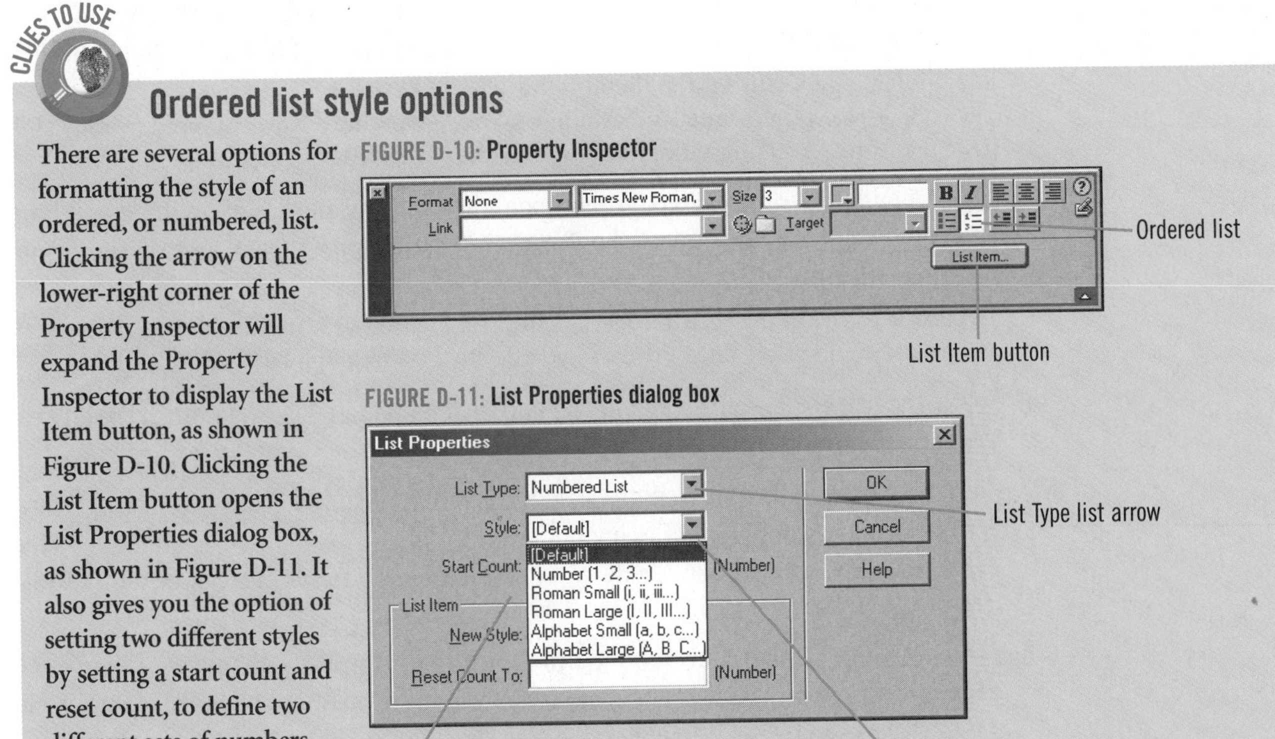

Dreamweaver 4

Dreamweaver 4

Editing Text with Code and Design Views

Even though it is easy to format text in Dreamweaver using the Property Inspector, a general knowledge of HTML can be useful at times. It is sometimes faster to enter changes directly in the HTML code rather than using Dreamweaver commands or inspectors. You can copy and paste HTML code in Code View just as easily as you can copy and paste text in Design View. You can also refer to the O'Reilly Reference Guide for HTML help by clicking the Reference icon on the toolbar. You would like to format the heading Avoiding Wrinkle Woes to match the heading Packing Essentials. Instead of using the Property Inspector, you decide to copy the HTML code for the Packing Essentials text and apply it to the Avoiding Wrinkle Woes text. You use the Show Code and Design Views to perform this task.

QuickTip

You can adjust the window percentage of either view by dragging the window border up or down.

1. Click the **Show Code and Design Views icon** on the toolbar to open the Code and Design View
   Notice how the document window is split between Code View and Design View, as shown in Figure D-12.
2. Click the insertion point in the **Design View window**, scroll until you can see the **Packing Essentials** text, then click in the **Packing Essentials** heading
   The insertion point is placed in the Packing Essentials text. Notice that another insertion point is placed in the Packing Essentials text in the Code View above.
3. Select the **HTML code for the Packing Essentials text**, as shown in Figure D-12
   The HTML code for the Packing Essentials text is selected. You are now ready to copy it.

QuickTip

You can undo and redo steps using the History panel.

4. Click **Edit** on the menu bar, click **Copy**, scroll down in the Code View window until you see the **Avoiding Wrinkle Woes** text, place the insertion point at the beginning of this line of code, click **Edit** on the menu bar, then click **Paste**
   The code is pasted in front of the Avoiding Wrinkle Woes text. Now you need to copy and paste the words "Avoiding Wrinkle Woes" over the words "Packing Essentials".
5. Select **Avoiding Wrinkle Woes** in the Code View window, click **Edit** on the menu bar, click **Cut** to cut the text, select the **Packing Essentials** text, click **Edit** on the menu bar, then click **Paste**
   The text is pasted in the HTML code, as shown in Figure D-13. You don't need extra paragraphs at the end of the line of code, so you delete the paragraph tags (<P></P>).
6. Select the extra **<P></P>** tags at the end of the line of code, then press **[Delete]**
   The extra paragraph tags are deleted from the code.
7. Click anywhere in Design View to deselect **Avoiding Wrinkle Woes** and see the formatting changes applied to the heading
   The format of the Avoiding Wrinkle Woes heading looks identical to that of the Packing Essentials heading.
8. Click the **Show Design View icon** to return to Design View, then save your work
   The two headings on the newsletter page have the same formatting applied to them, which gives the page an overall professional appearance.

FIGURE D-12: **Code and Design Views**

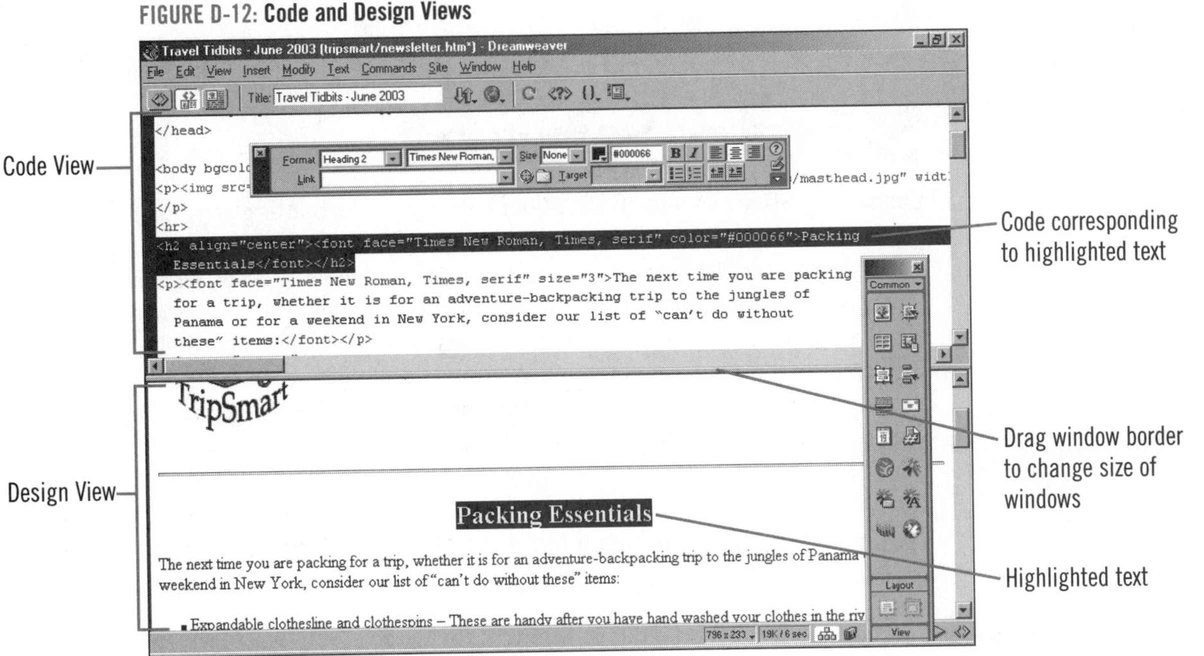

FIGURE D-13: **Code and Design Views**

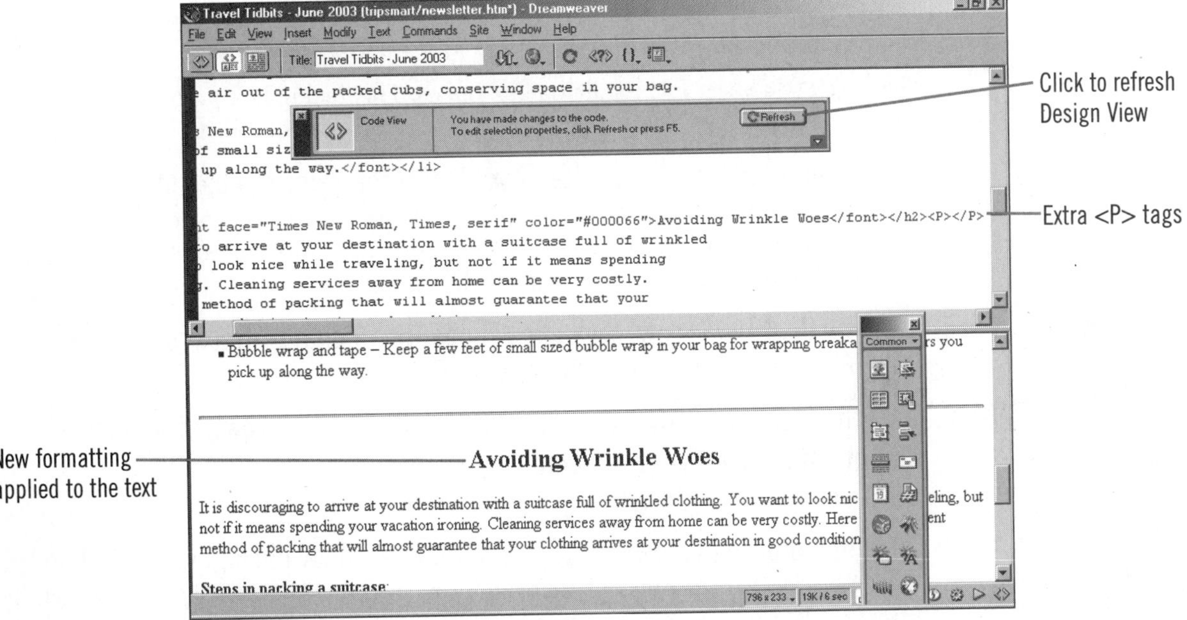

Quick Tag Editor

The Quick Tag Editor is an option for quickly editing HTML tags without changing to Code View or Code and Design View. The Quick Tag Editor shown below is found under the Modify menu. You type changes to the HTML code in the Quick Tag Editor window. You can also open the Quick Tag Editor by pressing [Ctrl][T] (Win) or [Command][T] (Mac).

FIGURE D-14: **Quick Tag Editor**

Edit Tag: <hr>

Quick Tag Editor displaying HTML code for a horizontal rule

Dreamweaver 4

Dreamweaver 4

Creating A Cascading Style Sheet

Cascading Style Sheets (CSS Styles) are sets of formatting attributes that are saved with a descriptive name. You can create CSS Styles when you want to apply the same formatting attributes to page elements, such as text, objects, and tables. CSS Styles can be applied to any element in a document or to all of the documents in a Web site. If an existing style is edited, the elements formatted with that style are automatically updated. CSS Styles save a lot of time and help create a look of continuity in a Web site. CSS Styles are individual files that are saved with the .css extension and stored in the root folder of a Web site. You decide to apply the same formatting to the ten items in the Packing Essentials list. Instead of formatting each item, one at a time, you create a Cascading Style Sheet and apply a style to each item in the list.

1. **Click Window on the menu bar, then click CSS Styles to open the CSS Styles panel**
   The CSS Styles panel opens. This panel is where you can add, delete, edit, and apply styles.

2. **Click the New Style icon on the CSS Styles panel, then verify that the New Style Sheet File option button and the Make Custom Style (class) option button are both selected**
   The New Style Sheet option makes the CSS Style available to use in the entire Web site, not just the current document and the Make Custom Style (class) option creates a new custom style and places it in the CSS Styles panel. See Figure D-15.

> **QuickTip**
> If you don't type the period before the style name, Dreamweaver will insert it for you.

3. **Type .bulleted_items in the Name text box, then click OK**
   The Save Style Sheet File As dialog box opens. This dialog box prompts you to name the Cascading Style Sheet Files and store it in the Web site's root folder.

4. **Type tripsmart in the File name text box (Win) or the Name text box (Mac), then click Save**
   The Style Definition for .bulleted_items in tripsmart.css dialog box opens. The .css extension stands for cascading style sheet. This dialog box allows you to choose attributes, such as font color and font size, for the CSS Style.

5. **Click the Font list arrow, then click Times New Roman, Times, serif**
   The three fonts are selected for the style sheet.

6. **Click the Size list arrow, click 12, click the Style list arrow, click normal, click the Weight list arrow, then click bold**
   You are now ready to choose a color for the style.

> **QuickTip**
> A few CSS Style attributes are not displayed in the Dreamweaver document window, such as blink and overline. However, they will display in a browser window. An * appears next to these attributes in the Style Definition dialog box, as shown in Figure D-16.

7. **Click the Color list arrow, click #000066, as shown in Figure D-16, then click OK**
   The CSS Style named bulleted_items appears in the CSS Styles panel as a style for the TripSmart Web site. CSS Style names in the CSS Styles panel do not show the period preceding the style name.

8. **Click the Show Site icon to view the TripSmart Web site**
   The tripsmart.css file appears in the file listing for the Web site, with a different icon than the HTML page icons.

9. **Close the Site window, then click the Show Code View icon on the toolbar to view the HTML code for the tripsmart.css file**
   The code for the tripsmart.css appears in the Head section, as shown in Figure D-17.

FIGURE D-15: New Style dialog box

Enter name of style here

Make Custom Style (class) option button

New Style Sheet File option button

FIGURE D-16: Style Definition for .bulleted_items in tripsmart.css dialog box

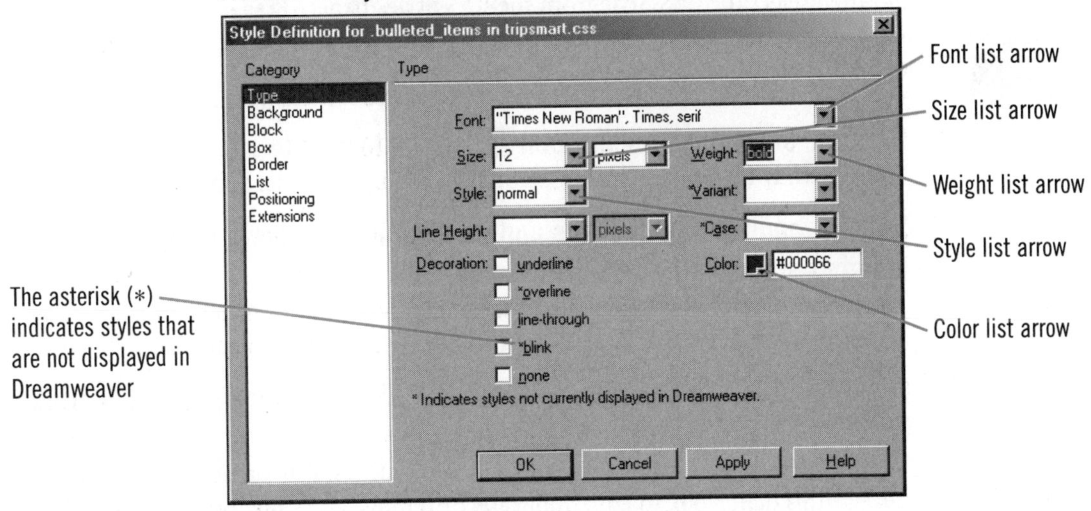

FIGURE D-17: Code View of tripsmart.css

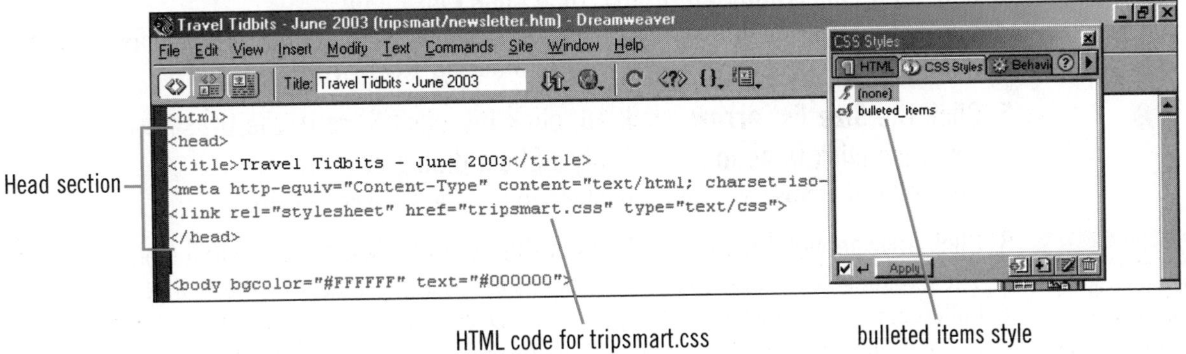

Dreamweaver 4

Using Cascading Style Sheets

Cascading Style Sheets are great timesavers. The ability to define a style and then apply it to page elements on hundreds of pages is a great benefit to Web developers. Cascading Style Sheets are not limited to one Web site. They can be exported into other Web sites, which makes them quite a powerful tool.

Unfortunately, not all browsers can read Cascading Style Sheets. Versions of Internet Explorer that are 4.0 or lower do not support Cascading Style Sheets. Only Netscape Navigator version 6.0 or higher supports Cascading Style Sheets. In the future, as viewers upgrade to newer browser software, this problem will be resolved.

Dreamweaver 4

Applying and Editing A Cascading Style Sheet

After creating a Cascading Style Sheet, it is easy to apply the styles to Web pages elements. If, after applying a style, the results are not satisfactory, the style can be edited to improve the formatting. To apply a CSS Style, you select the text or page element that you want to apply the style to, and then select the CSS Style from the CSS Styles panel. You are ready to apply the bulleted_items style to each item in the list of packing essentials, to place emphasis on them and make them easier to read.

Steps

1. Click the **Show Design View icon** on the toolbar to return to Design View
   You are ready to apply the new CSS Style to the list of bulleted items.
2. Select **Expandable clothesline and clothespins**, as shown in Figure D-18, then click **bulleted_items** in the CSS Styles panel
   The bulleted_items style is applied to the Expandable clothesline and clothespins text. You decide that the text is too small, so you edit the tripsmart.css file to change the text size to 16.
3. Click the **Edit Style Sheet icon** on the CSS Styles panel, then click **tripsmart.css (link)** in the Edit Style Sheet dialog box
   The Edit Style Sheet dialog box, shown in Figure D-19, lists each .css file in the Web site. You can use this dialog box to edit, duplicate, or remove a .css file. You can also link a .css file to a URL or create a new one.
4. Click **Edit**, click **.bulleted_items**, then click **Edit** again
   The Style Definition for .bulleted_items in tripsmart.css dialog box opens. This is the same dialog box you used to create the original .bulleted_items style.
5. Click the **Size list arrow**, click **16**, click **OK**, click **Save** in the tripsmart.css dialog box, then click **Done** in the Edit Style Sheet dialog box
   The bulleted_items style has been edited to include a larger text size.
6. Click anywhere on the page to deselect the Expandable clothesline and clothespins text
   The Expandable clothesline and clothespins text is larger, reflecting the changes made to the bulleted_items style applied to it. See Figure D-20. You are happy with the change you made to the bulleted_items style, so you apply it to rest of the items in the list.
7. Repeat Step 2 to apply the bulleted_items style to each of the nine remaining items
   All 10 items have the bulleted_items style applied to them. The list looks more attractive with emphasis placed on the item names.

QuickTip

If you click the insertion point in text that has an applied CSS style, that style is highlighted in the CSS Styles panel.

FIGURE D-18: **Applying a CSS Style to text**

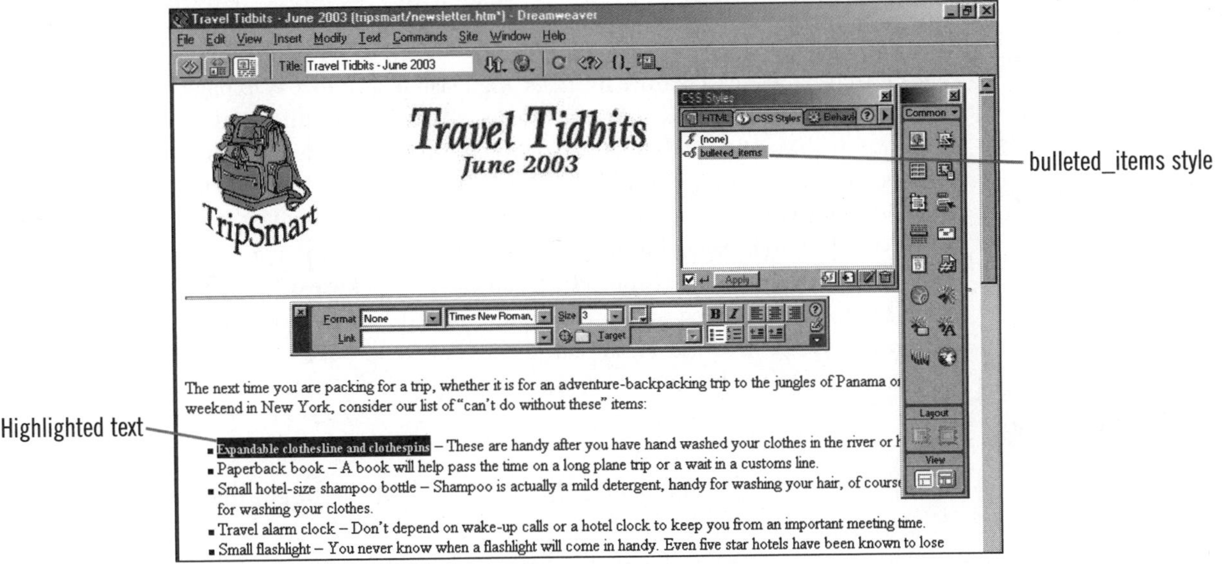

FIGURE D-19: **Edit Style Sheet dialog box**

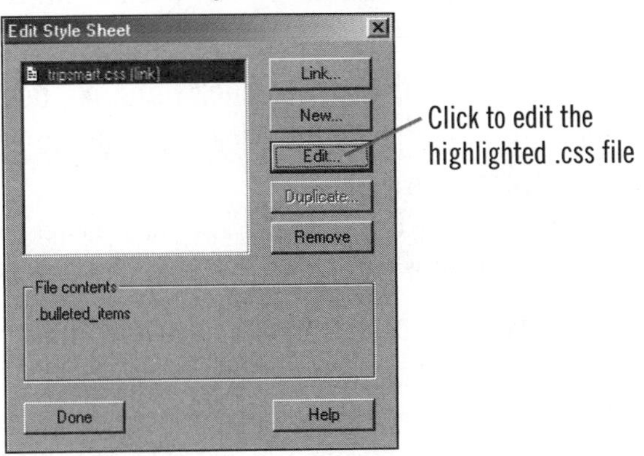

FIGURE D-20: **Viewing text with .bulleted_items style applied to it**

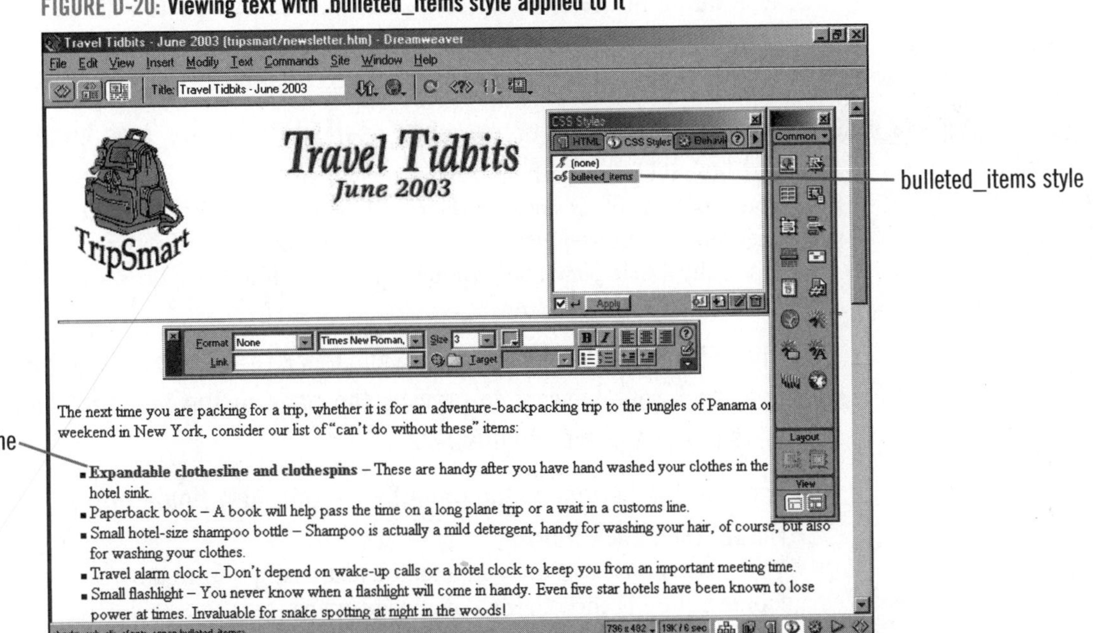

Dreamweaver 4

Dreamweaver 4

Inserting Flash Text

The Objects panel has a feature for inserting Flash text onto a Web page. **Flash** is a Macromedia software program that is used for creating vector-based graphics and animations. **Vector-based graphics** are based on mathematical formulas rather than the pixels that make up JPG and BMP images. Vector-based graphics have a smoother look and are smaller in file size, which makes them ideal for Web sites because they download quickly. Flash text may add visual interest to an otherwise dull Web page, and may help to deliver or reinforce a message. Flash files are saved with the .swf filename extension, which stands for Shockwave Flash. **Shockwave** is a player that you need to have installed on your computer in order to view movies created with Macromedia software. You add Flash text to the newsletter page to provide a link that viewers can click to return to the home page of the TripSmart Web site.

Steps 1 2 3 4

1. **Click the insertion point after the last word on the page, then press [Enter] (Win) or [return] (Mac) twice**
   The insertion point is positioned two lines below the last line of text, and ends the ordered list.
2. **Click the Insert Flash Text icon on the Objects panel**
   The Insert Flash Text dialog box opens. This dialog box allows you to set the formatting options for the Flash text. You choose the font, size, alignment, and style.
3. **Click the Font list arrow, click Dauphin, double-click the Size text box to highlight the current size, type 34, click the Bold icon, then click the Center Align icon to center the text**
   You next choose the text color and the rollover color. The **rollover color** is the color that the text appears in whenever the mouse pointer is "rolled over" it.
4. **Click the Color list arrow, click #000066, click the Rollover Color list arrow, then click #66CCFF, as shown in Figure D-21**
   When the mouse pointer rolls over the Flash text, the text will change from dark blue to light blue. You are ready to type the Flash text and create a link to link the Flash text to the home page.
5. **Type Home in the Text text box, click the Browse button next to the Link text box, as shown in Figure D-21, then double-click index.htm**
   The index.htm file is linked to the Flash text button.
6. **Click the Target list arrow, click _self, if necessary, type home.swf in the Save As text box, then click OK**
   The Flash text file is saved in the root folder for the Web site. The Flash text appears on the page, but the rollover effect works only in a browser window or when you click the Play button in the Assets panel. Setting the target to _self tells the browser to open the index page in the same browser window.
7. **Click File on the menu bar, click Save, click the Preview/Debug in Browser icon, then click your browser to preview the page in the browser. Compare your finished newsletter page with Figure D-22**
8. **Scroll to the bottom of the page to see your new Home button, roll your mouse over Home, then click Home**
   When the mouse rolls over Home, the text changes from dark blue to light blue. When the Home button is clicked, the home page opens.
9. **Exit (Win) or Quit (Mac) Dreamweaver**

Trouble?
If you don't have the Dauphin font, choose Arial instead.

Trouble?
If you choose the wrong color for the text or the rollover text, you can click the Strikethrough icon to start over.

QuickTip
Flash text files must be saved in the same folder as the page file that they are placed in.

FIGURE D-21: **Insert Flash Text dialog box**

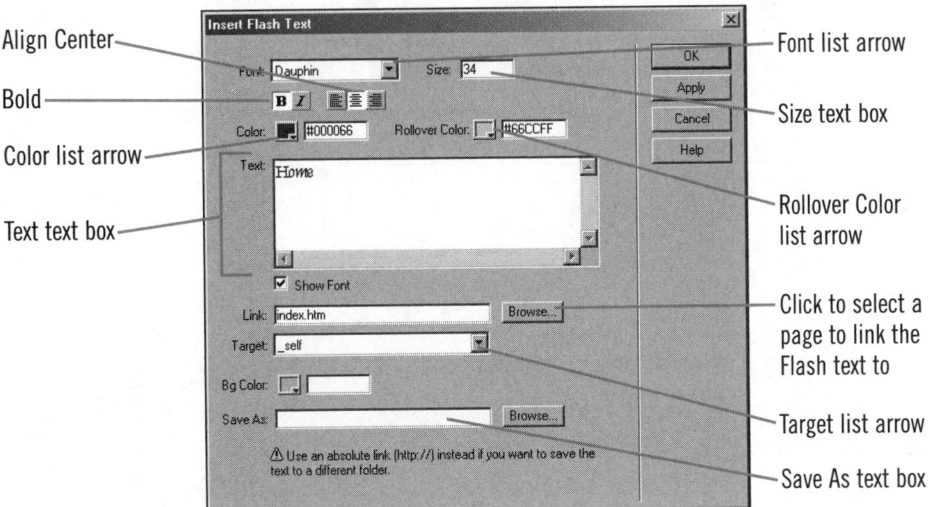

FIGURE D-22: **The finished product**

Travel Tidbits

June 2003

Packing Essentials

The next time you are packing for a trip, whether it is for an adventure-backpacking trip to the jungles of Panama or for a weekend in New York, consider our list of "can't do without these" items:

- **Expandable clothesline and clothespins** – These are handy after you have hand-washed your clothes in the river or hotel sink.
- **Paperback book** – A book will help pass the time on a long plane trip or a wait in a customs line.
- **Small hotel-size shampoo bottle** – Shampoo is actually a mild detergent, handy for washing your hair, of course, but also for washing your clothes.
- **Travel alarm clock** – Don't depend on wake-up calls or a hotel clock to keep you from an important meeting time.
- **Small flashlight** – You never know when a flashlight will come in handy. Even five-star hotels have been known to lose power at times. Invaluable for snake spotting at night in the woods!
- **Zippered plastic bags** – These are so handy for storing a number of things: snacks, dirty clothes, wet clothes, small items that would get "lost" in your bag, like pens, tape, and your expandable clothesline and clothespins!
- **Guidebook** – There are many great guidebooks that range from guides for students on a shoestring budget to guides on shopping for fine antiques in Italy. Take advantage of available research to obtain general background knowledge of your destination.
- **Backpack** – Backpacks are versatile, easy to carry, and have enough style variations to appeal to all ages and sexes. They hold a lot of your essential items!
- **Packing cubes** – Packing cubes are zippered nylon bags that are great for organizing your packed items. You can squeeze the air out of the packed cubes, conserving space in your bag.
- **Bubble wrap and tape** – Keep a few feet of small-sized bubble wrap in your bag for wrapping breakable souvenirs you pick up along the way.

Avoiding Wrinkle Woes

It is discouraging to arrive at your destination with a suitcase full of wrinkled clothing. You want to look nice while traveling, but not if it means spending your vacation ironing. Cleaning services away from home can be very costly. Here is an excellent method of packing that will almost guarantee that your clothing arrives at your destination in good condition.

Steps in packing a suitcase:

1. Decide what items to take.
2. Lay them out on a bed.
3. Arrange them in piles (socks, underwear, toiletries, shirts, ties, slacks, skirts, etc.).
4. Remove half of the items – you don't need all that!
5. Put small items, such as socks and underwear, in packing cubes (see p.26 of our Spring catalog).
6. Begin at the bottom of the suitcase with a folded cleaner's plastic bag.
7. Fold one of the larger items carefully; place it in the suitcase, and then top with another folded cleaner's bag.
8. Continue layering until the larger items are packed, ending with a plastic bag.
9. Tuck the smaller items into the side edges of the suitcase.
10. Walk around the block with the packed suitcase.
11. Is the suitcase too heavy for you to carry fairly easily? If so, remove half of the items.
12. Unpack as soon as you arrive, to shake out the clothes.

Flash text — *Home*

Practice

▶ Concepts Review

Label each element in the document window as shown in Figure D-23.

FIGURE D-23

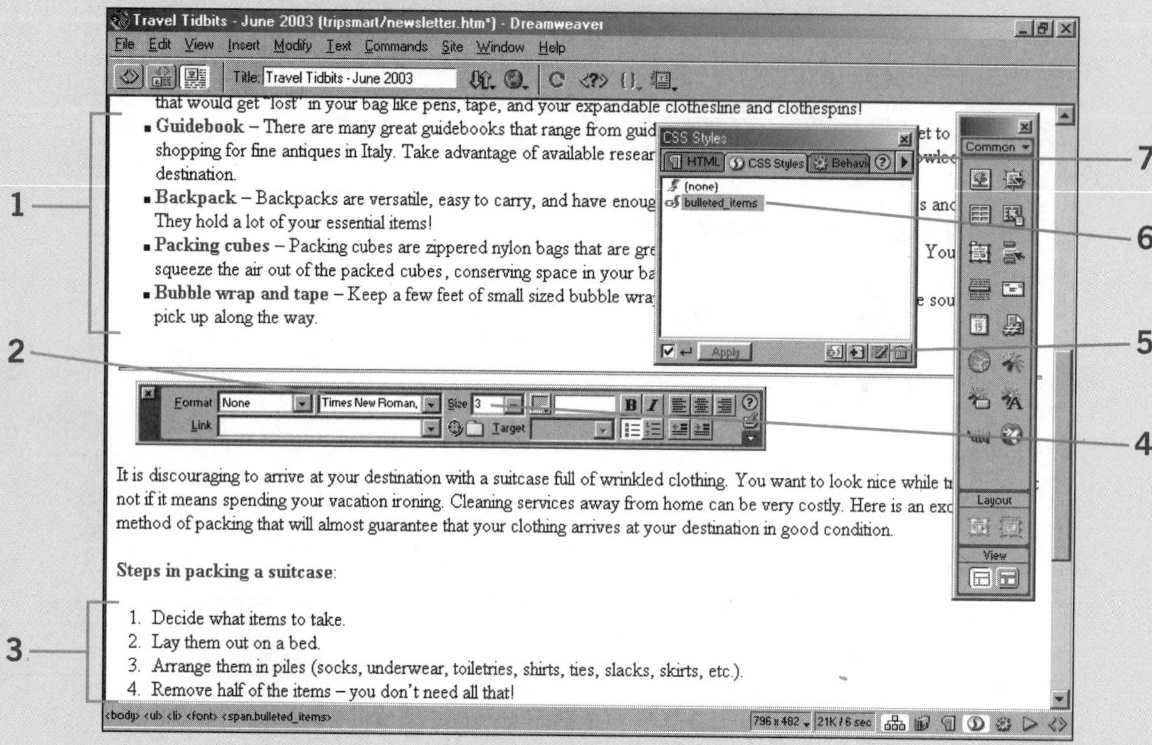

Match each of the following terms with the statement that describes its function.

8. Sans serif font	a. Numbered lists
9. Property Inspector	b. Block-style font
10. Ordered lists	c. Program that creates vector-based animation
11. Unordered lists	d. HTML help
12. Cascading Style Sheets	e. Based on mathematical formulas
13. Flash	f. Bulleted lists
14. O'Reilly Reference Guide	g. Edits text-formatting attributes
15. Vector-based graphic	h. Based on pixels
16. Bitmapped graphic	i. Font with extra strokes at the beginning and end of the characters
17. Serif font	j. Sets of formatting attributes

Select the best answer from the following list of choices.

18. The icon used to select color is:

a. [icon]
b. [icon]
c. [icon]
d. [icon]

19. Flash files are saved with the filename extension

a. PNG
b. JPG
c. SWF
d. GIF

20. A CSS Style name is preceded by a

a. Pound sign.
b. Period.
c. Dash.
d. Number.

21. The color of Flash text that appears when the mouse rolls over the text is called the:

a. Flash color.
b. Rollover color.
c. Button color.
d. Hyperlink color.

22. The default font is size ________.

a. 2
b. 4
c. 1
d. 3

Skills Review

***Important**: If you did not create this Web site in Unit B and maintain it during the preceding units, you will need to create a root folder for this Web site and define the Web site using files your instructor will provide. See the "Read This Before You Begin" section for more detailed instructions.*

1. Import text.

a. Start Dreamweaver.
b. Open the Blooms & Bulbs Web site.
c. Open dmd_2.htm from the drive and folder where your Project Files are stored in the Unit D folder.
d. Save the file as *tips.htm* in your blooms_and_bulbs Web site, overwriting the existing file.
e. Save the graphic planting_tips.jpg in the assets folder of the Blooms & Bulbs Web site.
f. Import the gardening_tips.htm file from the drive and folder where your Project Files are stored in the Unit D folder, using the Import Word HTML command.
g. Copy the imported text and close the gardening_tips.htm file.

h. Paste the text onto the tips.htm page below the horizontal rule.
i. Save the changes to the page.

2. Set text properties.
a. Select the Seasonal gardening checklist heading.
b. Use the Property Inspector to center the text.
c. Use the Property Inspector to format the text with the Heading 3 style.
d. Apply the color #006633 to the text.
e. Select the rest of the text on the page except for the Seasonal gardening checklist heading, then set the font as Times New Roman, Times, serif, size 3.
f. Select the Basic Gardening Tips heading.
g. Format this text as bold, with the color #006633 and a size of 3.
h. Save your work.

3. Create an unordered list.
a. Select the items in the Seasonal gardening checklist.
b. Format the list of items as an unordered list.
c. Save your work.

4. Create an ordered list.
a. Select the items in the Basic Gardening Tips list.
b. Format the items as an ordered list.
c. Save your work.

5. Edit text using Code and Design Views.
a. Change to the Code and Design View.
b. Place the insertion point in the Basic Gardening Tips heading in the Design View window.
c. Use the HTML code in the Code View window to change the text size of Basic Gardening Tips from size 3 to size 4.
d. Click the Refresh button on the Property Inspector.
e. Return to Design View.

6. Create a Cascading Style Sheet.
a. Open the CSS Styles panel, if necessary.
b. Create a new style.
c. Make sure that the New Style Sheet File option button is checked and that the Make Custom Style (class) option button is checked in the New Style dialog box.
d. Name the new style **.seasons**, then click OK.
e. Save the style sheet file with the name **blooms**, then click Save.
f. Set the font for the .seasons style as Times New Roman, Times, serif.
g. Set the font size as 12, the style as normal, and the weight as bold.
h. Set the font color as #006633.
i. Click OK, then save your work.

7. Apply and edit a Cascading Style Sheet.
a. Apply the seasons style to the words Fall, Winter, Spring, and Summer in the Seasonal gardening checklist.
b. Edit the style to increase the text size to a size 16.
c. Save your work.

8. **Insert Flash text.**
   a. Place your insertion point at the end of the last line of text on the page, then press [Enter] (Win) or [return] (Mac) twice.
   b. Using the Objects panel, insert Flash text.
   c. Set the font to Century Gothic, size 18. If you do not have Century Gothic as an option, choose Arial or a similar font.
   d. Set the font color to #006633, and the rollover color to #66FF99.
   e. Type **Home Page** in the Text text box.
   f. Use the Browse button to link the Flash text button to the index.htm file.
   g. Set the background color (Bg Color) to #FFFFFF.
   h. Save the Flash text as **home.swf**.
   i. Click OK, then save your work.
   j. Preview the page in your Web browser and test the Home Page button.
   k. Close your browser, then Exit (Win) or Quit (Mac) Dreamweaver.

***Important**: If you did not create the following Web sites in Unit B and maintain them during the preceding units, you will need to create a root folder for the Web sites in the following exercises and define the Web sites using files your instructor will provide. See the "Read This Before You Begin" section for more detailed instructions.*

► Independent Challenge 1

You are a Web developer for the rock band JW's Two Dog Band. Your boss, Julie Temple, asks you to simplify the band's Web site by creating a template for a page she uses to feature new CD releases. You begin by opening the Dreamweaver Guided Tour about adding content, to see if you can find information about using templates.

a. Open Dreamweaver and access the Guided Tour feature.
b. Select the fourth Guided Tour, Adding Content, as shown in Figure D-24.
c. Follow the directions on the screen and click on the movie icons to view the movies.
d. Using scrap paper or your word processor, write a few paragraphs explaining how consistency can be applied to a Web site with the use of templates.
e. Exit Help when you are finished.
f. Exit (Win) or Quit (Mac) Dreamweaver.

FIGURE D-24

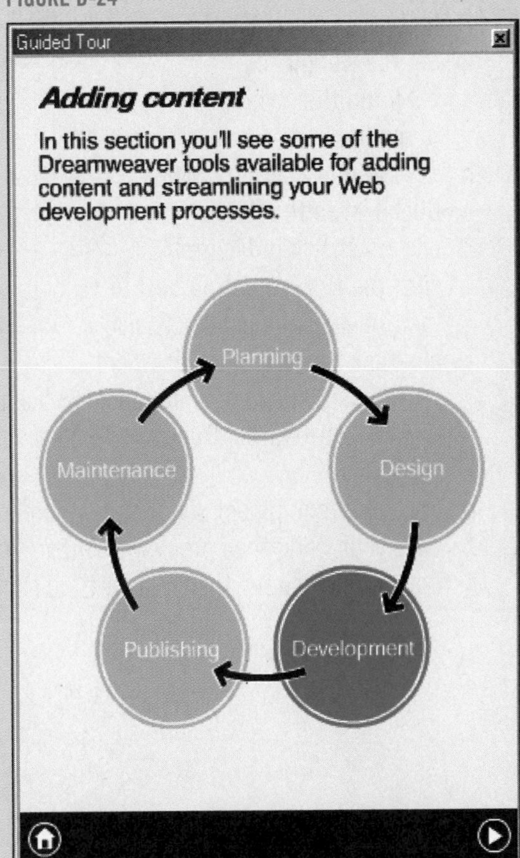

Dreamweaver 4

► Independent Challenge 2

The Over Under Dive Shop is a dive center in Nevis, West Indies. It is a certified Professional Association of Diving Instructors (PADI) dive center, offering PADI certification courses. They also conduct snorkeling and dive trips to various locations around the barrier reef surrounding Nevis. Open the Over Under Web site created in Unit B from the drive and folder where your Project Files are stored. In this exercise, you will create a new page for the Over Under store. The store carries diving equipment, snorkeling equipment, bathing suits, and various accessories for swimming and diving.

a. Start Dreamweaver.
b. Open the Over Under Web site, then open dmd_3.htm from the drive and folder where your Project Files are stored in the Unit D folder.
c. Save dmd_3.htm as **store.htm** in the Over Under Web site.
d. Change the path for the logo to a relative path, if necessary.
e. Add an appropriate title to the page.
f. Import the equip_list.htm file from the drive and folder where your Project Files are stored in the Unit D folder, using the Import Word HTML command.
g. Copy the text from the page and paste it onto the store.htm page, below the existing text.
h. Select the items in the list and use the Property Inspector to format them as an unordered list.
i. Create a new CSS Style named **.equipment**.
j. Save the Style Sheet File as **over_under.css**.
k. Set the font for the .equipment style to Arial, Helvetica, sans serif.
l. Set the font size to 14.
m. Set the weight to bold and the style to normal.
n. Set the font color to #336633.
o. Click List in the Category text box, as shown in Figure D-25, click the Browse button next to the Bullet Image list arrow, double-click the Unit D folder where your Project Files are store, double-click the assets folder, then click shell.jpg.
p. Click Select (Win) or Open (Mac), copy shell.jpg to the assets folder for the Web site, click Save, then click OK.
q. Apply the .equipment style to the unordered list.
r. Save your work, then preview the page in your browser to view the formatted list.
s. Close your browser, then Exit (Win) or Quit (Mac) Dreamweaver.

FIGURE D-25

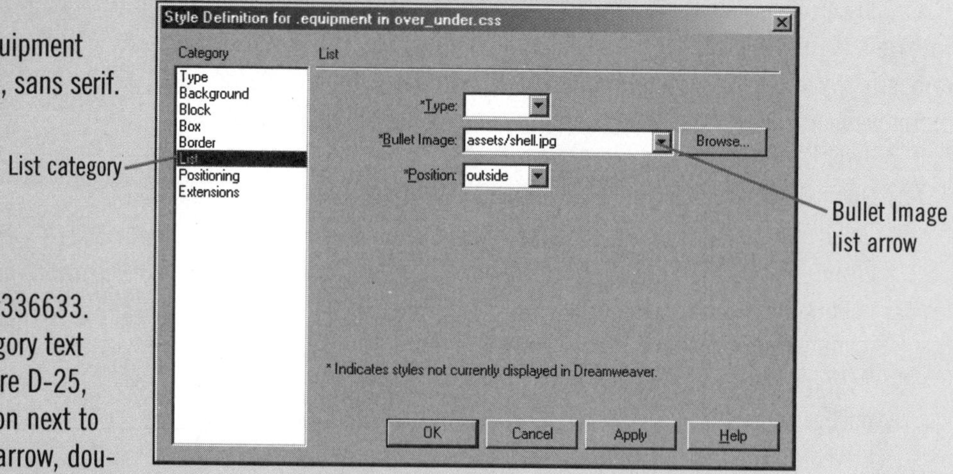

▶ Independent Challenge 3

Off Note is a music store specializing in classical, blues, rock, country, and jazz. Off Note is one of your Web Design company's clients. To keep the Web site fresh, you have been asked to add a page listing the top 10 jazz songs or jazz albums for the past week.

a. Start Dreamweaver.
b. Open the Off Note Web site.
c. Connect to the Internet and go to Yahoo! Music at *music.yahoo.com* (Note: do not put in www for this particular Web site.)
d. Click the Music Charts link.
e. Find the top 10 jazz singles or the top 10 jazz albums for the week. List your selections on a sheet of paper or copy them to the clipboard.
f. Return to the Off Note Web site and open jazz.htm to use for the top 10 list.
g. Add a page title and an appropriate opening paragraph.
h. List the songs or albums on the page in order from your notes or paste them from the clipboard.
i. Format the list as an ordered list.
j. Create a CSS Style called .hits, then save the Style Sheet File as *offnote.css.*
k. Refer to Figure D-26 for an example of settings you can use for the .hits style.
l. View the page in your browser.
m. Print the page from the browser window.
n. Click View on the menu bar, then click Source (Win) or Page Source (Mac) to view the code.
o. Print the code, exit the text editor window, then exit the browser.
p. Exit (Win) or Quit (Mac) Dreamweaver.

FIGURE D-26

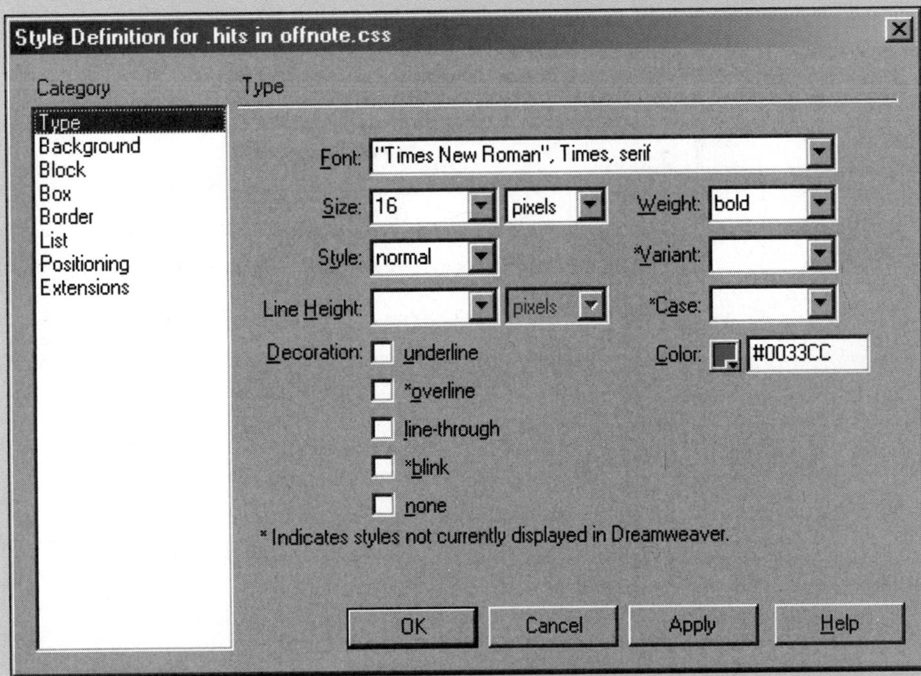

Dreamweaver 4

Independent Challenge 4

You are a student in Dr. Gwen Gresham's Web Design I class. She would like your class to learn more about Cascading Style Sheets. She has directed you to go to the Web site for The World Wide Web Consortium, the origin of the definition of the Cascading Style Sheet specification.

- **a.** Connect to the Internet and go to The World Wide Web Consortium at *www.w3.org*.
- **b.** Search the Web site for the most current definition of Cascading Style Sheets.
- **c.** Copy and paste the definition into a document you create in a word-processing program.
- **d.** List four topics that are covered in the Cascading Style Sheets Table of Contents.
- **e.** Exit the browser.

FIGURE D-27

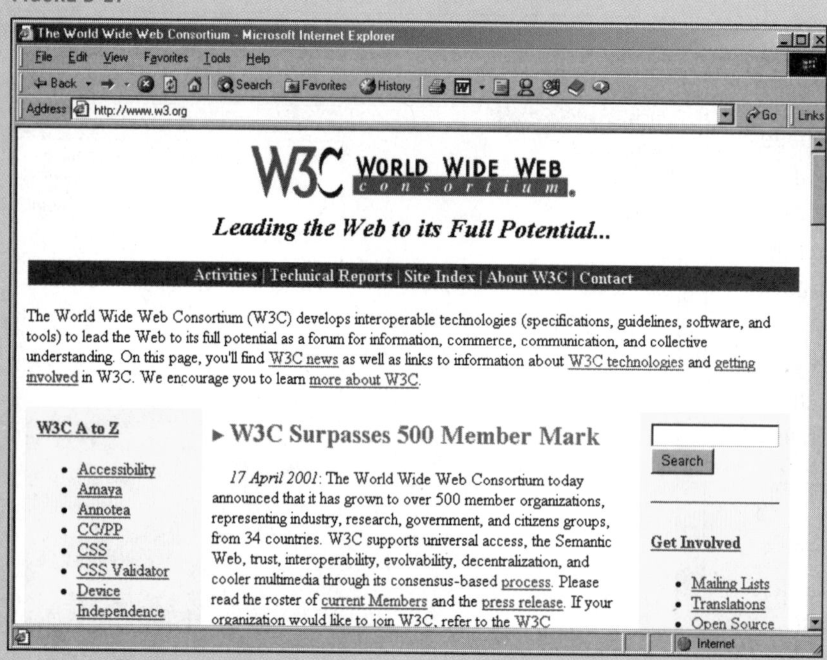

Independent Challenge 5

Dr. Chappell is a government historian who is conducting research on the separation of church and state. He has gone to the Library of Congress Web site to look for information he can use. Write your answers to the questions below on scrap paper or in your word processor.

- **a.** Connect to the Internet and go to The Library of Congress Web site at *www.loc.gov,* as shown in Figure D-28.
- **b.** Do you see text that was created and saved as a graphic? If so, on which page or pages? Was the use effective?
- **c.** What font or fonts are used on the pages for the main text? Are the same fonts used consistently on the other pages in the Web site?
- **d.** Do you see an ordered or unordered list on the Web site? If so, how was it used?
- **e.** View the source to see if a set of font faces was used. If so, which one?
- **f.** Go to Google at *www.google.com* or Alta Vista at *altavista.com* to find another Web site of interest. Compare the use of text on that site with the Library of Congress Web site.

FIGURE D-28

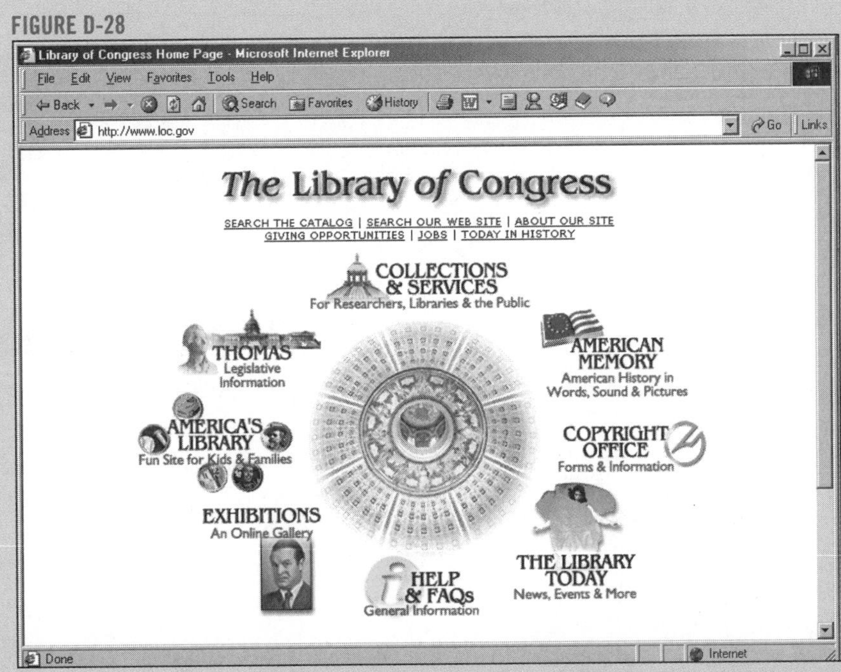

► Visual Workshop

Jacob's Restaurant is an upscale restaurant catering to business executives and theater patrons. They have an extensive menu including prix fixe dinners, pre-theater dinner specials, and after-theater specials. The cuisine is primarily French. If you have previously defined the Web site for Jacob's, open Dreamweaver and open the Web site. (If you have not maintained this Web site from the previous unit, then contact your instructor for assistance.) Create a new page and save it as recipes.htm. Duplicate Figure D-29 for the page content. (*Hint*: To align the text beside the Jacob's logo, select the logo, click the Align list arrow on the Property Inspector, then click Left.)

FIGURE D-29

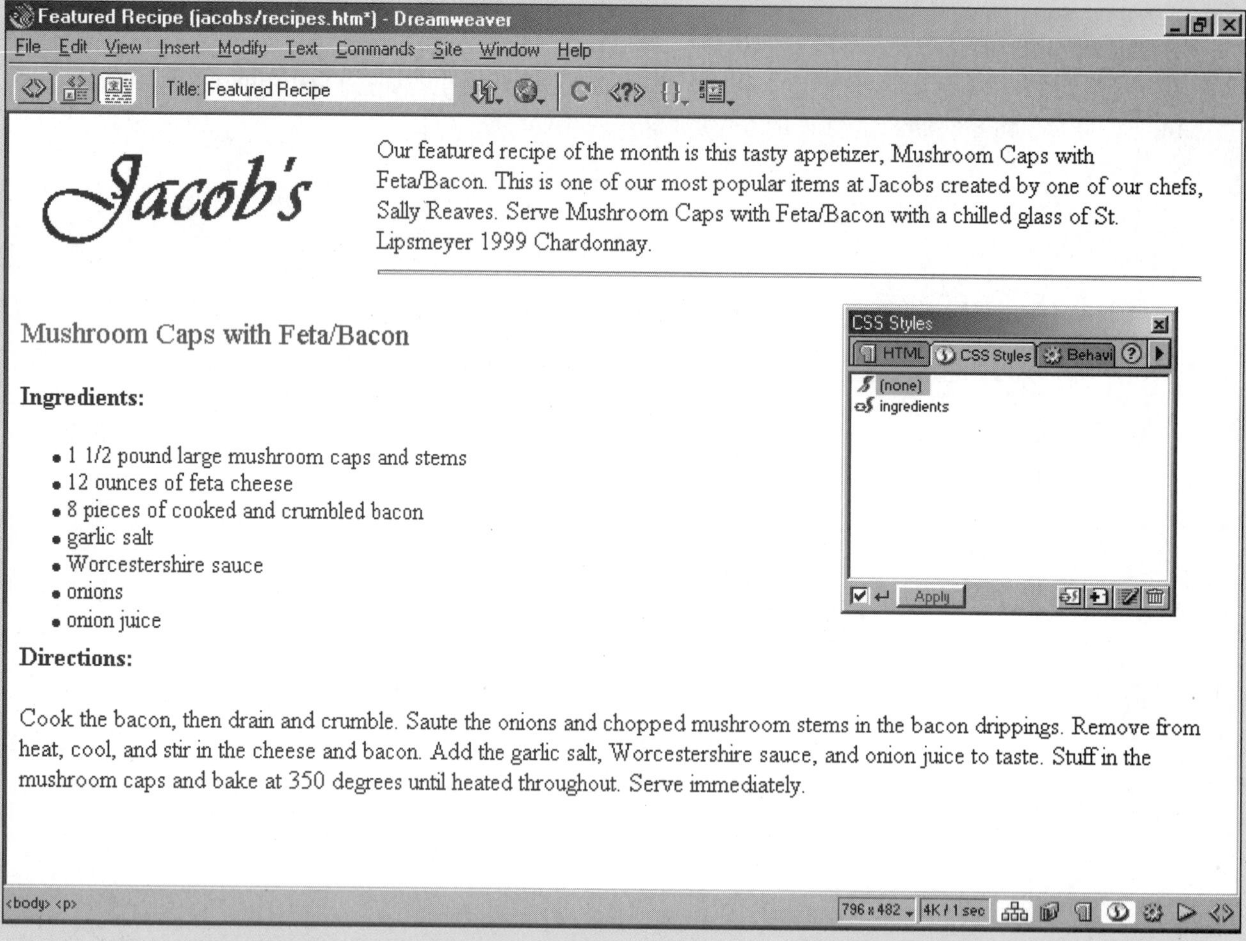

Featured Recipe (jacobs/recipes.htm*) - Dreamweaver

File Edit View Insert Modify Text Commands Site Window Help

Title: Featured Recipe

Jacob's

Our featured recipe of the month is this tasty appetizer, Mushroom Caps with Feta/Bacon. This is one of our most popular items at Jacobs created by one of our chefs, Sally Reaves. Serve Mushroom Caps with Feta/Bacon with a chilled glass of St. Lipsmeyer 1999 Chardonnay.

Mushroom Caps with Feta/Bacon

Ingredients:

- 1 1/2 pound large mushroom caps and stems
- 12 ounces of feta cheese
- 8 pieces of cooked and crumbled bacon
- garlic salt
- Worcestershire sauce
- onions
- onion juice

Directions:

Cook the bacon, then drain and crumble. Saute the onions and chopped mushroom stems in the bacon drippings. Remove from heat, cool, and stir in the cheese and bacon. Add the garlic salt, Worcestershire sauce, and onion juice to taste. Stuff in the mushroom caps and bake at 350 degrees until heated throughout. Serve immediately.

CSS Styles

HTML | CSS Styles | Behavi

(none)

ingredients

Apply

<body> <p>

796 x 482 | 4K / 1 sec

Using and Managing Graphics

Objectives

- Insert an image
- Align an image
- Enhance an image
- Use alternative text
- Understand the Assets panel
- Use the Assets panel to insert Flash text
- Insert a background image
- Delete graphic files from a Web site
- Create and find graphics for a Web site

Graphics can make Web pages more exciting than pages with just text. There are specific file formats in which graphics for Web sites should be saved, so as to provide maximum quality with minimum file size. In this unit you will learn how to incorporate graphics into a Web site and apply good management techniques for working with graphics. TripSmart is featuring a photo safari to Kenya as one of their travel package destinations. The Travel Department has asked you to contact Mary Bausch, the company photographer, to gather some photographs taken in Kenya. You'll use them to design a feature page on the Kenya trip. You'll use the Assets panel to manage the graphics that you add to the new Web page.

Dreamweaver 4

Inserting an Image

As you may remember from earlier units in this book, the three primary Web graphic file formats are GIF, JPEG, and PNG. As graphic files are added to a Web site, they are automatically added to the Assets panel. The **Assets panel** lists the assets, such as images and colors, in the Web site. As images are added to a Web page, the **download** time (time it takes to transfer file to viewer's computer) for the entire page increases. The status bar displays the download time for the current Web page. After meeting with Mary, you have selected several photos for the Package Tours Web page. As you place each graphic on the page, you check the file size in the Assets panel and the download time for the page on the status bar.

Steps

Trouble?

Images and internal links that display a broken link or an absolute path (extra characters, such as forward slashes and colons), can be fixed by selecting the graphic or the link, then clicking the Browse for File icon on the Property Inspector. Images should be saved in the assets folder overwriting the existing file, if necessary. For links, double-click the filename in the root folder, overwriting the existing file.

QuickTip

If you do not see the images in the Assets panel, click the Images icon on the Assets panel, as shown in Figure E-3.

QuickTip

You can also refresh the Assets panel by clicking the Assets panel list arrow, as shown in Figure E-4, then clicking Refresh Site List.

1. Open the **TripSmart Web site**, open **dme_1.htm** from the Unit E folder where your Project Files are stored, then save it as **packages.htm** in the tripsmart root folder, overwriting the existing file
   As shown in Figure E-1, the status bar shows that the page will take three seconds to download at your current connection speed setting.
2. Click the insertion point in front of **Our** in the first paragraph, show the Objects panel if necessary, click the **Insert Image icon** on the Objects panel, click the drive and folder where your Project Files are stored, double-click the **Unit E folder**, double-click the **assets folder**, double-click **zebra_mothers.jpg**, click **Yes** in the dialog box asking if you want to copy the file to your tripsmart root folder, double-click the **assets folder**, then click **Save**
   The picture is placed on the page at the beginning of the first paragraph, as shown in Figure E-2. You check the status bar and see that the page will now take eight seconds to download.
3. Click **Window** on the menu bar, click **Assets**, then click the **Refresh Site List icon** on the Assets panel
   After you click the Refresh Site List icon, you should see the three images you have added to the TripSmart Web site listed: masthead.jpg, tripsmart.gif, and zebra_mothers.jpg. The Assets panel, as shown in Figure E-3, is split into two windows. The lower window lists the graphic images in the Web site, and the top window displays a thumbnail of the selected image in the list.
4. Place the insertion point in front of **This** in the second paragraph, click , double-click **lion.jpg**, from the Unit E folder, click **Yes** in the dialog box asking if you want to copy the file to your tripsmart root folder, double-click the **assets folder**, then click **Save**
   The picture is placed on the page at the beginning of the second paragraph. The status bar indicates that the page will now take 12 seconds to download.
5. Click to refresh the list of images, if necessary
   The lion.jpg file is added to the list of images in the Assets panel.
6. Place the insertion point in front of **All safari vehicles** in the third paragraph, then insert **giraffe.jpg**, click **Yes** to copy the file to your tripsmart root folder, double-click the **assets folder**, then click **Save**
   You check the status bar again and see that the page will now take 16 seconds to download.
7. Click the **list arrow** on the Assets panel, then click **Refresh Site List** to refresh the site list
   Your Assets panel should list five images as shown in Figure E-4.

FIGURE E-1: **Status bar displaying download time for page**

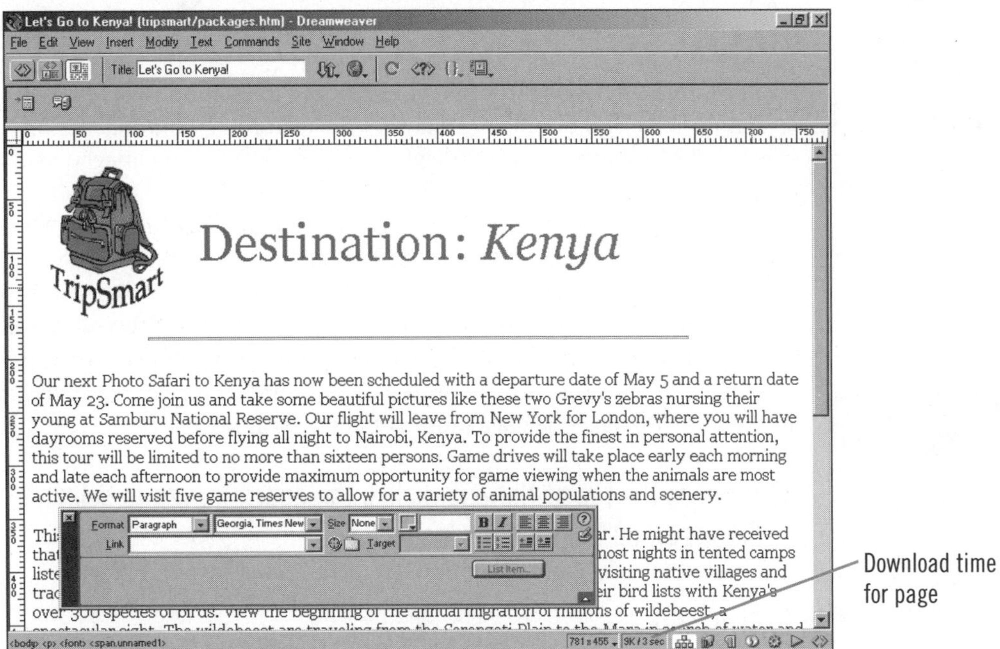

FIGURE E-2: **TripSmart packages page with inserted image**

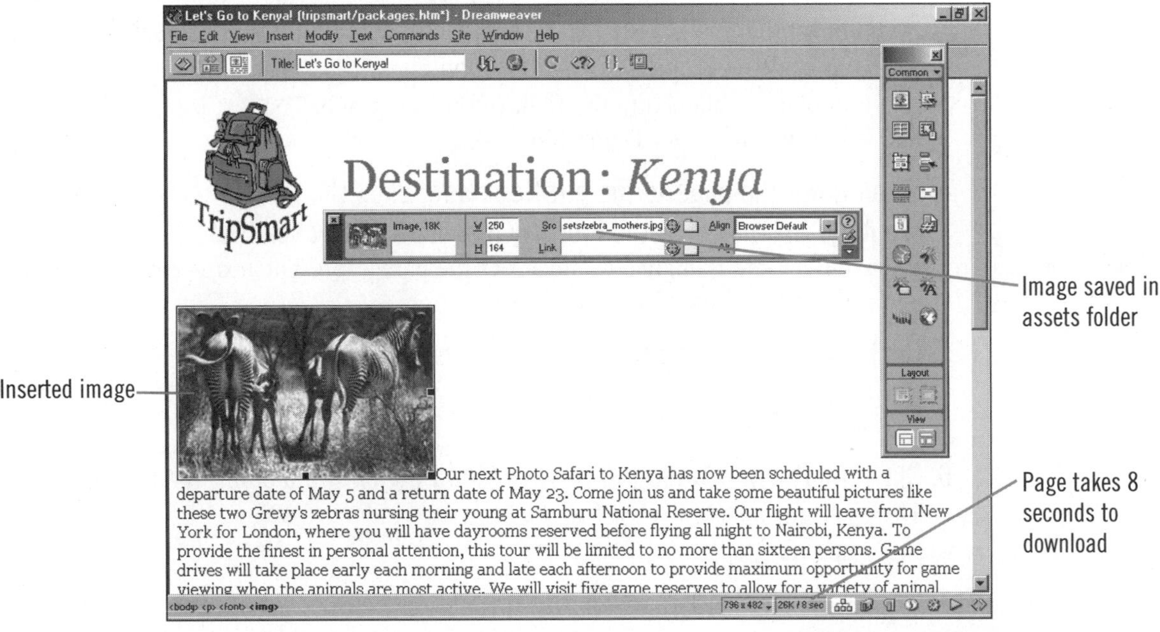

FIGURE E-3: **Assets panel listing for the TripSmart Web site**

FIGURE E-4: **Assets panel with five images**

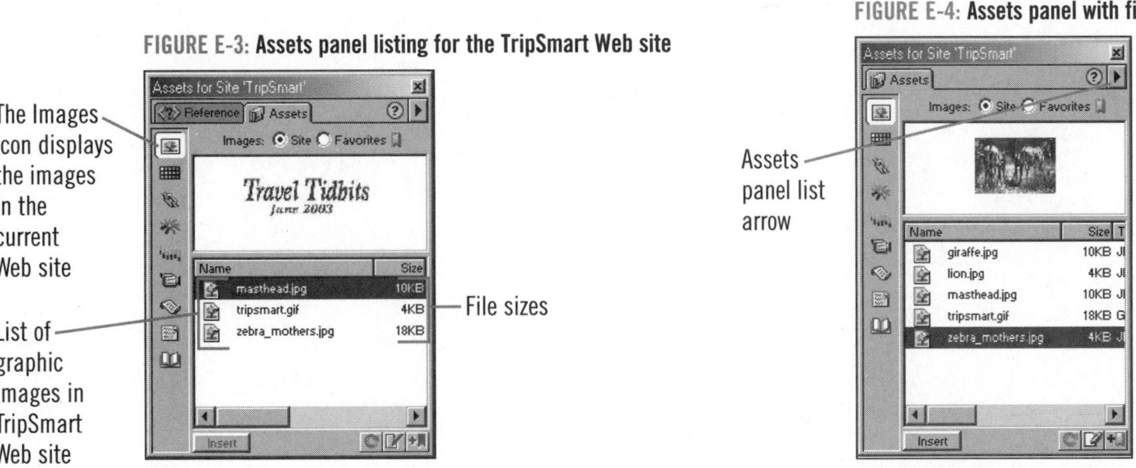

Dreamweaver 4

Aligning an Image

Like text, images can be positioned on the page in relation to other page elements, by means of several options. Positioning an image is referred to as **aligning** the image. When an image is selected, the Property Inspector displays options for aligning images, instead of for aligning text. An image can be aligned on the same line as text by using one of the following alignment options in the Property Inspector: Browser Default, Baseline, Top, Middle, Bottom, TextTop, Absolute Middle, Absolute Bottom, Left or Right. See Table E-1 for a description of each alignment option. You should experiment with each option to find the best alignment for your image. When an image is first placed on a page, it has the **Browser Default** alignment applied to it, which aligns the bottom of the image with the baseline of the text. After experimenting with several alignment options, you decide to stagger the alignment of the three images on the page, to make the page more visually appealing.

Steps 1 2 3 4

1. **Scroll to the top of the page, click the zebra image to select it, then click the Align list arrow on the Property Inspector**
   Notice the ten alignment options in the list, as shown in Figure E-5.

2. **Click Left**
   The zebra photo is aligned to the left side of the paragraph. The text is repositioned to align with the top of the photo.

3. **Scroll down the page to the lion image, click the lion image to select it, click the Align list arrow on the Property Inspector, then click Right**
   The lion photo is aligned to the right of the paragraph. The text is repositioned to the top and left of the photo. See Figure E-6.

4. **Scroll down the page to the giraffe image, click the giraffe image to select it, click the Align list arrow on the Property Inspector, then click Left**
   The giraffe photo is aligned to the left of the paragraph. The text is repositioned to the top and right of the photo. See Figure E-6.

5. **Click File on the menu bar, then click Save**
   The file is saved with the images aligned in staggered positions. You decide to preview the page in your browser.

6. **Click the Preview/Debug in Browser icon on the toolbar, then click your browser**
   The packages page is displayed in the browser window.

7. **Close the browser**
   You are back in the Design View of the packages page.

QuickTip

You may see an alignment icon such as at the top of your paragraph. This icon, called an Invisible Element, appears next to pictures that have alignment settings applied to them. You can hide Invisible Elements by clicking View on the menu bar, pointing to Visual Aids, then clicking Invisible Elements. The icon appears blue when it is selected and yellow when it is not selected.

FIGURE E-5: Alignment options for images

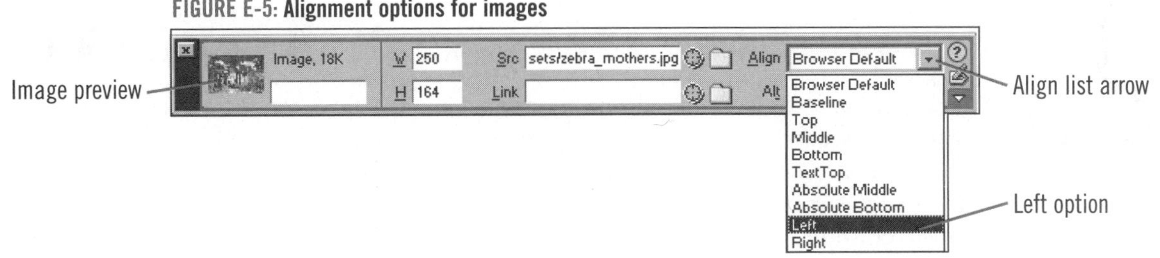

FIGURE E-6: Aligned images on the packages page

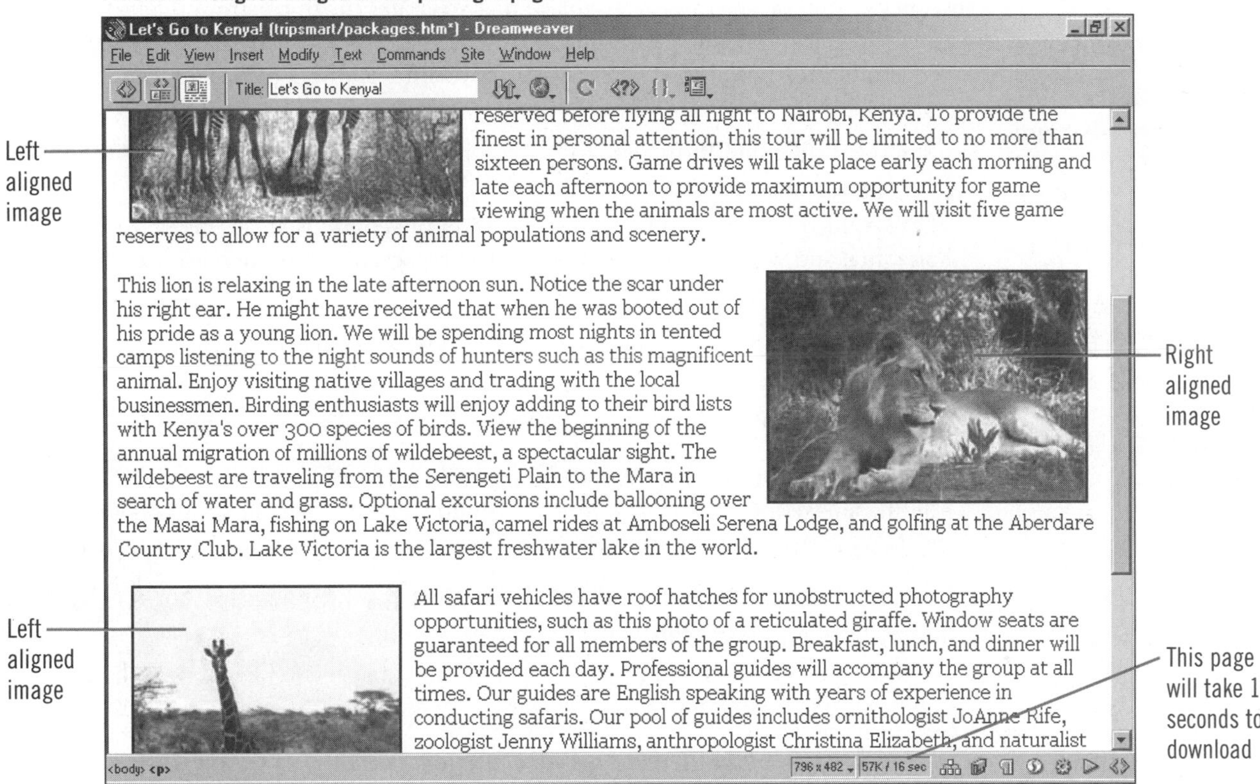

TABLE E-1: Aligning text to elements

alignment option	description
Browser Default	This is the default setting. The element is aligned with the baseline of the text in most browser default settings.
Baseline	The element is aligned with the baseline of the text regardless of the browser setting.
Bottom	The element is aligned with the baseline of the text or the bottom of another object, regardless of the browser setting.
Top	The element is aligned with the top of the tallest item, whether that item is text or another object.
Middle	The element is aligned with the baseline of the text or another object at the vertical middle of the image.
TextTop	The element is aligned with the top of the tallest character in a line of text.
Absolute Middle	The element is aligned with the absolute middle of the current line.
Absolute Bottom	The element is aligned with the bottom of a line of text or another object. This applies to letters that fall below the baseline, such as the letter y.
Left	The element is aligned to the left of the text.
Right	The element is aligned to the right of the text.

Dreamweaver 4

Enhancing an Image

After a graphic is selected, placed, and aligned on a Web page, there are still several options for enhancing an image. Enhancing an image means improving the appearance of the image. You'll need to use an image editor, such as Macromedia Fireworks or Adobe Photoshop, to make changes to the image itself, for example removing scratches from it, lightening it, or darkening it. However, you can enhance an image in Dreamweaver using borders and horizontal and vertical space. **Borders** are like frames that surround an image. Since linked images in Dreamweaver are displayed with blue borders, viewers may think other images with borders are also links. For this reason, you should use borders sparingly. **Horizontal** and **vertical space** is blank space above, below, and on the sides of an image that separates the image from the text or other elements on the page. You decide to enhance the images on the packages page by adding borders around the images and adjusting the horizontal and vertical space around each image.

QuickTip

You can click the arrow on the Property Inspector again to return it to its original size.

1. **Click the zebra image to select it, then click the arrow on the Property Inspector to expand it, if necessary**

   The expanded Property Inspector displays additional options, including image map settings, horizontal and vertical space settings, border size settings, Fireworks source, and additional alignment settings.

QuickTip

The default color of an image border is the same as the color of the text on the page.

2. **Type 2 in the Border text box, then press [Tab] to apply the border size, as shown in Figure E-7**

   A black border with a thickness of 2 pixels is placed around the image.

3. **Repeat Steps 1 and 2 for the lion and giraffe images**

   All three images now have black borders around them. The surrounding text wraps closer to the sides of the images than to the bottoms of the images, so you adjust the horizontal space.

4. **Click the zebra image to select it, type 10 in the H Space text box on the Property Inspector, then press [Tab]**

   H Space refers to the horizontal space around the image. You like the way the text is more evenly wrapped around the image, so you apply the same option to the other two images.

5. **Repeat Step 4 for the lion and giraffe images**

   The three images reflect the horizontal space setting. The spacing is still not exactly even under each picture because of the difference in the lengths of the paragraphs that the pictures are next to.

QuickTip

The [Shift] key is used to resize a graphic proportionately.

6. **Click the zebra image to select it, press and hold [Shift], then slowly drag the right corner selection handle on the image to slightly resize it until the space between the bottom of the image and the text looks equal to the space on the right side of the image**

   The spacing on the right side and on the bottom of the graphic now looks even.

QuickTip

To restore an image to its original height or width setting, click the Reset Size button Reset Size on the Property Inspector.

7. **Repeat Step 6 for the lion and giraffe images, if necessary**

   All three graphics now have even spacing on the sides and bottoms. Notice that the W and H Size numbers on the Property Inspector have changed, and are bold. This means that the original size of the selected image has been altered. See Figure E-8.

8. **Click File on the menu bar, then click Save to save changes to the page**

FIGURE E-7: **Property Inspector showing options for images**

FIGURE E-8: **Property Inspector with altered width and height settings**

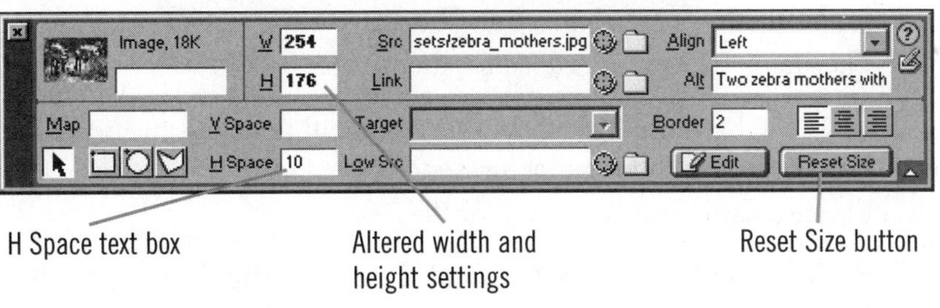

Resizing graphics using an external editor

Each image on a Web page takes a specific number of seconds to download, depending on the size of the file. Larger files (in kilobytes, not width and height) take longer to download than smaller files. You should figure out the smallest acceptable size that an image can be for your Web page, and then, if you need to resize the image, use an external image editor to do so, instead of resizing it in Dreamweaver. Dreamweaver does have width and height settings on the Property Inspector that can be used for resizing the image on the screen, but these settings do not affect the file size. If you decrease the size of an image using the H Size (height) and W Size (width) settings on the Property Inspector, you are not reducing the time it will take the file to download. The ultimate goal is to use graphics that have the smallest file size and the highest quality possible. An ideal page will download in eight seconds or less.

Dreamweaver 4

Using Alternative Text

One of the easiest ways to make your Web page viewer-friendly and handicapped accessible is through the use of alternative text. **Alternative text** is descriptive text that can be set to appear in place of an image, while the image is downloading or when a mouse pointer is placed over an image. Some browsers can be programmed to display only text and to download images manually. In such instances, alternative text is used in place of graphic images. Alternative text can be "read" by a **screen reader**, a device used by the visually impaired to convert written text on a computer monitor to spoken words. Using a screen reader and alternative text, visually impaired viewers can have an image described to them in detail. You add alternative text that describes each of the four images on the packages page.

Steps

Trouble?

Some older browsers may not show alternative text.

1. Click the **zebra image** to select it, type **Two zebra mothers with their babies** in the Alt text box on the Property Inspector, then press **[Tab]**
   The alternative text is entered for the image, as shown in Figure E-9. You preview the page in your browser to view the alternative text.
2. Click the **Preview/Debug in Browser icon** on the toolbar, select your browser, then place your pointer over the zebra image
   When the pointer is placed over the image, a small text box containing the alternative text is displayed on the screen, as shown in Figure E-10.
3. Close your browser window
   You return to the Dreamweaver window and add alternative text to the other three images on the page.
4. Click the **TripSmart logo** to select it, type **TripSmart logo** in the Alt text box on the Property Inspector, then press **[Tab]**
   The alternative text is entered for the image.
5. Click the **lion image** to select it, type **Lion relaxing in the Kenyan sun** in the Alt text box on the Property Inspector, then press **[Tab]**
   The alternative text is entered for the image.
6. Click the **giraffe image** to select it, enter **Reticulated giraffe posed among acacia trees and brush** in the Alt text box on the Property Inspector, then press **[Tab]**
   The alternative text is entered for the image.
7. Click , select your browser, then place the pointer over each image on the page
   Each image now displays alternative text.
8. Close your browser to return to the Dreamweaver window, then save your work

FIGURE E-9: Alternative text setting on the Property Inspector

FIGURE E-10: Alternative text displayed in browser

Dreamweaver 4

Dreamweaver 4

Understanding the Assets Panel

The **Assets panel** is a panel containing all of the assets in a Web site. There are nine categories of assets, represented by icons, on the Assets panel. These include Images, Colors, URLs, Flash, Shockwave, Movies, Scripts, Templates, and Library. There are two options for viewing the assets in each category. You can click the Site option button to view all the assets in a Web site, or the Favorites option button to view those assets that you have designated as **favorites**—assets that you expect to use repeatedly while you work on the site. So far, your Web site includes several images, several colors, and a Flash text button. You explore the Assets panel to understand how Dreamweaver organizes your assets.

Steps

1. Click **Window** on the menu bar, then click **Assets**, if necessary
   The Assets panel opens.

QuickTip

The first time that the Assets panel is used, it displays the Images category; subsequently, it displays the category that was clicked in the last Dreamweaver working session.

2. Click each category icon on the Assets panel
   Each time you click an icon, the contents in the Assets panel window change. Figure E-11 displays the Images category, and lists the five images in the Web site.
3. Click the **Colors icon** to display the Colors category
   You notice a non-Websafe color is listed in the Colors category. **Non-Websafe colors** are those that may not be displayed uniformly across platforms. You realize that color #252084 is the color of the blue text on the home page. You decide to replace it with a Websafe color.
4. Click the **Show Site icon**, double-click **index.htm** in the Local Folder list, then click **OK** to close the Design Notes dialog box
   The home page opens.
5. Select the **The smart way to go!**, click the **Text Color list arrow** on the Property Inspector, click the **Strikethrough icon** in the Color Picker to clear the text color, click again, then click **#003399**
   A Websafe color is applied to the text and added to the Colors category of the Assets panel. See Figure E-12.

Trouble?

If the Assets panel does not refresh when you click , press [Ctrl] (Win) or [Command] (Mac) while you click .

6. Click **File** on the menu bar, click **Save**, press and hold **[Ctrl]** (Win) or **[Command]** (Mac), then click to refresh the Assets panel
   The list of colors used in the Web site is updated. You have removed all non-Websafe colors from the Web site.
7. Click **File** on the menu bar, then click **Close** to close the home page
   You realize how easy it is to keep your Web site's assets organized using the Assets panel.

FIGURE E-11: The Assets panel

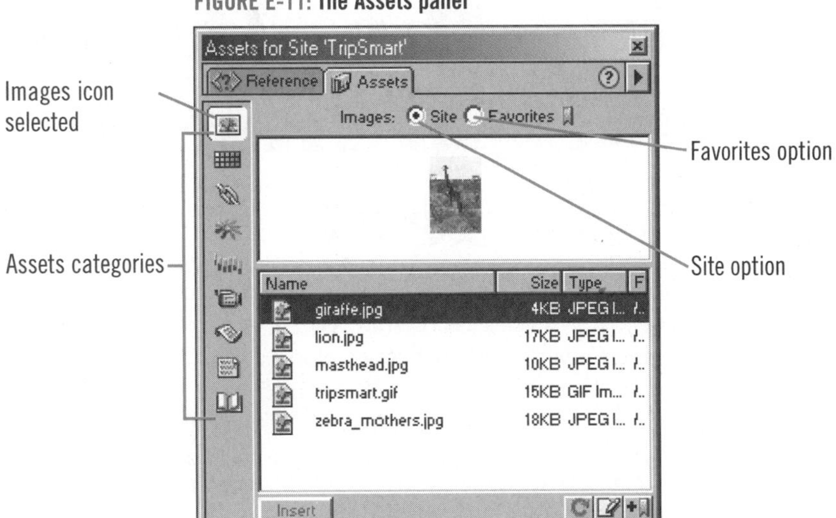

FIGURE E-12: Assets panel showing Colors category

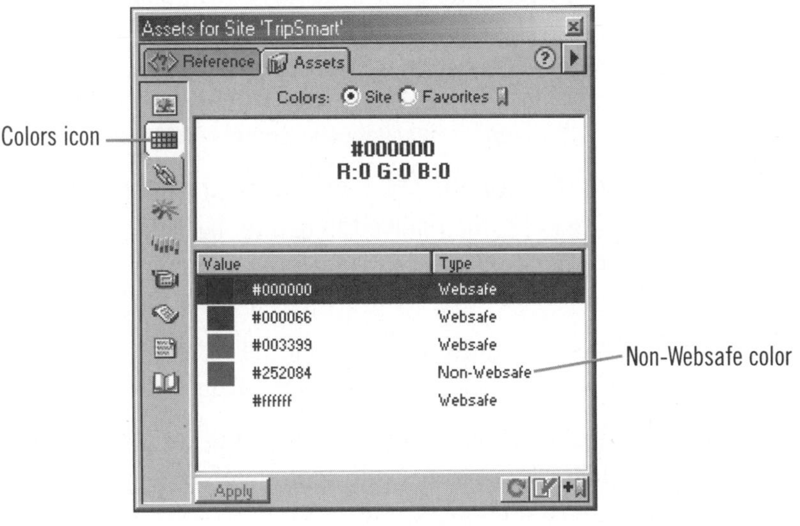

Using Favorites in the Assets panel

There are a few ways to add favorites to the Favorites list in the Assets panel. You can right-click (Win) or [control] click (Mac) an image on a Web page, then click Add to Image Favorites. When you click the Favorites option button in the Assets panel, you will see the image in the list. You can also right-click (Win) or [control] click (Mac) the name of an image in the Site list (when the Site option button is selected in the Assets panel), then click Add to Favorites. You can also create a folder for storing assets by category by clicking the Favorites option button in the Assets panel, clicking the Assets panel list arrow, then clicking New Favorites Folder. You can give the folder a descriptive name, then drag assets in the Favorites list on top of the folder to place them in the folder. You can create nicknames for assets in the Favorites list by right-clicking (Win) or [control] clicking (Mac) the asset in the Favorites list, then clicking Edit Nickname.

Dreamweaver 4

Using the Assets Panel to Insert Flash Text

So far you have used the Objects panel to insert new elements, such as images and horizontal rules, onto Web pages. You can also insert elements that are currently in your Assets panel onto Web pages. This feature is especially handy with the Colors category. You can highlight text, then click a color in the Colors list of the Assets panel. You can insert page elements easily by clicking the asset, then clicking the Insert button or dragging the asset's icon onto the Web page. You would like to place the same home page button you created with Flash on the packages page. You use the Assets panel to insert the Flash text at the bottom of the packages page.

Steps

1. Press and hold **[Ctrl]** (Win) or **[Command]** (Mac), press **[End]** (Win) or **[end]** (Mac) to place the insertion point at the bottom of the page, then press **[Enter]** (Win) or **[return]** (Mac)
   The insertion point is positioned two spaces below the last line of text on the page.
2. Show the Assets panel, if necessary, then click the **Flash icon** to view the Flash category in the Assets panel
   The home.swf file (which is a Shockwave movie) appears in the list of Flash assets, as shown in Figure E-13. This is the home page button used on the newsletter page. Before you insert it at the bottom of the packages page, you play the movie in the Assets panel preview window.
3. Click the **Play button** in the top-right corner of the Assets preview window, shown in Figure E-13, then move the pointer over the word Home
   The Play button changes to a Stop button. As the pointer moves over the text, the text turns light blue. When the pointer is no longer over the text, it returns to the dark blue color.
4. Click the **Stop button** to stop the movie
   The movie stops and the Stop button becomes the Play button again.
5. Click **home.swf** in the Assets panel if necessary, then click the **Insert button** Insert
   The Flash text is inserted at the bottom of the page. You preview the page in your browser to test the Flash text.
6. Click **File** on the menu bar, click **Save**, click the **Preview/Debug in Browser icon** on the toolbar, then choose your browser
   The page is displayed in the browser. You scroll to the bottom of the page to locate the Flash text.
7. Scroll to the bottom of the page, then click **Home**
   Clicking the home page button brings you to the TripSmart home page.
8. Close your browser window
   You return to the Dreamweaver window and decide to examine the source code for the Flash text.
9. Click the **Show Code View icon** on the toolbar to view the code for the Flash text, as shown in Figure E-14, then click the **Show Design View icon** to return to the Design View
   The code displays the URL for the Macromedia Web site. If a page that requires Flash Player is viewed in an older browser that does not support Flash, the viewer will be prompted to download Flash Player using the Macromedia URL. **Flash Player** is a software extension that is added to a Web browser to display animation, video, or sound.
10. Save your work

Trouble?

If you cannot see complete lines of code on the screen without scrolling to the right, while in Code View, click View on the menu bar, point to Code View Options, then click Word Wrap.

FIGURE E-13: Flash category in the Assets panel

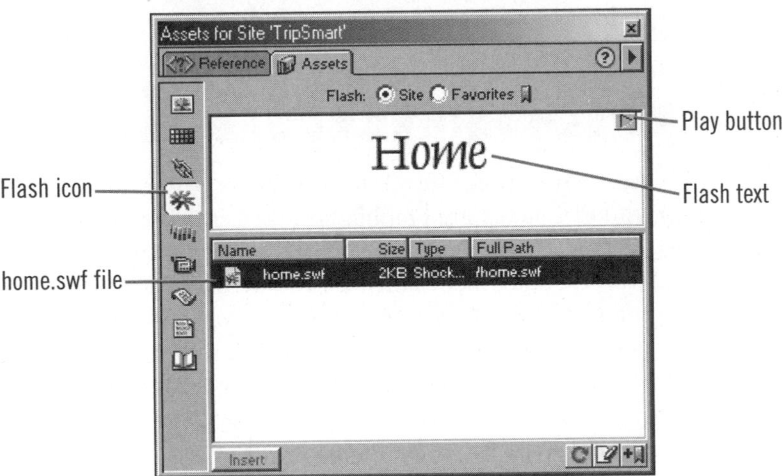

FIGURE E-14: Code View for Flash text

```
<p><object classid="clsid:D27CDB6E-AE6D-11cf-96B8-444553540000"
codebase="http://download.macromedia.com/pub/shockwave/cabs/flash/swflash.cab#version=5,0,0,0"
width="76" height="27">
    <param name=movie value="home.swf">
    <param name=quality value=high>
    <embed src="home.swf" quality=high
pluginspage="http://www.macromedia.com/shockwave/download/index.cgi?P1_Prod_Version=ShockwaveFl-
ash" type="application/x-shockwave-flash" width="76" height="27">
    </embed>
  </object></p>
</body>
</html>
```

Object tags

Embed tags

Macromedia URL for Flash download

Deleting assets from the Assets panel

If you want to remove an asset from your Web site, right-click (Win) or [control] click (Mac) the asset in the Assets panel, then click Locate in Site. Dreamweaver switches to the Site window and highlights the name of the asset in the list of files in the Web site. Click [Delete] to remove the asset, then click OK in the warning message that asks you if you really want to remove it.

Dreamweaver 4

Inserting a Background Image

Some Web pages have a background image in order to provide depth and visual interest to the page. **Background images** are graphic files used in place of background colors. Background images may certainly create a dramatic effect; however, they may not be practical for Web pages that have lots of text and other elements. Although they may be considered too plain, standard white backgrounds are usually the best choice for Web pages. If you choose to use a background image on a Web page, it should be small in file size, preferably in GIF format. If tiled, it should be a seamless image. A **tiled image** is a small graphic that repeats across and down a Web page, appearing as individual squares or rectangles. A **seamless image** is a tiled image that is blurred at the edges so that it appears to be all one image. A tiled image can be converted into a seamless image by using an image editor to blend the edges. You experiment with the background of the packages page by choosing a tiled image and then a seamless image.

Steps 1 2 3 4

1. Click **Modify** on the menu bar, then click **Page Properties**
2. Click the **Browse button** next to the Background Image text box, click the drive and folder where your Project Files are stored, double-click the **Unit E folder**, double-click the **assets** folder, then double-click **tile_bak.gif**
   A message appears, asking if you want to copy the file to the root folder of the TripSmart Web site.
3. Click **Yes**, double-click the **assets** folder, click **Save**, then click **OK** to close the Page Properties dialog box
   A tiled blue background replaces the white background on the packages page. Notice that the background is made up of individual squares, as shown in Figure E-15. You realize that the Flash text does not display well against the tiled background, so you decide to replace it with a seamless background.
4. Click **Modify** on the menu bar, click **Page Properties**, click the **Browse button** next to the Background Image text box, click the drive and folder where your Project Files are stored, double-click the **Unit E folder**, double-click the **assets** folder, then double-click **seamless_bak.gif**
   A message appears, asking if you want to copy the file to the root folder of the TripSmart Web site.
5. Click **Yes**, double-click the **assets** folder, click **Save**, then click **OK**
   The tan background serves as the page background now, rather than the tiled blue background. Notice that it is now harder to tell where one square stops and the other begins, as shown in Figure E-16. If you scroll to the bottom of the page, you will see that the Flash text still does not display well against the textured background. You decide to return to the white background.
6. Click **Modify** on the menu bar, then click **Page Properties**
   You can remove a background image from a Web page by removing the background image filename in the Page Properties dialog box.
7. Highlight the information in the Background Image text box, press **[Delete]**, then press **OK** to close the Page Properties dialog box
   Much better! The background returns to white. You decide to leave it that way.
8. Save your work

QuickTip

You should use either a background color or a background image, but not both on the same page, unless you have a need for the background color to be displayed while the background image finishes downloading.

QuickTip

Even when you have removed a graphic image from a Web page, it is still in the assets folder in the local root folder of the Web site.

FIGURE E-15: **Packages page with a tiled background**

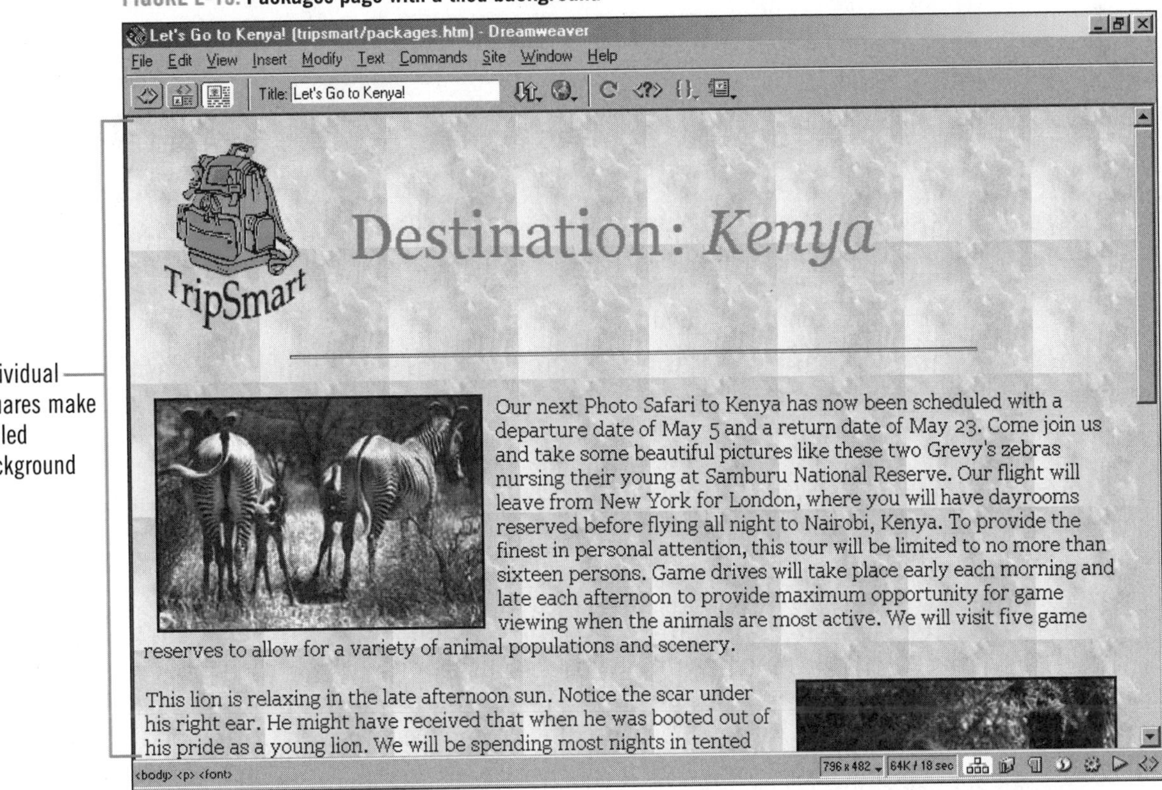

FIGURE E-16: **Packages page with a seamless background**

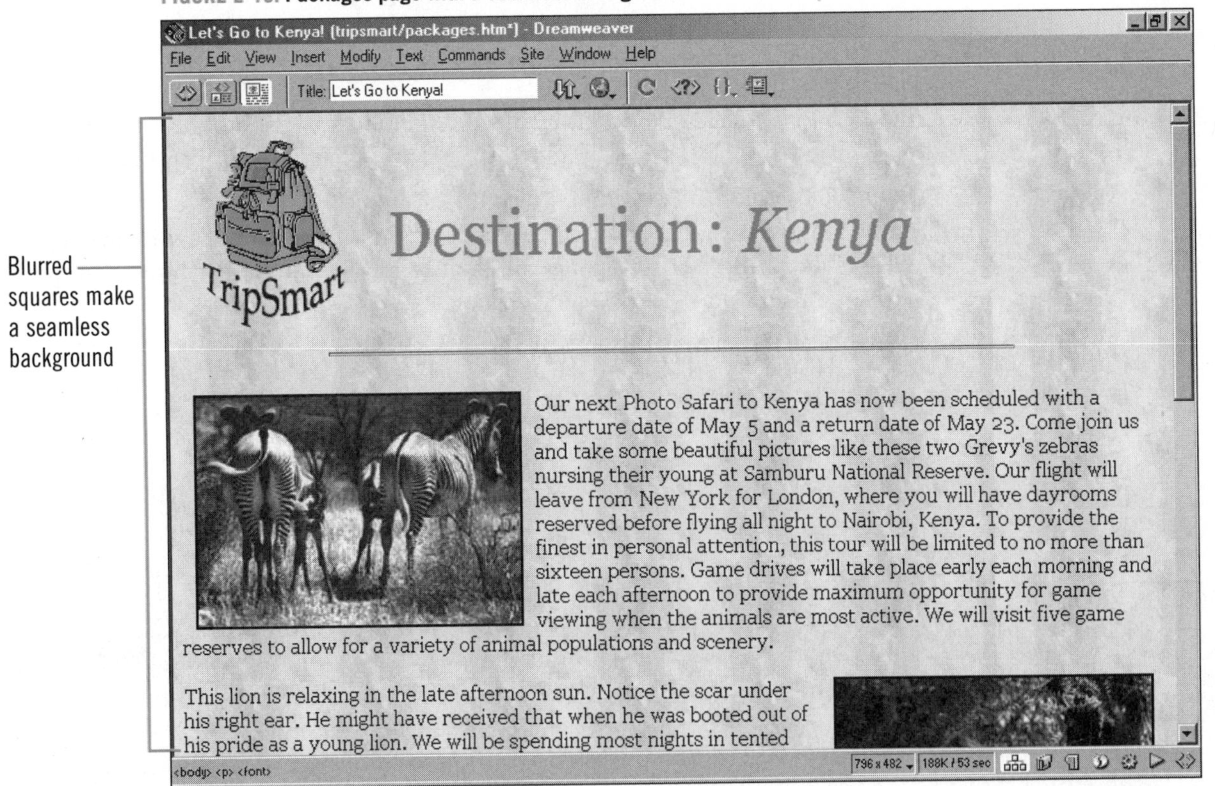

Dreamweaver 4

Deleting Graphic Files from a Web Site

As you work on a Web site, it is very common to accumulate files that are never used on any page in the site. One way to avoid this is to look at a graphic on a page first, before you copy it to the root folder. If the file has been copied to the root folder, however, it should be deleted or at least moved to another location to ensure that the Assets panel only lists the assets actually used in the Web site. This practice is considered good Web site management. You delete the two background graphics from the Assets panel, since you decided not to use them on the packages page.

Steps

1. Open the Assets panel, if necessary, click the **Images icon** on the Assets panel, then click the **Refresh Site List icon** to refresh the list of images
   The two background files are listed in the Images list, even though you have deleted them from the page. You navigate to the location of the images in the Web site folder structure.
2. Right-click (Win) or [control] click (Mac) **seamless_bak.gif** in the Assets panel, then click **Locate in Site**, as shown in Figure E-17
   The Site window opens, and the seamless_bak.gif file is highlighted.
3. Click **seamless_bak.gif**, press **[Delete]** to delete the file, click **OK** in the dialog box asking if you really want to delete the file, close the Site window to return to the packages page, then click on the Assets panel to refresh the list of images
   The file is no longer listed in the Site list, as it has been deleted from the Web site.
4. Right-click (Win) or [control] click (Mac) **tile_bak.gif** in the Assets panel, then click **Locate in Site**
   The Site window opens, and the tile_bak.gif file is highlighted.
5. Click **tile_bak.gif**, press **[Delete]** to delete the file, click **OK** in the dialog box asking if you really want to delete the file, close the Site window to return to the packages page, then click to refresh the list of images
   The file is no longer listed, as it has been deleted from the Web site. You have cleaned up the Web site list of images in the Assets panel and in the root folder for the Web site. Your packages page is finished for now, and should resemble Figures E-18 and E-19.
6. **Exit** (Win) or **Quit** (Mac) **Dreamweaver**

Graphic file management

It is a really good idea to have an additional storage space for your Web site graphic files, besides the assets folder in the Web site. Keep all original graphic files outside of the Web site and save them once with their original settings. As you edit them, save them using a different name. This way, if you need to find the original file before it is resized or compressed, it will be there for you. You may have files you don't want to use now, but may need later. Store them outside your Web site to keep from cluttering up the assets folder.

FIGURE E-17: Locate in Site option in Assets panel

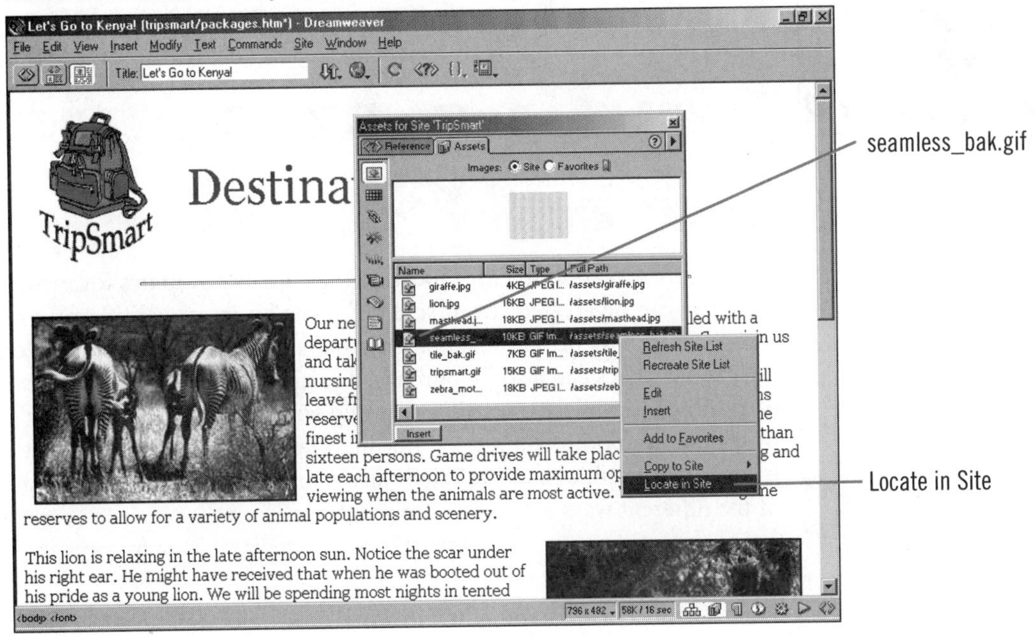

FIGURE E-18: The finished project

Destination: *Kenya*

Our next Photo Safari to Kenya has now been scheduled with a departure date of May 5 and a return date of May 23. Come join us and take some beautiful pictures like these two Grevy's zebras nursing their young at Samburu National Reserve. Our flight will leave from New York for London, where you will have dayrooms reserved before flying all night to Nairobi, Kenya. To provide the finest in personal attention, this tour will be limited to no more than sixteen persons. Game drives will take place early each morning and late each afternoon to provide maximum opportunity for game viewing when the animals are most active. We will visit five game reserves to allow for a variety of animal populations and scenery.

This lion is relaxing in the late afternoon sun. Notice the scar under his right ear. He might have received that when he was booted out of his pride as a young lion. We will be spending most nights in tented

FIGURE E-19: The finished project

with Kenya's over 300 species of birds. View the beginning of the annual migration of millions of wildebeest, a spectacular sight. The wildebeest are traveling from the Serengeti Plain to the Mara in search of water and grass. Optional excursions include ballooning over the Masai Mara, fishing on Lake Victoria, camel rides at Amboseli Serena Lodge, and golfing at the Aberdare Country Club. Lake Victoria is the largest freshwater lake in the world.

All safari vehicles have roof hatches for unobstructed photography opportunities, such as this photo of a reticulated giraffe. Window seats are guaranteed for all members of the group. Breakfast, lunch, and dinner will be provided each day. Professional guides will accompany the group at all times. Our guides are English speaking with years of experience in conducting safaris. Our pool of guides includes ornithologist JoAnne Rife, zoologist Jenny Williams, anthropologist Christina Elizabeth, and naturalist Richard Newland. Private air transport will whisk us to our more distant game reserves. This is truly a trip of a lifetime. We expect the openings to fill quickly, so make your reservation now!

The price schedule is as follows: Land Tour and Supplemental Group Air, $4,500.00; International Air, $1,350.00; and Single Supplement, $1,000.00. Entrance fees, hotel taxes, and services are included in the Land Tour price. A deposit of $500.00 is required at the time the booking is made. Trip Insurance and Luggage Insurance are optional and are also offered at extra charge. A passport and visa will be required for entry into Kenya. Call us at *(555) 433-7844* for further information from 8:00 a.m. to 6:00 p.m. (Central Standard Time).

Home

Dreamweaver 4

Creating and Finding Graphics for a Web Site

There are several resources for locating high-quality graphics for incorporation into a Web site. Graphics can be created "from scratch" using an image-editing program such as Macromedia Fireworks or Adobe Photoshop. Original photography is another option for colorful, rich images. Graphics can also be purchased as clip art collections. **Clip art collections** are groups of graphic files collected on CDs and sold with an **index**, or directory of the files. The Internet, of course, is another source for finding graphics. Now that you understand how to incorporate graphics into the TripSmart Web site, you explore the advantages and disadvantages of the different ways to accumulate graphics.

Details

Original graphics

Programs such as Macromedia Fireworks and Adobe Photoshop give you the ability to create and modify original artwork. These image-editing programs have numerous features for manipulating images. For example, you can adjust the color, brightness, or size of an image. You can also set a transparent background for an image. **Transparent backgrounds** have transparent pixels, rather than pixels of another color, resulting in images that blend easily on a Web page background. Figure E-20 shows an example of an image with a colored background, while Figure E-21 has a transparent background. You can save images as **interlaced graphics**, which are graphics that appear on a Web page before the browser has fully downloaded them, giving viewers something to look at while they are waiting for the entire image to download.

Original photography

High-quality photographs can greatly enhance a Web site. Fortunately, digital cameras and scanners have made this venture much easier than in the past. Once you scan a photograph or shoot it with a digital camera, you can further enhance your images using an image-editing software program.

Clip art collections

Clip art collections can be purchased in computer software stores, from office supply stores, and over the Internet. When using clip art collections, you should read the terms of the copyright statement in the user's manual. Some limitations may be placed on the use of the clip art. Not all clip art is **royalty free**, free for the purchaser to copy and publish without having to pay a royalty to the company that made the clip art.

The Internet

There are many Web sites that allow you to copy their graphics, but, again, look carefully for copyright statements regarding the use of the graphics. There are many collections of clip art online that are free for you to use, but some sites ask that you give them credit on your Web site with either a simple statement or a link to their Web site. *If you copy and paste images you find while accessing other Web sites and use them for your own purposes, you may be violating copyright laws.*

FIGURE E-20: **Graphic with colored background**

FIGURE E-21: **Graphic with transparent background**

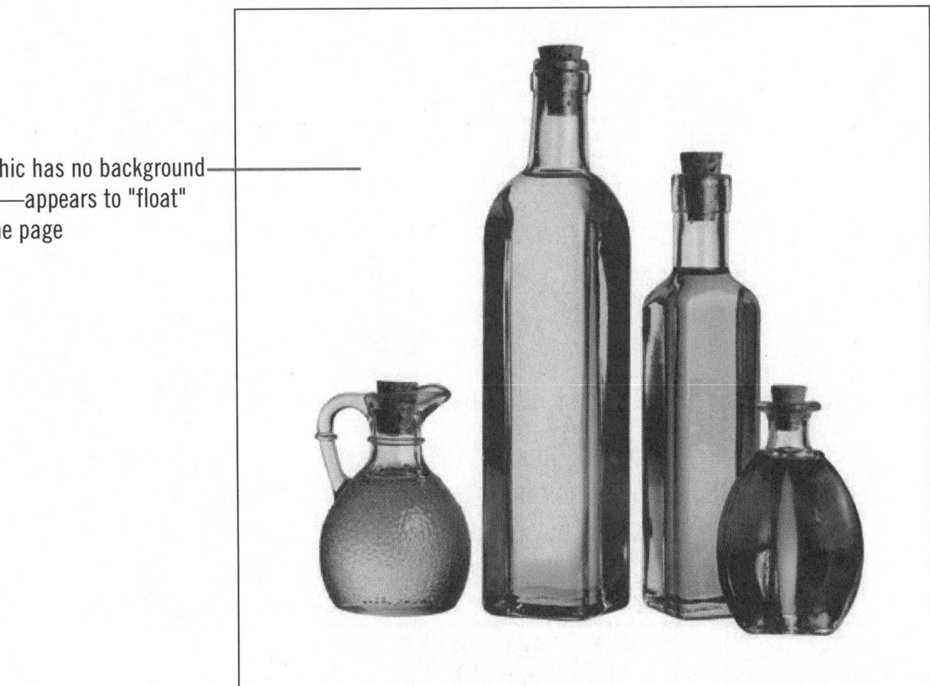

Dreamweaver 4

Practice

▶ Concepts Review

Label each element shown in Figure E-22.

FIGURE: E-22

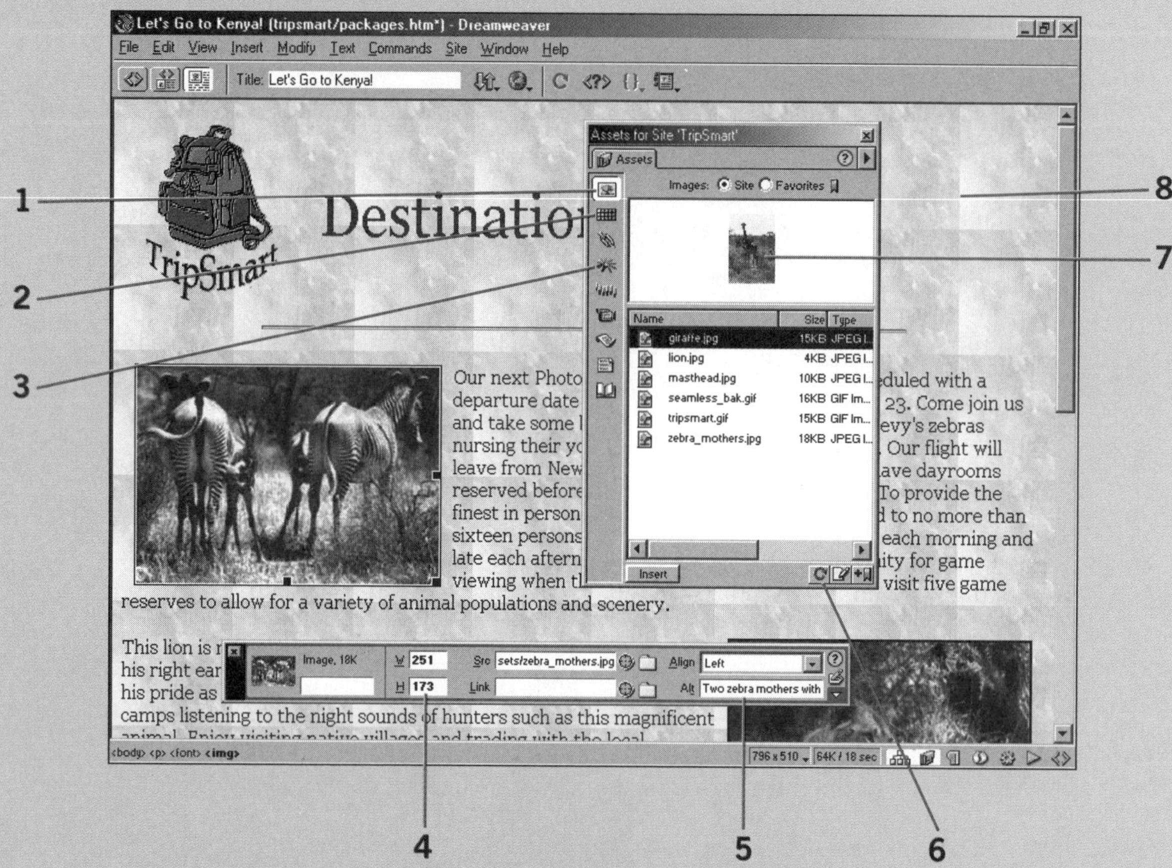

Match each of the following terms with the statement that describes its function.

9. Assets panel	a. Positioning an image on a page
10. JPEG	b. Updates the current list of assets in the Assets panel
11. Aligning an image	c. Includes only those assets designated as favorites
12. Site option button	d. Small graphic that repeats across and down a Web page
13. Favorites list	e. Used to manage graphics and other elements of a Web site
14. Refresh Site List icon	f. Describes an image on a Web page
15. Tiled image	g. A frame placed around an image
16. Seamless image	h. A graphic file format
17. Alternative text	i. Small background graphic that is blurred at the edges
18. Border	j. Lists all the assets of the Web site, including favorites

Select the best answer from the following list of choices.

19. The following category is not found on the Assets panel:
- **a.** URLs.
- **b.** Colors.
- **c.** Tables.
- **d.** Movies.

20. Files that are no longer needed in a Web site:
- **a.** Should be left in the Assets panel.
- **b.** Should be dragged off the Web page to the Recycle Bin (Win) or the Trash icon (Mac).
- **c.** Should be placed in the Site list.
- **d.** Should be deleted from the Web site.

21. Background images:
- **a.** Are never appropriate.
- **b.** Are always appropriate.
- **c.** Cannot be tiled.
- **d.** Can be seamless.

22. Tiled background images generally:
- **a.** Appear as one graphic on a Web page.
- **b.** Appear as many small squares on a Web page.
- **c.** Appear as many rows across a Web page.
- **d.** Appear as many columns down a Web page.

▶ Skills Review

Important: *If you did not create this Web site in Unit B and maintain it during the preceding units, you will need to create a root folder for this Web site and define the Web site using files your instructor will provide. See the "Read This Before You Begin" section for more detailed instructions.*

1. Insert an image.
- **a.** Start Dreamweaver.
- **b.** Open the Blooms&Bulbs Web site from the drive and folder where your Project Files are stored.
- **c.** Open dme_2.htm from the drive and folder where your Project Files are stored in the Unit E folder, then save it as plants.htm in the Blooms&Bulbs Web site, overwriting the existing plants.htm file. (*Hint:* Images and internal links that display a broken link or an absolute path (extra characters, such as forward slashes and colons), can be fixed by selecting the graphic or the link, then clicking the Browse for File icon on the Property Inspector. Images should be saved in the assets folder overwriting the existing file, if necessary. For links, double-click the filename in the root folder, overwriting the existing file.)
- **d.** Insert the iris.jpg file from the drive and folder where your Project Files are stored for Unit E, in front of the words Beautiful spring iris.
- **e.** Copy the file to the assets folder of the Web site.
- **f.** Insert the tulips.jpg file in front of the words Dramatic masses.
- **g.** Copy the file to the assets folder of the Web site.
- **h.** Insert the pansies.jpg file in front of the words Pretty pansies.
- **i.** Copy the file to the assets folder of the Web site.
- **j.** Save your work.

2. Align an image.
- **a.** Click the iris.jpg and use the Property Inspector to left-align the image.
- **b.** Left-align the tulips.jpg.
- **c.** Left-align the pansies.jpg.
- **d.** Save your work.

3. Enhance an image.
- **a.** Select the iris.jpg and apply a size 2 border to it.
- **b.** Select the tulips.jpg and apply a size 2 border to it.

   c. Select the pansies.jpg and apply a size 2 border to it.
   d. Save your work.
4. **Use alternative text.**
   a. Select the iris.jpg, then type **Purple Iris** in the Alt text box on the Property Inspector.
   b. Select the tulips.jpg and type **Red and Yellow Tulips** in the Alt text box.
   c. Select the pansies.jpg, then type **Deep Violet Pansies** in the Alt text box.
   d. Save your work.
5. **Understand the Assets panel.**
   a. Open the Assets panel, if necessary.
   b. View the Images list to verify that there are five images in the list. Refresh the site list, if necessary.
   c. View the Colors list to verify that there are three Websafe colors.
   d. View the Flash list to verify that there is one Flash file.
6. **Use the Assets panel to insert Flash text.**
   a. Click the insertion point after the last sentence on the plants page, then press [Enter] (Win) or [return] (Mac).
   b. Click home.swf in the Assets panel to select it, and insert the Flash text on the page by pressing the Insert button on the Assets panel or dragging the filename to the bottom of the page.
   c. View and test the Flash text in your browser, then close the browser window.
   d. View the Flash text code in Code View.
   e. Return to Design View.
   f. Save your work.
7. **Insert a background image.**
   a. Click Modify on the menu bar, then click Page Properties.
   b. Insert the daisies.gif file as a background image. (This file is in the assets folder in the Unit E folder in the drive and folder where your Projects Files are stored.)
   c. Save the daisies.gif file in the assets folder of your Web site.
   d. View the Web page in your browser.
   e. Close the browser window.
   f. Remove the daisies.gif graphic from the background. You may have to refresh the site list first.
   g. Save your work.
8. **Delete graphic files from a Web site.**
   a. Delete the daisies.gif file from the list of images in the Assets panel.
   b. Refresh the Assets panel and verify that the daisies.gif file has been removed from the Web site.
   c. Save your work, then Exit (Win) or Quit (Mac) Dreamweaver.

Important: *If you did not create the following Web sites in Unit B and maintain them during the preceding units, you will need to create a root folder for the Web sites in the following exercises and define the Web sites using files your instructor will provide. See the "Read This Before You Begin" section for more detailed instructions.*

Independent Challenge 1

Green Matters is an environmental consulting firm that markets its services over a media-rich Web site. The Production Department would like to begin creating its own animations for the Web site. The vice president of marketing, Rick Williams, and the vice president of production, Larry Stroud, are considering either Macromedia Flash or Adobe Live Motion for creating animation. They ask you to research both products and recommend one of them on the basis of your findings.

   a. Connect to the Internet and go to Macromedia at *www.macromedia.com.*
   b. Find out as much information as you can about Flash. You may want to take notes on your findings or print out information from the Web site as needed.

c. Go to Adobe at *www.adobe.com.*
d. Find out as much information as you can about Live Motion. You may want to take notes on your findings or print out information from the Web site as needed.
e. Go to your favorite search engine, such as Google, at *www.google.com*.
f. Search for information comparing these two products.
g. Write a summary of your findings and recommendation to Rick and Larry in your word-processing software.
h. Print the summary.

▶ Independent Challenge 2

The Over Under Dive Shop in Nevis, West Indies, is a certified Professional Association of Diving Instructors (PADI) dive center offering PADI certification courses. They also conduct snorkeling and dive trips to various locations around the barrier reef surrounding Nevis. They need to add a new page to their Web site, featuring the favorite diving sites of Jon Moseley, the dive master. Refer to Figure E-23 as you work on this page.

a. Start Dreamweaver and open the Over Under Web site.
b. Open dme_3.htm from the drive and folder where your Project Files are stored in the Unit E folder.
c. Save dme_3.htm as *diving.htm*, overwriting the existing diving.htm file.
d. Insert one or more of the fish images fish_1.jpg, fish_2.jpg, fish_3.jpg from the drive and folder where your Project Files are stored in the Unit E assets folder. Insert the fish images wherever you like.
e. Align the images using either the Left or Right alignment option.
f. Add borders to the images. Choose a border size that you like.
g. Create alternative text for each image.
h. Create and insert a Flash text button at the bottom of the page that links to the home page. *Hint*: Use the same color as the background page color for the background color of the Flash text.
i. Note the time the page will take to download in the browser.
j. Save your work, then Exit (Win) or Quit (Mac) Dreamweaver.

FIGURE E-23

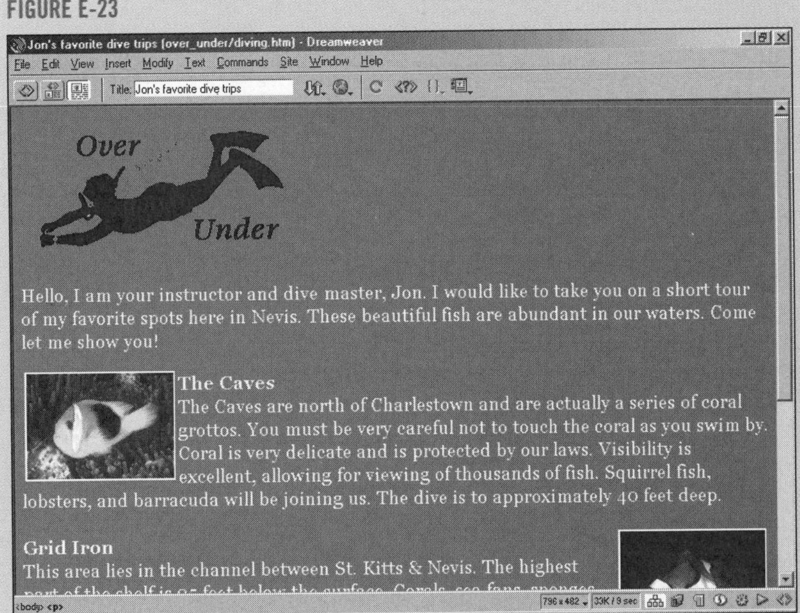

► Independent Challenge 3

Rapids Transit is a river expedition company. They are located on the Buffalo River in Northwest Arkansas. In addition to renting canoes, kayaks, and rafts, they have a country store and snack bar. River guides are available if requested by clients to accompany them on float trips. The clients range from high-school and college students to families to vacationing professionals. Mike Andrew, the owner of Rapids Transit, has asked you to redesign the logo and replace the old logo in the Web site. Refer to Figure E-24 as you work on this page.

- **a.** Start Dreamweaver and open the Rapids Transit Web site.
- **b.** Open the index.htm file in the Web site.
- **c.** Delete the current logo and insert rapids_logo.gif from the drive and folder where your Project Files are stored in the Unit E assets folder.
- **d.** Save the new logo in your assets folder.
- **e.** Refresh the list of images in the Assets panel.
- **f.** Open dme_4.htm from the drive and folder where your Project Files are stored in the Unit E folder and save it in the Rapids Transit Web site as *guides.htm*, overwriting the existing guides file.
- **g.** Insert image buster_tricks.jpg at an appropriate place on the page. (This file is in the drive and folder where your Project Files are stored in the Unit E assets folder.)
- **h.** Create alternative text for the buster_tricks.jpg image, add a border to the image, then choose an alignment setting for the image.
- **i.** Create Flash text that serves as a link to the home page.
- **j.** Save your work, then Exit (Win) or Quit (Mac) Dreamweaver.

FIGURE E-24

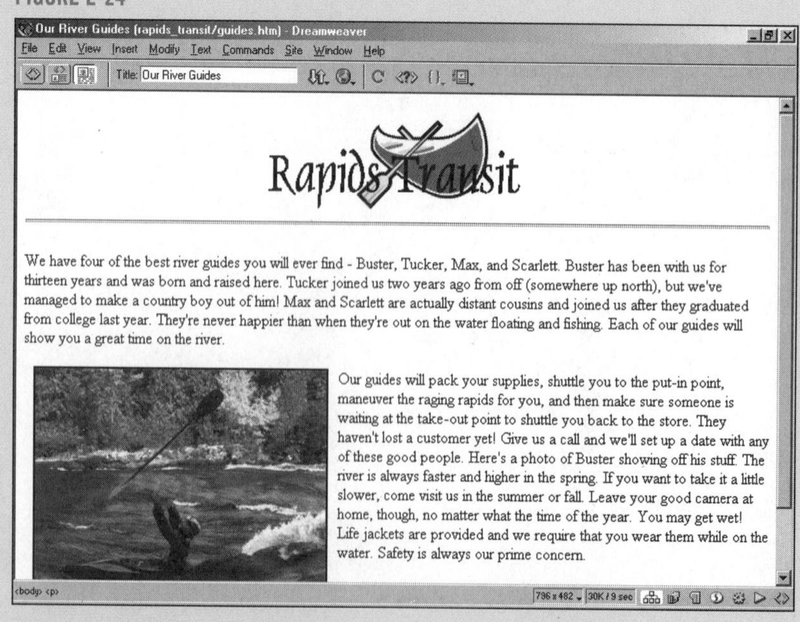

Independent Challenge 4

Off Note is a music store specializing in classical, blues, rock, country, and jazz. You have been asked to find suitable graphics for their country music Web page in their Web site. You decide to look for some royalty-free images on the Internet

a. Connect to the Internet and go to Alta Vista at *www.altavista.com.*
b. Click Tools, then click Image Search.
c. Type **country music** in the Search for text box.
d. Check the Photos, Graphics, and Color check boxes, as shown in Figure E-25. Make sure no other option buttons are checked.
e. Click the Search button to begin the search.
f. Choose one of the pictures found in your search, then click the more info link to see if you can locate copyright information on the page that opens.
g. Summarize on paper the information that you found about the picture, including the copyright information if you were able to find it.

FIGURE E-25: Alta Vista search engine

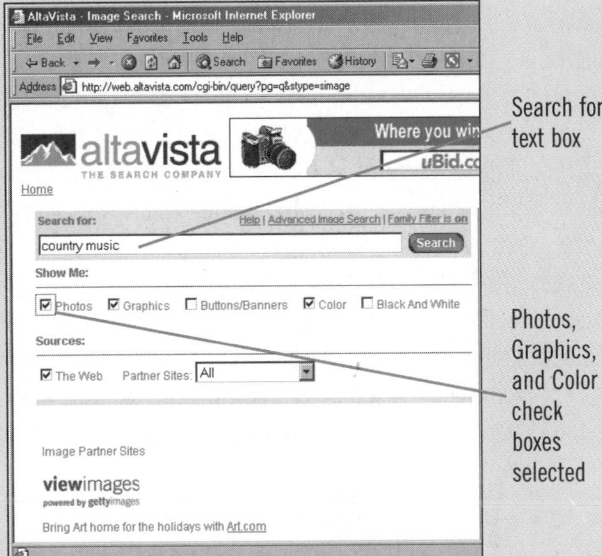

Independent Challenge 5

John Wesley is a golf pro who tours nationally and offers private lessons at a resort golf course. He endorses a line of golf equipment and occasionally provides commentary about golf trivia at the Masters Tournament. He is learning Dreamweaver to be able to create a Web site for his company, Wesley Enterprises. He would like to look at some golf Web sites to get a feel for the types of graphics he may want to use in his Web site. Use a word processor or scrap paper to answer the questions below.

a. Connect to the Internet and go to PGA of America at *www.pga.com.*
b. What color is the background? Would you have selected a different one? Why, or why not?
c. Evaluate the graphics used in the Web site. Do they add interest to the pages, or are they distracting? Was alternative text used for any or all of the images?
d. How long did the home page take to download on your computer? In your opinion, was it too slow?
e. Are there too few graphics, too many, or just enough to add interest?
f. Go to Google at *www.google.com* or Yahoo!at *www.yahoo.com* to find another golf Web site.
g. Compare the site you found to the PGA site by answering questions b through e above.

► Visual Workshop

Your company has been creating a Web site for Jacob's, a new restaurant located in the theater district in New York City. This is an upscale restaurant catering to business executives and theater patrons. They have an extensive menu including prix fixe dinners, pre-theater dinner specials, and after-theater specials. The cuisine is primarily French. Jacob has recently sent photos of some of his fabulous desserts to your company. He has asked you to design a Web page featuring his desserts to add to his Web site.

If you did not maintain this Web site from the previous unit, then contact your instructor for assistance. Open dme_5.htm from the drive and folder where your Project Files are stored in the Unit E folder. Save dme_5.htm as *after_theater.htm,* in the Jacob's web site, then add the poached_pear.jpg, oranges.jpg, and triple_cheesecake.jpg images from the Unit E assets folder to create the page shown in Figure E-26. (*Hint:* Images and internal links that display a broken link or an absolute path (extra characters, such as forward slashes and colons), can be fixed by selecting the graphic or the link, then clicking the Browse for File icon on the Property Inspector. Images should be saved in the assets folder overwriting the existing file, if necessary. For links, double-click the filename in the root folder, overwriting the existing file.) Create and format a caption, such as "To complete a perfect evening…" below the horizontal rule.

FIGURE E-26

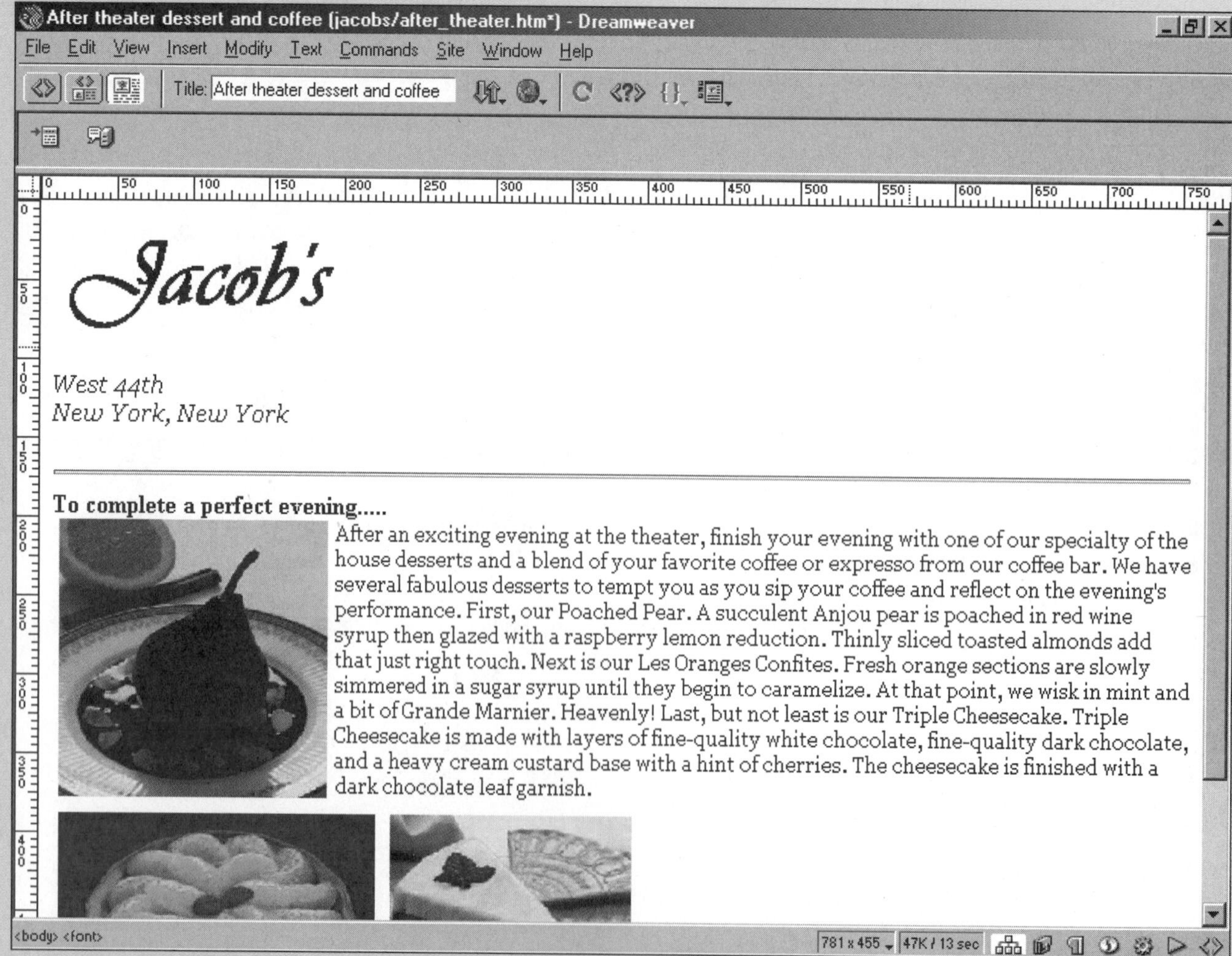

Creating Links and Navigation Bars

Objectives

- Understand links and paths
- Create an external link
- Create an internal link
- Insert a named anchor
- Create an internal link to a named anchor
- Create a navigation bar
- Modify a navigation bar
- Copy a navigation bar to other pages in a Web site
- Manage Web site links

Hyperlinks, also known as links, are the real strength of a Web site because they give viewers the freedom to open the various pages of a Web site as they choose. Links intuitively guide the viewer to the Web pages in the same Web site, or may lead viewers to Web pages in different Web sites. It is imperative that all links work correctly. A **navigation bar** is a series of text or button links that the viewer can use to navigate between pages of a Web site. In this unit, you will learn how to set up links to guide viewers between the pages of Web sites and to point them to other related Web sites. You decide to start working on the link structure for the TripSmart Web site. You also add links to the services page and create a navigation bar.

Understanding Links and Paths

There are two types of links found on Web pages. **Internal links** are links to Web pages within the same Web site, and **external links** are links that connect to Web pages in other Web sites. Both internal and external links have two important parts that work together. The first part of a link is what the viewer actually sees and clicks on a Web page, such as a word, an icon, or an animated button. When the pointer is placed over a link, the pointer's appearance changes to a pointing finger icon. The second part of a link is the **path**: the name and physical location of the Web page file that will open when the link is clicked. The information in a path depends on whether a link is internal or external. A link that returns an error message when it is clicked is referred to as a **broken link**. Broken links occur when files are renamed or deleted from the Web site, or if the filename is misspelled. You spend some time studying the various types of paths used for internal and external links.

- **Absolute paths**

  Absolute paths are used with external links. They reference links on Web pages outside of the current Web site, and include "http" (the hypertext protocol) and the URL (Uniform Resource Locator), or address, of the Web page. In some cases the Web page filename and folder hierarchy where it is located are also part of an absolute path. Figure F-1 shows an example of an absolute path.

- **Relative paths**

  Relative paths are used with internal links. They reference Web pages and graphic files within one Web site, and include the filename and the folder hierarchy where the file resides. Figure F-1 also shows an example of a relative path. Relative paths are further classified as root-relative and document-relative.

- **Root-relative paths**

  Root-relative paths are referenced from a Web site's root folder. As shown in Figure F-2, a root-relative path begins with a forward slash, which represents the Web site's root folder. This method is used when several Web sites are being published to one server, or when a Web site is so large that it uses more than one server.

- **Document-relative paths**

  Document-relative paths reference the path in relation to the Web page that is displayed. A document-relative path includes only a filename if the referenced file resides in the same folder as the current Web page. For example, index.htm and accessories.htm both reside in the root folder for TripSmart. However, when a graphic is referenced in the assets folder, since the assets folder is a subfolder of the root folder, you must include the word assets/ in front of the filename, for example, assets/tripsmart.gif. In *most* cases, document-relative paths are recommended. See Figure F-2 for an example of a document-relative path.

FIGURE F-1: Absolute and relative paths

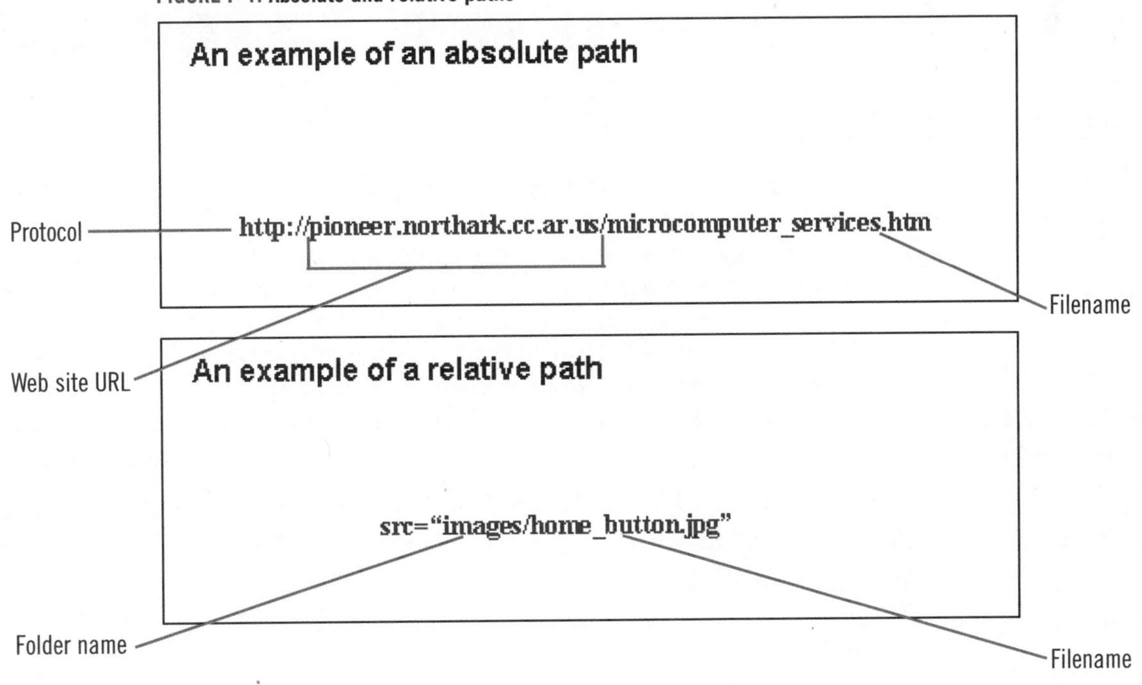

FIGURE F-2: Root-relative and document-relative paths

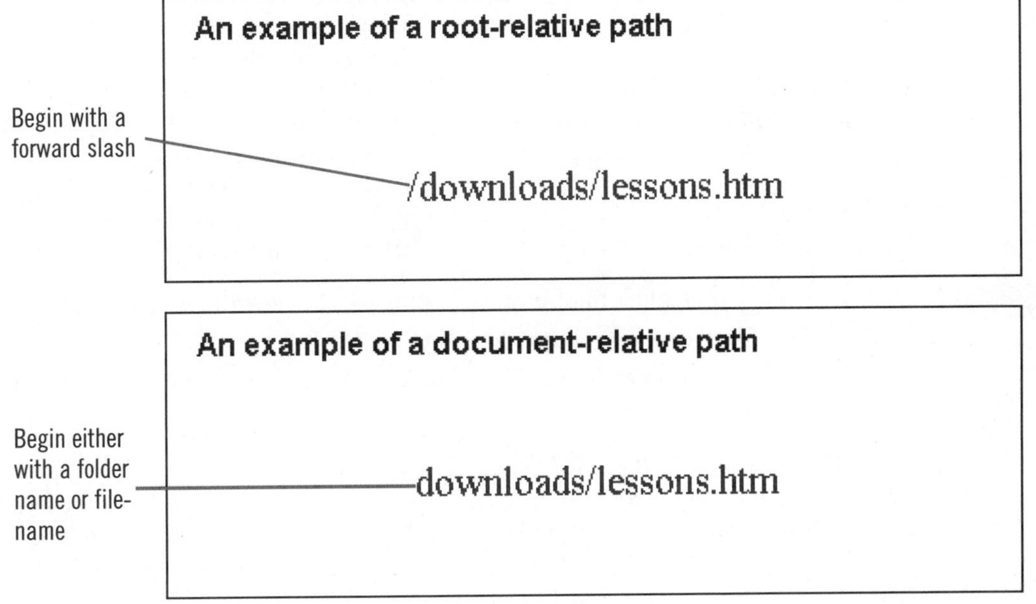

Dreamweaver 4

Dreamweaver 4

Creating an External Link

As you know, external links use absolute paths. Absolute paths must include the complete name and path of the Web address in order to link to the destination Web page successfully. Since the World Wide Web is a constantly changing environment, it is necessary to check external links frequently. Web sites may be up one day and down the next day. If a Web site changes server locations or goes down as a result of technical difficulties or a power failure, the links to it become broken. An external link can also become broken when an Internet connection is not working properly. Broken links, like misspelled words on a Web page, indicate that the Web site is not being maintained diligently. You create external links on the services page.

Steps 1 2 3 4

Trouble?

Images and internal links that display a broken link or an absolute path (extra characters, such as forward slashes and colons), can be fixed by selecting the graphic or the link, then clicking the Browse for File icon on the Property Inspector. Images should be saved in the assets folder overwriting the existing file, if necessary. For links, double-click the filename in the root folder, overwriting the existing file.

Trouble?

You need to find and highlight the name of the Web site on the services page before you type the link information in the Link text box in the Property Inspector.

QuickTip

If you do not see the page titles in the Site Map, click View on the menu bar, then click Show Page Titles (Win), or click Site on the menu bar, point to Site Map View, then click Show Page Titles (Mac).

1. Open the **TripSmart Web site**, open **dmf_1.htm** from the Unit F folder where your Project Files are stored, then save it as **services.htm** in the tripsmart root folder overwriting the existing file
   The new services page opens in Design View. The services page lists many Web sites related to travel.

2. Scroll to the bottom of the page, click the insertion point before **CNN**, then select **CNN Travel Channel**, as shown in Figure F-3
   You are ready to make the CNN Travel Channel text into an external link that will lead viewers to the CNN Travel Channel Web site.

3. Click the **Link text box** on the Property Inspector, type **http://www.cnn.com/travel**, then press **[Enter]** (Win) or **[return]** (Mac)
   The link information is complete. You want to make sure the link works correctly.

4. Click **File** on the menu bar, click **Save**, click the **Preview/Debug in Browser icon**, choose your browser, click **CNN Travel Channel** on the Web page, then close your browser
   You are ready to finish creating the external links on the services page.

5. Repeat Steps 3 and 4 to create links for the following Web sites listed on the services Web page:

Centers for Disease Control and Prevention	**http://www.cdc.gov/travel**
US State Department	**http://travel.state.gov**
Yahoo!	**http://www.yahoo.com/Recreation/Travel**
United States Tour Operators Association	**http://www.ustoa.com**
CNN Time Zone Map and Converter	**http://www.cnn.com/WEATHER/worldtime**
MapQuest	**http://www.mapquest.com**
randmcnally.com	**http://www.randmcnally.com**
AccuWeather	**http://www.accuweather.com**
The Weather Channel	**http://www.weather.com**

6. Save your work, then click the **Show Site icon** to view the Site window, press and hold the **Site Map icon**, then click **Map and Files**
   The services page appears in the Site Map, displaying the page title "We are here to serve you." as shown in Figure F-4.

7. Click the **plus sign** to the left of the services page icon
   The external links on the services page are displayed. There are eleven links: the ten external links that you created and the e-mail link. See Figure F-4.

FIGURE F-3: **Creating an external link to the CNN Travel Channel**

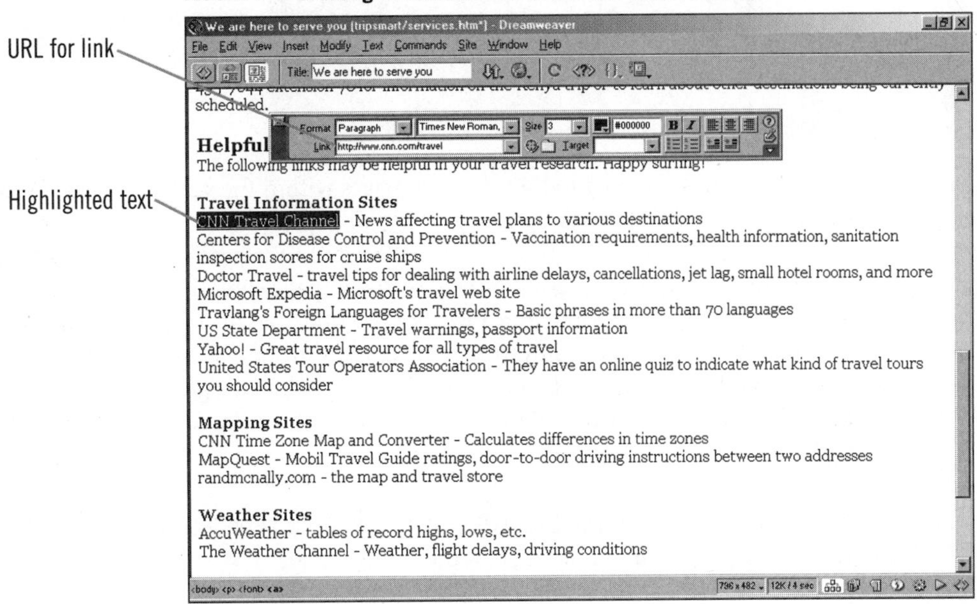

FIGURE F-4: **Site Map displaying external links on the services page**

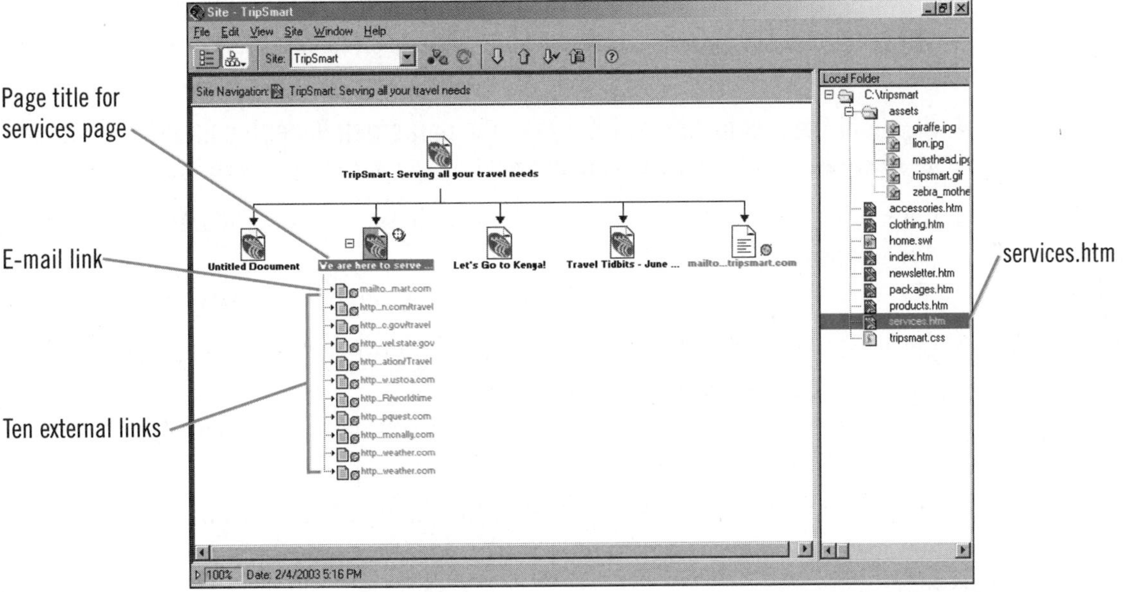

Typing URLs

Typing URLs can be very tedious, and it is easy to make mistakes when you type long and complex URLs. URLs that contain mistakes cause broken links. If you know of a Web page that you would like to include as an external link in your Web site, open the Web page, then copy the link information in the Address text box (Internet Explorer) or the Location text box (Netscape Navigator and Communicator). Then, select the link on your Web page and paste the link information in the Link text box in the Property Inspector in Dreamweaver. Copying and pasting a URL ensures that the URL is entered correctly.

Creating an Internal Link

As you know, internal links are used to link the Web pages within the same Web site. Web sites usually have individual pages for each category or major topic of the Web site. Within those pages, viewers may be able to link to other pages that relate to the particular topic. Much care should be taken in managing your internal links. The home page should provide intuitive navigation to each category or major topic in a Web site. A good rule of thumb is to design your Web site so that viewers are always only three clicks away from the page they are seeking. Referring to storyboards is very helpful when you are creating the navigation structure of your Web site. You create internal links on the services page that will link to other pages in the TripSmart Web site.

Steps

1. **Double-click services.htm in the Site window to open the services page in Design View**
   You are ready to create the internal links on the services page.
2. **Using Figure F-5 as a reference, highlight on-line catalog in the paragraph under the Travel Outfitters heading**
   The on-line catalog text will become an internal link to the products page.
3. **Click the Browse for File icon on the Property Inspector, then double-click products.htm in the Select File dialog box**
   Figure F-5 shows products.htm in the Link text box on the Property Inspector. When the on-line catalog link is clicked, the products page will open.

QuickTip

Make sure that the Relative To text box is set to Document in the Select File dialog box.

4. **Highlight the first instance of Kenya in the paragraph under the Escorted Tours heading**
   The Kenya text will be used as an internal link to the packages page.
5. **Click on the Property Inspector, then double-click packages.htm in the Select File dialog box**
   The word Kenya is now a link to the packages page in the TripSmart Web site.
6. **Click the Show Site icon to view the Site window, press and hold the Site Map icon, click Map and Files, if necessary**
   There are now thirteen links on the services page: one e-mail link, ten external links, and two internal links, as shown in Figure F-6.

Trouble?

If you do not see the thirteen links, click the plus sign to the left of the services page icon.

7. **Double-click services.htm to return to the page in Design View**
   You have successfully created internal and external links for the services page.
8. **Save your work**

FIGURE F-5: Creating internal links on the services page

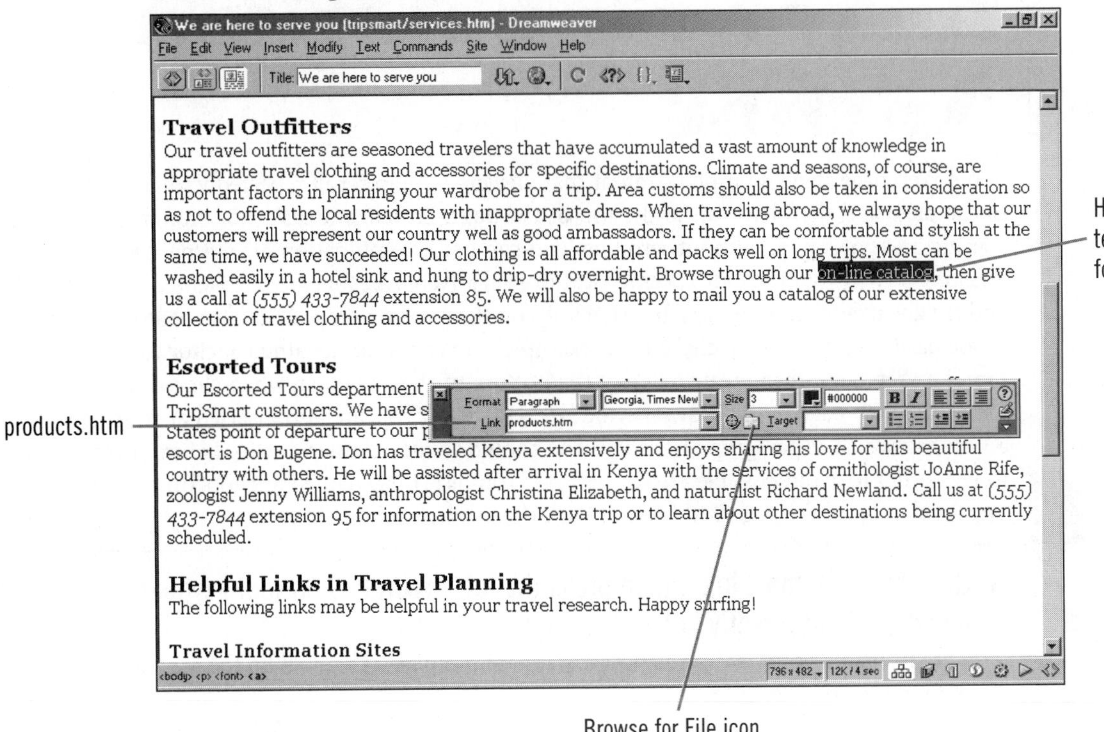

FIGURE F-6: Site Map displaying internal and external links on the services page

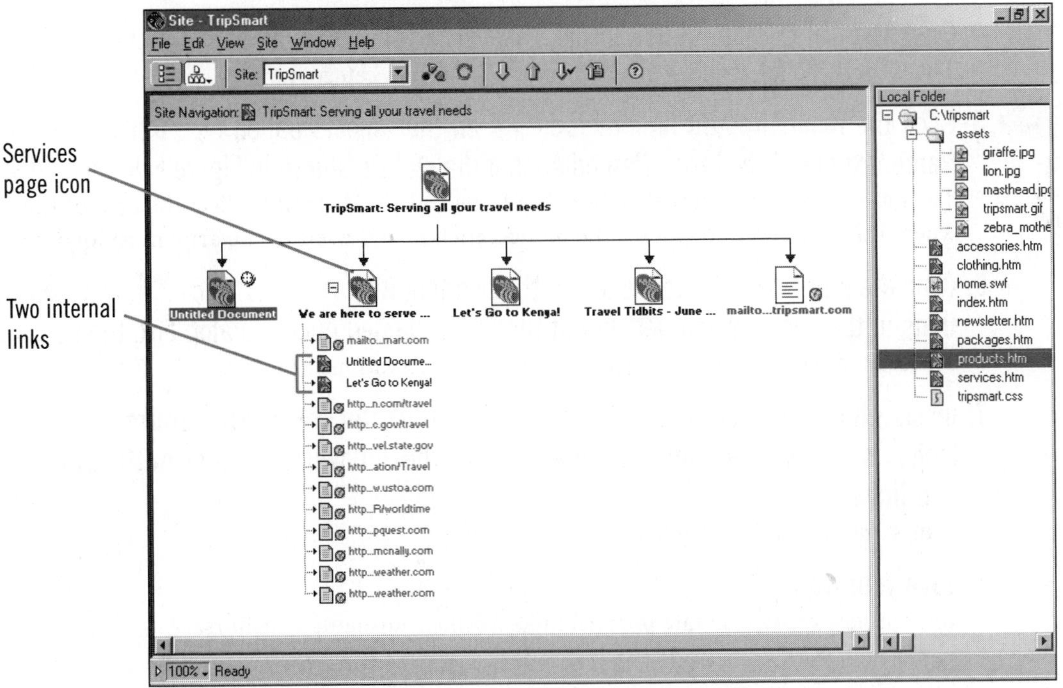

Dreamweaver 4

Dreamweaver 4

Inserting a Named Anchor

Some Web pages have so much content that viewers have to scroll repeatedly to get to the bottom of the page and then back up to the top of the page. To make it easier for viewers to navigate to specific areas of a page without scrolling, you can use a combination of internal links and named anchors. **Named anchors** are specific locations on a Web page that are represented by a special icon and are given descriptive names. Internal links on the page are programmed to jump to the location of the named anchor, when clicked. For example, you can insert a named anchor called "top" at the top of a Web page, then create a link at the bottom of the page that, when clicked, will display the top of the Web page in the browser window. Named anchors are also inserted at strategic spots on a Web page, such as paragraph headings. You should create a named anchor before you create a link to it in order to avoid possible errors. You insert five named anchors on the services page: one for the top of the page and four for each department subheading.

Steps

1. Click the **TripSmart logo**, then press the **left arrow key** on your keyboard to place the insertion point directly before the logo

   The insertion point is now at the very top of the page. This will be the location for the first named anchor.

2. Click **View** on the menu bar, point to **Visual Aids**, then click **Invisible Elements** to select it, if necessary

   Named anchors are an example of Invisible Elements. Invisible Elements must be "on" in order to reveal where named anchors are located on the page. A checkmark to the left of the Invisible Elements menu item indicates that the feature is turned on.

3. Click **Window** on the menu bar, then click **Objects**, if necessary

4. Click the **Objects panel list arrow**, then click **Invisibles**, as shown in Figure F-7

   The Objects panel displays the icons in the Invisibles category.

5. Click the **Insert Named Anchor icon** on the Objects panel, type **top** in the Anchor Name text box of the Insert Named Anchor dialog box, shown in Figure F-8, then click **OK**

   The name used for a named anchor should be short and should reflect the area of the page where it is inserted. You can see the named anchor to the left of the TripSmart logo.

6. Click the insertion point to the left of the heading **Reservations**, click , type **reservations** in the Anchor Name text box of the Insert Named Anchor dialog box, then click **OK**

   The second named anchor appears before the Reservations heading.

7. Insert named anchors in front of the **Travel Outfitters**, **Escorted Tours**, and **Helpful Links in Travel Planning** headings, using the following names: **outfitters**, **tours**, and **links**

   Your screen should resemble Figure F-9.

8. Save your work

   You are now ready to create internal links for the four named anchors.

QuickTip

You should only use lowercase characters for named anchor names. You should not use spaces or special characters in the name.

FIGURE F-7: Objects panel displaying Invisibles icons

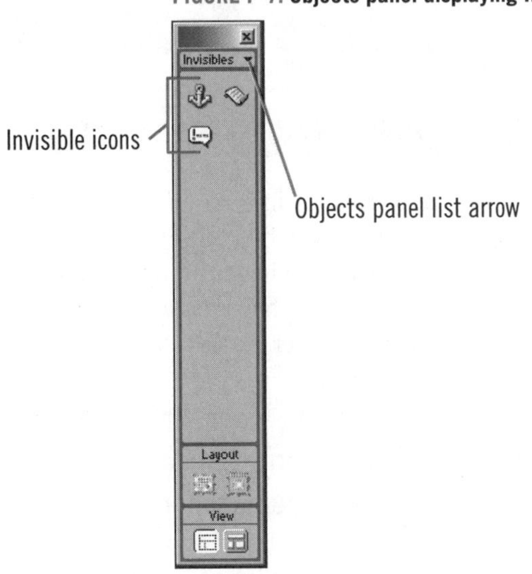

FIGURE F-8: Insert Named Anchor dialog box

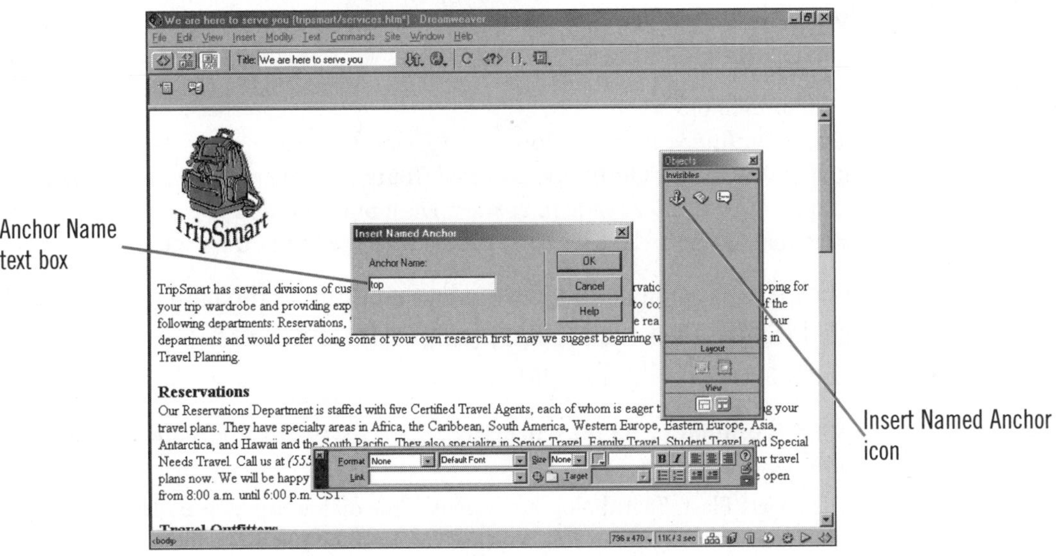

FIGURE F-9: Named anchor icons

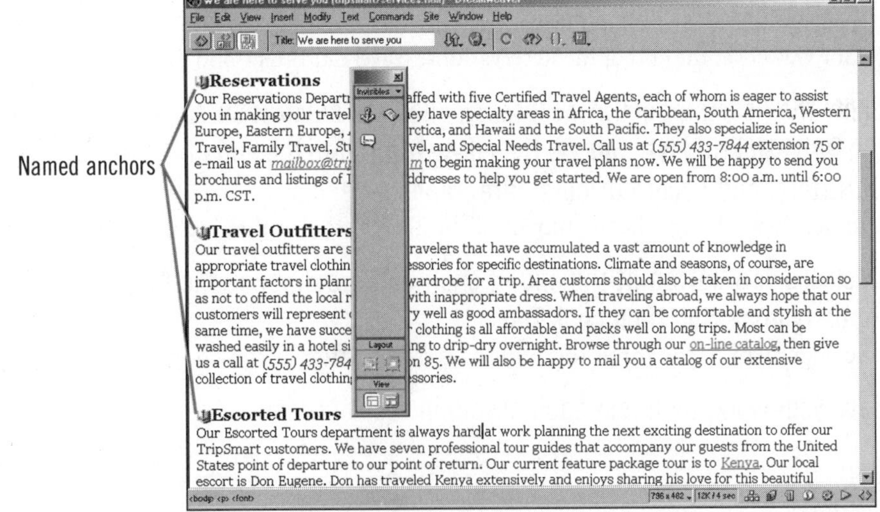

Dreamweaver 4

Dreamweaver 4

Creating Internal Links to Named Anchors

Named anchors act as targets for internal links. A **target** is the location on a Web page that the browser will display in full view when an internal link is clicked. You use the Point to File icon on the Property Inspector to connect an internal link to a named anchor. You create internal links and link them to each named anchor on the services page. You also create a link at the bottom of the page that viewers can use to return to the top of the page.

Steps

QuickTip

The name of a named anchor is always preceded by a pound (#) sign in the Link text box on the Property Inspector, as shown in Figure F-10.

QuickTip

You can hide named anchors by clicking View on the menu bar, pointing to Visual Aids, then clicking Invisible Elements.

QuickTip

As shown in Figure F-11, services.htm is entered in front of #top in the Link text box because the Top button is a separate Flash file from the services page file.

1. Using Figure F-10 as a guide, highlight **Reservations** in the second sentence of the first paragraph, then click-and-drag the **Point to File icon** on the Property Inspector on top of the **reservations named anchor**
   The word Reservations is now a link that, when clicked, will display the Reservations paragraph at the top of the browser window, because the reservations named anchor is the target of the Reservations link.
2. Create internal links for **Travel Outfitters**, **Escorted Tours**, and **Helpful Links in Travel Planning** by first highlighting each phrase in the second and third sentences of the first paragraph, then clicking-and-dragging on top of the **outfitters**, **tours**, and **links** named anchors
   Travel Outfitters, Escorted Tours, and Helpful Hints in Travel Planning are now links that link to the Travel Outfitters, Escorted Tours, and Helpful Links in Travel Planning paragraphs. You are now ready to create a Flash button called Top at the bottom of the services page that, when clicked, will bring viewers to the top of the page.
3. Click the insertion point after the **Home button** at the bottom of the page, press and hold **[Shift]**, then click **[Enter]** (Win) or **[return]** (Mac) to insert a space below the Home button for the Top button
4. Click the **Objects panel list arrow**, click **Common**, then click the **Insert Flash Text icon**
   The Insert Flash Text dialog box opens. This dialog box is used to create and format Flash text. You can also enter a link for the Flash text in this dialog box.
5. Type **Top** in the Text text box, match the settings in the Insert Flash Text dialog box on your screen with those shown in Figure F-11, then click **OK**
   The Top button appears below the Home button. When the Top button is clicked, the top of the page will be displayed in the browser window. You think the Top button would also be useful for viewers at the end of the Reservations, Travel Outfitters, and Escorted Tours paragraphs.
6. Show the Assets panel, if necessary, click the **Flash icon** on the Assets panel, click the **Refresh Site List icon** then drag **top.swf** to the end of the Reservations, Travel Outfitters, and Escorted Tours paragraphs
   You decide to change the alignment of the Top button so that it aligns better with the text.
7. Click the **Top button** at the end of each paragraph, click the **Align list arrow** on the Property Inspector, then click **Top**
   The alignment of the three Top buttons is much better as shown in Figure F-12.
8. Save your work, then test each button in your browser

FIGURE F-10: Using the Point to File Icon

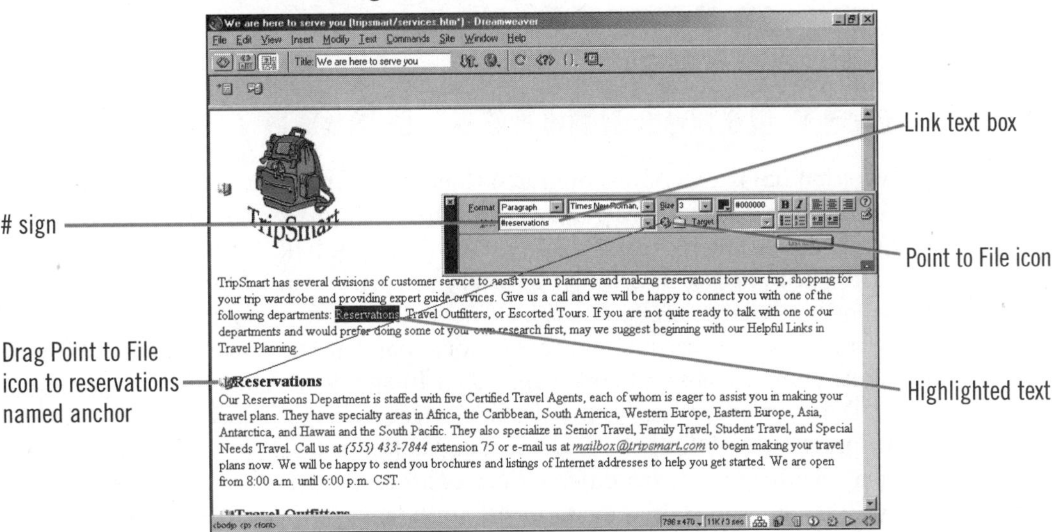

FIGURE F-11: Insert Flash Text dialog box

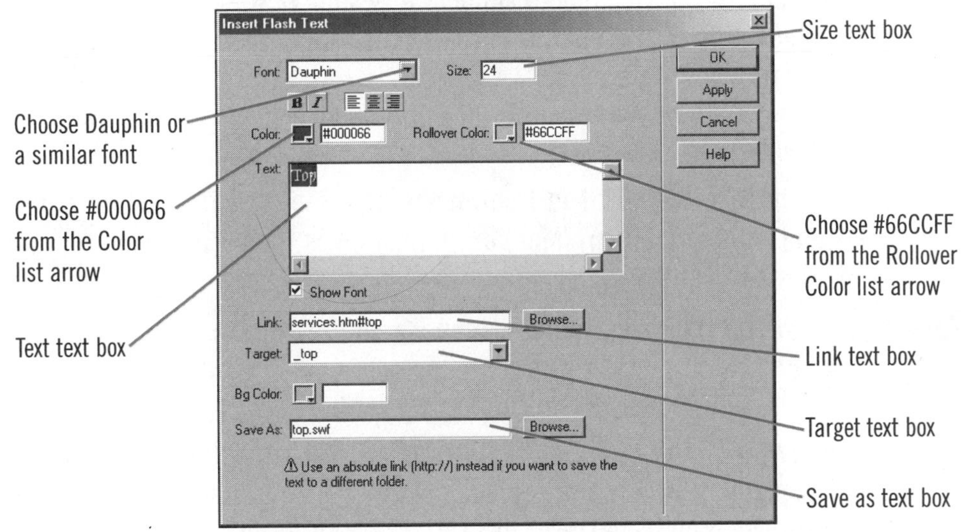

FIGURE F-12: Top button placed on services page

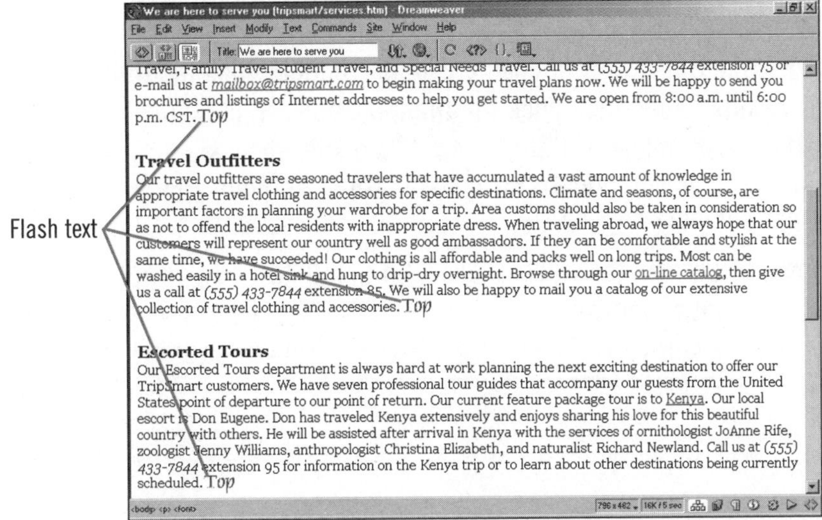

Dreamweaver 4

Dreamweaver 4

Creating a Navigation Bar

A **navigation bar** is a set of text or graphic links that viewers can use to navigate between pages of a Web site. When you create a navigation bar with images rather than text, you create the images in another graphics software program. All graphic links created for a navigation bar must be exactly the same size in order to be displayed correctly in a browser. The Insert Navigation Bar dialog box refers to each link as an element. Each element can have four possible **states**, or appearances, based on the location of the mouse pointer. These states include **Up Image** (when the mouse pointer is not on the element), **Over Image** (when the mouse pointer is over the element), **Down Image** (when you click the element with the mouse pointer), and **Over While Down Image** (when you click the element and continue holding with the mouse pointer). You can create a rollover by using different images to represent each button state. When the mouse rolls over the button or link, the pointer's appearance changes. You begin creating a navigation bar that will have five navigation elements: home, services, products, tours, and newsletter.

1. Make sure the services page is open in Design View, click the **TripSmart logo**, click the **Align list arrow** on the Property Inspector, then click **Left** to left-align the TripSmart logo
   Your first task is to make room for the navigation bar. You want to place it before the first paragraph.
2. Click the insertion point in front of the first sentence in the first paragraph, press **[Enter]** (Win) or **[return]** (Mac) once, then press the **up arrow** on your keyboard
   You can insert a navigation bar using the Objects panel or the Insert menu.
3. Click the **Insert Navigation Bar icon** on the Objects panel
   The Insert Navigation Bar dialog box opens. You use this dialog box to name each element and assign graphics for each element's four states.
4. Type **home** in the Element Name text box, click the **Insert list arrow**, then click **Horizontally**, if necessary, to place the navigation bar horizontally on the page
   The Element Name is the name that you choose for the link that will appear on the navigation bar. The home link will have two appearances: one for the Up Image state, and a different one for the Over Image, Down Image, and Over While Down Image states.
5. Using Figure F-13 as a reference, click each **Browse button** next to the Up Image, Over Image, Down Image, and Over While Down Image text boxes, click the drive and folder where your Project Files are stored, double-click the **Unit F folder**, double-click the **assets** folder, then click the **filenames** shown in Figure F-13, and save each file in the assets folder of the TripSmart Web site when you are prompted to do so
   You need to link the home element to the TripSmart home page. The TripSmart home page's filename is index.htm.
6. Type **index.htm** in the When Clicked, Go To URL text box, as shown in Figure F-13, click **OK**, then save your work
   The home element, which is the first element in your navigation bar, appears on the services page and remains selected, as shown in Figure F-14.

QuickTip

You can only place one navigation bar on a Web page.

Trouble?

Click Yes when you are asked if you want to replace the existing down image files in the Copy File As dialog box.

FIGURE F-13: Insert Navigation Bar dialog box

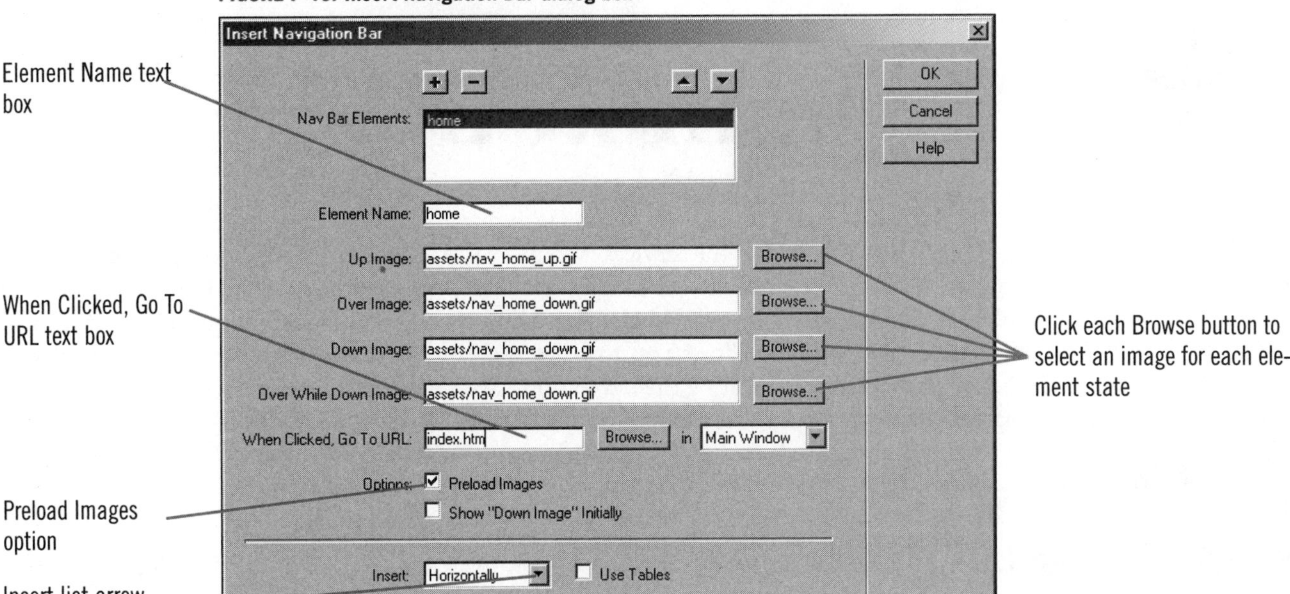
Insert Navigation Bar
Element Name text box
Nav Bar Elements:
home
OK
Cancel
Help
Element Name:
home
Up Image:
assets/nav_home_up.gif
Browse...
When Clicked, Go To URL text box
Over Image:
assets/nav_home_down.gif
Down Image:
assets/nav_home_down.gif
Over While Down Image:
assets/nav_home_down.gif
Click each Browse button to select an image for each element state
When Clicked, Go To URL:
index.htm
in
Main Window
Options:
Preload Images
Show "Down Image" Initially
Preload Images option
Insert:
Horizontally
Use Tables
Insert list arrow

FIGURE F-14: The first element of the navigation bar

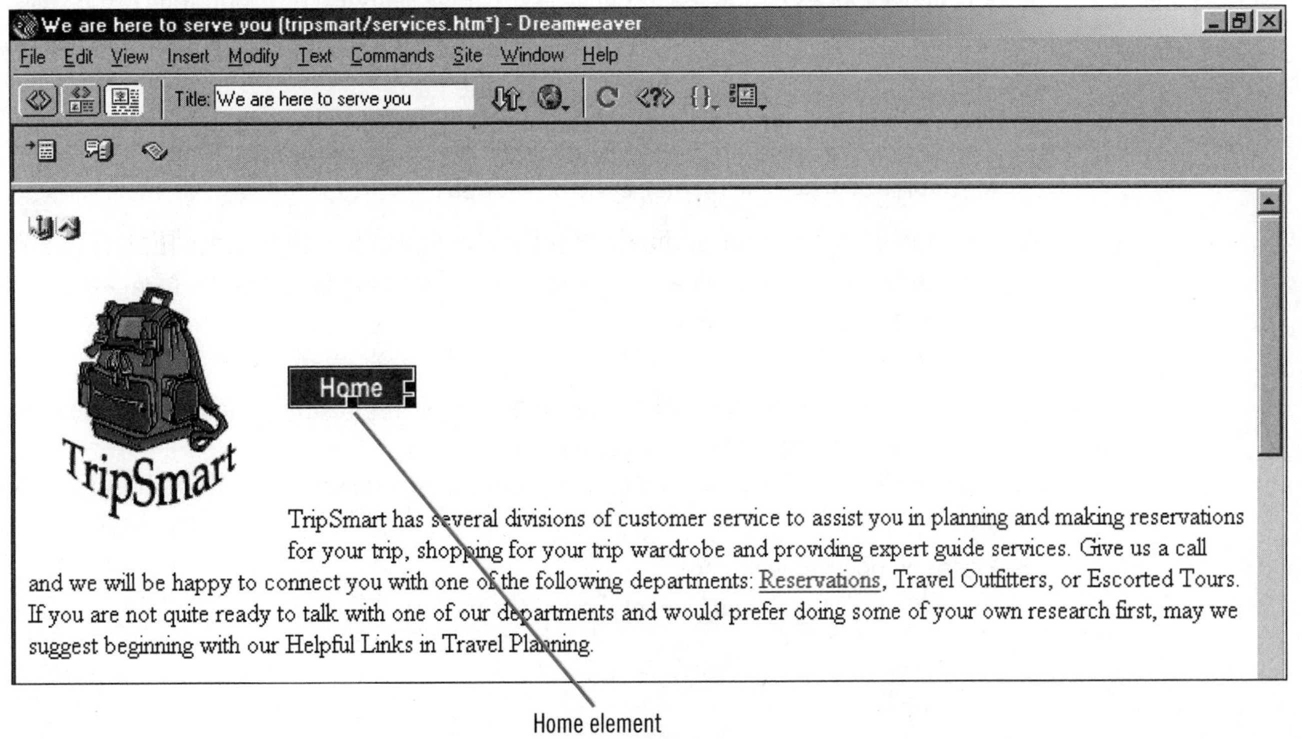
We are here to serve you (tripsmart/services.htm*) - Dreamweaver
File Edit View Insert Modify Text Commands Site Window Help
Title: We are here to serve you
Home
TripSmart
TripSmart has several divisions of customer service to assist you in planning and making reservations for your trip, shopping for your trip wardrobe and providing expert guide services. Give us a call and we will be happy to connect you with one of the following departments: Reservations, Travel Outfitters, or Escorted Tours. If you are not quite ready to talk with one of our departments and would prefer doing some of your own research first, may we suggest beginning with our Helpful Links in Travel Planning.
Home element

Dreamweaver 4

Dreamweaver 4

Modifying a Navigation Bar

After you create a navigation bar, you can modify it using the Modify Navigation Bar dialog box. Modifying a navigation bar allows you to customize its appearance on various Web pages. For example, if you are viewing the services Web page, you can change the graphic for the Up Image state of the services element to the graphic used for the Down Image state (which is a different color). This method acts as a visual clue to remind viewers which page, or section of a Web site, they are viewing. It also allows you to place the same navigation bar on all pages in a Web site. You finish creating the navigation bar, then modify the services element by changing the Up Image state to the Down Image state.

QuickTip

You can click any part of the navigation bar to modify it.

1. Click the **navigation bar**, click **Modify** on the menu bar, then click **Navigation Bar**
   The Modify Navigation Bar dialog box opens.
2. Click the **Add Navigation Bar Element icon** + at the top of the Modify Navigation Bar dialog box, type **services** in the Element Name text box, as shown in the Services section of Figure F-15
   You click + to add a new navigation element to the navigation bar and click − to delete a navigation element from the navigation bar.
3. Using the four sections in Figure F-15 as a guide, finish the services element and create three more elements called **products**, **tours**, and **newsletter** by filling in the Insert Navigation Bar dialog box text boxes and the When Clicked, Go to URL text boxes
   You are now ready to modify the services element.

QuickTip

The Modify Navigation Bar dialog box does not include the Insert list arrow, which allows you to choose Horizontally or Vertically as a layout choice for your navigation bar.

4. Click **services** in the Nav Bar Elements text box, then click **Show "Down Image" Initially check box**, as shown in Figure F-16
   An asterisk appears next to services in the Nav Bar Elements text box, indicating that this element will be initially displayed in the Down Image state.
5. Click **OK** to close the dialog box, then save the file
   The Up Image state of the services element displays the light blue graphic normally used for the Down Image state of the navigation bar elements. This "trick" reminds viewers which page of a Web site they are currently viewing.
6. Click the insertion point to the right of the navigation bar, then press [**Enter**] (Win) or [**return**] (Mac) until you are pleased with the spacing between the navigation bar and the first paragraph
   The page looks more balanced with the added white space.
7. Click the **Preview/Debug in Browser icon** on the toolbar, choose your browser, then click **Services** on the navigation bar
   The page loads with the services element in the Down Image state. The services element remains in the Down Image state after it is clicked..
8. Close the browser window
   You are back in the Design View of the services page.

FIGURE F-15: Creating four navigation elements

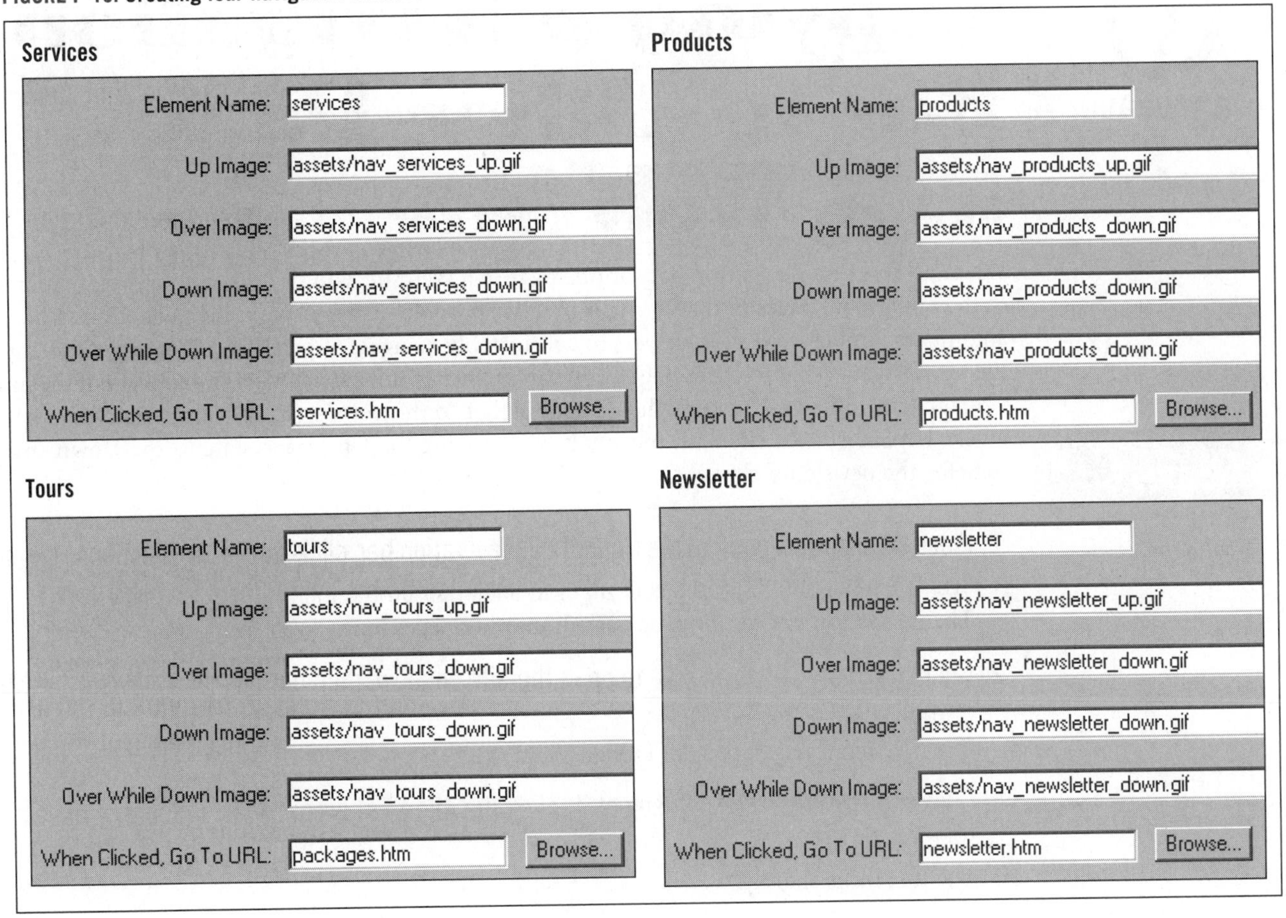

Services
Element Name: services
Up Image: assets/nav_services_up.gif
Over Image: assets/nav_services_down.gif
Down Image: assets/nav_services_down.gif
Over While Down Image: assets/nav_services_down.gif
When Clicked, Go To URL: services.htm
Browse...
Products
Element Name: products
Up Image: assets/nav_products_up.gif
Over Image: assets/nav_products_down.gif
Down Image: assets/nav_products_down.gif
Over While Down Image: assets/nav_products_down.gif
When Clicked, Go To URL: products.htm
Browse...
Tours
Element Name: tours
Up Image: assets/nav_tours_up.gif
Over Image: assets/nav_tours_down.gif
Down Image: assets/nav_tours_down.gif
Over While Down Image: assets/nav_tours_down.gif
When Clicked, Go To URL: packages.htm
Browse...
Newsletter
Element Name: newsletter
Up Image: assets/nav_newsletter_up.gif
Over Image: assets/nav_newsletter_down.gif
Down Image: assets/nav_newsletter_down.gif
Over While Down Image: assets/nav_newsletter_down.gif
When Clicked, Go To URL: newsletter.htm
Browse...

FIGURE F-16: The Modify Navigation Bar dialog box

Modify Navigation Bar
OK
Cancel
Help
Nav Bar Elements:
home
services *
products
tours
Element Name: services
Up Image: assets/nav_services_up.gif
Browse...
Over Image: assets/nav_services_down.gif
Browse...
Down Image: assets/nav_services_down.gif
Browse...
Over While Down Image: assets/nav_services_down.gif
Browse...
When Clicked, Go To URL: services.htm
Browse...
in
Main Window
Options:
Preload Images
Show "Down Image" Initially

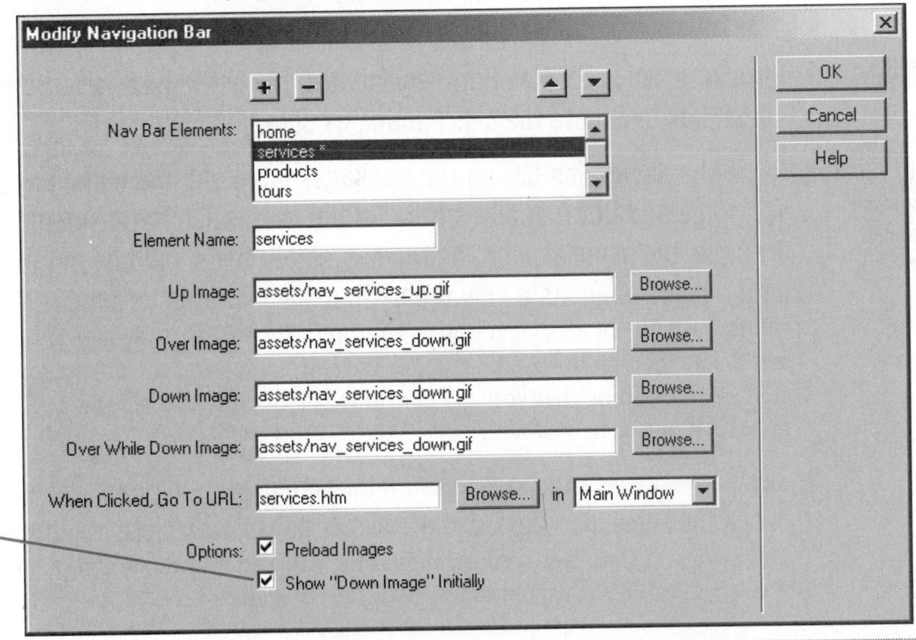

Show "Down Image" Initially check box

Dreamweaver 4

Dreamweaver 4

Copying a Navigation Bar to Other Pages in a Web Site

When you create a navigation bar for one page in a Web site, you should copy and paste it on all of the other main pages in the site. This practice provides continuity in the navigation structure and makes it much easier for viewers to comfortably navigate to pages in a Web site. After copying the navigation bar to other pages, you can further modify it to reflect the content of the individual pages. You copy the navigation bar to the newsletter, home, and packages pages in the TripSmart Web site, and modify it by changing the Up Image state to the Down Image state for the newsletter element.

Steps 1 2 3 4

1. **Place the insertion point to the right of the navigation bar, click-and-drag the mouse pointer over the navigation bar to select all of it, click Edit on the menu bar, then click Copy**
   The navigation bar can now be pasted on other pages in the Web site.
2. Click the **Show Site icon** to open the Site window, then double-click **newsletter.htm** in the Local Folder list
   The newsletter page opens in Design View.
3. Click the **TripSmart logo** to select it, click the **Align list arrow** on the Property Inspector, then click **Left**
   The text shifts slightly.
4. Click the **horizontal rule** to select it, click **Edit** on the menu bar, then click **Paste**
   The navigation bar replaces the horizontal rule.
5. Click the **navigation bar**, click **Modify** on the menu bar, then click **Navigation Bar**
   The Navigation Bar dialog box opens. You need to set the Down Image state to show initially when the page opens.
6. Click **newsletter** in the Nav Bar Elements text box, then click the **Show "Down Image" Initially** check box, as shown in Figure F-17
   Now you are ready to modify the services element so it displays in the Up Image state.
7. Click **services** in the Nav Bar Elements text box, click the **Show "Down Image" Initially check box** to remove the check mark, as shown in Figure F-18, then click **OK**
8. Paste the navigation bar on the packages page and the home page, then modify the Up Image and Down Image states for the navigation bar elements, as necessary (for example, the home element on the navigation bar should be in the Down Image state on the home page, as a visual clue that the viewer is looking at the home page)
   (Hint: Paste the new navigation bar on top of the existing navigation bar on the home page and delete the first horizontal rule on the page. A copy of the navigation bar remains on the clipboard, meaning that you can continue pasting it without copying it each time you want to paste it onto a new page.)
9. Save your work on each page, preview the current page in your browser, test the navigation bar on the home, packages and newsletter pages, then close the browser window
   The navigation bar is placed on the home, newsletter and packages pages of the TripSmart Web site. Feel free to adjust the page elements as necessary.

Trouble?

If you closed the Modify Navigation Bar dialog box too early, click the navigation bar, click Modify on the menu bar, point to Navigation Bar, then repeat Step 7.

FIGURE F-17: Changing settings for the newsletter element

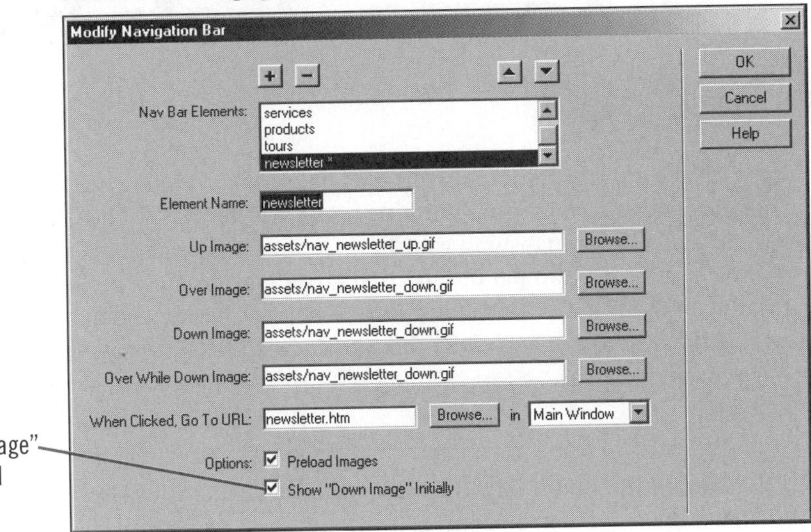

FIGURE F-18: Changing settings for the services element

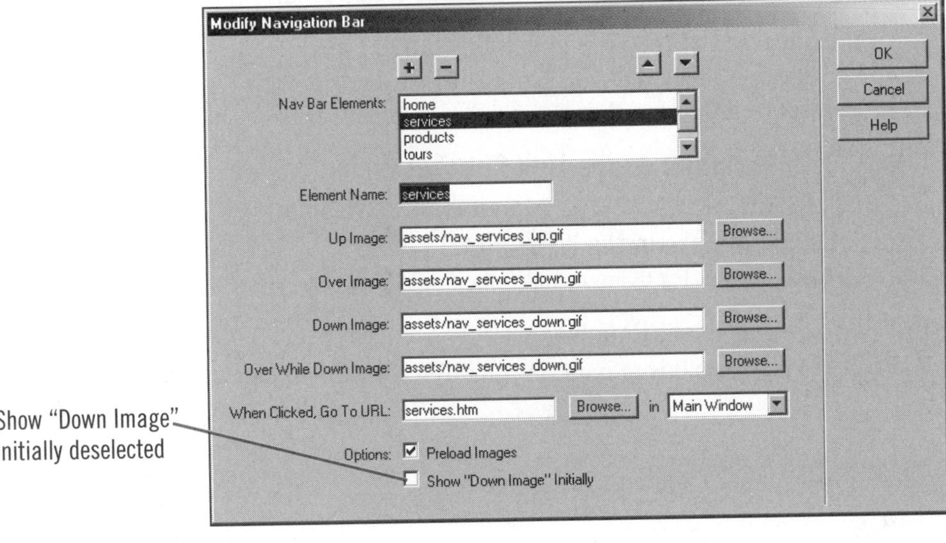

Creating an image map

Another way to create navigation links for Web pages is to create an image map. An **image map** is a graphic that has one or more hotspots placed on top of it. A **hotspot** is a clickable area on a graphic that, when clicked, links to a different location on the page or to another Web page. For example, a map of the United States could have a hotspot placed on each individual state so that viewers could click a state to link to information about that state. You can create hotspots by first selecting the image that you want to place hotspots on top of, then using one of the hotspot tools on the Property Inspector. Figure F-19 displays the pointer, rectangular, oval, and polygon hotspot tools on the Property Inspector.

FIGURE F-19: The hotspot drawing tools in the Property Inspector

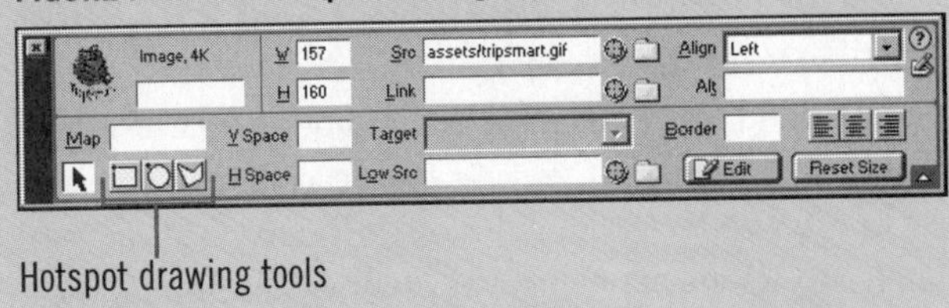

Dreamweaver 4

Managing Web Site Links

As your Web site grows, so will the number of links in it. Checking links to make sure they work is an ongoing and crucial task that must be performed regularly. The Check Links Sitewide feature is a helpful tool for managing your links. It checks your entire Web site for the total number of links and for the number of links that are OK, external, or broken, and then displays the information in the Link Checker dialog box. The Link Checker dialog box also provides a list all the files used in a Web site, including those that are **orphaned files**, files that are not linked to any pages in the Web site. You check the TripSmart Web site for any broken links or orphaned files.

Steps

QuickTip

Broken links can be displayed by double-clicking the name of the broken link in the Link Checker dialog box. Dreamweaver will then locate that link in the Web site and display the broken link on the page for you to repair.

Trouble?

Your number of files may differ from those shown in the figures on page F-19.

1. Click **Site** on the menu bar, then click **Check Links Sitewide**
   The Link Checker dialog box opens. By default the Link Checker dialog box initially displays any broken internal links found in the Web site. The TripSmart Web site has no broken links.
2. Click the **Show list arrow**, then click **External Links**
   Some external links are listed more than once because the Link Checker displays each external link each time it is used in the Web site. See Figure F-20.
3. Click the **Show list arrow**, then click **Orphaned Files**
   The Link Checker displays the orphaned files for the Web site. See Figure F-21. Eventually these files will be linked to other pages and will no longer be orphaned files.
4. Click the **Close button** on the **Link Checker** dialog box, click **Window** on the menu bar, click **Assets**, if necessary, then click the **URLs icon** on the Assets panel to display the list of links in the Web site
   The Assets panel displays the external links used in the Web site. See Figure F-22.
5. **Exit** (Win) or **Quit** (Mac) Dreamweaver
   You now see how easy it is to manage your Web site links in Dreamweaver.

Navigation design considerations

As you work on the navigation structure for a Web site, you should try to limit the number of links on each page to no more than 10. Too many links may confuse visitors to your Web site. Another consideration is to design links so that viewers can reach the information they are seeking within three or four clicks. Otherwise viewers may become discouraged or lost in the site. You should also provide visual clues on each page to let viewers know where they are, much like a "You are here" marker on a store directory at the mall.

FIGURE F-20: Link Checker displaying external links

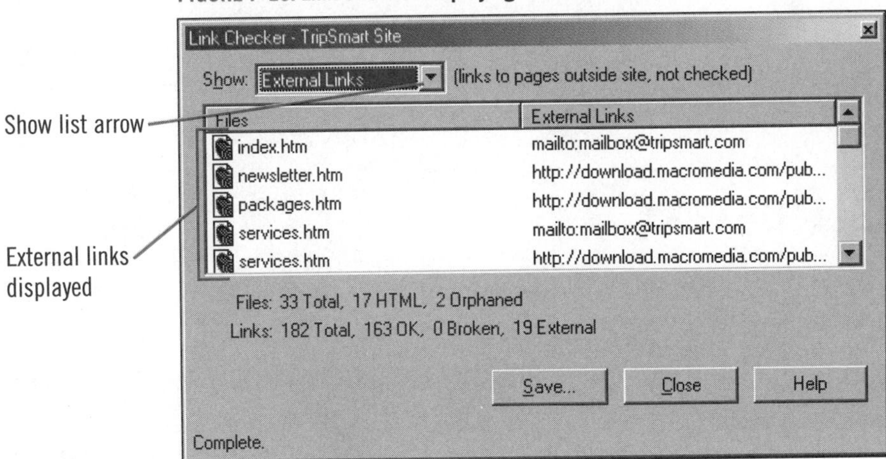

FIGURE F-21: Link Checker displaying orphaned files

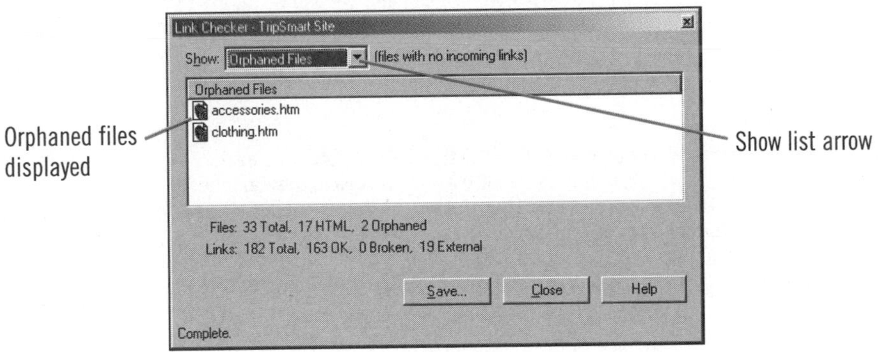

FIGURE F-22: Assets panel displaying links

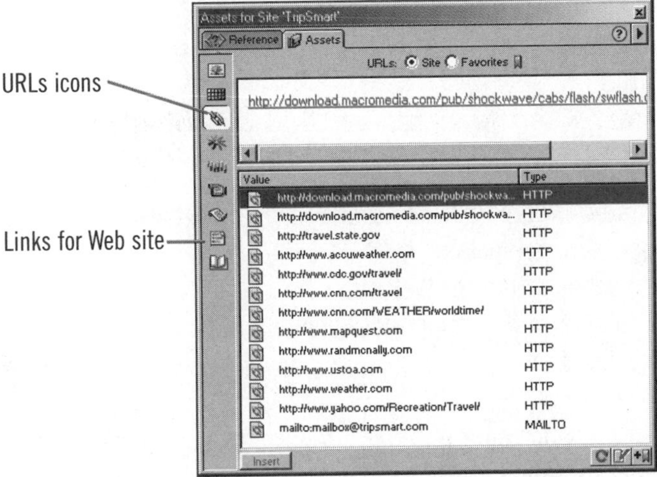

Dreamweaver 4

Practice

► Concepts Review

Label each element in the Dreamweaver window shown in Figure F-23.

FIGURE F-23

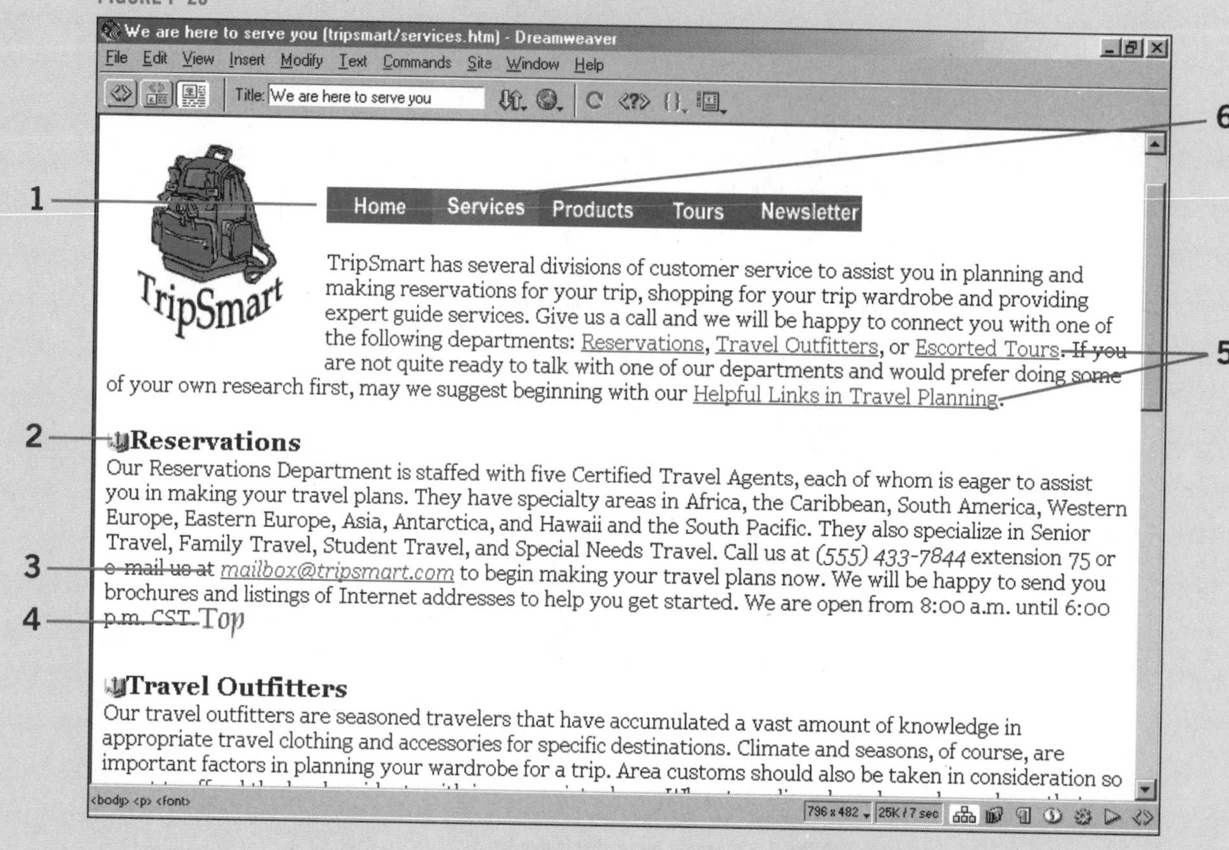

Match each of the following terms with the statement that describes its function.

7. Internal links
8. External links
9. Broken link
10. Named anchor
11. Navigation bar
12. Rollover
13. Image map
14. Hotspot
15. Orphaned file

a. A link that does not work correctly
b. A set of text or graphic links used to navigate between pages of a Web site
c. A graphic with hotspots on it
d. Links to pages within the Web site
e. Clickable area on a graphic that links to a URL
f. The effect of an image changing its appearance when the mouse pointer is positioned over it
g. A specific location on a Web page, represented by a special icon, that will fully display in the browser window when a user clicks the link tagged to it
h. A file that is not linked to any pages in a Web site
i. Links to pages outside the Web site

Select the best answer from the following list of choices.

16. Which type of path begins with a forward slash?

a. Document-relative
b. Root-relative
c. Absolute
d. Site-relative

17. Which icon on the Property Inspector do you use to connect an internal link to a named anchor?

a. Point to File
b. Point to Anchor
c. Anchor to File
d. Point to Named Anchor

18. The four possible states of an element in a navigation bar are:

a. Up Image, Over Image, Down Image, Under Image.
b. Up Image, Over Image, Down Image, Over While Down Image.
c. Up Image, Over Image, Down Image, Up While Down Image.
d. Up Image, Over Image, Down Image, Up While Under Image.

19. To see all links in a Web site, you click which icon on the Assets panel?

a. Links
b. Paths
c. URLs
d. Anchors

20. Which dialog box shows you a list of orphaned files?

a. Orphaned Files
b. Link Checker
c. Check Links Sitewide
d. Assets

Skills Review

Important: *If you did not create this Web site in Unit B and maintain it during the preceding units, you will need to create a root folder for this Web site and define the Web site using files your instructor will provide. See the "Read This Before You Begin" section for more detailed instructions.*

1. Create an external link.

a. Start Dreamweaver and open the Blooms&Bulbs Web site.
b. Open dmf_2.htm from the Unit F folder where your Project Files are stored, then save it as *master_gardener.htm* in the blooms root folder. (*Hint:* Images and internal links that display a broken link or an absolute path (extra characters, such as forward slashes and colons), can be fixed by selecting the graphic or the link, then clicking the Browse for File icon on the Property Inspector. Images should be saved in the assets folder overwriting the existing file, if necessary. For links, double-click the filename in the root folder, overwriting the existing file.)
c. Scroll to the bottom of the page and link the National Gardening Association text to *http://www.garden.org.*
d. Link the United States Department of Agriculture text to *http://gardening.usda.gov/region.html.*
e. Link the United States Department of Agriculture Home Gardening text to *http://www.usda.gov/news/garden.htm.*
f. Link the Better Homes and Gardens Gardening Home Page text to *http://bhg.com/gardening.*
g. Link the Southern Living text to *http://www.southernliving.com.*
h. Save the file and preview it in your browser.
i. Test each link to make sure they all work correctly.

2. Create an internal link.

a. Scroll to the paragraph about plants. Select the water plants text and link it to the water_plants.htm file in the blooms_and_bulbs root folder, using the Browse for File icon.
b. Select the annuals text in the same paragraph and link it to the annuals.htm file in the blooms_and_bulbs root folder, using the Browse for File icon.
c. Select the perennials text in the same paragraph and link it to the file perennials.htm in the Web site, using the Browse for File icon.
d. Scroll to the bottom of the page and insert the Flash home.swf file at the bottom of the page.
e. Save the file and test the links in your browser.

3. Insert a named anchor.

a. Click View on the menu bar, point to Visual Aids, then click Invisible Elements, if necessary.
b. Click the Objects panel list arrow, then click Invisibles, if necessary.
c. Insert a named anchor in front of the Grass subheading, then name it **grass**.
d. Insert a named anchor in front of the Trees subheading, then name it **trees**.
e. Insert a named anchor in front of the Plants subheading, then name it **plants**.
f. Save the file.

4. Create an internal link to a named anchor.

a. Using the Point to File icon on the Property Inspector, create a link from the word grass in the Gardening Issues paragraph to the grass named anchor.
b. Create a link from the word trees in the Gardening Issues paragraph to the trees named anchor.
c. Create a link from the word plants in the Gardening Issues paragraph to the plants named anchor.
d. Save the file and test the links in your browser.

5. Create a navigation bar.

a. Using the Objects panel, create a navigation bar at the top of the master_gardener page under the logo.
b. Type **home** as the first element name, and use the nav_bhome.up.gif file for the Up Image state and the nav_bhome_down.gif file for the three remaining states. These files are in the assets folder of the Unit F folder where your Project Files are stored. Click Yes when you are asked if you want to replace the existing down image files in the Copy File As dialog box.
c. Copy the gif files in the blooms_and_bulbs assets folder when prompted.
d. Set the index.htm file as the link for the home element.
e. Create a new element named **plants**, and use the nav_plants_up.gif file for the Up Image state and the nav_plants_down.gif file for the remaining three states. These files are in the assets folder of the Unit F folder where your Project Files are stored.
f. Copy the gif files in the blooms_and_bulbs assets folder when prompted.
g. Set the plants.htm file as the link for the plants element.
h. Create a new element named **events**, and use the nav_events_up.gif file for the Up Image state and the nav_events_down.gif file for the remaining three states.
i. Copy the gif files in the blooms_and_bulbs assets folder when prompted.
j. Set the events.htm file as the link for the events element.
k. Create a new element named **tips**, and use the nav_tips_up.gif file for the Up Image state and the nav_tips_down.gif file for the remaining three states.
l. Copy the gif files in the blooms_and_bulbs assets folder when prompted.
m. Set the tips.htm file as the link for the tips element.

n. Create a new element named **ask**, and use the nav_ask_up.gif file for the Up Image state and the nav_ask_down.gif file for the remaining three states.
o. Copy the gif files in the blooms_and_bulbs assets folder when prompted.
p. Set the master_gardener.htm file as the link for the ask element.
q. Save the page and test the links in your browser.

6. Modify a navigation bar
a. Modify the navigation bar to show the Down Image state initially for the ask element.
b. Save the page and test the links in your browser.

7. Copy a navigation bar to other pages in a Web site.
a. Select and copy the navigation bar.
b. Use the Site window to open the index.htm page.
c. Delete the current navigation bar and paste the new navigation bar on the home page.
d. Modify the ask element on the navigation bar to remove the checkmark from the Show "Down Image" Initially check box, in the Modify Navigation Bar dialog box.
e. Modify the home element on the navigation bar so that it shows the down state initially, by placing a checkmark in the Show "Down Image" Initially check box.
f. Save the page and test the links in your browser.
g. Copy the navigation bar to the plants.htm page and the tips.htm page, making the necessary modifications.

8. Manage Web site links.
a. Use the Check Links Sitewide command to view broken links, external links, and orphaned files.
b. Refresh the Site list in the Site window if you see broken links or orphaned files.
c. View the external links in the Assets panel.
d. Save the file and Exit (Win) or Quit (Mac) Dreamweaver.

Important: *If you did not create the following Web sites in Unit B and maintain them during the preceding units, you will need to create a root folder for the Web sites in the following exercises and define the Web sites using files your instructor will provide. See the "Read This Before You Begin" section for more detailed instructions.*

► Independent Challenge 1

Your company has been creating a Web site for Jacob's, a new restaurant located in the theater district in New York City. This is an upscale restaurant catering to business executives and theater patrons. They have an extensive menu including prix fixe dinners, pre-theater dinner specials, and after-theater specials. Chef Jacob has sent you a copy of this month's featured pre-theater dinner to place on the Web site. He has included some links to New York theater reviews to add interest to the page.

a. Start Dreamweaver and open the Jacob's Web site from the location where your Project Files are stored.
b. Open dmf_3.htm from the drive and folder where your Project Files are stored.
c. Save the file as *pre_theater.htm*, overwriting the existing file.
d. Verify that the Jacob's logo path is set correctly to the assets folder in the Src text box of the Property Inspector. (*Hint:* Images and internal links that display a broken link or an absolute path (extra characters, such as forward slashes and colons), can be fixed by selecting the graphic or the link, then clicking the Browse for File icon on the Property Inspector. Images should be saved in the assets folder overwriting the existing file, if necessary. For links, double-click the filename in the root folder, overwriting the existing file.)

e. Select the prix fixe tasting menus text in the fifth sentence of the first paragraph and link it to the prix_fix.htm page.
f. Select the Playbill on Line text and link it to *http://www1.playbill.com.*
g. Select the NYC Tourist text and link it to *http://www.nyctourist.com.*
h. Select the newyorktoday.com text and link it to *http://www.nytoday.com/theaterdance.*
i. Select the New York Theatre Experience text and link it to *http://www.botz.com/nytheatre/.*
j. Save the file and check for broken links and orphaned files.
k. Design a navigation bar, using either text or graphics, and place it on each completed page of the Web site. The navigation bar should include links to Home, Pre-theater Offerings, Prix Fixe Menu, After-Theater Desserts, and Recipes.

Independent Challenge 2

Rapids Transit is a river expedition company. They are located on the Buffalo River in Northwest Arkansas. In addition to renting canoes, kayaks, and rafts, they have a country store and snack bar. River guides are available if requested by clients to accompany them on float trips. The clients range from high-school and college students to families to vacationing professionals. Mike Andrew, the owner of Rapids Transit, has asked you to create a new page for the Web site that lists helpful links for his customers.

a. Start Dreamweaver and open the Rapids Transit Web site from the drive and folder where your Project Files are stored.
b. Open dmf_4.htm in the Unit F folder from the drive and folder where your Project Files are stored.
c. Save dmf_4 as *before.htm*. You'll need to save the buffalo_fall.gif file on the page in your assets folder of the Rapids Transit Web site.
d. Create the following links:

Buffalo National River in the Arkansas Ozarks:	*http://www.ozarkmtns.com/buffalo*
Map of the Buffalo National River:	*http://www.ozarkmtns.com/buffalo/buffmap.html*
Arkansas Game and Fish Commission:	*http://www.agfc.com*
Arkansas, the Natural State:	*http://www.arkansas.com*
Buffalo River Floater's Guide:	*http://www.ozarkmtns.com/buffalo/bfg.html*

e. Drag the home.swf button from the Assets panel below the list of links.
f. Design a navigation bar, using either text or graphics, and place it on each completed page of the Web site. The navigation bar should include links to Home, Our Guides, Equipment Rentals, Country Store, and Before You Go.
g. Save the file and test all links in your browser.

 Independent Challenge 3

John Wesley is a golf pro who tours nationally and offers private lessons at a resort golf course. He endorses a line of golf equipment and occasionally provides commentary for golf tournaments. He is learning Dreamweaver to be able to create a Web site for his company, Wesley Enterprises. He is having difficulty with a broken link in his Web site. He has also noticed two orphaned files. Use scrap paper or your word-processing software to answer the questions below.

a. What could have caused the broken link?
b. Explain a probable reason for the two orphaned files in his Web site.
c. How can he correct the orphaned files?

 Independent Challenge 4

Dr. Elaine Collins' patients often ask her questions about the current treatment protocol for Parkinson's disease. Parkinson's disease is a debilitating neurological disease. She would like to post some helpful links in her clinic Web site to use to inform her patients.

a. Connect to the Internet and go to your favorite search engine, for example Google at *www.google.com.*
b. Type in keywords that would help you find Web sites that have helpful medical information about Parkinson's disease.
c. List at least five helpful links that Dr. Collins should consider for her site, including the National Parkinson Foundation. Use scrap paper or your word-processing software to record your links.

 Independent Challenge 5

Jon Moseley, the dive master at the Over Under Dive Shop in Nevis, West Indies, would like you to create a navigation bar for his Web site that includes both images and text. He asks you to look at a navigation bar he saw in a competitor's Web site. He likes the look of it and wants something similar but warns you not to violate copyright laws by copying it. Use scrap paper or your word-processing software to answer the questions below.

a. Connect to the Internet and go Scuba Safaris Web site at *www.divenevis.com/* to view the navigation bar.
b. What do you like about the navigation bar?
c. What do you dislike about the navigation bar?
d. How would you describe the quality of the site? Excellent? Good? Fair? Poor? Defend your answer.
e. Why do you think the navigation bar was repeated as plain text links at the bottom of the page?
f. Do you see any copyright information on the page?
g. Print the source code and find the code for the first navigation bar. How do you think it was created?
h. Create either a text navigation bar or a navigation bar object for all completed pages of the Web site.
i. Save the files and test all links.

► Visual Workshop

Off Note is a music store specializing in classical, blues, rock, country, and jazz. They have asked you to create a Web page that will be used to list the GRAMMY Award nominees and winners for this year. Open the Off Note Web site and create a page called grammy.htm that looks like the page in Figure F-24. (If you have not maintained this web site from the previous unit, then contact your instructor for assistance.) You will need to create a new page called categories.htm to use with the Music Categories link on the navigation bar.

FIGURE F-24

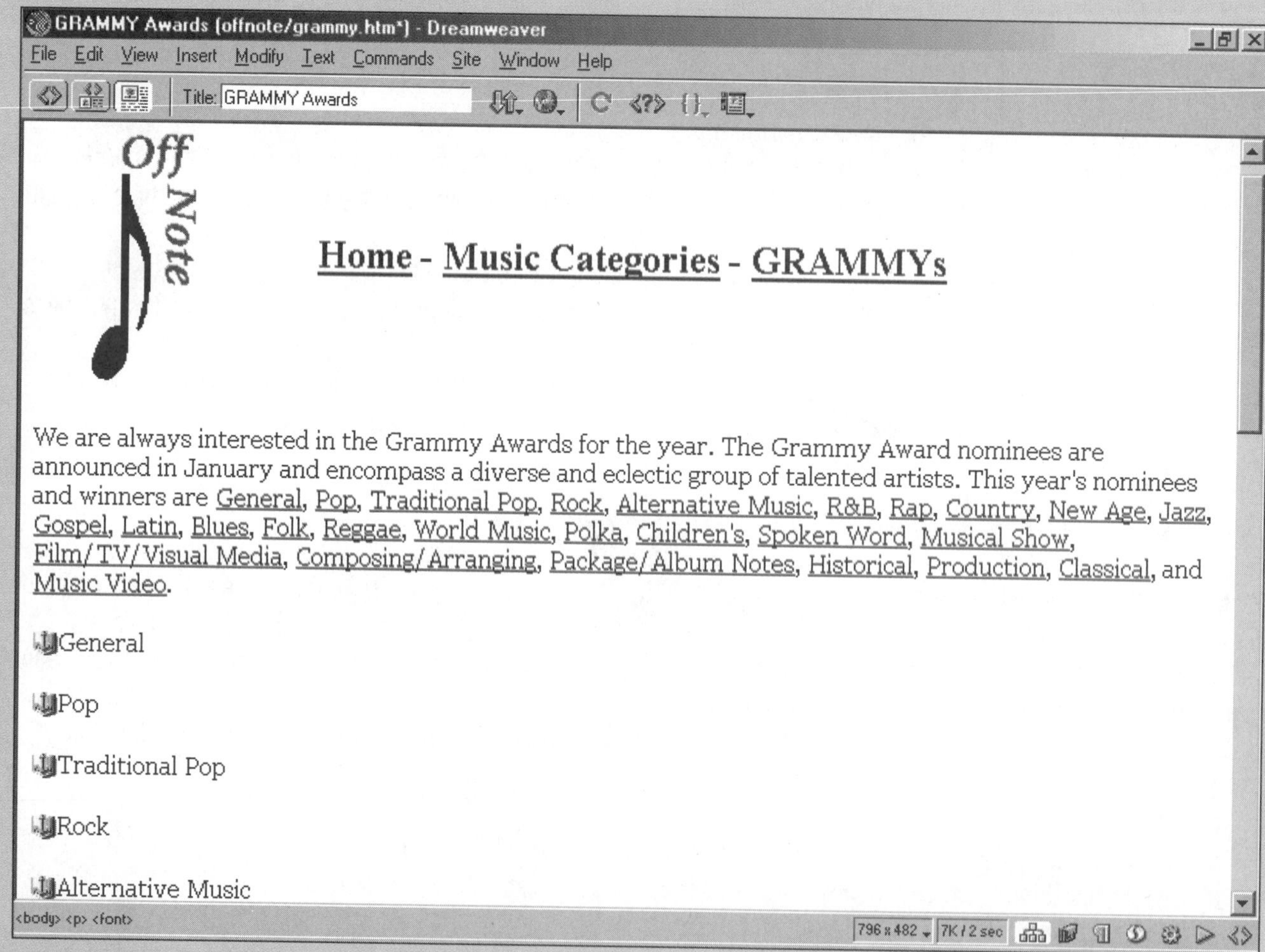

Working with Tables

Objectives

- Understand table views
- Create a table
- Resize rows and columns
- Insert and align graphics in table cells
- Split and merge cells
- Insert text
- Format cell content
- Insert and delete a row

You have learned how to place elements on a page, align them, and enhance them through various formatting options. **Tables** are placeholders made up of small boxes called **cells**, where text and graphics are inserted. Cells are arranged horizontally in **rows**, and vertically in **columns**. Using tables on a Web page gives you total control over the placement of each object on the page. In this unit you will learn how to create and format tables, work with table rows and columns, and format the contents of table cells.

The vice president of catalog sales, Betty Pipkin, has asked you to create a new page for the Trip Smart Web site, featuring new travel accessories. She would like the page to include pictures and descriptions of the items, and price information. You decide to use tables to lay out the information on the new page.

Dreamweaver 4

Understanding Table Views

There are two ways to create a table in Dreamweaver. You can use the Insert Table icon on the Objects panel, or draw your own table using tools on the Objects panel. Each method for creating a table requires a specific view. **Standard View** is the view that is used when you insert a table using the Insert Table icon. **Layout View** is required when you draw your own table. Layout View shows only the cells you create, then generates a table on the page. You can choose the view that you want by clicking the Standard View icon or the Layout View icon on the Objects panel, as shown in Figure G-1. It is common to switch between both views as you work with tables in Dreamweaver. You review both methods for creating tables using the Standard and Layout Views, so that you can pick the most appropriate method for creating your table.

Details

- **Creating a table in Standard View**
  Standard View is the view you have been using for page layout up to this point. Creating a table in Standard View is useful when you want to create a table with a specific number of columns and rows. To create a table in Standard View, you click the Insert Table icon on the Objects panel, as shown in Figure G-1. The Insert Table dialog box opens, and allows you to enter values for the number of rows and columns, the border size, table width, cell padding, and cell spacing. The **border** is the outline or frame around the table and the individual cells. It is expressed in pixels. The **width** refers to the width of the table. The width is expressed either in pixels or as a percent. When expressed as a percent, the table width will adjust to the width of the browser window. When expressed in pixels, the table width does not change, regardless of the size of the browser window. **Cell padding** is the distance between the cell content and the cell walls, the lines inside the cell borders. **Cell spacing** is the distance between cells. Figure G-1 shows an example of a table created in Standard View.

- **Drawing a table in Layout View**
  Layout View is the view that you use when you want to draw your own table. Layout View is a good choice when you know where you want to place page elements on a Web page, and do not need a specific number of rows and columns. You can use the Draw Layout Cell or the Draw Layout Table icons on the Objects panel to draw a cell or a table. You do not have to draw a table before you can draw an individual cell, because Dreamweaver will plot a table for you automatically after you draw your first cell. You may experience a decrease in your computer's processing speed if there are a large number of cells drawn on a page. Figure G-2 shows an example of a table created in Layout View.

FIGURE G-1: Table created in Standard View

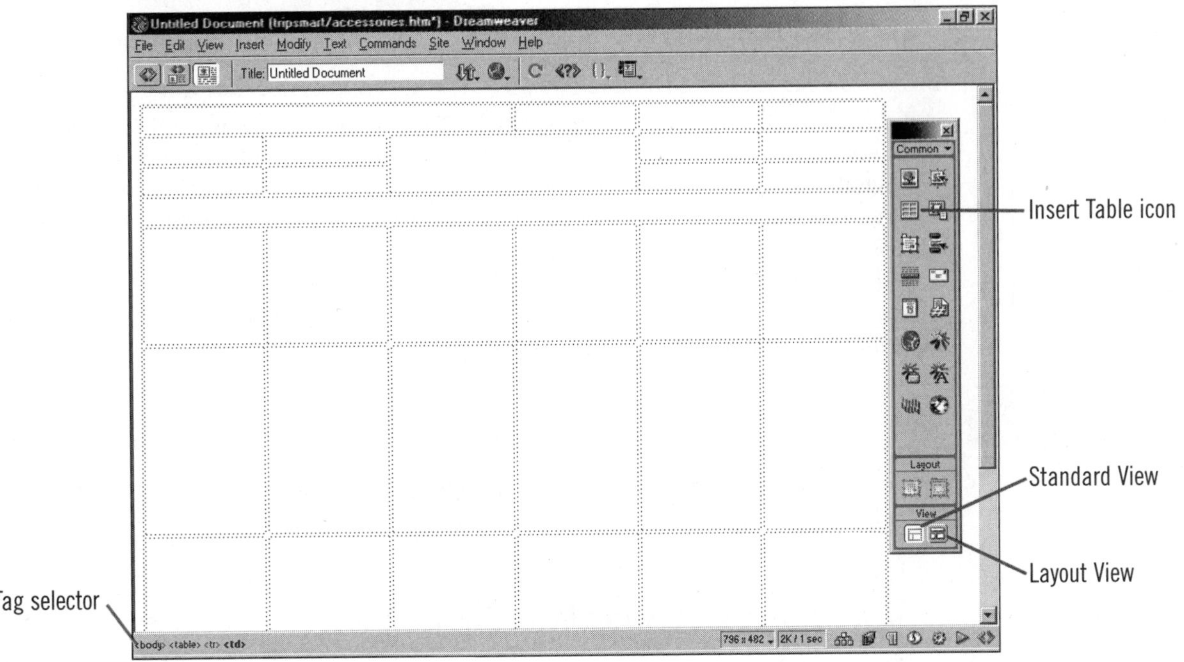

FIGURE G-2: Table created in Layout View

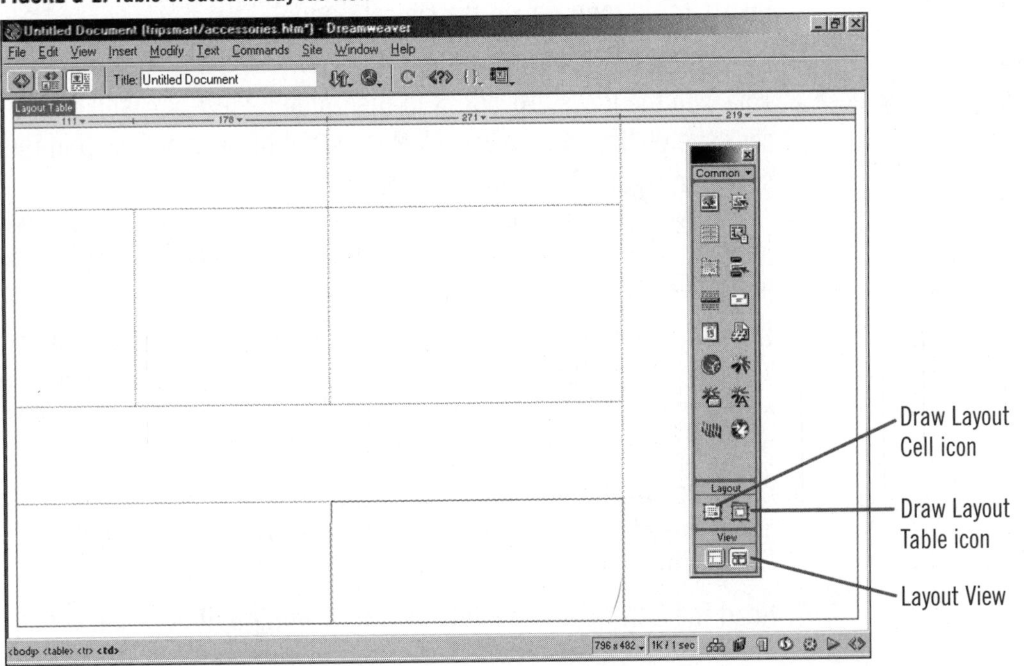

HTML table tags

When formatting a table, it is important to understand the basic HTML table tags. The tags used for creating a table are **<table></table>**. The tags used to create table rows are **<tr></tr>**. The tags used to create table cells are **<td></td>**. Dreamweaver places the   code into each empty table cell at the time it is created. The   code represents a nonbreaking space. A **nonbreaking space** is a space that will be left on the page by a browser. Some browsers will collapse an empty cell, which can ruin the look of a table. The nonbreaking space will hold the cell until content is placed in it, at which time the nonbreaking space will be automatically removed.

Dreamweaver 4

Creating a Table

Before you begin creating a table in either view, it is imperative that you plan in advance where you want the table to be placed on the Web page and how you want it to look. If you plan to insert graphics into a table, you should know exactly where you want them to appear on the page. Having an overall plan before you begin will save you a lot of time. You should also consider whether you want the table borders and the cell walls to appear in the browser window. You can make a table "invisible" by setting the border value to zero. Thus, the viewer will never know that a table was used for the page layout. After consulting with Betty, you sketch your ideas for the new accessories page in the TripSmart catalog, as shown in Figure G-3. You then insert a table, using the Insert Table icon on the Objects panel.

1. Open the TripSmart Web site, click the **Show Site icon** to switch to the Site window, then double-click **accessories.htm** to open it in Design View
   The accessories page needs a descriptive title.
2. Type **Featured Accessories** in the Title text box of the accessories page.
3. Show the Objects panel and the Property Inspector, if necessary, expand the Property Inspector by clicking the small arrow in the lower-right corner of it, then click the **Insert Table icon** on the Objects panel
   The Insert Table dialog box opens.
4. Type **3** in the Rows text box, **3** in the Columns text box, and **100** in the Width text box, click the **Width list arrow**, click **Percent**, if necessary, type **0** in the Border text box, as shown in Figure G-4, then click **OK**
   A table with three rows and three columns is placed on the page. The Property Inspector displays the table settings that you entered in the Insert Table dialog box. You can make changes to the table by changing the values in the Property Inspector.
5. Click the **Align list arrow**, then click **Center** to center the table on the page
   The table shifts slightly and is now centered on the page. Since the width has been set using a percent instead of pixels, and the table has been center-aligned, it will appear in proportion and centered position in all browser window sizes.
6. Click the **Layout View icon** on the Objects panel
   The Getting Started in Layout View window may open. It includes instructions on creating and editing a table in Layout View.
7. Read the Getting Started in Layout View window, if necessary, then click **OK** to close it
   The table appears in Layout View, as shown in Figure G-5. The Property Inspector now displays the properties for tables shown in Layout View. The **Autostretch** option in the Property Inspector means that the table will "stretch" to fit the browser window, since the table width was set as a percent.
8. Click the **Standard View icon** on the Objects panel to return to Standard View, then save your work
   The table is displayed in Standard View. As content is placed into the table cells, the table will expand on the page.

Trouble?

If the Insert Table icon is not available, click the Standard View icon on the Objects panel.

Trouble?

The Property Inspector will not display information about the table if it is not selected. To select a table, move the pointer slowly to the edge of the table until you see the pointer change to a four-sided arrow, then click the table border.

FIGURE G-3: Sketch of a table on the accessories page

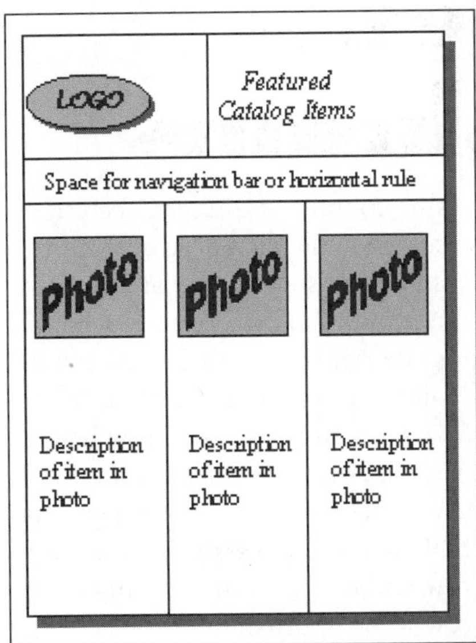

FIGURE G-4: Insert Table dialog box

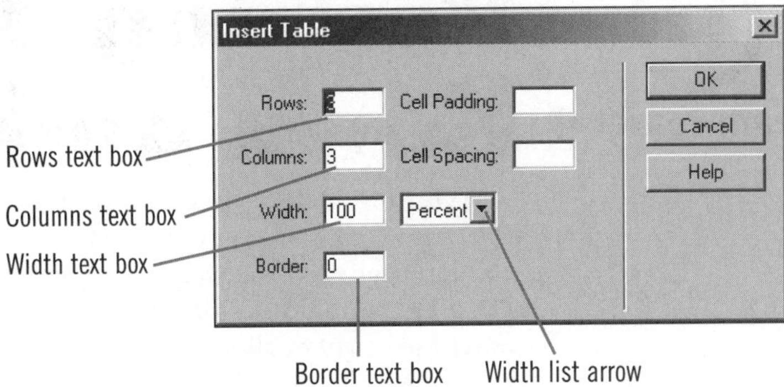

FIGURE G-5: Table in Layout View

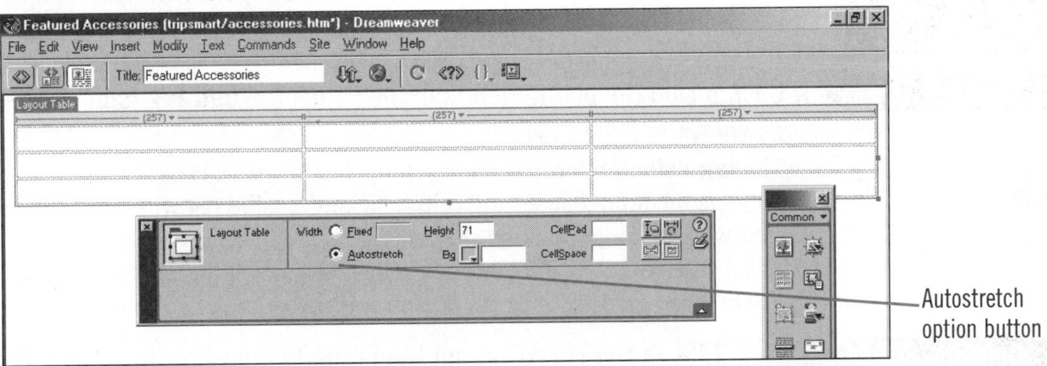

Options for selecting a table in Dreamweaver

There are several ways to select a table in Dreamweaver. First, you can click the insertion point in the table, click Modify on the menu bar, point to Table, then click Select Table. Second, you can click the insertion point in the table, click Edit on the menu bar, then click Select All or use the quick keys for Select All: [Ctrl][A] (Win) or [command][A] (Mac). Third, you can select a table by clicking the table border when the pointer changes to a four-sided arrow ✥. Finally, you can click the table tag <table> on the tag selector.

Setting table and cell widths

If you use a table for positioning text and graphics on an entire Web page, it is wise to set the width of the table as a percent of the browser window. The table will resize itself proportionately if the browser window size is changed. If you set the width of a table using pixels, the table will remain one size, regardless of the browser window size. It is difficult to create a table that covers the entire browser window, because of page margin issues; however, if you want the table to cover most of the browser window, set its width to 100% and enter 0 in the Border text box. You should also set each cell width as a percent of the table if you want the columns to keep their original proportion in the table when viewed in different window sizes. Sometimes this is not possible because a cell may require a specific width to fully display contents such as a large graphic. In these situations, it is fine to set the width to pixels, using the Property Inspector.

Dreamweaver 4

Resizing Tables, Rows, and Columns

After creating a table, you can resize the table and its rows or columns manually. To resize a table, a row, or a column proportionately, you must first select the table, then drag one of three selection handles. If you want to change all of the columns in a table so that they are the same size, drag the middle-right selection handle. Dragging the middle-bottom selection handle resizes the height of all rows simultaneously, while dragging the right-corner selection handle resizes the entire table. To resize a row or column individually, you drag the interior cell borders up, down, to the left, or to the right. You can also resize column widths and row heights using the W and H text boxes on the Property Inspector. Cell sizes can be resized using pixels or a percent as a measurement. Cells resized as a percent will maintain that percent in relationship to the width or height of the entire table, if the table is resized. You want to make sure that the contents of the three cells in the last row will be distributed evenly across the table. You set the width of the three cells in the last row to be approximately 33% of the table width. It is a good idea to set the cell widths before you enter data, because the widths will shift as the data is entered if you do not. You also experiment with resizing a row height.

Steps

QuickTip

To select the table, click the table tag on the tag selector <table>.

1. **Click inside the bottom left cell, then click the cell tag icon on the tag selector <td>, as shown in Figure G-6**

   The **tag selector**, located on the status bar, displays HTML tags for the various page components including tables and cells. Clicking a table tag will select the table element associated with that tag. Clicking the cell tag icon will select the corresponding cell in the table. This is the HTML tag for that cell. The cell is now selected with a dark border surrounding it. The Property Inspector displays properties of the selected cell.

QuickTip

Type the % sign next to a number you want expressed as a percent. Otherwise, it will be expressed in pixels.

2. **Type 33% in the W text box on the Property Inspector to change the width of the cell to 33% of the table width, then press [Tab]**

   The cell width is set to 33%. Now, as content is added to the table, you can be sure that each column will remain 33% of the width of the table.

3. **Repeat Steps 1 and 2 for the next two cells in the last row, using 33% for the middle cell and 34% for the last cell**

   The combined widths of the three cells now add up to 100%. Now you experiment with changing the row height of the first row.

QuickTip

The height of a row automatically increases to accommodate the height of the contents placed in it.

4. **Click inside one of the cells to deselect the last selected cell, place the pointer over the bottom row border of the first row until the pointer changes to a resizing pointer ÷, as shown in Figure G-7, then click-and-drag ÷ downward to slightly increase the height of the row**

   The color of the border becomes darker once you select it and drag it. You undo the row size, using the History panel.

5. **Click Window on the menu bar, click History, then drag the slider in the History panel up, to undo the Set Height command**

   The row returns to the original height.

6. **Save the file**

   You realize how easy it is to resize table rows and columns.

FIGURE G-6: Selecting a cell

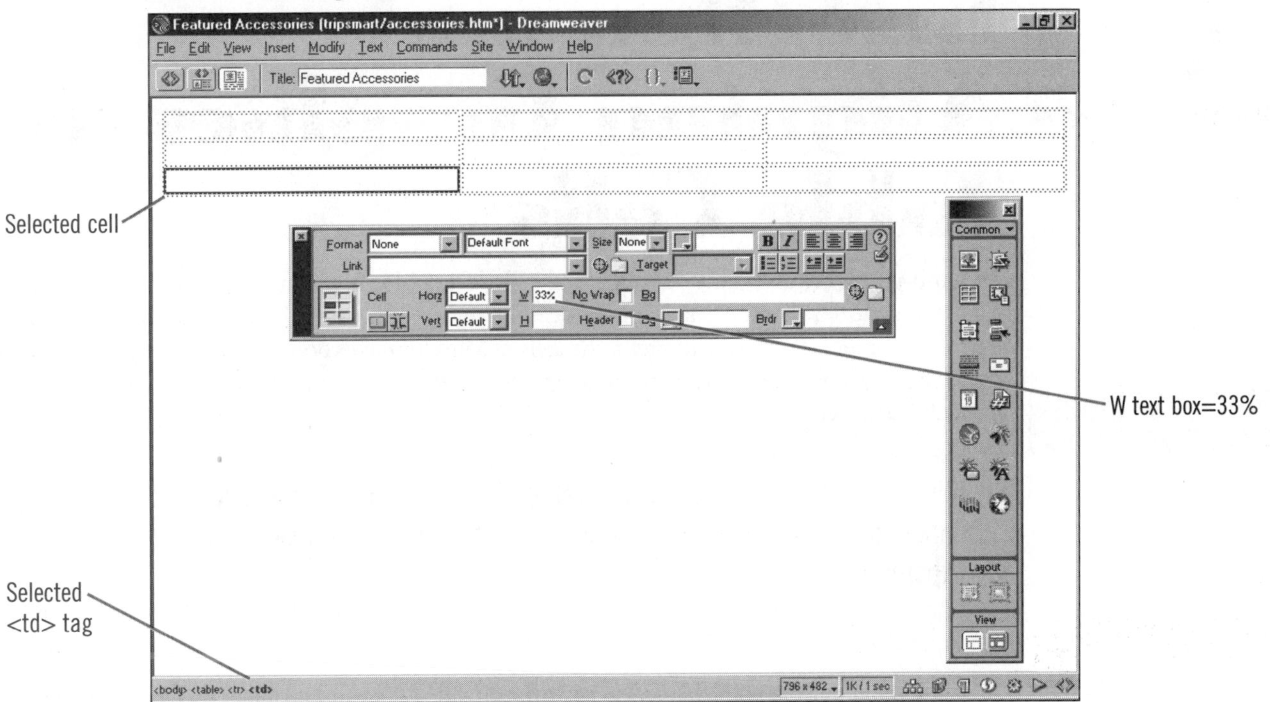

FIGURE G-7: Resizing the height of a row

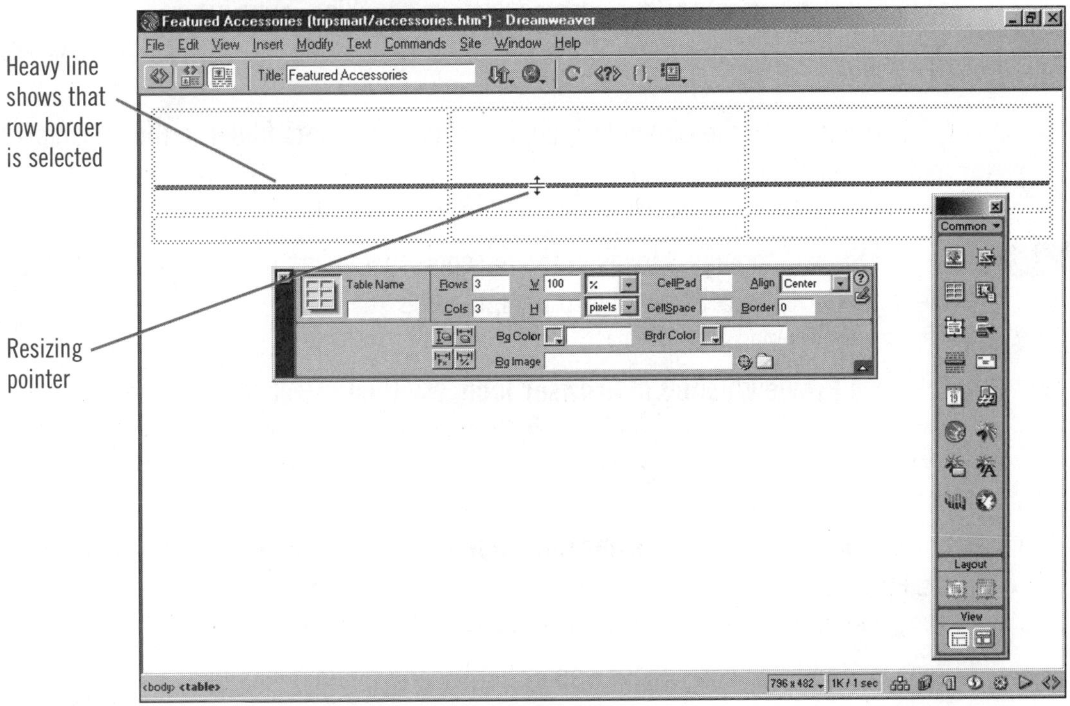

Resetting table widths and heights

After resizing columns and rows in a table, you may want to return your table to the original column and row sizes. To reset columns and rows to their original widths and heights, you can click Modify on the menu bar, point to Table, then click Clear Cell Heights or Clear Cell Widths. You can also use this feature to tighten up any extra white space in a cell. Using the Clear Cell Heights command will force the cell border to snap to the bottom of the inserted graphic.

Dreamweaver 4

Dreamweaver 4

Inserting and Aligning Graphics in Table Cells

Text and graphics can be inserted into the cells of a table. Text can be typed directly in cells or copied and pasted into the cells. Graphics can be inserted by using the Objects panel or the Insert menu. As content is added to the cells, the cells expand to make room for the content. You insert the TripSmart logo and three catalog images into the table on the accessories page, then center each image within its cell.

1. Click the insertion point in the **top-left cell**, click the **Insert Image icon** on the Objects panel, double-click the **assets** folder in the tripsmart root folder, then double-click **tripsmart.gif**
   The TripSmart logo is placed in the top-left cell of the table. Notice how the cell has expanded to adjust to the height of the image.
2. Click the insertion point in the **lower-left cell**, click on the Objects panel, click the drive and folder where your Project Files are stored for Unit G, double-click the **Unit G folder**, double-click the **assets folder**, then double-click **packing_cube.jpg**
   A message appears, asking you if you want to copy the packing_cube.jpg file to your Web site. You want to place this file in your assets folder.
3. Click **Yes** to close the dialog box, double-click the **assets** folder in the tripsmart root folder, then click **Save**
   The image is placed in the cell and is saved in the assets folder of the Web site.
4. Repeat Steps 1 through 3 to insert the passport_holder.jpg file and the headphones.jpg file in the next two cells, as shown in Figure G-8
   The images are placed on the page and saved in the assets folder.
5. Click the **Preview/Debug in Browser icon**, then select your browser
   The accessories page is displayed in the browser window. The images are not distributed evenly on the page. Your next step is to horizontally center each image in the cell it occupies, to improve the spacing.
6. Close your browser, click the **packing cube image**, then click the **Align Center icon** on the Property Inspector
   The packing cube image is horizontally centered in the cell it occupies.
7. Repeat Step 6 to center the passport holder and headphones images
   Each image is horizontally centered in its respective cell. See Figure G-9.
8. Preview the page in your browser, then close the browser window
   The images look much better centered in their cells.

QuickTip

You can press [Tab] to move your insertion point to the next cell in a row and press [Shift][Tab] to move your insertion point to the previous cell.

CLUES TO USE

Vertically aligning cell contents

The contents of a cell can be aligned both horizontally and vertically. When you vertically align an object in a cell, your choices are to place the object at the top, middle, or bottom of the cell. To vertically align a graphic, click the division tag <div> on the tag selector, click the Vert list arrow on the Property Inspector, then choose a type of alignment. See Figure G-10.

FIGURE G-8: Graphics inserted into table cells

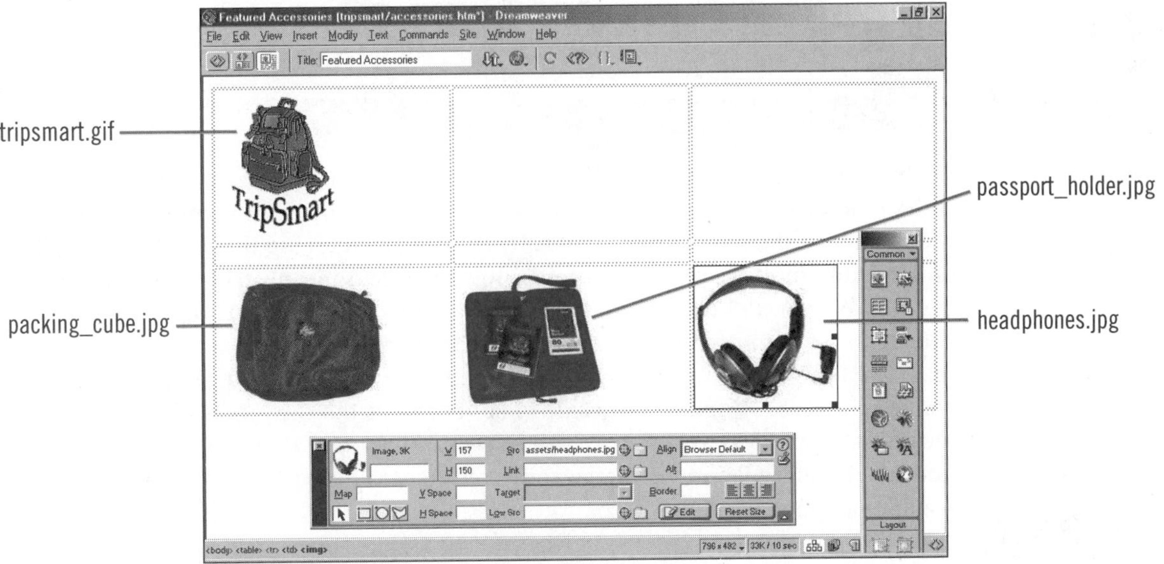

FIGURE G-9: Centering images in a cells

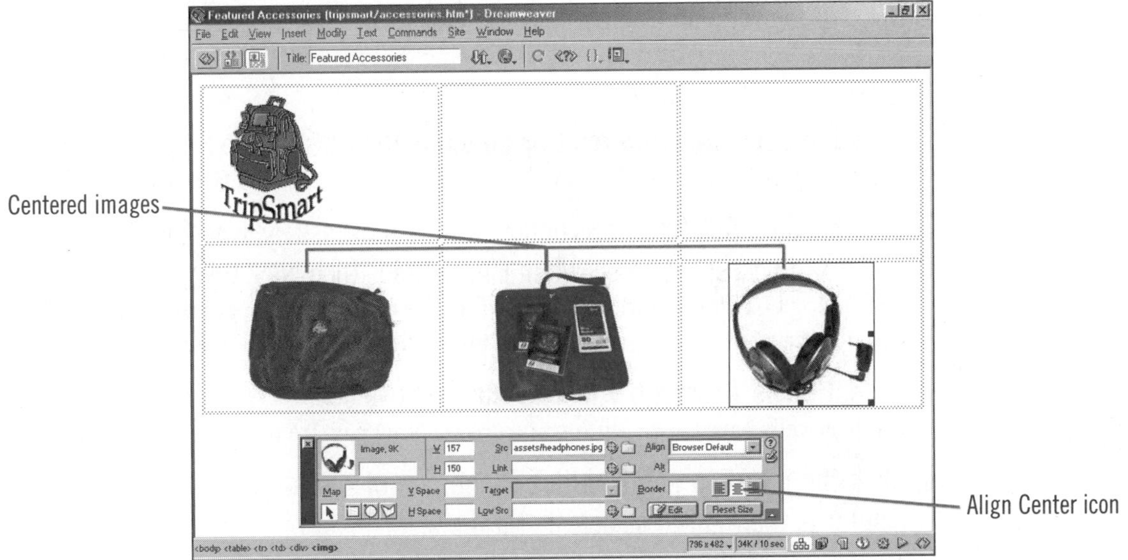

FIGURE G-10: Vertically aligning cell contents

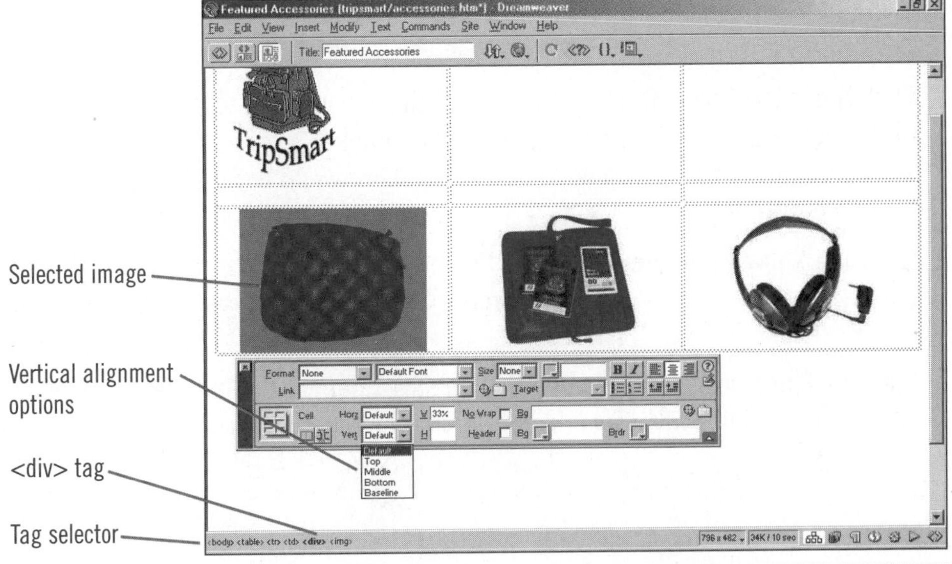

Dreamweaver 4

Splitting and Merging Cells

A table created using the Insert Table command on the Objects panel or menu bar is created with evenly spaced columns and rows. In addition to resizing the columns and rows, you may need to adjust the cells in such a table by splitting or merging them. To **split** a cell means to divide it into multiple rows or columns. To **merge** cells means to combine multiple cells into one cell. When cells are merged, the HTML tag used to describe them changes from a width size tag to a column span or row span tag. For example, <td colspan="2"> refers to two cells that have been merged into one cell that spans two columns. You can split merged cells and merge split cells. You decide to split each of the three cells that contain the catalog images into two rows, one row for the image, and another that you'll use to enter a description of the image. You also merge some cells, anticipating that you'll need room for large graphics and text blocks.

Steps

1. Click inside the **bottom-left cell** to the left of the packing cubes graphic, then press the **cell tag icon** on the tag selector <td>
   A black border surrounds the cell, indicating that the cell is selected. The entire cell must be selected in order to split it.
2. Click the **Splits cell into rows or columns icon** on the Property Inspector
   The Split Cell dialog box opens. You want to split the cell into two rows.
3. Click the **Split Cell Into Rows** option button, if necessary, type **2** in the Number of Rows text box, if necessary, as shown in Figure G-11, then click **OK**
   The dialog box closes, and the cell is split into two rows. The graphic occupies the top row, and a description of the packing cubes item will eventually be placed in the bottom row.
4. Repeat Steps 1 through 3 to split the next two cells
   All three cells have been split into two rows. Now you are ready to merge cells in your table.
5. Click the insertion point in the second cell of the top row, then click-and-drag the pointer to the right to select the third cell
   The second and third cells in the top row are selected so that they can be merged into one cell. This space is perfect for a large page heading.
6. Click the **Merges selected cells using spans icon** on the Property Inspector
   The two cells are merged into one cell, as shown in Figure G-12.
7. Click the insertion point in the first cell of the second row, click-and-drag the pointer to the right to select the next two cells, then click
   The entire row of cells is merged into one cell. This would be an ideal cell for a navigation bar or a horizontal rule.
8. Click the **Show Code View icon** to view the code for the split and merged cells
   Notice the table tags denoting the column span and the nonbreaking spaces inserted in the empty cells.
9. Click the **Show Design View icon**, then save changes to the accessories page
   Splitting and merging cells gives you more flexibility for inserting graphics or text into your table.

QuickTip

You can only merge cells that, together, form a rectangle.

FIGURE G-11: **Splitting a cell into two rows**

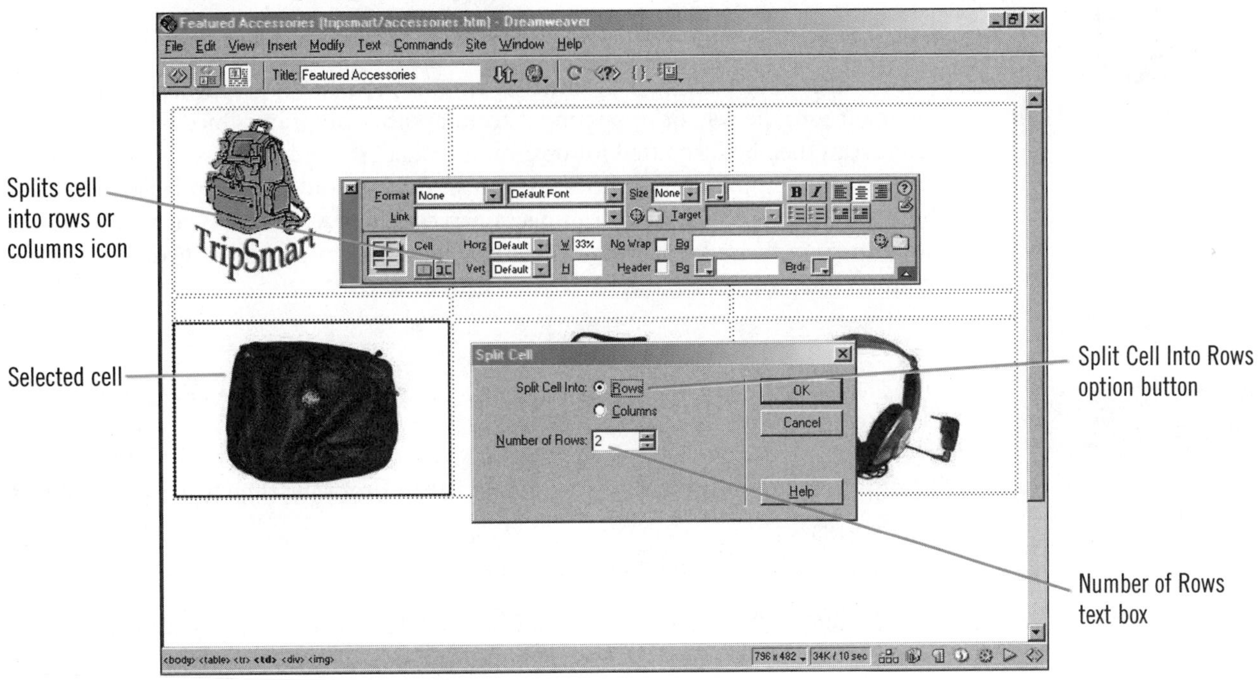

FIGURE G-12: **Merging selected cells into one cell**

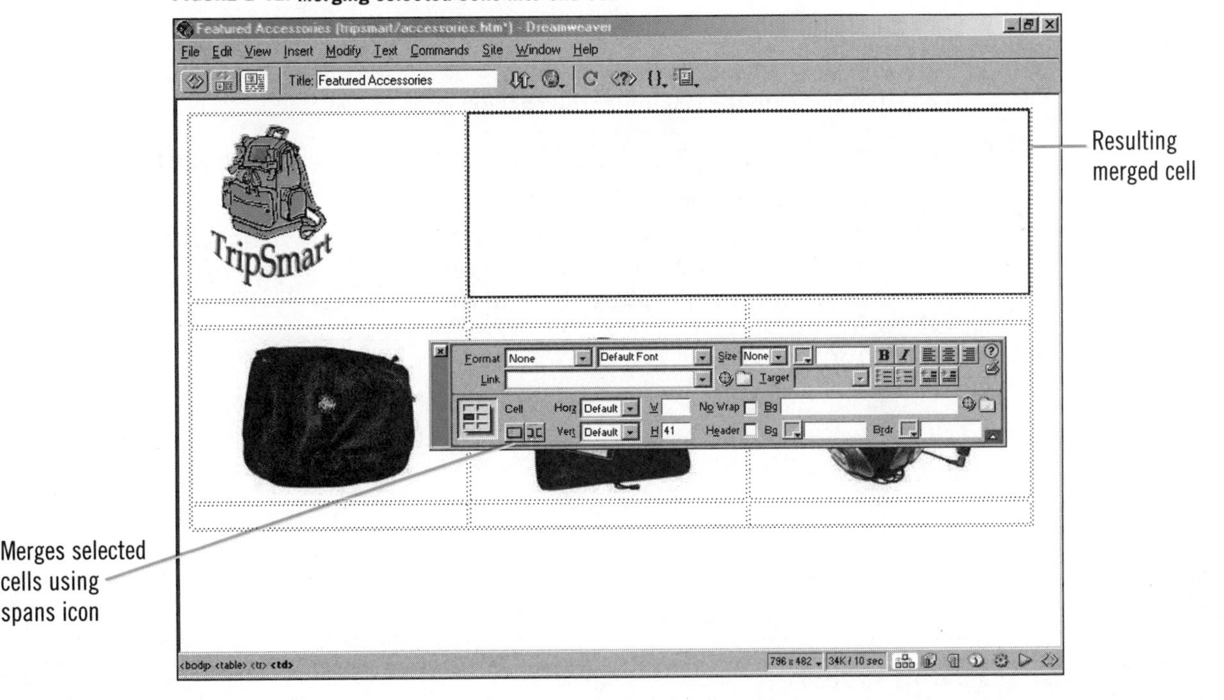

CLUES TO USE

Merging and splitting cells in Layout View

As you draw cells of different sizes in Layout View, you may not realize that you are merging and splitting cells as you draw them. Drawing cells of different sizes and shapes in Layout View generates different HTML code than splitting or merging cells. This is important to keep in mind if you are trying to resize cells in Standard View that were originally drawn in Layout View. If you are having problems formatting a table created in Layout View, check the HTML code to correct your problem.

Dreamweaver 4

Inserting Text

Text can be entered in table cells by either typing in the cell, copying it from another source and pasting it into the cell, or importing it from another program. Once the text is placed in the table, it can then be formatted for optimum readability and appearance on the Web page. If you import text from another program, you should use the Clean Up HTML or Clean Up Word HTML command to remove unnecessary code. You type a heading for the accessories page in the cell next to the TripSmart logo, then copy and paste descriptive text for each item on the page.

Steps

1. Click the insertion point in the **second cell in the first row**, then type **Featured Catalog Accessories**
   The text is placed in the cell to serve as a heading for the page.
2. Open **packing_cube.htm** from the Unit G folder where your Project Files are stored, click **Edit** on the menu bar, click **Select All**, click **Edit** on the menu bar, click **Copy**, then close packing_cubes.htm
   The text from the file is placed on the clipboard. You will paste it on the accessories page under the packing cube image.
3. Click the insertion point in the cell under the packing cube image, click **Edit** on the menu bar, then click **Paste**
   The text is placed in the cell under the packing cube image.
4. Repeat Steps 2 and 3 to paste the text from the passport_holder.htm and headphones.htm files in the cells under their respective images
   All three images now have descriptive text under them, as shown in Figure G-13.
   You like the placement of the text descriptions but not the formatting. You remember that text is always formatted *after* being placed in Dreamweaver.
5. Save your work

Using nested tables

Inserting another table inside a table is similar to adding a new row or column to a table. This is called a nested table. To create a nested table, click the insertion point inside the cell where you want the nested table to appear, click the Insert menu, then click Table or click the Insert Table icon on the Objects panel. The nested table is a separate table that can be formatted differently than the table it is placed in. Nested tables can be used effectively if you would like part of your table data to have visible borders and part to have invisible borders. For example, you can nest a table with red borders inside a table with invisible borders. Careful planning is important when you work with nested tables. It is easy to get carried away and have too many nested tables. You may be able to achieve the same results by adding rows and columns or splitting cells instead of inserting a nested table.

FIGURE G-13: Copying and pasting text into cells

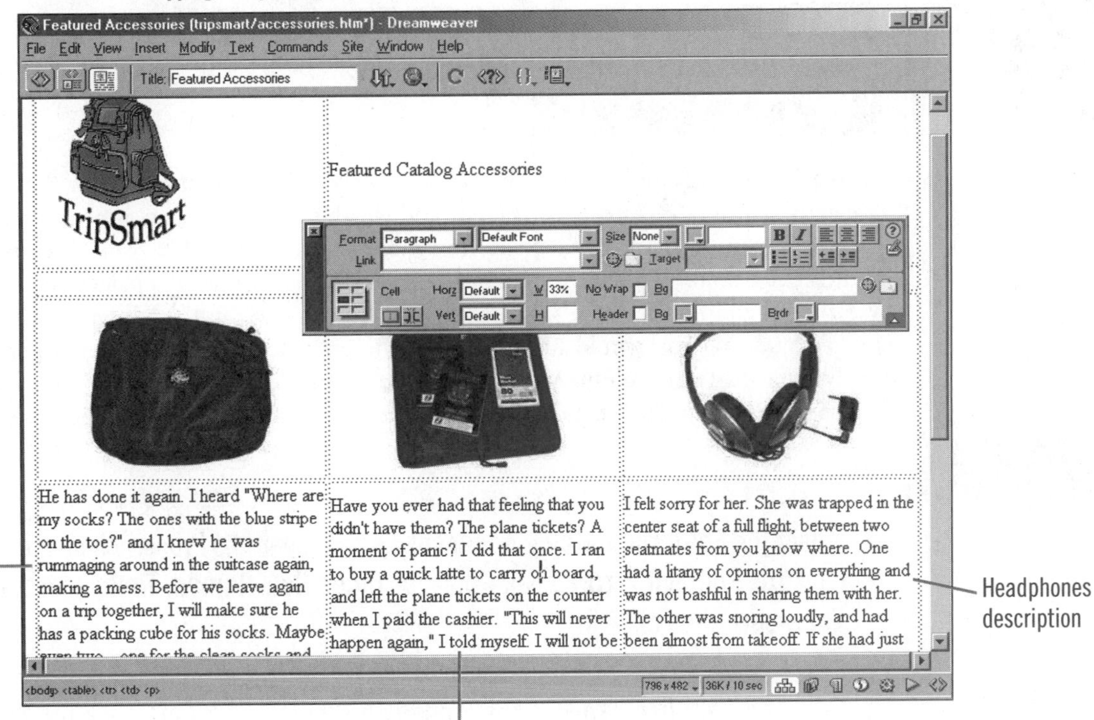

Importing and exporting tabular data

You can import and export tabular data into and out of Dreamweaver. **Tabular data** is data that is arranged in columns and rows and separated by a **delimiter**: a comma, tab, colon, semicolon, or similar character. **Importing** means to bring data created in another software program into Dreamweaver, and **exporting** means to save data that was created in Dreamweaver as a special file format. Files that are imported into Dreamweaver must be saved as delimited files. Programs such as Microsoft Word and Excel offer many file formats for saving files. To import a delimited file, you click File on the menu bar, point to Import, then click Import Tabular Data. The Import Table Data dialog box opens, offering you choices for the table that will appear on the Web page as a result. To export a table that you created in Dreamweaver, you click File on the menu bar, point to Export, then click Export Table. The Export Table dialog box opens, letting you choose the type of delimiter you want for the delimited file.

Dreamweaver 4

Dreamweaver 4

Formatting Cell Content

It is easier to modify and format a table and its contents in Standard View than it is in Layout View. In addition to resizing the height and width of cells, you can apply a background color or a background image to fill the entire table or individual cells. Border colors and border widths can also be applied to the table. You can format text that is placed in cells in Standard View by changing the font, size, or color of the text. Graphics placed in cells can also be resized. You would like to format the page heading by using a larger font size and applying a shade of the blue used in the TripSmart Web site to the text. You also format the descriptions of the three catalog items to give them a more uniform appearance.

Steps

1. Select the **Featured Catalog Accessories** text, open the Property Inspector if necessary, click the **Font list arrow**, click **Georgia**, **Times New Roman**, **Times**, **serif**, click the **Size list arrow**, then click **5**

   The text is now larger and formatted with a new font.

2. Click the **Horz list arrow** on the Property Inspector, click **Left**, click the **Vert list arrow**, then click **Middle**

   The text is now horizontally aligned to the left and vertically aligned to the middle of the cell, as shown in Figure G-14.

QuickTip

You can also change the color of text by selecting it, then dragging a color from the Assets panel on top of the text.

3. Make sure that Featured Catalog Accessories is still highlighted, open the Assets panel, if necessary, click the **Colors icon** on the Assets panel, then drag the color icon on top of the highlighted text

   Your screen should resemble Figure G-14.

4. Select the entire description of the packing cube image, click the **Horz list arrow** on the Property Inspector, click **Left**, click the **Vert list arrow** on the Property Inspector, then click **Top**

   The text jumps to the top of the cell and is left-aligned. Now you'll change the size and font of the text.

5. Click the **cell tag** <td> on the tag selector, click the **Font list arrow**, click **Georgia**, **Times New Roman**, **Times**, **serif**, click the **Size list arrow**, then click **3**

   You are happy with the new look of the text, so you apply the same formatting to the next two cells.

6. Repeat Steps 4 and 5 to format the text in the next two cells, using the same formatting applied to the first cell

   Your screen should resemble Figure G-15. After viewing the text descriptions, you decide to add some space between them.

7. Click the **table tag** <table> on the tag selector to select the entire table, type **12** in the CellSpace text box, as shown in Figure G-16, then press **[Enter]** (Win) or **[return]** (Mac)

   The descriptions are easier to read now because you have inserted a little white space between them.

8. Save your work, preview the accessories page in your browser window, then close your browser

   Formatting the text in the table cells makes the accessories page look more professional.

FIGURE G-14: Formatting text using the Property Inspector and the Assets panel

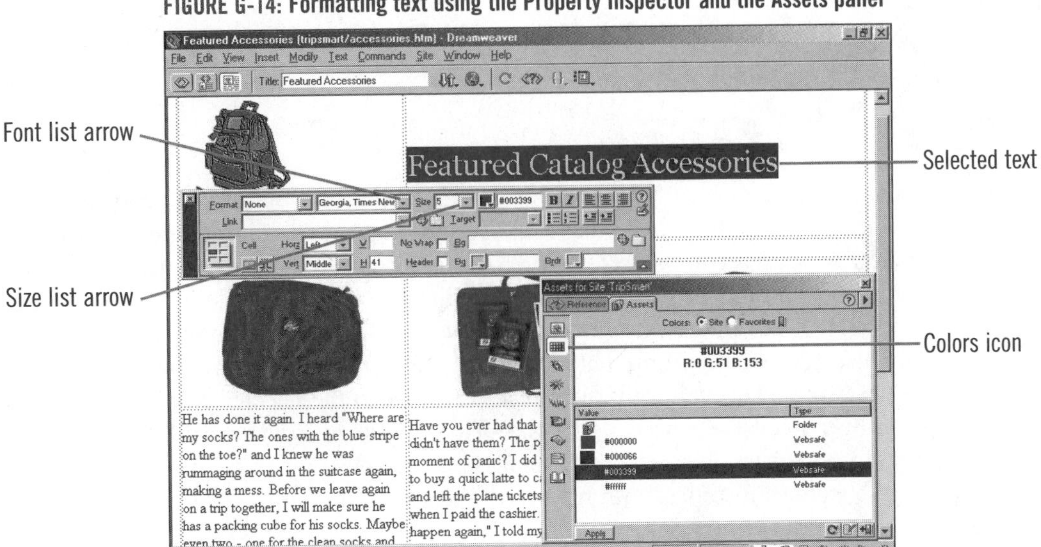

FIGURE G-15: Formatting catalog item descriptions

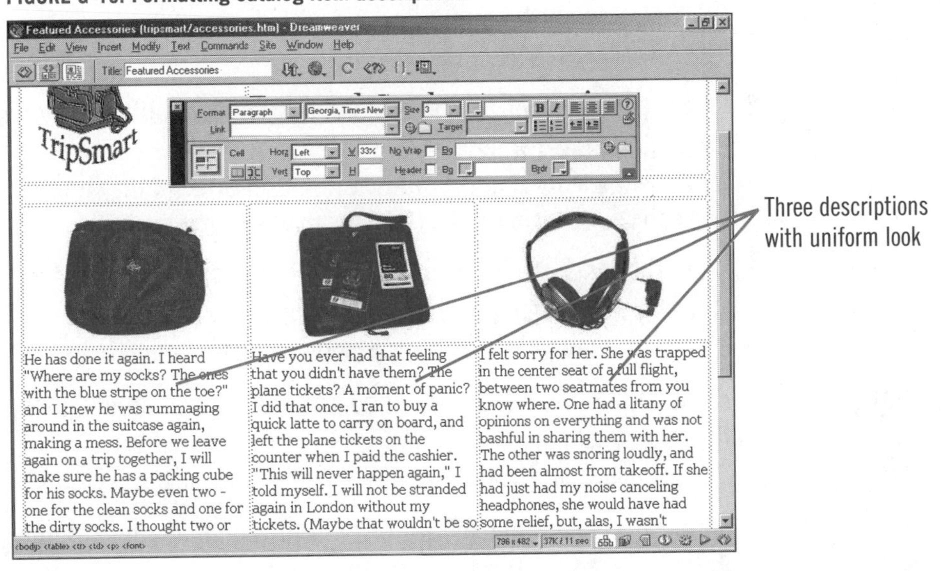

FIGURE G-16: Changing the CellSpace amount

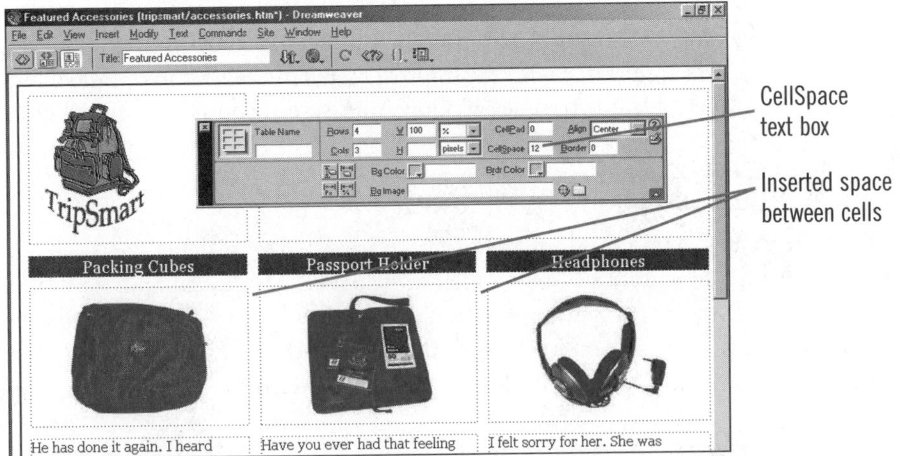

Dreamweaver 4

Dreamweaver 4

Deleting or Adding a Row

As you add new content to your table, you may find that you have too many rows or columns, or not enough rows or columns. You can add one row or column at a time or add several at once. The same is true when deleting rows or columns. You use commands under the Modify menu to add and delete table rows and columns. When you add a new column or row, you must first select an existing column or row that the new column or row will be adjacent to. The Insert Row or Column dialog box lets you choose how many rows or columns you want to insert and where you want them placed relative to the selected row or column. You no longer need the row beneath the TripSmart logo, so you delete it. You need to place descriptive names above the three images, so you select the row with the images, then insert a new row above it so that both rows have the same number of cells.

Steps

1. Position the pointer so that it is pointing to the second row, then when the pointer becomes an arrow ➡, click the pointer to select the row, as shown in Figure G-17
2. Click **Modify** on the menu bar, point to **Table**, then click **Delete Row**
   The row is deleted from the table.
3. Select the three cells in the second row, click **Modify** on the menu bar, point to **Table**, then click **Insert Row**
   A new row, identical to the one below it, is inserted in the table. When you insert a new row, it has the same formatting as the row that was first selected.
4. Click the insertion point in the first cell of the new row, type **Packing Cubes**, press **[Tab]**, type **Passport Holder**, press **[Tab]**, then type **Headphones**
   Three labels are placed in the cells above the images and help to identify the items.
5. Using Figure G-18 as a reference, format the text labels, using the settings shown on the Property Inspector
   The white text labels show up nicely against the blue background.
6. Scroll to the bottom of the page and select **Item number 20486**, then click the **Bold icon** **B** on the Property Inspector
7. Apply the bold style to the item numbers in the next two cells
   All three item numbers are bold, which make them easier to find quickly.
8. Save your work, then preview the accessories page in your browser
   You are pleased with the improvements in the Featured Catalog Accessories page as you preview it in the browser window. Your screen should resemble Figure G-19.

Trouble?

If the Delete Row menu option is not available, the row is not properly selected. Repeat Step 1 and try again.

QuickTip

You can also choose colors for the text using the Assets panel.

CLUES TO USE

Formatting cells and cell content

Contents in cells can be formatted using the Property Inspector. Formatting cells is not the same as formatting the contents inside them. You can format a cell by simply clicking the insertion point inside the cell that you want to format, then choosing options in the Property Inspector. For example, you can click a cell, then choose a fill color for the cell by clicking the Bg list arrow in the Property Inspector. Don't forget, you'll have to expand the Property Inspector to see these options. To format the contents of a cell, you must select the contents in the cell, not the cell itself. For example, to change the formatting of text in a cell, select all of the text, then format it as you wish.

FIGURE G-17: **Selected row**

Selected row
Click when pointer becomes an arrow
TripSmart
Vert
Default
H
Header
Bg
Brdr

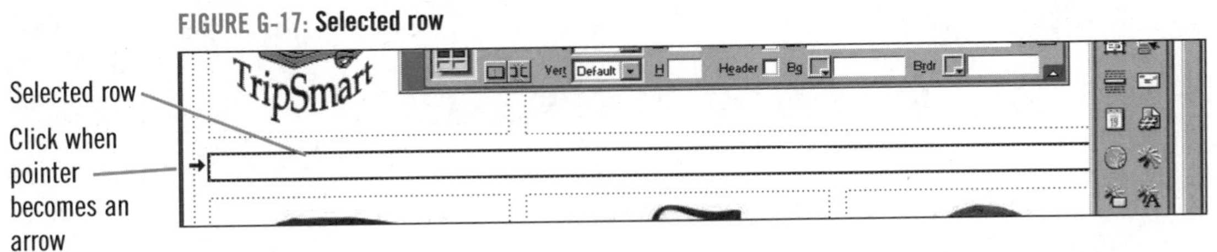

FIGURE G-18: **Formatted text labels**

Font=Georgia, Times New Roman, Times, serif
Highlighted text labels
Click to choose #FFFFFF as the text color
Alignment=Center
Size=4
Click to choose #003399 as the background
Format
None
Georgia, Times New
Size
4
#FFFFFF
Link
Target
Row
Horz
Default
W
No Wrap
Bg
Vert
Default
H
Header
Bg
#003399
Brdr
TripSmart
Packing Cubes
Passport Holder
Headphones

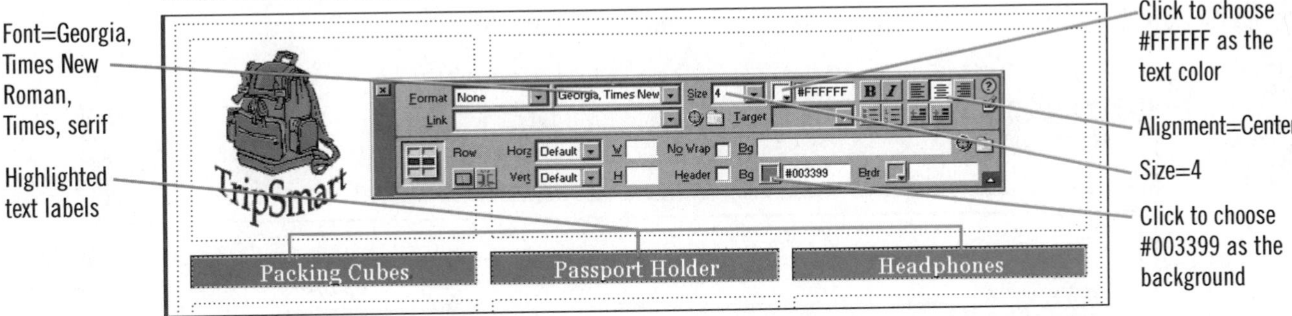

FIGURE G-19: **The finished project**

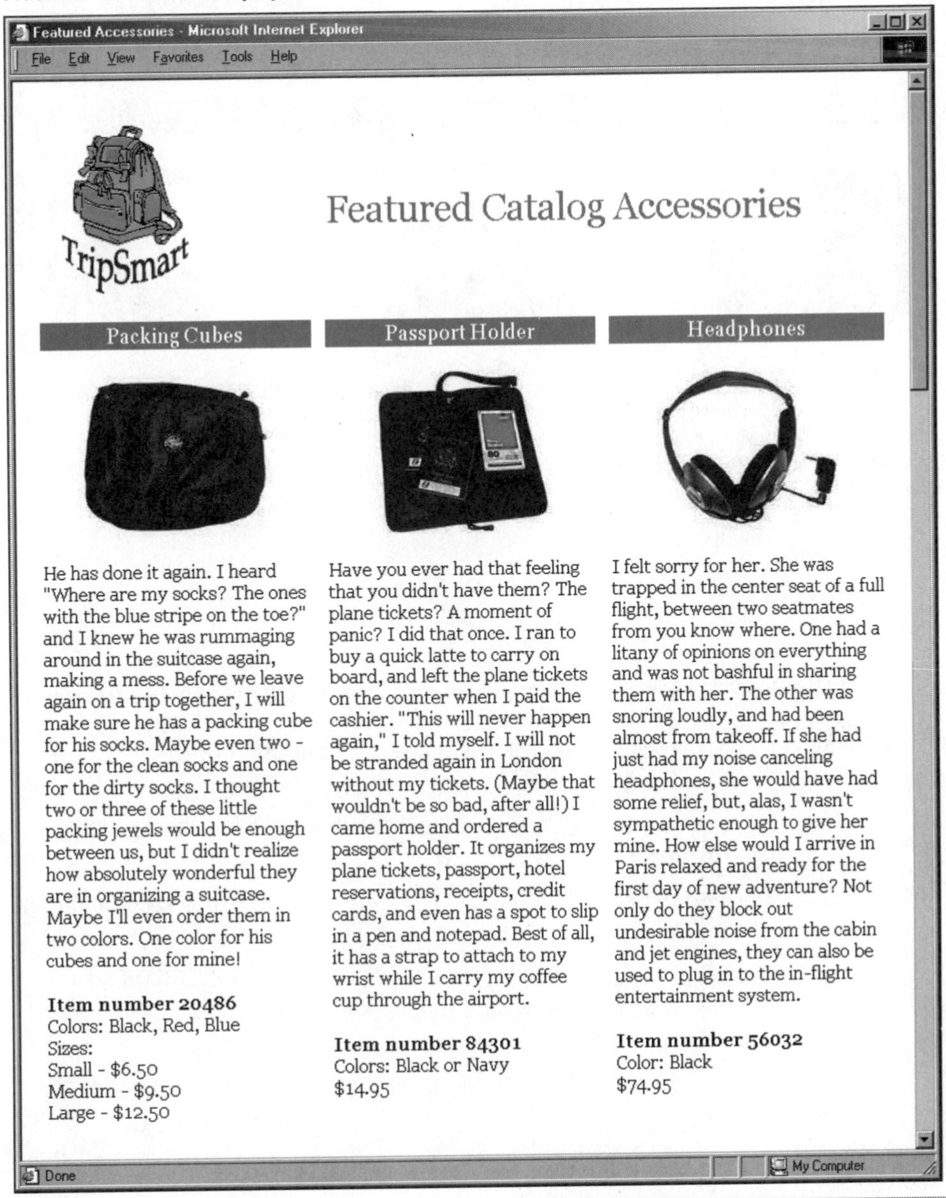

Featured Accessories - Microsoft Internet Explorer
File Edit View Favorites Tools Help
TripSmart
Featured Catalog Accessories
Packing Cubes
Passport Holder
Headphones
He has done it again. I heard "Where are my socks? The ones with the blue stripe on the toe?" and I knew he was rummaging around in the suitcase again, making a mess. Before we leave again on a trip together, I will make sure he has a packing cube for his socks. Maybe even two - one for the clean socks and one for the dirty socks. I thought two or three of these little packing jewels would be enough between us, but I didn't realize how absolutely wonderful they are in organizing a suitcase. Maybe I'll even order them in two colors. One color for his cubes and one for mine!
Item number 20486
Colors: Black, Red, Blue
Sizes:
Small - $6.50
Medium - $9.50
Large - $12.50
Have you ever had that feeling that you didn't have them? The plane tickets? A moment of panic? I did that once. I ran to buy a quick latte to carry on board, and left the plane tickets on the counter when I paid the cashier. "This will never happen again," I told myself. I will not be stranded again in London without my tickets. (Maybe that wouldn't be so bad, after all!) I came home and ordered a passport holder. It organizes my plane tickets, passport, hotel reservations, receipts, credit cards, and even has a spot to slip in a pen and notepad. Best of all, it has a strap to attach to my wrist while I carry my coffee cup through the airport.
Item number 84301
Colors: Black or Navy
$14.95
I felt sorry for her. She was trapped in the center seat of a full flight, between two seatmates from you know where. One had a litany of opinions on everything and was not bashful in sharing them with her. The other was snoring loudly, and had been almost from takeoff. If she had just had my noise canceling headphones, she would have had some relief, but, alas, I wasn't sympathetic enough to give her mine. How else would I arrive in Paris relaxed and ready for the first day of new adventure? Not only do they block out undesirable noise from the cabin and jet engines, they can also be used to plug in to the in-flight entertainment system.
Item number 56032
Color: Black
$74.95
Done
My Computer

Dreamweaver 4

Practice

► Concepts Review

Label each element in the Dreamweaver window shown in Figure G-20.

FIGURE G-20

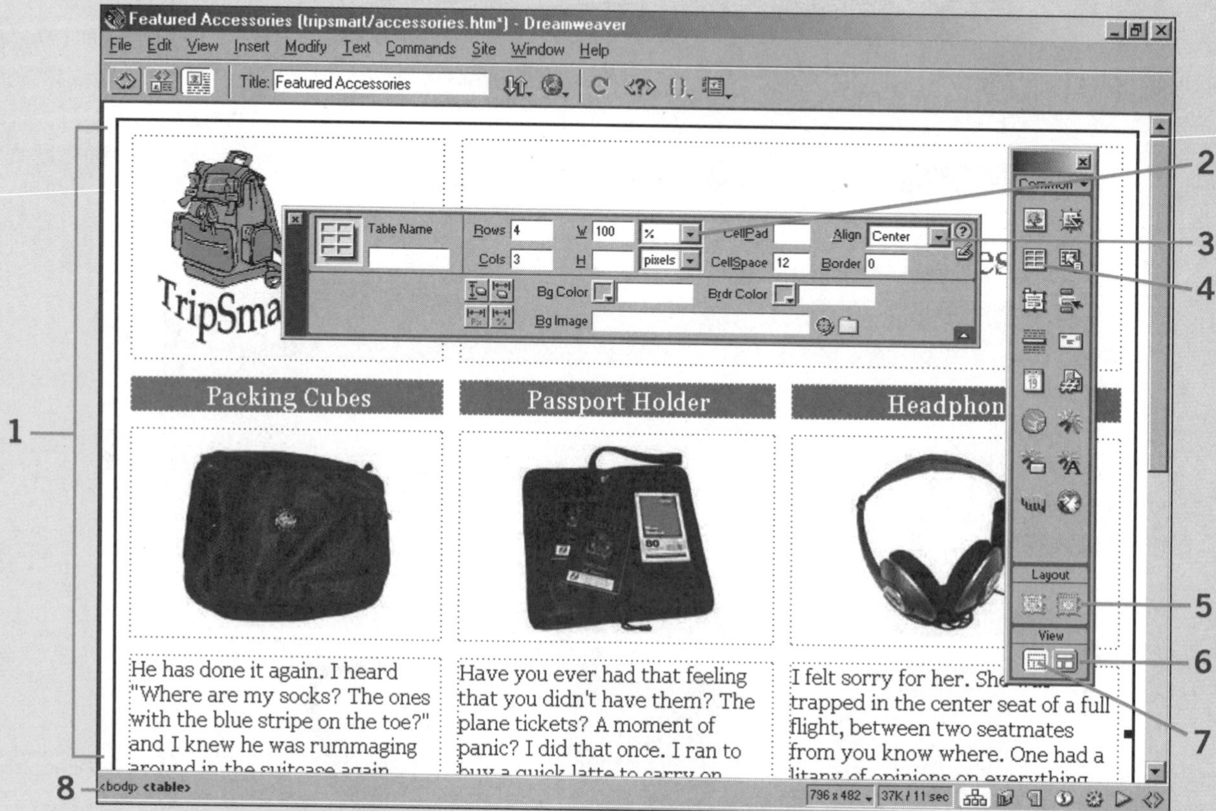

Match each of the following terms with the statement that describes its function.

9. Small boxes that make up columns and rows
10. Layout View
11. Cell padding
12. Standard View
13. Border
14. Import
15. Cell spacing
16. Export
17. Tag selector

a. The view that only displays the cells you draw
b. The space between cell content and cell walls
c. Displays HTML tags for the various page components, including tables and cells
d. Cells
e. The view that you use to create a table with a specific number of rows and columns
f. Saving data that was created in Dreamweaver as a special file format
g. The space between table cells
h. The outline of a table or an individual cell
i. To bring data into Dreamweaver from another program

Select the best answer from the following list of choices.

18. Which of the following is true about nested tables?
- **a.** Only one nested table can be inserted into a table.
- **b.** Nested tables are inserted using the Insert Nested Table icon.
- **c.** Nested tables can have visible or invisible borders.
- **d.** Nested tables cannot be formatted like regular tables.

19. Which of the following is used to select a row in a table?
- **a.** <tr>
- **b.** <div>
- **c.** <table>
- **d.** <td>

20. Which pointer is used to select a row?
- **a.**
- **b.**
- **c.**
- **d.**

Skills Review

Important: *If you did not create this Web site in Unit B and maintain it during the preceding units, you will need to create a root folder for this Web site and define the Web site using files your instructor will provide. See the "Read This Before You Begin" section for more detailed instructions. You can refer to Figure G-21 for guidance during this exercise.*

1. Understand table views.
- **a.** Open the Blooms&Bulbs Web site from the drive and folder where your Project Files are stored.
- **b.** Using the Site window, create a new page for the Web site and save it as *rose_tour.htm.*
- **c.** Using the Objects panel, click the Standard View icon, then click the Layout View icon. Close the Getting Started in Layout View window, if it opens.
- **d.** Click the Draw Layout Cell icon, then click the Draw Layout Table icon.
- **e.** Click the Standard View icon again.

2. Create a table.
- **a.** Double-click rose_tour.htm to open it in Design View.
- **b.** Type **Texas Rose Festival Tour** in the Title text box on the toolbar.
- **c.** Insert a table on the page with the following settings:
  Rows = 3
  Columns = 3
  Width = 100%
  Border = 0
- **d.** Center the table on the page.
- **e.** Type **5** in the CellSpace text box.
- **f.** Save the file.

3. Resize rows and columns.
- **a.** Select the first cell in the first row and set the cell width to 35%.
- **b.** Select the second cell in the same row and set the cell width to 35%.
- **c.** Select the third cell in the same row and set the cell width to 30%.
- **d.** Save your work.

4. Insert and align graphics in table cells.
- **a.** Use the Assets panel to insert the Blooms&Bulbs logo in the first cell in the first row of the table.
- **b.** Use the Objects panel to insert the yellow_rose.jpg file in the second cell in the second row. You can find the yellow_rose.jpg file in the Unit G folder where your Project Files are stored.

c. Insert the tearoom.jpg file from the drive and folder where your Project Files for Unit G are stored in the second cell of the last row.
d. Select the yellow_rose.jpg and set its alignment to Left.
e. Keeping yellow_rose.jpg selected, select the cell tag on the tag selector, click the Vert list arrow on the Property Inspector, then click Top.
f. Select the tearoom.jpg and center it.
g. Keeping tearoom.jpg selected, select the cell tag on the tag selector, click the Vert list arrow on the Property Inspector, then click Top.
h. Save your work.

5. Split and merge cells.

a. Merge the third cell in the first row with the third cell in the second row, then insert the texas_rose.jpg in the merged cell. You can find the texas_rose.jpg file in the Unit G folder.
b. Save texas_rose.jpg to the assets folder when prompted.
c. Center the graphic.
d. Using the tag selector, select the first cell in the second row and split it into two rows.
e. Save your work.

6. Insert text.

a. Type **Texas Rose Festival** in the second cell in the top row, press and hold [Shift] and press [Enter] (Win) or [return] (Mac) to create a soft return, then type **Tyler**, **Texas**.
b. Click the insertion point in the third cell in the first column (two cells below the Blooms & Bulbs logo), then copy the text from the agenda.htm file in the drive and folder where your Project Files for Unit G are stored, and paste it into the cell.
c. Click the insertion point in the cell with the yellow roses, copy the text from the nursery.htm file in the drive and folder where your Project Files for Unit G are stored, and paste it into the cell.
d. Click the insertion point in the first cell in the last row, copy the text from the tearoom.htm file in the drive and folder where your Project Files for Unit G are stored, and paste it into the cell.
e. Click the insertion point in the last cell of the last row, copy the text from the exhibition.htm file in the drive and folder where your Project Files for Unit G are stored, and paste it into the cell.
f. Click the insertion point to the right of the texas_rose.jpg, press [Enter] (Win) or [return] (Mac) to create a soft return. (Hint: A soft return begins a new line of type without creating a new paragraph.) Type **Price: $60**, create a soft return, type **Includes:**, create a soft return, type **Admissions, lunch**, create a soft return, then type **snacks, and tea**.
g. Type **Agenda**: in the cell directly below the Blooms & Bulbs logo.
h. Save your changes to the page.

7. Format cell content.

a. Select the Texas Rose Festival text and format it using Georgia, Times New Roman, Times, serif for the font, 5 for the size, Bold, Right for the alignment, and #336633 for the color.
b. Select the Tyler, Texas text and format it using Georgia, Times New Roman, Times, serif for the font, 4 for the size, Bold, Right for the alignment, and #336633 for the color.
c. Select the cell containing Texas Rose Festival, Tyler, Texas, then set the vertical alignment to Middle.
d. Select each of the paragraphs of text and format them using Georgia, Times New Roman, Times, serif for the font and 2 for the size.
e. Select each cell containing a paragraph of text, then set the vertical alignment to Top for each.
f. Select the text under the texas_rose.jpg and format it using Georgia, Times New Roman, Times, serif for the font and 2 for the size, Bold, and Center for the alignment.
g. Select the cell with the word Agenda in it and change the cell background color to #336633.

h. Format the word Agenda: using Georgia, Times New Roman, Times, serif for the font, 3 for the size, Bold, Center for the alignment, and #FFFFFF for the color.
i. Save the file.

8. **Insert and delete a row.**
   a. Select the last row, then insert one row above it.
   b. Insert a centered, horizontal rule in each cell of the new row.
   c. Insert a new row below the last row of the table.
   d. Merge the three cells in this new row.
   e. Insert a centered horizontal rule in the last row.
   f. Save the file and view the page in your browser.

FIGURE G-21

Texas Rose Festival
Tyler, Texas

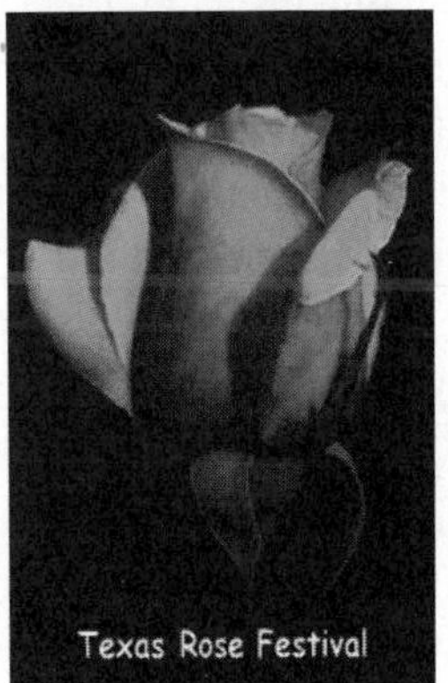

Agenda:

The van will leave from the greenhouse parking lot at 7:00 a.m. on October 12. We will have coffee and warm muffins ready to take on the bus. Water and soft drinks will be available in coolers on the van all day. Our tour is limited to 20 people, so make your reservations early.

We will arrive for a tour at the Yellow Rose Nursery at approximately 10:00. The Yellow Rose Nursery is owned by Maude Key and her daughter, Floy. They have been a premier rose supplier for major markets for over 70 years. Their specialty is yellow roses. You will learn how the roses are planted, cultivated, and prepared for shipping.

Price: $60
Includes:
Admissions, lunch, snacks, and tea

After the tour, we will have lunch at Sue and Cathy's Little Tearoom in Tyler. Sue and Cathy have an excellent tearoom. People have been known to drive from Dallas just to have lunch there. They always have fresh rose arrangements on each table and will make you feel so welcome. The homemade rolls and rose jelly are their specialties.

After lunch, we will drive to the Tyler Municipal Rose Garden for the main event. This 14-acre garden displays over 400 varieties of roses blooming from over 30,000 bushes. You won't believe it! After the exhibition we will enjoy the Queen's tea and come home. We expect to arrive by 7:00 p.m.

Important: *If you did not create these Web sites in Unit B and maintain them during the preceding units, you will need to create a root folder for each Web site and define the Web site using files your instructor will provide. See the "Read This Before You Begin" section for more detailed instructions.*

► Independent Challenge 1

Jacob's Restaurant is an upscale restaurant catering to business executives and theater patrons. They have an extensive menu including prix fixe dinners, pre-theater dinner specials, and after-theater specials. The cuisine is primarily French. Jacob is planning a tasting menu in conjunction with Howard Vineyards. He would like you to design a page featuring this special occasion. Refer to Figure G-22 for ideas.

a. Open the Jacob's Web site from the drive and folder where your Project Files are stored.
b. Open the prix_fix.htm file in the Jacob's Web site and type **An Evening with Howard Vineyards** for the page title. (*Hint*: Images and internal links that display a broken link or an absolute path (extra characters, such as forward slashes and colons), can be fixed by selecting the graphic or the link, then clicking the Browse for File icon on the Property Inspector. Images should be saved in the assets folder overwriting the existing file, if necessary. For links, double-click the filename in the root folder, overwriting the existing file.)
c. Create a table on the page that has three rows, three columns, a width of 100%, and a border of 0.
d. Insert the Jacob's logo in the first cell in the first row.
e. Click the insertion point to the right of the Jacob's logo in the same cell to deselect it, then press [Enter] (Win) or [return] (Mac).
f. Copy the address from the index page and paste it in the same cell under the logo.
g. Merge the top-middle and top-right cells.
h. Copy the Jacob's navigation bar from the index.htm page into the merged cells.
i. Merge the first and second cells in the second row.
j. Split the new merged cell below the Jacob's logo and address into two rows, then type **Special dinner honoring Tony nominees ~ May 8** in the top new row.
k. Open the dinner.htm file from the Unit G folder from the drive and folder where your Project Files are stored.
l. Copy the text from the dinner.htm file and paste it in the cell under the Special dinner heading.
m. Close the dinner.htm file.
n. Insert grapes.jpg in the second cell in the middle row and save the graphic to your assets folder. The grapes.jpg file is in the assets folder of the Unit G folder in the drive and folder where your Project Files are stored.
o. Type **For reservations: (555) 991-6668** in the cell directly below the grapes image.
p. Merge the first and second cells in the last row, then type **Jacob's selections will be announced as each course is presented.** in the merged cell.
q. Use the Property Inspector to format the cells and the cell content to make the page more attractive.
r. Save the file.

FIGURE G-22

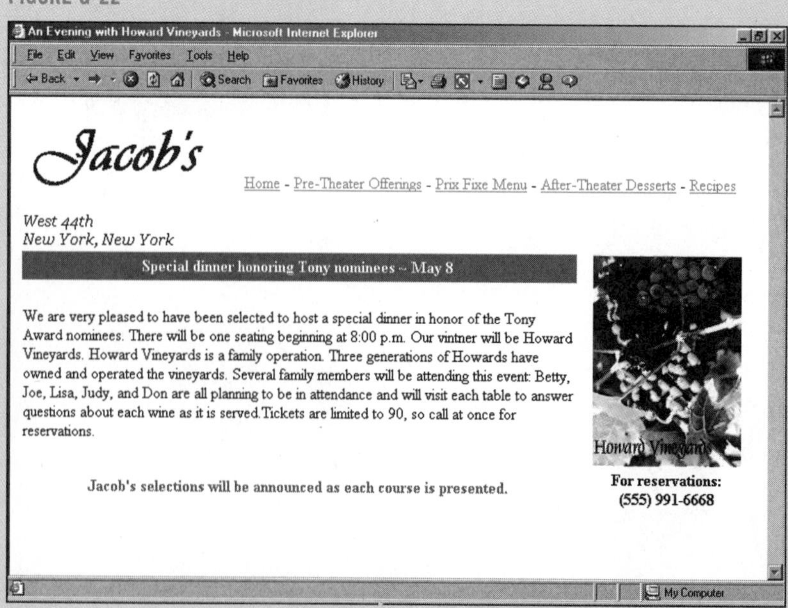

Independent Challenge 2

The Over Under Dive Shop is a dive center in Nevis, West Indies. It is a certified Professional Association of Diving Instructors (PADI) dive center offering PADI certification courses. They also conduct snorkeling and dive trips to various locations around the barrier reef surrounding Nevis. Jon, the dive master, has asked you to create a table on one of their pages that lists the PADI courses he offers, and the price of each course.

a. Open the Over Under Web site from the drive and folder where your Project Files are stored.
b. Connect to the Internet and go to PADI at *www.padi.com.*
c. Find out the names of the recreational courses offered as PADI courses, such as PADI Open Water Diver.
d. Open the padi.htm file in the Over Under Web site.
e. Title the page PADI Courses Offered by Over Under.
f. Add a table to the page that will include the Over Under Logo, the navigation bar for the Web site, the name of each course offered (offer at least five of them), and the course prices.
g. Format the page and table and add any additional text or graphics that would make the page attractive. Refer to Figure G-23 for a design example. (*Hint*: A table with a white background might look nice on a page with the same sea-green background found on the Web site's home page.)
h. Save the file.

FIGURE G-23

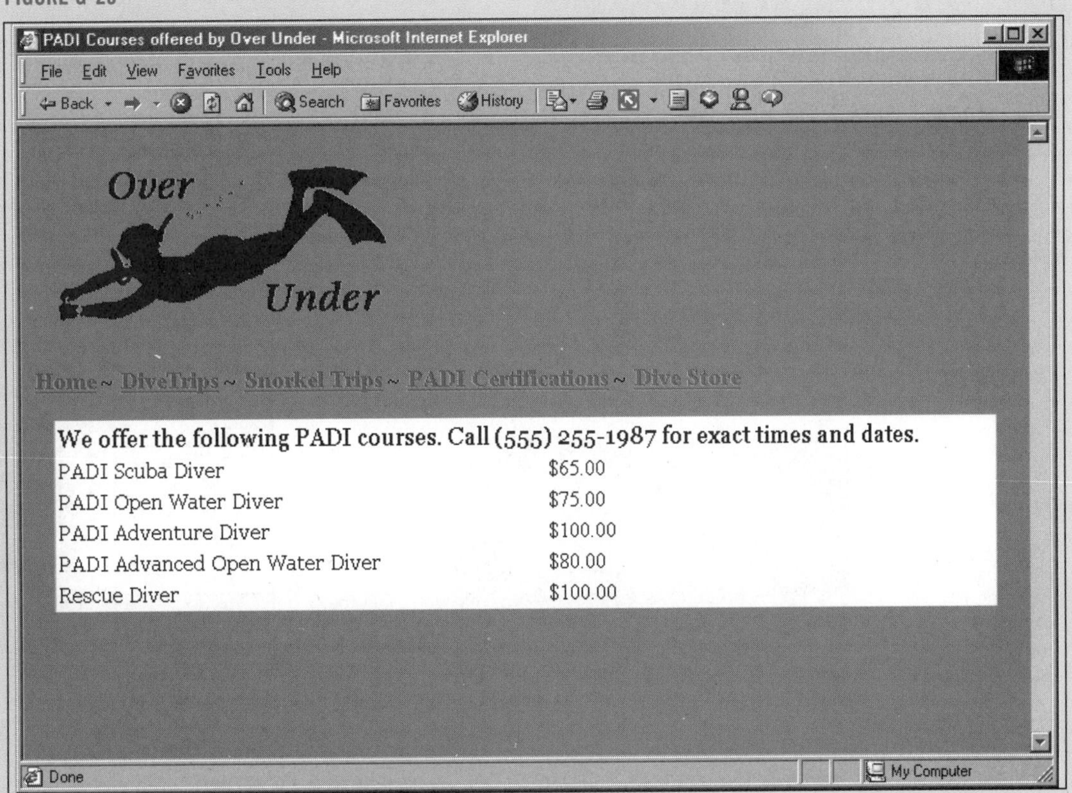

Dreamweaver 4

► Independent Challenge 3

Off Note is a music store specializing in classical, blues, rock, country, and jazz. The home page was started, but was never completed. You would like to redesign the home page, using a table to lay out the information on the home page.

a. Open the Off Note Web site created in Unit B from the drive and folder where your Project Files are stored.
b. Open the index.htm page.
c. Place the insertion point after the last sentence on the page and press [Enter] (Win) or [return] (Mac).
d. Using the Objects panel, create a table with three rows and columns, a width of 100%, and a border of 0.
e. Center the table and set the cell spacing to 0.
f. Click-and-drag the Off Note logo into the first cell in the first row.
g. Select and drag the paragraph on the page to the second cell in the second row.
h. Refer to Figure G-24 as you create the rest of the page layout. (*Hint*: There are two nested tables: one for the navigation bar and one for the Featured Events.)
i. Insert the cd_sale.jpg file from the Unit G folder where your Project Files are stored and save it in the offnote assets folder.
j. Make any adjustments you would like in the design layout without removing any information from the page.

FIGURE G-24

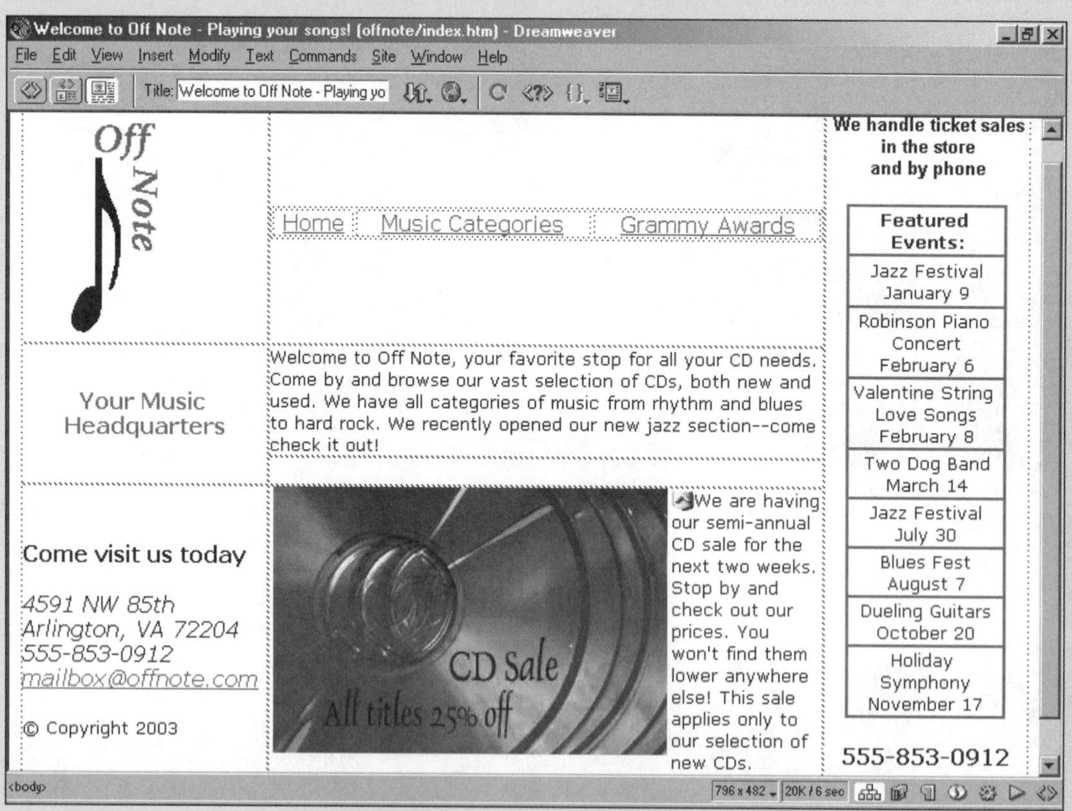

Independent Challenge 4

Sally Reeves has asked you to design a Web site for her interior design shop that will incorporate the use of tables for both basic page layout and for detailed tabular merchandise and pricing data. She has directed you to go to the Web site for The World Wide Web Consortium before you begin work to research accessibility issues regarding the use of tables in designing Web pages.

a. Connect to the Internet and go to the World Wide Web Consortium at *www.w3.org*
b. Search the Web site for guidelines regarding the use of tables in Web content.
c. Copy and paste any information you find into a document using your word processing software.
d. Type a short paragraph summarizing your findings.
e. Exit the browser.

Independent Challenge 5

Carolyn Raney has opened a new shop called Needles and Thread that carries needlepoint, cross-stitching, and smocking supplies. She is considering going "on the Web" with a Web site and would like to gather some ideas before she hires a Web designer. She decides to visit the L.L. Bean and Neiman Marcus Web sites to look for design ideas.

a. Connect to the Internet and go to Neiman Marcus at *www.neimanmarcus.com.*
b. Save the Neiman Marcus home page as **neiman.htm** in the drive and folder where your Project Files are stored.
c. Close the browser, return to Dreamweaver, then open neiman.htm in Dreamweaver to see the table layout.
d. Return to the Internet and go to L.L. Bean at *www.llbean.com.*
e. Save the L.L. Bean home page as *bean.htm* and open it in Dreamweaver to see the table layout.
f. Compare the two by:
   1. Selecting the tables on each page and viewing the table properties.
   2. Selecting a few cell tags on each page and viewing the cell properties.
   3. Selecting a few row tags on each page and viewing the row properties.
g. Using your word-processing software or scrap paper, list five design ideas that you like from either of these pages and tell which page was the source of each idea.

► Visual Workshop

Rapids Transit is a river expedition company. They are located on the Buffalo River in Northwest Arkansas. In addition to renting canoes, kayaks, and rafts, they have a country store and snack bar. Mike Andrew, the owner of Rapids Transit, has asked you to work on the page for his equipment rentals. (If you have not maintained this Web site from the previous Unit, then contact your instructor for assistance.) Open the rentals.htm file in the Web site and use a table to create the layout pictured in Figure G-25. (*Hint*: The table with the rental items is a nested table. The picture shown below is called kayak.jpg, and it is located in the Unit G assets folder.)

FIGURE G-25

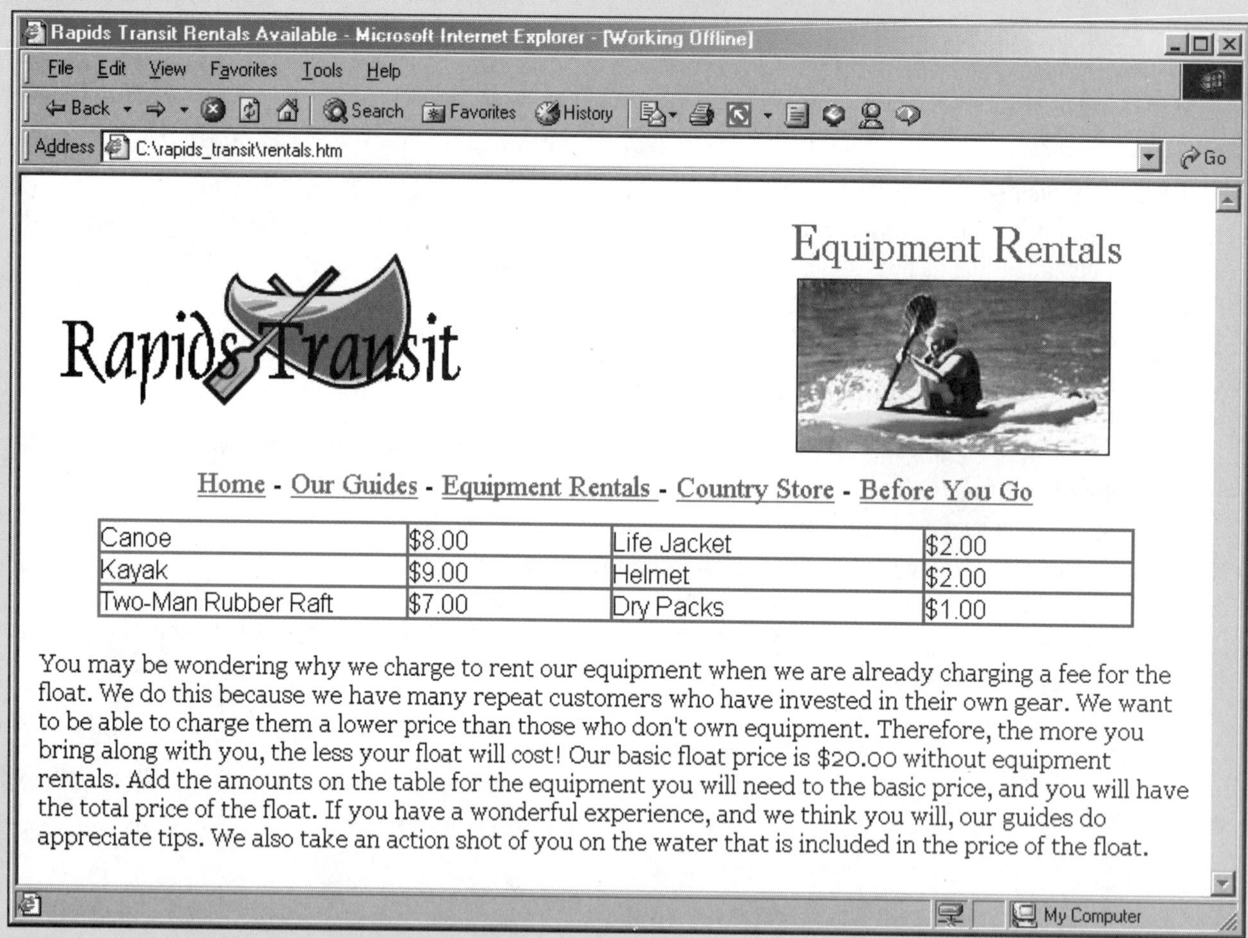

Dreamweaver 4

Working with Frames

Objectives

- Understand frames and framesets
- Create a frameset
- Save a frameset and view the Frames panel
- Format a frameset using the Property Inspector
- Format a frame using the Property Inspector
- Edit and format frame content
- Link frames
- Perform Web site maintenance

It is possible to display multiple Web pages simultaneously in the browser window. These multiple pages that appear in one window are called **frames**. There are mixed feelings about using frames in Web design. Some designers feel that frames are an effective way to display information and provide strong navigation between a Web site and its pages. Others feel that frames can be visually confusing. Frames may also take longer to download than single pages. Betty Pipkin, the vice president of catalog sales, was so impressed with the accessories Web page that you created, she asks you to create a similar page for displaying travel clothing. You explain to her that combining the accessories page and the new clothing page, using frames, would be a great way to allow viewers to view the clothing and accessories on one page.

Dreamweaver 4

Understanding Frames and Framesets

A **frame** is a Web page displayed as an individual window in your browser. As shown in Figure H-1, a Web page can display multiple frames simultaneously. Each frame is an individual Web page. A **frameset** is a Web page that is used to tie the frame pages together. A frameset page is never seen and contains no content. Think of it as a Web page that works behind the scenes rather than in the spotlight. The two terms can be confusing. Frames are the individual pages that you see in a browser window. The Web page that is responsible for linking the frames together, but is never seen, is the frameset. Multiple frames in a window are referred to as being "in a frameset." If there are three frames in a frameset, there are four corresponding HTML files: three for the individual frames and one for the frameset. Before you begin working on the new frames page, you take time to learn more about the differences between frames and framesets and the differences in their HTML code.

Frame

A frame is an individual Web page that contains page content. It is displayed in a browser window along with one or more frames. The HTML code used for a frame is the same as that for other individual Web pages. It contains opening and closing HTML tags, heading tags, title tags, and body tags, as shown in Figure H-2. Each frame in a frameset can have individual scroll bars that work independently without affecting the others.

Frameset

A frameset is a Web page that provides HTML code to coordinate the individual pages, or frames, to display them together in a browser window. The HTML code for a frameset is quite different from the code used for a frame. It has opening and closing HTML tags, heading tags, and title tags, but does not have body tags. Instead, it has opening and closing frameset tags. Inside the frameset tags are short instructions for the way the individual frames are displayed inside the frameset. The code for a frameset is quite short compared to the code for a frames page, as shown in Figure H-2.

FIGURE H-1: Example of a Web page using frames

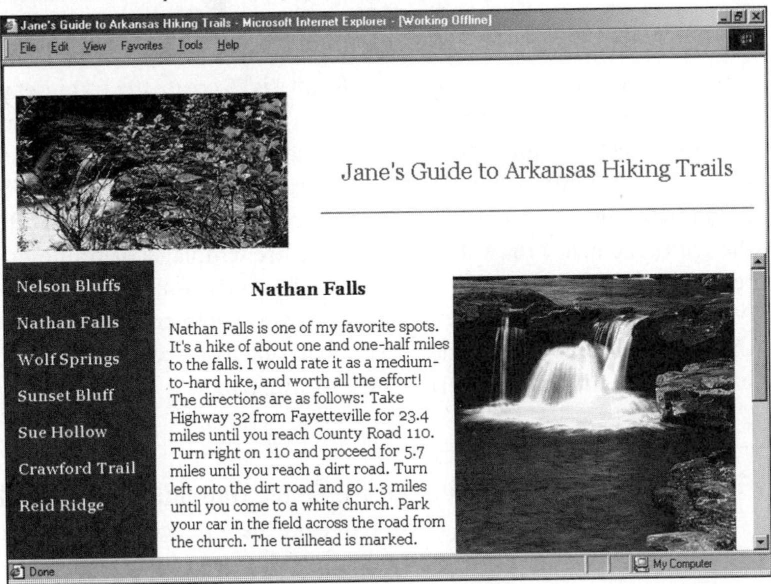

FIGURE H-2: HTML code for a frame and a frameset

HTML code for frame

Opening body tag

```
<html>
<head>
<title>Featured Accessories</title>
<meta http-equiv="Content-Type" content="text/html; charset=iso-8859-1">
</head>
<body text="#000000" bgcolor="#FFFFFF">
<table width="100%" border="0" cellspacing="12" align="center">
  <tr>
    <td height="41"><img src="assets/tripsmart.gif" width="157" height="160"></td>
    <td height="41" colspan="2" valign="middle" align="left">
      <p><font face="Georgia, Times New Roman, Times, serif" size="6" color="#003399">I
        Catalog Accessories</font></p>
    </td>
  </tr>
  <tr bgcolor="#003399">
    <td width="33%">
      <div align="center"><font face="Georgia, Times New Roman, Times, serif" size="4"
color="#FFFFFF">Packing
        Cubes</font></div>
```

HTML code for frameset

Frameset tags

```
<html>
<head>
<title>Product</title>
<meta http-equiv="Content-Type" content="text/html; charset=iso-8859-1">
</head>

<frameset rows="*" cols="80,*" frameborder="NO" border="0" framespacing="0">
  <frame name="leftFrame" scrolling="NO" noresize src="left.htm">
  <frameset rows="80,*" frameborder="NO" border="0" framespacing="0">
    <frame name="topFrame" noresize scrolling="NO" src="top.htm">
    <frame name="mainFrame" src="main">
  </frameset>
</frameset>
<noframes><body bgcolor="#FFFFFF" text="#000000">

</body></noframes>
</html>
```

Design Matters

Setting the number of frames in a frameset

If you have decided to create a frameset, consider limiting the number of frames to two or three. Using more than two or three may be too confusing or distracting for viewers. Viewing too many frames in a frameset can be compared to watching television with multiple channels being displayed simultaneously on one screen. Some people find it difficult to view two screens at once. Even when they are only concentrating on one screen at a time, the other is distracting to them. The same may be true for viewers of multiple frames.

Dreamweaver 4

Creating a Frameset

The first step in creating a page using frames is to create the frameset page. Even before that, you must decide how many frames you want to use and how you want them arranged in the browser window. Sketching your ideas on paper may be very helpful at this stage. You have two choices for creating a frameset. You can design a frameset yourself, using the Modify menu, by pointing to Frameset then choosing a frameset option, or you can use one of the predefined framesets on the Objects panel. **Predefined framesets** are templates of frameset designs with borders that represent the outline of each frame in the frameset. You don't have to complete the frame pages before you create the frameset. You decide to create a frameset with three pages: one for the TripSmart logo and the navigation bar, one to show the accessories and clothing pages, and one with links to the accessories and clothing pages.

Steps

1. Start Dreamweaver, open the TripSmart Web site, then close the Site window
   You will use the Untitled Document page that opened when you started Dreamweaver to create the frameset page using a predefined frameset.

QuickTip
You can drag frameset icons from the Objects panel to the page.

2. Show the Objects panel and Property Inspector if necessary, click the **Objects panel list arrow**, then click **Frames**
   The Objects panel displays eight icons representing the predefined frameset styles. You are now ready to create a frameset. Framesets can only be created in Design View.

Trouble?
If you accidentally clicked the page and deselected the frameset, click one of the outside borders of the frameset to select all of it. If you click an inside border, you are only selecting a frame, not the entire frameset.

3. Click the **Insert Top and Nested Left Frame icon** on the Objects panel to insert the frameset on the page
   The frameset is displayed on the page. The dotted line on top of the frameset borders indicates that the frameset is selected. As shown in Figure H-3, the Property Inspector displays the properties of the frameset. As with other Web pages, it's a good idea to give the frameset page a descriptive page title.

4. Make sure that the frameset is still selected, type **TripSmart Catalog Items** in the Title text box, then press **[Enter]** (Win) or **[return]** (Mac)
   As soon as you press Enter (Win) or [return] (Mac), the insertion point is placed in the top frame. The frameset is no longer selected, so the title in the Title text box displays Untitled Document. To see the title again, you must select the border of the frameset.

Trouble?
If you don't see the frameset borders, click View on the menu bar, point to Visual Aids, then click Frame Borders.

5. Click the **outside border of the frameset** to select the frameset, then click the **Show Code View icon** to look at the HTML code for the frameset
   The frameset code is displayed as shown in Figure H-4.

6. Locate the tags for the individual frames
   You notice that the frameset code refers to leftFrame, topFrame, and mainFrame, the default frame names for the untitled frame pages that you will use. Each page in the frameset needs to be set in the code for the individual frame.

7. Click the **Show Design View icon** to return to Design View
   The view icons on the toolbar make it easy to switch back and forth between Design View and Code View.

FIGURE H-3: Frameset page for TripSmart

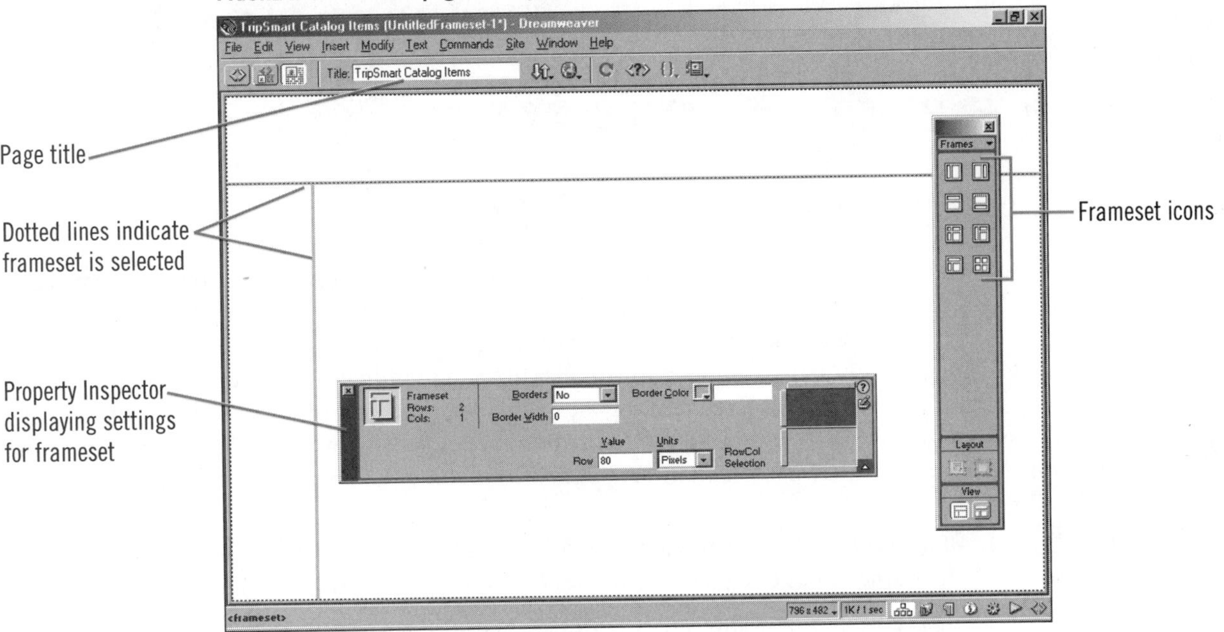
Page title
Dotted lines indicate frameset is selected
Property Inspector displaying settings for frameset
Frameset icons
TripSmart Catalog Items (UntitledFrameset-1*) - Dreamweaver
Title: TripSmart Catalog Items
<frameset>

FIGURE H-4: HTML code for frameset page

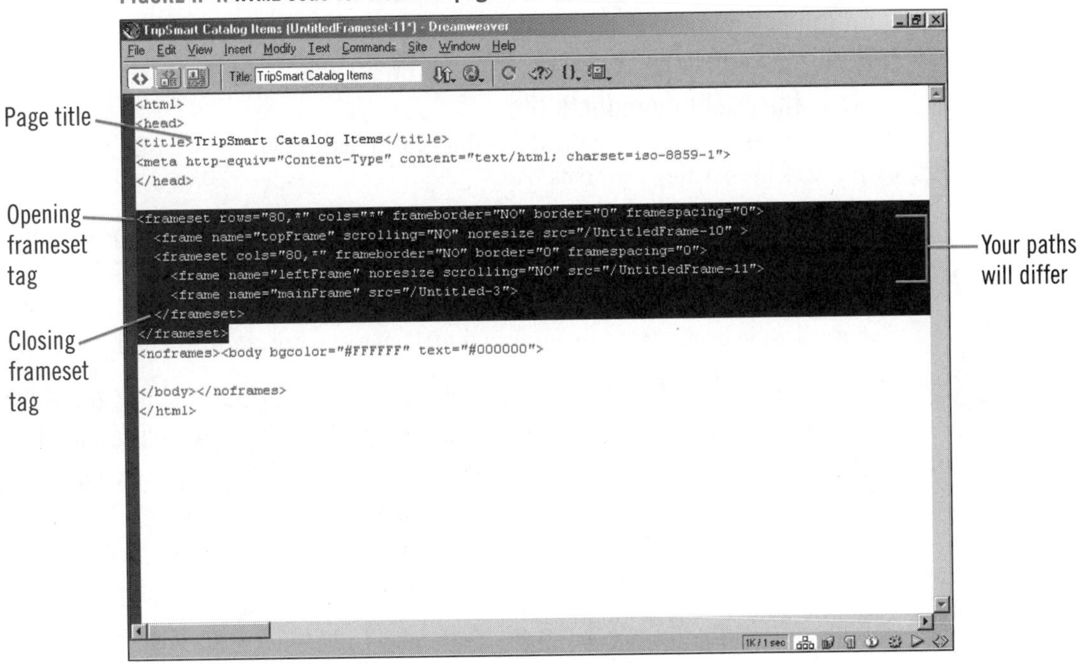
Page title
Opening frameset tag
Closing frameset tag
Your paths will differ
TripSmart Catalog Items (UntitledFrameset-11*) - Dreamweaver
Title: TripSmart Catalog Items
<html>
<head>
<title>TripSmart Catalog Items</title>
<meta http-equiv="Content-Type" content="text/html; charset=iso-8859-1">
</head>
<frameset rows="80,*" cols="*" frameborder="NO" border="0" framespacing="0">
<frame name="topFrame" scrolling="NO" noresize src="/UntitledFrame-10" >
<frameset cols="80,*" frameborder="NO" border="0" framespacing="0">
<frame name="leftFrame" noresize scrolling="NO" src="/UntitledFrame-11">
<frame name="mainFrame" src="/Untitled-3">
</frameset>
</frameset>
<noframes><body bgcolor="#FFFFFF" text="#000000">
</body></noframes>
</html>

Design Matters

Using fake frames

There is a very effective trick that is often used to create the illusion of a frameset, without actually making one. You create a graphic file to use as a background for a Web page. The graphic has a colored rectangle down the side of the page, and the navigation links can be placed over it, thus creating the illusion of a frameset, as in Figure H-5. Another method is to use a table for the page layout and use the top row and the left column for a "frames look" by using background colors in those cells.

FIGURE H-5: Creating a fake frame effect

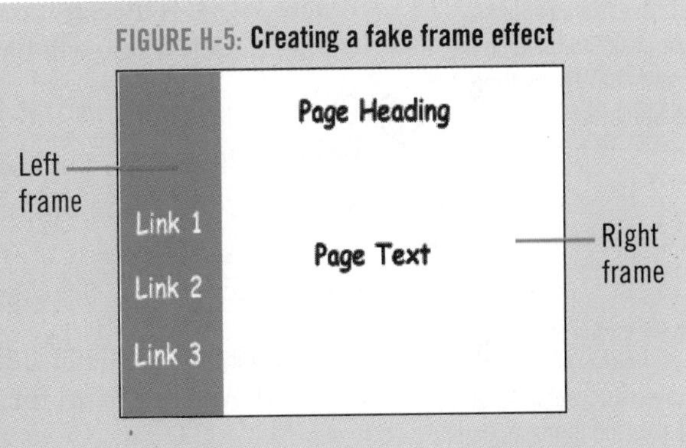
Page Heading
Left frame
Link 1
Link 2
Link 3
Page Text
Right frame

Dreamweaver 4

Dreamweaver 4

Saving a Frameset and Viewing the Frames Panel

When a frameset page is open in Design View, you can save it just as you would save an ordinary Web page. When you save a frameset, you are only saving the frameset page, not the individual pages that make up the frames in the frameset. Each frames page must be saved individually. The **Frames panel** can be used to help you identify and modify the frameset structure as you work with the frames pages. The Frames panel displays a graphic layout of the frameset to help you visualize the way the frames relate to the frameset. You open the Frames panel to view the frameset, then save the frameset page before adding the frames pages to it.

QuickTip

You must be in Design View to save a frameset.

1. **Make sure that the frameset is selected by clicking one of the frameset borders**
   The frameset has to be selected in order to save it.
2. **Click File on the menu bar, click Save Frameset As, click the drive and folder where your TripSmart root folder is located, double-click tripsmart, highlight the filename in the File name text box (Win) or the Name text box (Mac), type products.htm, click Save, then click Yes (Win) or Replace (Mac) when you are asked if you want to overwrite the existing products file**
   The frameset page is renamed products.htm, as shown in the title bar in Figure H-6. It replaces the existing products page.
3. **Click Window on the menu bar, click Frames to open the Frames panel, then click topFrame in the Frames panel**
   The top frame will contain the TripSmart logo and the navigation bar. These two elements have already been placed on an individual page and are ready to be placed in the top frame.

Trouble?

Images and internal links that display a broken link or an absolute path (extra characters, such as forward slashes and colons), can be fixed by selecting the graphic or the link, then clicking the Browse for File icon on the Property Inspector. Images should be saved in the assets folder overwriting the existing file, if necessary. For links, double-click the filename in the root folder, overwriting the existing file.

4. **Click the Browse for File icon on the Property Inspector, click the drive and folder where your Project Files are stored for Unit H, click, dmh_1.htm, click Select (Win) or Open (Mac), click Yes to copy the file to the root folder when asked to do so, type navigation.htm in the File name text box (Win) or the Name text box (Mac), then click Save**
   Only part of the navigation page shows in the top frame of the frameset. The frame border can be adjusted to show more of the page later.
5. **Click leftFrame in the Frames panel to select the left frame, click , click dmh_2.htm from the drive and folder where your Project Files are stored for Unit H, click Select (Win) or Open (Mac), click Yes to copy the file to the root folder, then save it as left_frame.htm**
   A new page fills the left frame. It contains links called Accessories and Clothing. Like the top frame, the left frame will have to be adjusted later to make room for the links.
6. **Click mainFrame in the Frames panel to select the main frame, click , on the Property Inspector, click accessories.htm from the TripSmart root folder, then click Select (Win) or Open (Mac)**
   The accessories page is now displayed in the main frame. All three frames have individual files placed in them. See Figure H-7.

QuickTip

The Save Frameset command only saves the frameset page.

7. **Click File on the menu bar, then click Save All Frames**
   The Save All Frames command saves each frame in the frameset as well as the frameset file.

FIGURE H-6: The products page

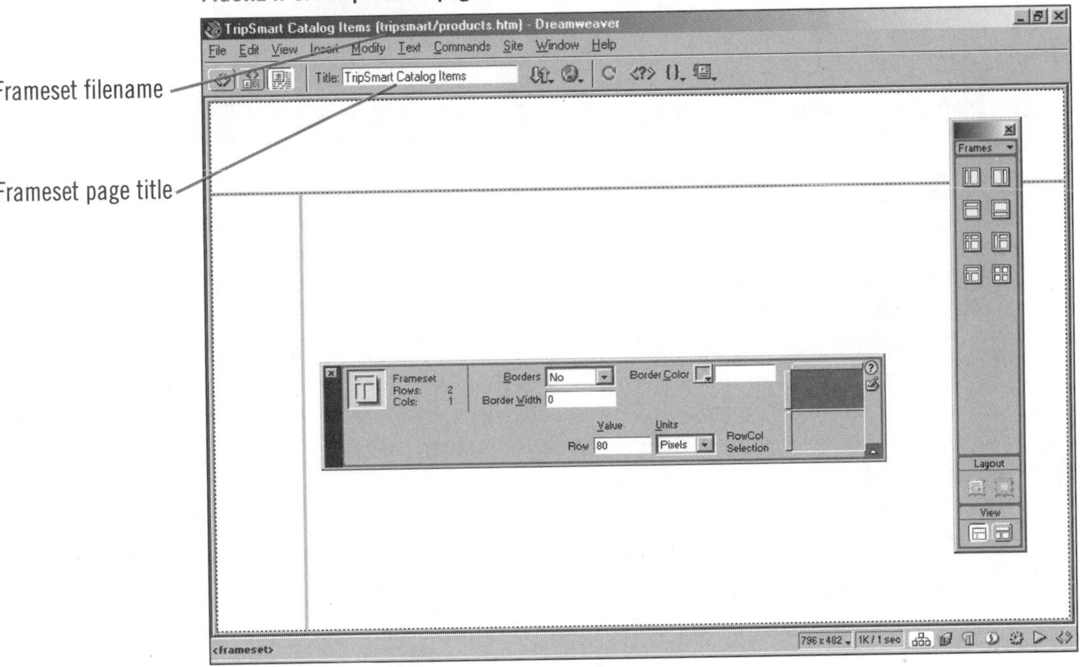

FIGURE H-7: Files inserted into the three frames on the products page

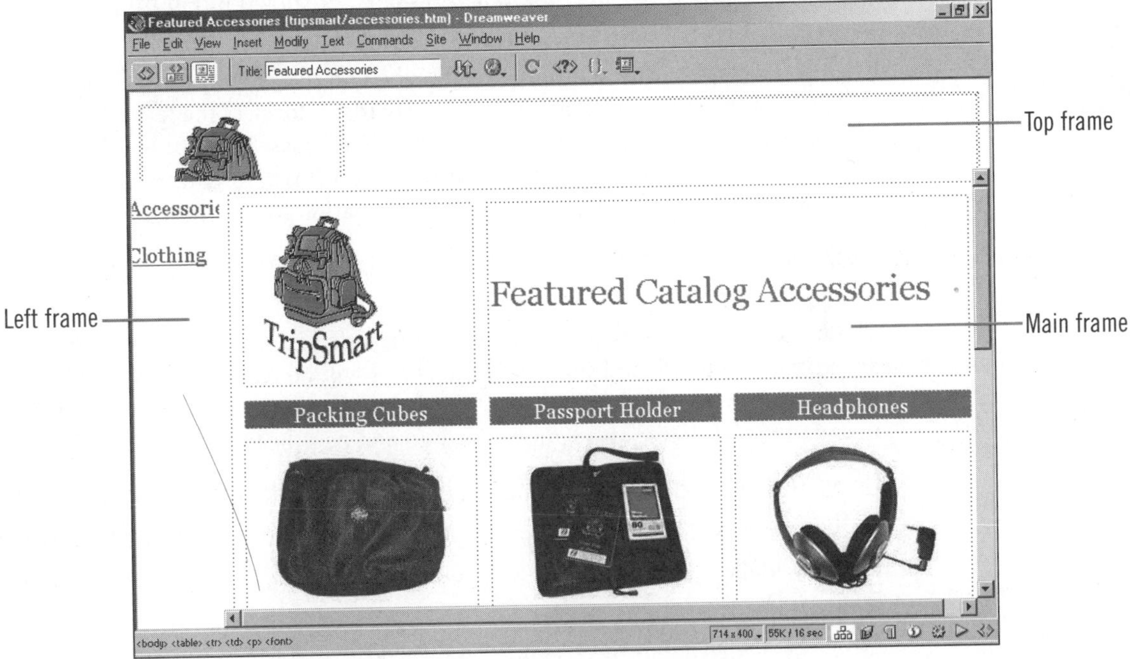

Saving individual frames

When working with frames and framesets, you have the option of saving individual frames, the frameset, or both the frames and the frameset. To save an individual frame, click the insertion point inside the frame you want to save, click File on the menu bar, then click Save Frame. To save a frameset, use the Save Frameset command, and if you want to save all frames and the frameset they are in, use the Save All Frames command.

Dreamweaver 4

Dreamweaver 4

Formatting a Frameset Using the Property Inspector

When a frameset is selected, the Property Inspector displays formatting options for framesets. You can change the size of a frame using pixels or percent as a unit of measure. You can set frame border widths and colors. You can also opt to hide frame borders. This provides a seamless window where it is not obvious where one frame starts and another one ends, if the page is designed skillfully. You use the Property Inspector to reallocate the space each frame occupies in the frameset on the products page, so that you can see the navigation bar and the links in the left frame.

Steps

1. Show the Frames panel, if necessary, then click the **frameset border** in the Frames panel to select the frameset, as shown in Figure H-8
   The Frames panel displays a dark border around the frameset image.The top and bottom frames are represented by the image in the Frames panel. You view the default settings on the Property Inspector.

QuickTip

The rectangles displayed in the Property Inspector depend on which frameset border you click in the Frames panel.

2. Click the **small arrow** on the Property Inspector to expand it, if necessary, click the **top row tab** in the RowCol Selection box, as shown in Figure H-8, type **170** in the Row Value text box, then press **[Enter]** (Win) or **[return]** (Mac)
   The two rectangles in the RowCol Selection box on the Property Inspector represent the top and bottom frames on the page. The Property Inspector uses the term Row in the Value text box. The Row Value is used to change the height of the selected frame. The top frame (row) in the frameset becomes taller, and the frame below it is automatically resized as a result. You can now see the entire TripSmart logo and navigation bar, as shown in Figure H-8.
3. Click the **bottom row tab** in the RowCol Selection box to view the current settings for the bottom frame
   The bottom frame is set to one pixel, the default size for an empty frame. As content is added, the height of the frame will increase. It will be resized relative to the top frame, or row, in the browser window. You leave the default setting for the bottom frame. You still need to widen the left frame and remove the logo and page heading from the main frame.
4. Using Figure H-9 as a guide, click the border around the **mainFrame** and the **leftFrame** in the **Frames panel**, click the **left column tab** in the RowCol Selection box on the Property Inspector, type **100** in the Column Value text box, then press **[Enter]** (Win) or **[return]** (Mac)
   The two rectangles on the Property Inspector represent the left and right bottom frames on the page. Since these two frames are considered columns, the Property Inspector uses the term Column in the Value text box. The Column Value is used to change the width of the selected frame. The left frame (column) is now 100 pixels wide.
5. Click the **right column tab** in the RowCol Selection box on the Property Inspector to view the settings for the right frame
   The right frame has been resized as a result of the left column being resized.
6. Click **File** on the menu bar, click **Save Frameset**, then click the **Preview/Debug in Browser icon** to view the frameset
   You are happy with the size of the frames and will continue working on the content in each frame.

FIGURE H-8: **Frameset properties for top frame**

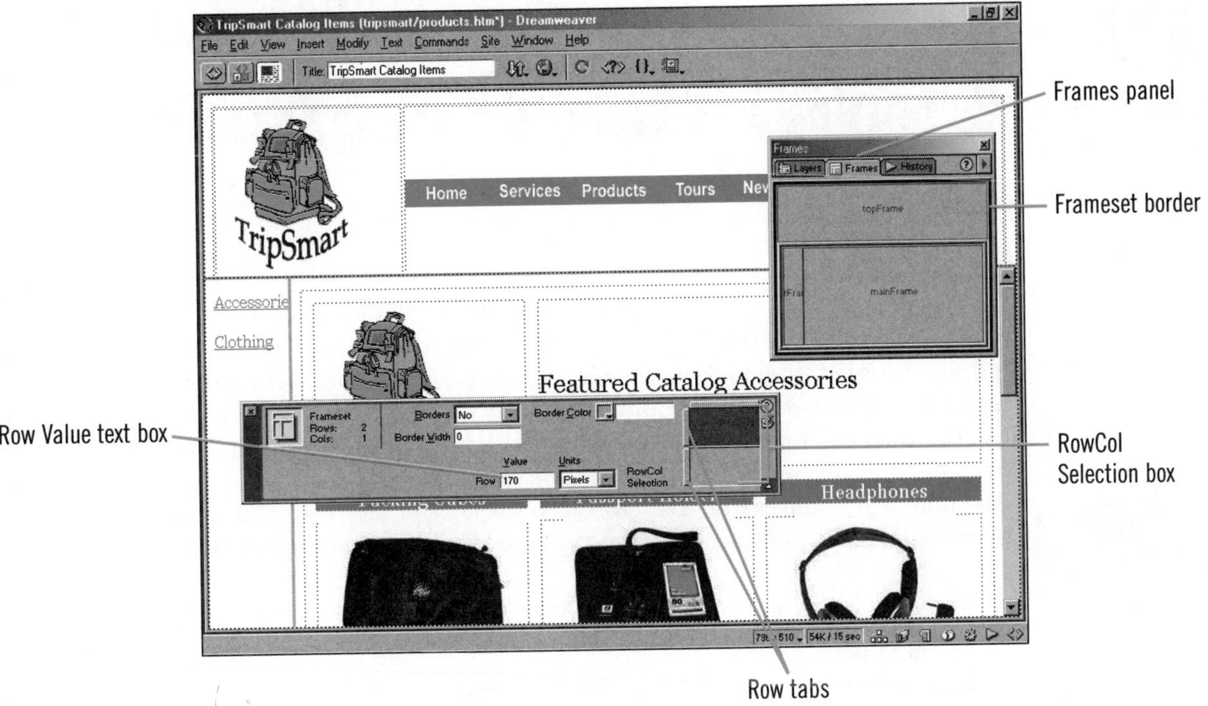

FIGURE H-9: **Frameset properties for left frame**

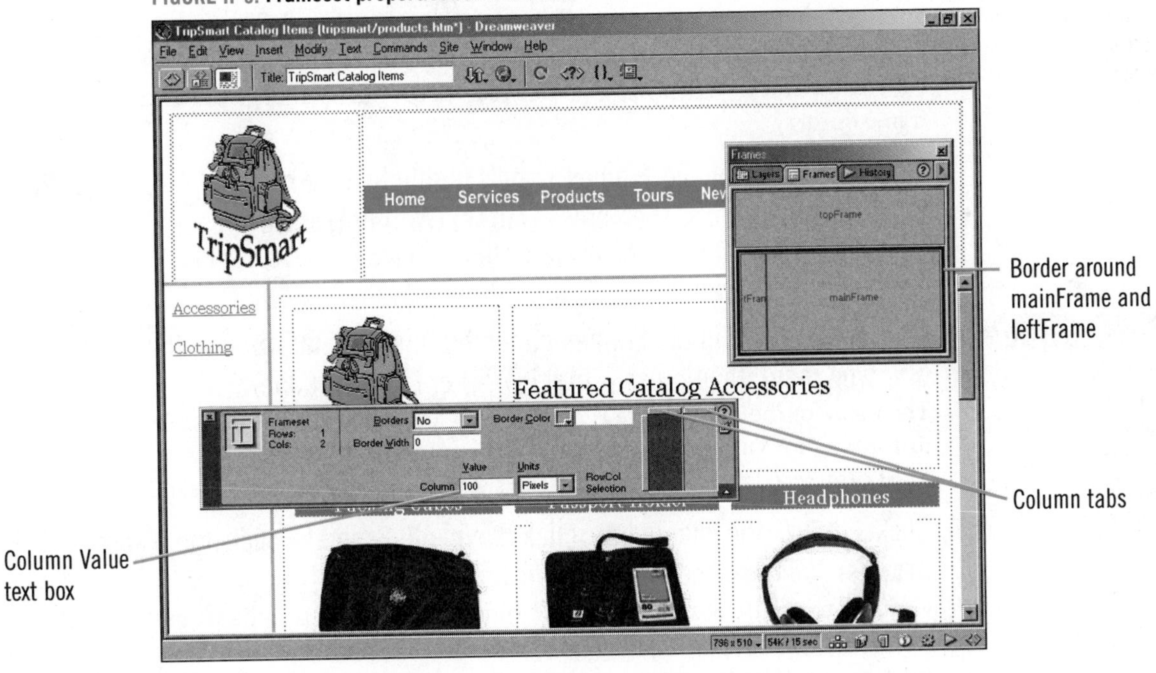

Design Matters

Using a frameset for the home page

Although you can create a frameset for the initial page in a Web site, it is not a good idea because it might cause the page to be overlooked by search engines. As you have seen, the frameset does not contain page content. Since it only contains instructions for the coordination of the individual frames within the frameset, a search engine would not find content to use to index the page.

Dreamweaver 4

Formatting a Frame Using the Property Inspector

As with framesets, the Property Inspector is used to format and choose settings for individual frames. After selecting a frame, you can set the height and width of its page margin and set its border size and border color. You can also choose whether or not to show a scroll bar in the frame if the frame is too small to display the entire Web page in the browser window. Each frame must have a descriptive name in order for the links between the frames to work properly. You can name a frame using the Property Inspector. You use the Property Inspector to change the name of each frame, ensure that the frame borders cannot be resized by visitors to your Web site, and determine which frames will have scroll bars. The top and left frames will not scroll, but the main frame will scroll because the page content is too long for the browser window.

Steps

1. Show the Frames panel and the Property Inspector, if necessary, then click **topFrame** in the Frames panel
   The top frame is selected, and the Property Inspector displays the information pertinent to the top frame.

QuickTip

To prevent linking errors, you should not use hyphens, periods, or spaces in a frame name.

2. Highlight **topFrame** in the Frame Name text box on the Property Inspector, type **navigation_bar**, then press **[Enter]** (Win) or **[return]** (Mac)
   The name of the top frame is now navigation_bar. As shown in Figure H-10, you leave the **No Resize** check box checked so that visitors to your Web page cannot manually resize the frame borders.
3. Click **leftFrame** in the Frames panel, highlight **leftFrame** in the Frame Name text box, type **page_links**, then press **[Enter]** (Win) or **[return]** (Mac)
   The name of the left frame is now page_links. You leave the rest of the settings alone, including the No Resize option.

QuickTip

When you click inside a frame, the Property Inspector will display the properties for the contents of the frame. To display the frame properties, select the frame in the Frames panel.

4. Click **mainFrame** in the Frames panel, highlight **mainFrame** in the Frame Name text box, type **main**, then press **[Enter]** (Win) or **[return]** (Mac)
   The name of the main frame is now main. Notice that the Scroll text box displays Default, instead of No. This means that the main frame will show scroll bars in a browser window. Most browsers default to automatically show scroll bars when necessary.
5. Click **File** on the menu bar, click **Save All Frames**, click the **Preview/Debug in Browser icon**, then choose your browser
   Changes to the three frames and the frameset are saved simultaneously, and the products frameset page is displayed in the browser window. To save only one frame at a time, place the insertion point in that frame, click File on the menu bar, then click Save Frame.
6. Close your browser window
   You return to the Design View in Dreamweaver. You are now ready to make changes to the content in the frames.

FIGURE H-10: Setting the frame properties for the top frame

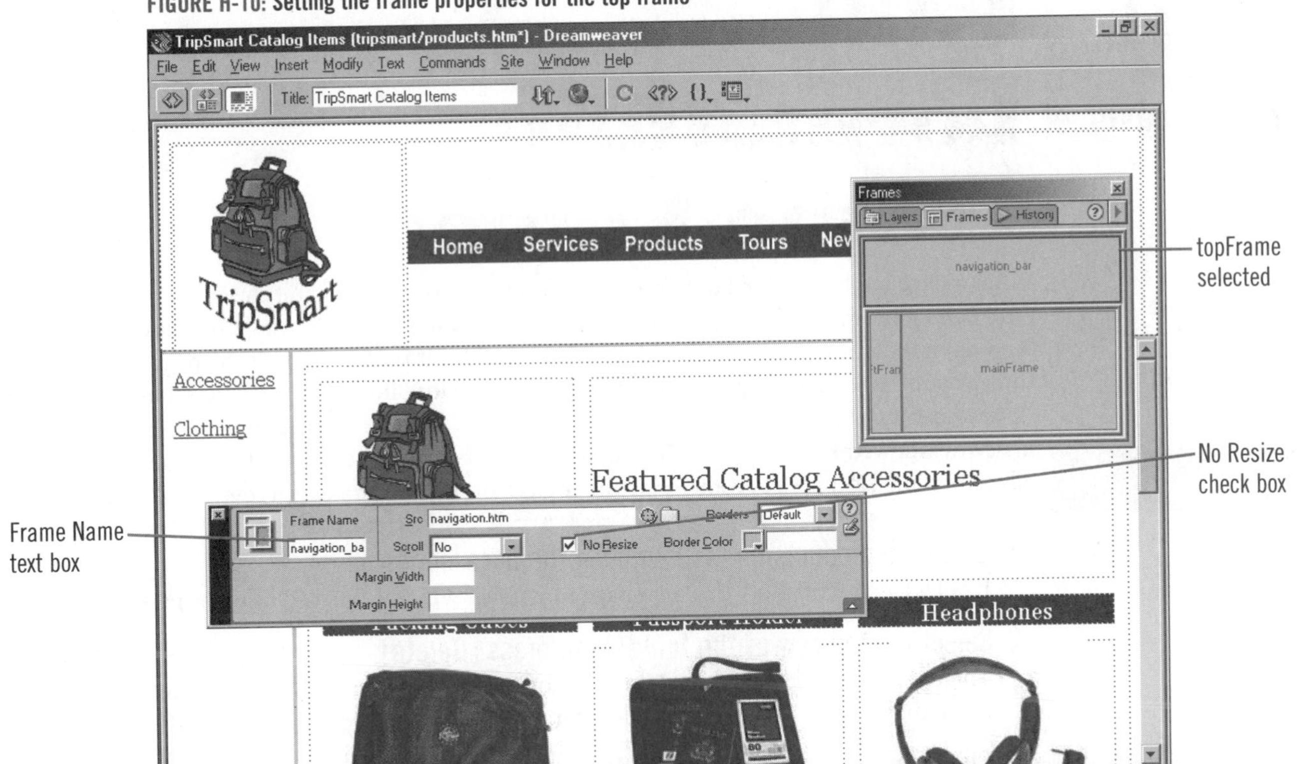

Frameset considerations

When a viewer clicks a link to a Web page containing multiple frames, he or she must wait for all of the frame page files and the frameset page file to download before the entire page is displayed. For example, if a frameset contains three frames, four files are downloaded to display the frameset. For this reason, you should keep each frame's file size as small as possible. Large files take longer to download, which may cause visitors to your Web site to become impatient.

Dreamweaver 4

Editing and Formatting Frame Content

After a page has been added to a frame in a frameset, you can still edit the contents of that page. You can either make changes to the page while it is open in the frameset or close the frameset and open the frame page in a new document window. It is easier to edit the page in a new document window. After the page is modified, you can close it, then open it again in the frameset to see how the changes look when viewed as a frame. You open the accessories page in a new window, then remove the TripSmart logo and change the size of the text on the page. You also open the clothing page and copy the images on it to your assets folder.

1. **Close the products page, then open the accessories page**
   It is less distracting to work on a page in its own window, instead of within the frameset.
2. **Select the top row of the table, then press [Delete]**
   The top row is deleted, which takes care of the extra TripSmart logo and page heading. You think that the text in the three columns in the main frame would look nicer if it were smaller.
3. **Click the insertion point in the first cell in the third row, click the cell tag icon on the tag selector <td>, click the Size list arrow on the Property Inspector, then click 2**
   The size of the text in the first cell changes to size 2, as shown in Figure H-11.

Trouble?

Be careful not to click +2 instead of 2 in the list of sizes on the Property Inspector.

4. **Repeat Step 3 to change the size of the text in the next two cells to 2**
   The text in all three cells is set to size 2. You save your changes and close the page.
5. **Click File on the menu bar, click Save to save the page, click File on the menu bar, then click Close to close the page**
   When the accessories page is displayed in the main frame of the products frameset, the type size will appear as size 2.
6. **Open products.htm, click the Preview/Debug in Browser icon, then choose your browser**
   The products page looks much better now. Viewers can use the scroll bars in the main frame to read the text on the accessories page.
7. **Close the browser window**
   You are ready to work on setting the frameset links.
8. **Open clothing.htm from the drive and folder where your Project Files are stored for Unit H, then save it as clothing.htm, replacing the original clothing.htm file in the tripsmart root folder**
   The new clothing page opens. The clothing page will replace the accessories page in the main frame whenever the Clothing link is clicked.
9. **Copy the hat.jpg, pants.jpg, and vest.jpg images in your assets folder, then save and close the page**
   The images are saved in the assets folder.

FIGURE H-11: Editing and formatting a frame

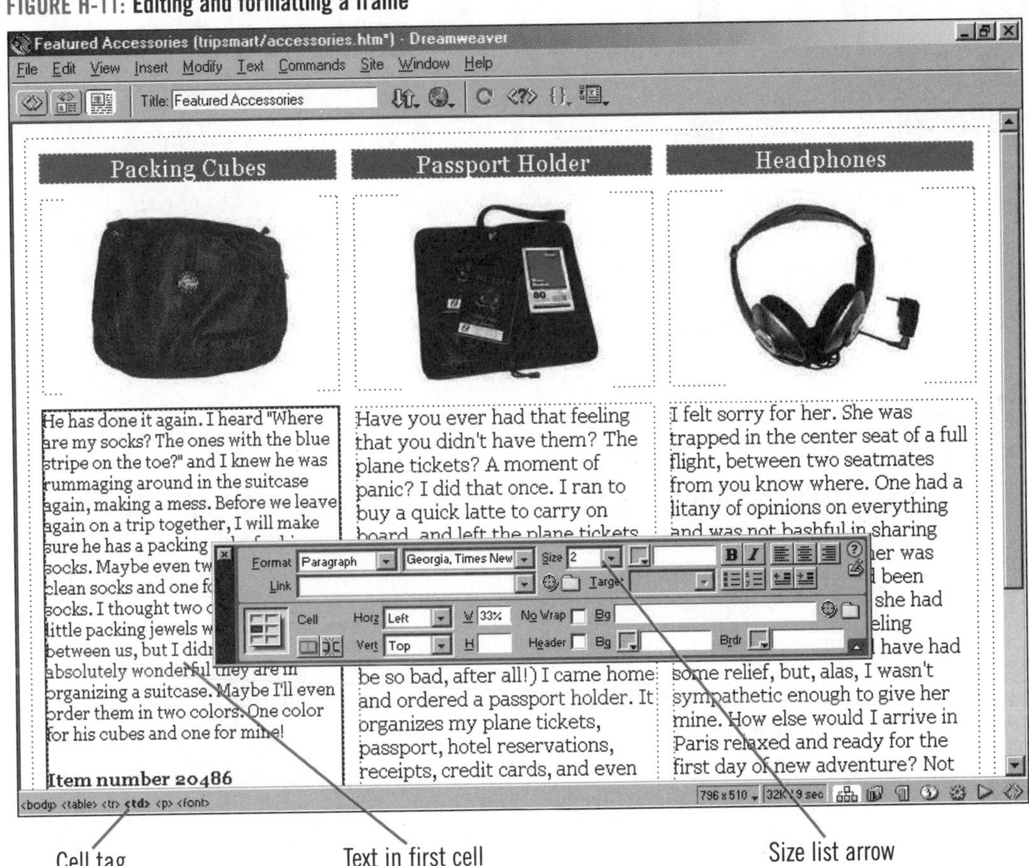

Creating a noframes option

As discussed earlier, framesets are controversial. Some people do not enjoy using framesets. Others may have older versions of browser software that do not support frames. You should provide an option for viewers to view your pages without using frames. This is called a **noframes** option. To create a noframes option, click Modify on the menu bar, point to Frameset, then click Edit NoFrames Content. The NoFrames Content window that opens is used to create the content that will be displayed in place of the frameset. If you create a noframes option, you should create a No Frames link on your Web page. When it is clicked, viewers will see your noframes content instead of the frames in the frameset.

Dreamweaver 4

Dreamweaver 4

Linking Frames

The purpose of creating a frameset is to be able to click a link in a frame in the frameset and have another file open in the same frame or in a different frame in the frameset. Typically, designers place the changing content in one frame, such as the main frame, and the navigation links in another frame that does not change. To link frames together, each link must have a target. A **target** is the frame that will open when the link is clicked. When you assign a target to a link, you use the name given to the frame in the Property Inspector. You set the target for the Accessories and Clothing links. The navigation bar in the top frame and the links in the left frame will not change, but the main frame will display either the accessories page or the clothing page, depending on which link is clicked.

Steps

1. **Open the products.htm page, show the Property Inspector, if necessary, then double-click Accessories in the left frame to select it**
   The properties of the highlighted text appear in the Property Inspector. When a viewer clicks the Accessories link, you want the accessories.htm page to open in the main frame of the products page. You need to set the target for the Accessories link.

2. **Click the Target list arrow on the Property Inspector, then click main**
   The target is now set so that the accessories.htm page will open in the main page if it is not already displayed. As shown in Figure H-12, the three named frames appear in the Target list arrow in addition to four default target settings provided by Dreamweaver. They include _blank, _parent, _self, and _top and are described in much more detail in Table H-1.

3. **Double-click Clothing in the left frame, click the Target list arrow, then click main**
   The target is now set so that the clothing.htm page will open in the main page when the Clothing link is clicked.

4. **Click File on the menu bar, then click Save all Frames**
   Changes to the frames and the frameset are saved.

5. **Click the Preview/Debug in Browser icon, choose your browser, then click each link in the left frame and top frame to make sure that each one works correctly**
   The links in the left frame work correctly, but the links in the navigation frame do not. You need to set targets for the links in the navigation frame.

6. **Close your browser, click the Home element on the navigation bar in the navigation frame to select it, click the Target list arrow, then click _top, as shown in Figure H-13**
   Now, when the Home link is clicked, the home page will open in the whole window, rather than in the frameset. The home page is not part of the frameset.

7. **Repeat Step 6 for the Services, Products, Tours, and Newsletter elements on the navigation bar in the navigation frame, then save all frames**
   Each element on the navigation bar is set to open the respective page in a window by itself, replacing the entire frameset.

8. **Click the Preview/Debug in Browser icon, choose your browser, then click each link in both the left and navigation frames to make sure that each works correctly**
   All links now work correctly.

9. **Close your browser window**
   Your finished project should resemble Figure H-14.

Trouble?

Images and internal links that display a broken link or an absolute path (extra characters, such as forward slashes and colons), can be fixed by selecting the graphic or the link, then clicking the Browse for File icon on the Property Inspector. Images should be saved in the assets folder overwriting the existing file, if necessary. For links, double-click the filename in the root folder, overwriting the existing file.

Trouble?

To return to the products page after checking a link in the navigation bar, click the Products link.

FIGURE H-12: Setting a target for Accessories

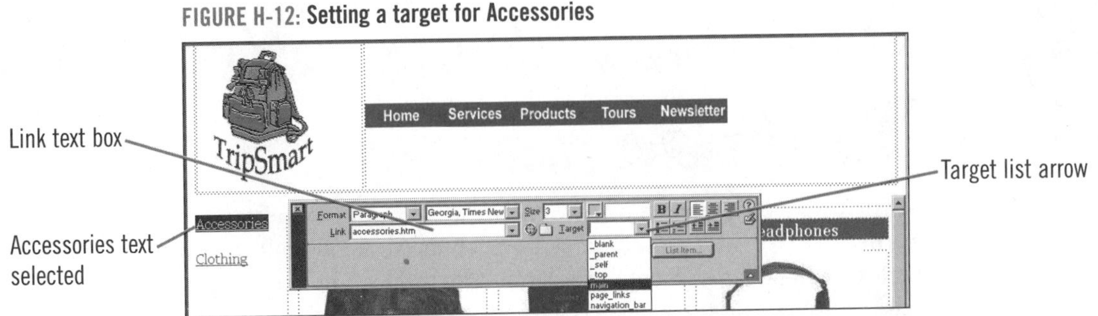

FIGURE H-13: Setting a target for Home

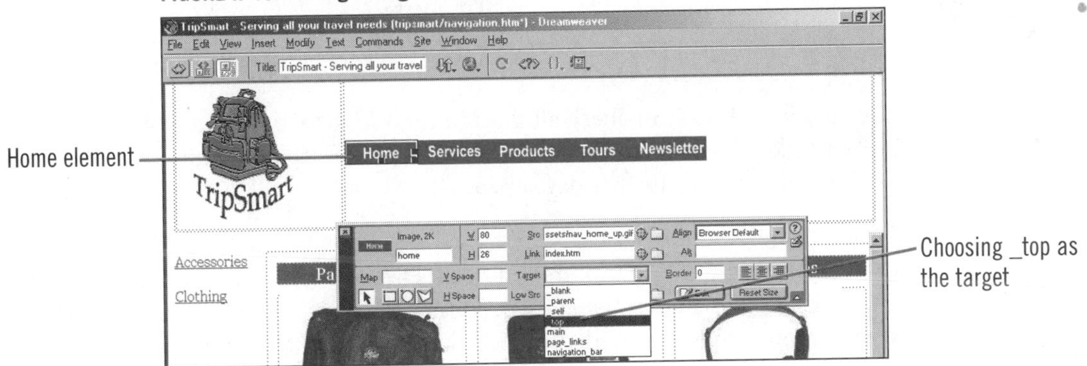

FIGURE H-14: The finished project

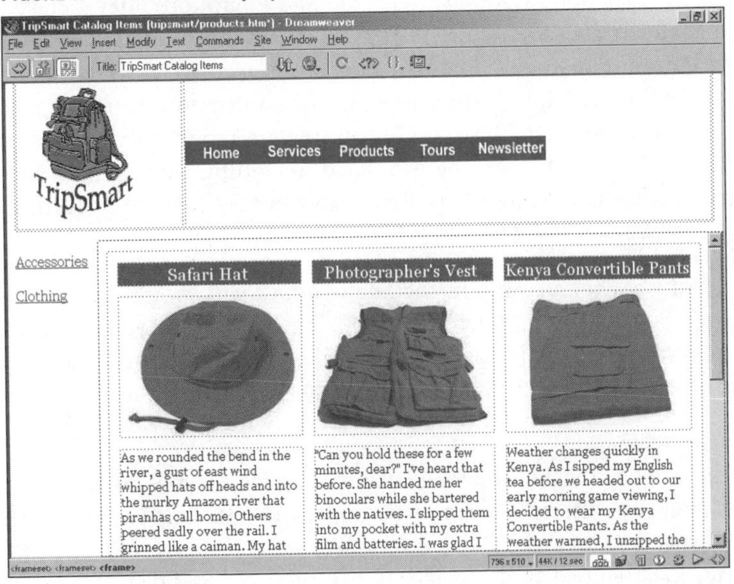

TABLE H-1: Target locations

_blank	Opens the linked document in a separate browser window
_parent	Opens the linked document in the parent frameset
_self	Opens the linked document in the same frame
_top	Opens the linked document in the whole browser window, replacing the original frameset

Dreamweaver 4

Performing Web Site Maintenance

At fairly frequent intervals you should perform routine Web site maintenance tasks. As you have learned, as Web sites grow they can quickly become difficult to manage if maintenance is not performed regularly. There are several tasks that can be quickly performed to keep a Web site "clean." You are pleased with your progress on the TripSmart Web site. Before you add more to the Web site, you review the checklist of routine maintenance tasks below, to make sure the site is in great shape.

- **Check Links Sitewide**
  Use the Link Checker to check all links in the Web site, both external and internal. Repair any broken links. Check for orphaned files. If there are orphaned files, evaluate whether the files need to be deleted or further developed.

- **Assets panel**
  Use the Assets panel to check the list of images and colors used in your Web site. If there are images listed that are not being used, consider moving them to a storage folder outside of the Web site until they are needed. Check the Colors list to make sure that all colors listed are Websafe. If there are non-Websafe colors in the list, locate the elements that the non-Websafe colors are applied to and re-apply Websafe colors to them.

- **Site reports**
  The Reports option, found under the Site menu, provides a checklist of reports that you can generate for your Web site. Figure H-15 shows the Reports dialog box. You can create reports for the current document, the entire local site, selected files in the site, or a selected folder by clicking the Report On list arrow and choosing an option. You can create a Workflow report to see files that have been Checked Out or create a report to view the Design Notes. There are five HTML Reports that can be generated, including Combinable Nested Font Tags, Missing Alt Text, Redundant Nested Tags, Removable Empty Tags, and Untitled Documents.

- **Site Map**
  Looking at the Site Map in the Site window, you should ask yourself the following questions: Does the navigation structure reflect a logically organized flow chart? Is each page three or four clicks from the home page? If not, make any adjustments that would improve the navigation structure. Figure H-16 is an example of a Site Map.

- **Test pages**
  Test each page again for design layout, using many types and versions of browsers. Test each page using many different screen resolutions, and test your Web site on different platforms. Test all external links to make sure they connect to valid, active Web sites. Notice how long it takes each page to download, and consider trimming pages that download slowly.

- **Enjoy positive feedback and respond to negative feedback**
  Everyone enjoys hearing positive feedback. When you receive positive feedback, record the positive comments so that you can refer to them in the future as you edit the site. Listen to the negative feedback and use it to your advantage to improve the Web site.

FIGURE H-15: **Reports dialog box**

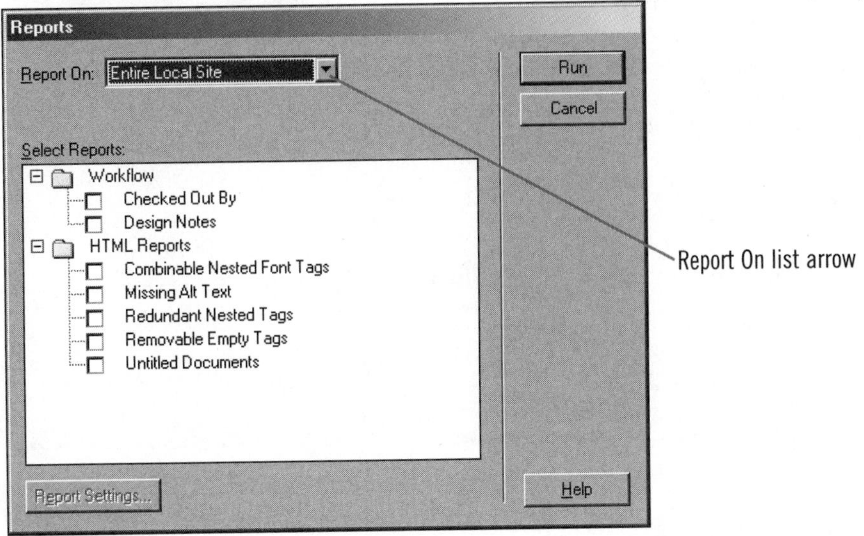

FIGURE H-16: **A Site Map**

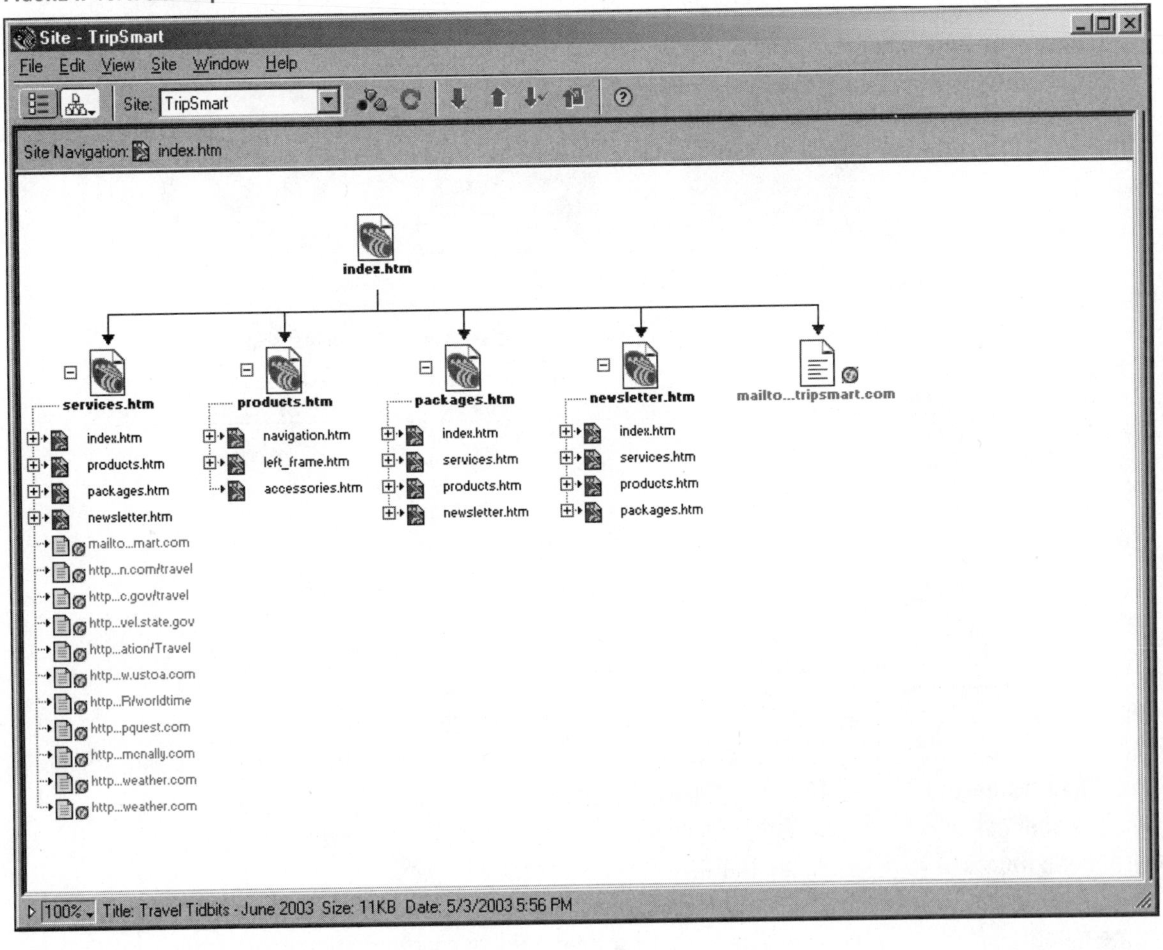

Site - TripSmart
File Edit View Site Window Help
Site: TripSmart
Site Navigation: index.htm
index.htm
services.htm
products.htm
packages.htm
newsletter.htm
mailto...tripsmart.com
index.htm
products.htm
packages.htm
newsletter.htm
mailto...mart.com
http...n.com/travel
http...c.gov/travel
http...vel.state.gov
http...ation/Travel
http...w.ustoa.com
http...R/worldtime
http...pquest.com
http...mcnally.com
http...weather.com
http...weather.com
navigation.htm
left_frame.htm
accessories.htm
index.htm
services.htm
products.htm
newsletter.htm
index.htm
services.htm
products.htm
packages.htm
100% Title: Travel Tidbits - June 2003 Size: 11KB Date: 5/3/2003 5:56 PM

Practice

▶ Concepts Review

Label each element in the Site window shown in Figure H-17.

FIGURE H-17

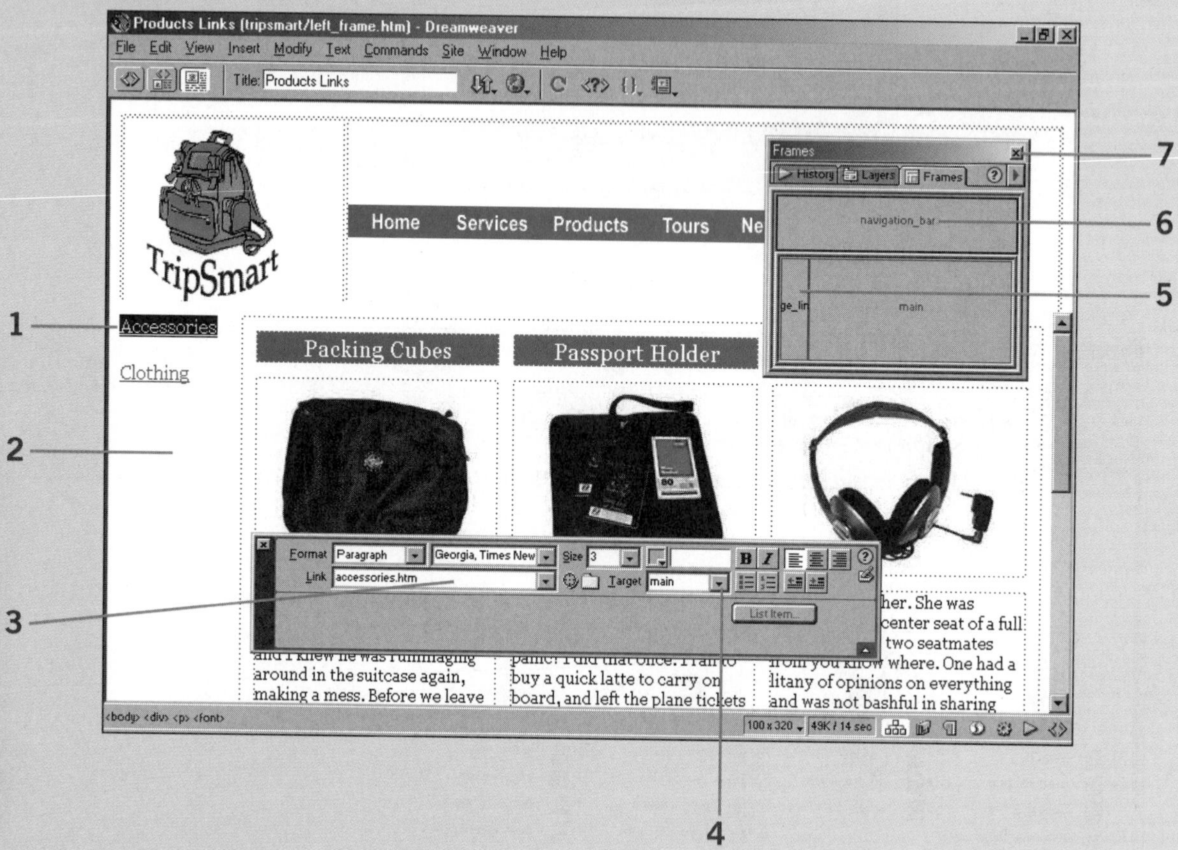

Match each of the following terms with the statement that describes its function.

8. Frame
9. Frameset
10. Predefined frameset
11. Frames panel
12. Noframes option
13. Target
14. Frame name

a. Automatically created by Dreamweaver
b. Used to view and modify the frameset structure as you work with frames pages
c. Option for viewing frames pages outside of frames
d. A Web page displayed in an individual window in your browser
e. Name that is used when setting targets
f. Frame that will open when a link is clicked
g. A Web page that provides code to coordinate individual pages, or frames

Select the best answer from the following list of choices.

15. The type of target that will open a page in a separate browser window is called:
- **a.** _blank.
- **b.** _top.
- **c.** _parent.
- **d.** _self.

16. The RowColumn Selection box is used:
- **a.** To delete rows and columns.
- **b.** To add rows and columns.
- **c.** To select frames, also referred to as rows and columns.
- **d.** To select the frameset.

17. A target can be set by using the:
- **a.** Property Inspector.
- **b.** Target Inspector.
- **c.** Frames panel.
- **d.** Frameset tag icon.

Skills Review

***Important**: If you did not create this Web site in Unit B and maintain it during the preceding units, you will need to create a root folder for this Web site and define the Web site using files your instructor will provide. See the "Read This Before You Begin" section for more detailed instructions.*

1. Create a frameset.
- **a.** Open the Blooms&Bulbs Web site.
- **b.** Open plants.htm, then save it as *featured_plants.htm.*
- **c.** Create a new page in Design View.
- **d.** Show the Objects panel, click the Objects panel list arrow, then click Frames to display the frame options.
- **e.** Click the Insert Top and Nested Left Frame icon on the Frames panel.
- **f.** Type **Our Greenhouse Plants** as the page title.

2. Save a frameset and view the Frames panel.
- **a.** Make sure the frameset is selected, then save the frameset as *plants.htm*, overwriting the existing file.
- **b.** Open dmh_3.htm from the drive and folder where your Project Files are stored for Unit H.
- **c.** Save dmh_3.htm as *navigation.htm* and store it in the root folder of the Blooms&Bulbs Web site.
- **d.** Click each image on the navigation bar and remove any absolute paths, if necessary, by clicking each element, clicking Modify on the menu bar, clicking Navigation Bar, then clicking the Browse button for each state.
- **e.** Use the Navigation Bar command under the Modify menu to check and set relative paths for all links, if necessary, then save and close the page.
- **f.** Open dmh_4.htm from the drive and folder where your Project Files are stored for Unit H.
- **g.** Save dmh_4.htm as *left_frame.htm* in the root folder of the Blooms&Bulbs Web site, then close the page.
- **h.** Open annuals.htm from the drive and folder where your Project Files are stored for Unit H, then save it in your root folder, using the same name and overwriting the existing file.
- **i.** Select the image on the page and use the Browse for File icon on the Property Inspector to save the image in the assets folder.

j. Repeat Steps h and i for the perennials.htm and water_plants.htm files.
k. Close all of the open files except for the plants.htm file. (Hint: If the plants.htm file was closed, you will see several messages warning you of unsaved pages when you open it. Close the messages and proceed. You have not linked the frames to page files yet.)
l. Display the Frames panel, if necessary.
m. Click topFrame in the Frames panel, then type **navigation.htm** in the Src text box on the Property Inspector. (*Hint*: If you do not see frame borders, click View on the menu bar, point to Visual Aids, then click Frame Borders.)
n. Click leftFrame in the Frames panel, then type **left_frame.htm** in the Src text box on the Property Inspector.
o. Click mainframe in the Frames panel, then type **featured_plants.htm** in the Src text box on the Property Inspector.
p. Save all frames.

3. Format a frameset using the Property Inspector.

a. Using the Property Inspector and the Frames panel, change the height of the top navigation frame to 85 pixels. (*Hint*: Click the entire frameset border in the Frames panel.)
b. Using the Property Inspector, change the width of the left frame to 100 pixels. (*Hint*: Click the border around the mainFrame and LeftFrame in the Frames panel.)
c. Save all frames.

4. Format a frame using the Property Inspector.

a. Click topFrame in the Frames panel.
b. Type **navigation_bar** in the Frame Name text box on the Property Inspector.
c. Click the leftFrame border in the Frames panel and change the name of leftFrame to **page_links**.
d. Click the mainFrame border in the Frames panel and change the name of mainframe to **main**.
e. Save all frames.

5. Edit and format frame content.

a. Open featured_plants.htm.
b. Delete the logo, the text around the logo, and the navigation bar.
c. Save and close the file.

6. Link the frames together.

a. Place the insertion point in the left frame of the plants page.
b. Highlight Featured Plants and use the Property Inspector to link the text to featured_plants.htm and target the main frame.
c. Highlight Annuals and use the Property Inspector to link the source to annuals.htm and target the main frame.
d. Highlight Perennials and use the Property Inspector to link the source to perennials.htm and target the main frame.
e. Highlight Water Plants and use the Property Inspector to link the source to water_plants.htm and target the main frame.
f. Use the Property Inspector to set targets for all the navigation links in the navigation bar to _top.
g. Save all frames.
h. Preview each page in the browser and check all links.
i. Close your browser.

***Important**: If you did not create these Web sites in Unit B and maintain them during the preceding units, you will need to create a root folder for these Web sites and define the Web sites using files your instructor will provide. See the "Read This Before You Begin" section for more detailed instructions.*

► Independent Challenge 1

Off Note is a music store specializing in classical, blues, rock, country, and jazz. Rose Lyons, the store manager, has asked you to create a frameset page for her Web site that will link pages about music categories together. You can use Figure H-18 as a reference to get you started. (*Hint*: It is easier to open each page that you are editing in a new window than to edit frame pages in a frameset.)

FIGURE H-18

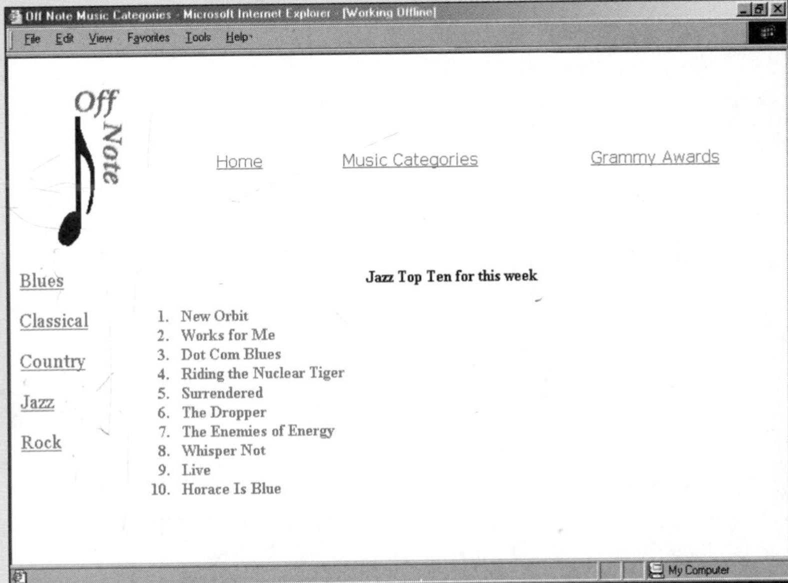

a. Open the Off Note Web site, then open categories.htm.
b. Create a frameset on this page, using your choice of frameset options.
c. Title the page **Off Note Music Categories**.
d. Create a navigation bar in one frame with links to the Home, Music Categories, and Grammy Awards pages.
e. Create a navigation bar in another frame with links to the Blues, Classical, Country, Jazz, and Rock pages.
f. Use the Frames panel to name each frame.
g. Name the individual pages for music categories that will open in the main frame as blues.htm, classical.htm, country.htm, jazz.htm, and rock.htm.
h. Create page content, such as a title or descriptive text, to help identify each page, so you will know that your links are opening the correct pages.
i. Set targets for the Home, Music Categories, and Grammy Awards pages to _top.
j. Preview the page in your browser, then test all links.
k. Save all pages.

 Independent Challenge 2

Jacob's Restaurant is an upscale restaurant catering to business executives and theater patrons. They have an extensive menu including prix fixe dinners, pre-theater dinner specials, and after-theater specials. The cuisine is primarily French. Customers have recently asked Jacob to keep the monthly, featured recipes up on his Web site, rather than take them down, after each month is over.

a. Open the Jacob's Web site.

b. Open recipes.htm.

c. Select all of the page elements. (*Hint*: Click Edit on the menu bar, then click Select All.) Click Edit on the menu bar, then click Copy to copy all of the page elements.

d. Create a new page in Design View, click Edit on the menu bar, click Paste, then save the new page as *mushroom_caps.htm*.

e. Title the page **Mushroom Caps**.

f. Since this page is going to be a frames page, delete any unnecessary page content, such as the navigation bar.

g. Create a frameset with at least three frames, then save the frameset as recipes.htm, replacing the existing recipes.htm file in the Jacob's root folder.

h. Title the frameset **Favorite Recipes**.

i. Create a navigation bar on one of the frames that will link to the Home, Pre-theater Offerings, Prix Fixe Menu, After-Theater Desserts, and Recipes pages.

j. Open dmh_5.htm from the drive and folder where your Project Files are stored for Unit H, then save it as *rolls.htm*.

k. Create two links in one frame called Mushroom Caps and Grandmother's Rolls.

l. Link Mushroom Caps to mushroom_caps.htm, then set the target of mushroom_caps.htm so that it opens in the main frame.

m. Link Grandmother's Rolls to rolls.htm, then set the target of rolls.htm so that it opens in the main frame.

n. Edit any or all of the pages used in the frameset to create the look you want.

o. Save all frames and pages, then test your links in your browser.

FIGURE H-19

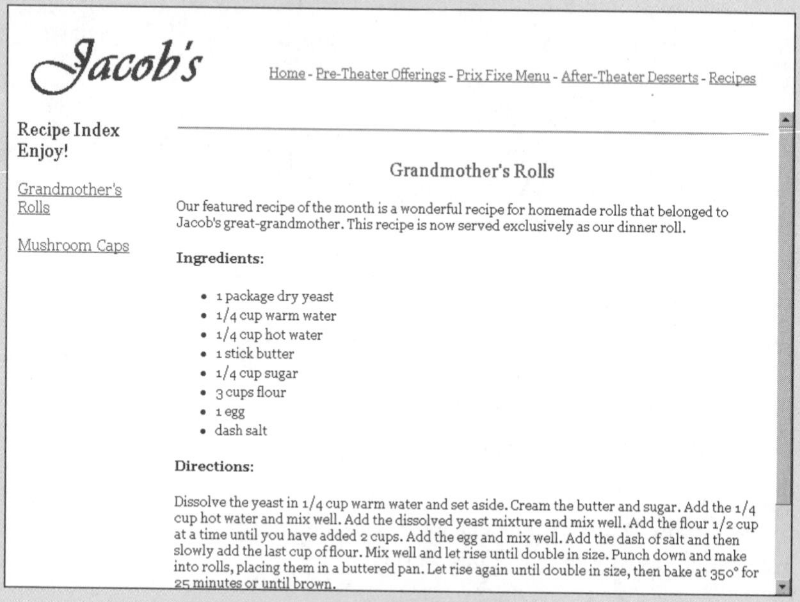

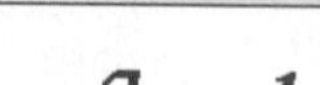

Independent Challenge 3

Rapids Transit is a river expedition company. They are located on the Buffalo River in Northwest Arkansas. In addition to renting canoes, kayaks, and rafts, they have a country store and snack bar. Mike, the owner of Rapids Transit, has asked you to work on a page for his country store. The store page will be a frameset that will contain a page for their snack items with another page to be added later.

a. Open the Rapids Transit Web site.
b. Create a frameset on a new page and save it as *store.htm*, overwriting the existing file.
c. Title it **Our Country Store**.
d. Create a navigation bar out of text or buttons on one of the frames.
e. Set the snacks.htm file to display in the main frame.
f. Using Figure H-20 as a guide, create page content for snacks.htm. You may include the fruit_basket.jpg graphic from the drive and folder where your Project Files are stored in the assets folder in the Unit H folder.
g. Make sure that all frames have page titles.
h. Save all frames.

FIGURE H-20

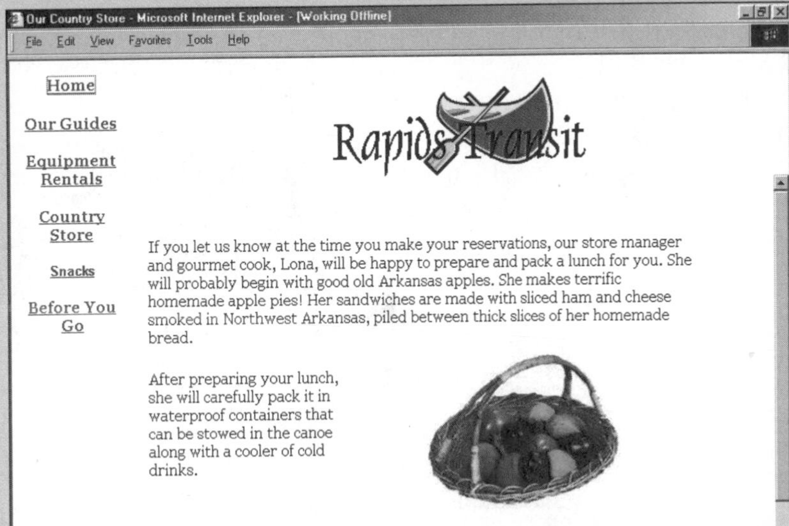

Independent Challenge 4

Grace Keiko is an artist who specializes in watercolor paintings. Grace would like to have a professional Web site designed to help to advertise her paintings. Grace would like to incorporate the use of frames in her Web site, but needs to learn a little more about them.

a. Connect to the Internet and go to Macromedia at *www.macromedia.com* as shown in Figure H-21.
b. Type **frames** in the Search text box, then click Go.
c. Browse several articles to gather information about frames.
d. Print the article that you find most informative.

FIGURE H-21

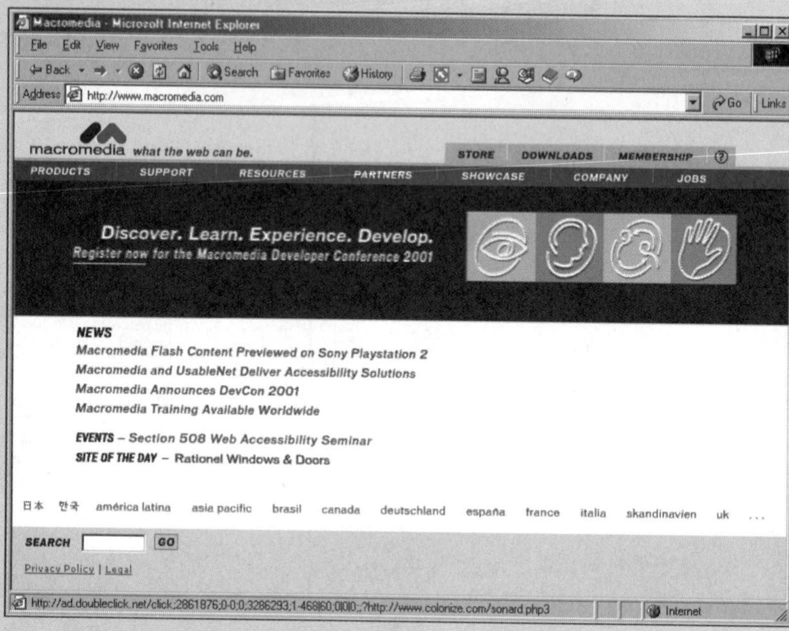

Independent Challenge 5

Paula Melton owns a small computer-consulting firm. She has found a real niche in her area making house calls for small computer problems such as installing printers and software, adding memory, and updating hardware. She would like to create a Web site to advertise her business and is interested in using either frames or "fake frames." She views several Web sites that use frames pages. Record your answers to the questions below on scrap paper or using your word-processing software.

a. Connect to the Internet and go to the University of Arkansas' athletic programs Web site at *www.hogwired.com* as shown in Figure H-22.

b. Does the page use a frameset or the illusion of a frameset?

c. Do you see Flash content?

d. Go to Fisher Scientific at *www.fisherscientific.com/html/frameset.htm.*

e. How long did the page take to load?

f. Do you like the design of the frameset?

g. Which layout in general do you prefer—framesets or fake framesets? Why?

h. Find one more example of a Web site that uses a frameset or a fake frameset, record the name of the Web site, and state whether it uses a frameset or a fake frameset.

FIGURE H-22

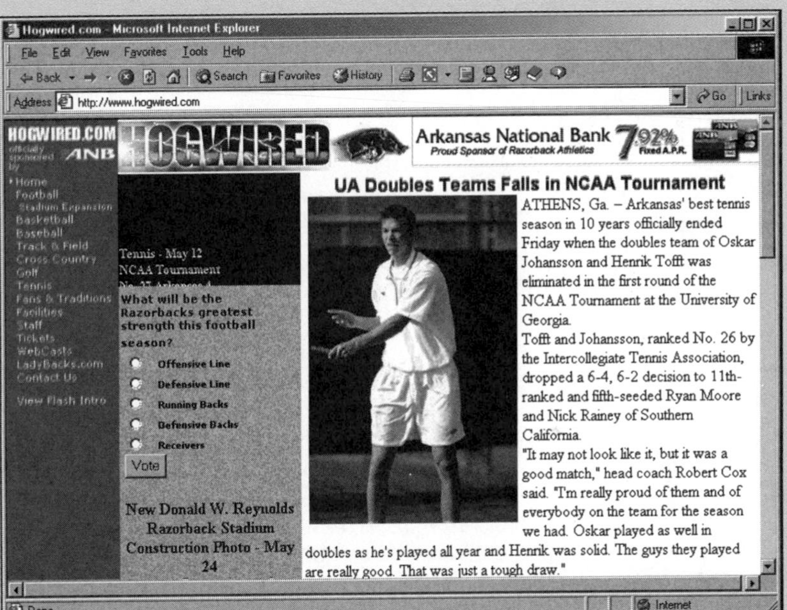

► Visual Workshop

The Over Under Dive Shop is a dive center in Nevis, West Indies. It is a certified Professional Association of Diving Instructors (PADI) dive center offering PADI certification courses. They also conduct snorkeling and dive trips to various locations around the barrier reef surrounding Nevis. Jon, the dive master, would like you to create a frameset for the snorkeling page. He wants to feature night snorkeling with a short description and a photograph taken at night. (If you have not maintained this website from the previous unit, then contact your instructor for assistance. Create the frameset shown in Figure H-23, using night_coral.jpg and mask_fins.jpg, found in the drive and folder where your Project Files are stored for Unit H. The images are in the assets folder.

FIGURE H-23

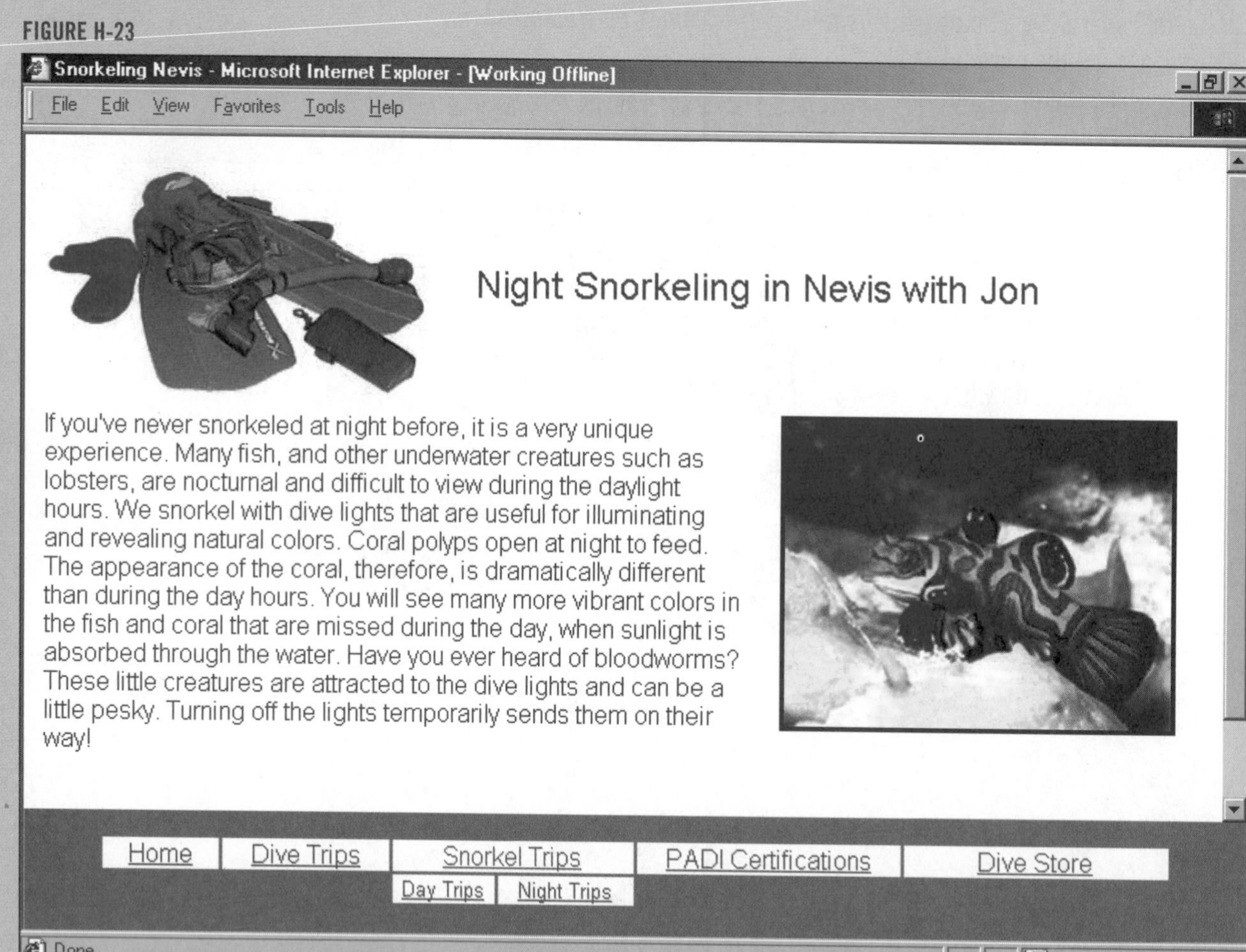

Project Files List

To complete the lessons and practice exercises in this book, students need to use Project Files that are supplied by Course Technology. Once obtained, students select where to store the files, such as to the hard disk drive, network server, or Zip disk. Below is a list of the files that are supplied, and the unit or practice exercise to which the files correspond. For information on how to obtain Project Files, please see the inside cover of this book. The following list only includes Project Files that are supplied; it does not included the files students create from scratch or the files students create by revising the supplied files.

Unit	File supplied on Project Disk	Location file is used in unit
Unit A	**Unit A folder:** dma_1.htm **Unit A/assets folder:** tripsmart.gif	Lessons
	Unit A folder: dma_2.htm **Unit A/assets folder:** blooms_logo.gif	Skills Review
Unit B	**Unit B folder:** dmb_1.htm **Unit B/assets folder:** tripsmart.gif	Lessons
	Unit B folder: dmb_2.htm **Unit B/assets folder:** blooms_logo.gif	Skills Review
	Unit B folder: dmb_3.htm **Unit B/assets folder:** rapids_logo.gif	Independent Challenge 2 Independent Challenge 3
	Unit B folder: dmb_4.htm **Unit B/assets folder:** over_logo.gif	
	Unit B folder: dmb_5.htm **Unit B/assets folder:** jacobs_logo.gif	Independent Challenge 4
	Unit B folder: dmb_6.htm **Unit B/assets folder:** offnote_logo.gif	Visual Workshop
Unit C	No files supplied	
Unit D	**Unit D folder:** dmd_1.htm	Lessons

Unit	File supplied on Project Disk	Location file is used in unit
	how_to_pack.htm packing_essentials.htm **Unit D/assets folder:** tripsmart.gif masthead.jpg	
	Unit D folder: dmd_2.htm gardening_tips.htm **Unit D/assets folder:** blooms_logo.gif planting_tips.jpg	Skills Review
	Unit D folder: dmd_3.htm equip_list.htm **Unit D/assets folder:** shell.jpg over_logo.gif	Independent Challenge 2
	UnitD/assets folder: offnote_logo.gif	Independent Challenge 3
	Unit D/assets folder: jacobs_logo.gif	Visual Workshop
Unit E	**Unit E folder:** dme_1.htm **Unit E/assets folder:** giraffe.jpg lion.jpg seamless_bak.gif tile_bak.gif tripsmart.gif zebra_mothers.jpg	Lessons
	Unit E folder: dme_2.htm **Unit E/assets folder:** blooms_logo.gif daisies.gif iris.jpg pansies.jpg tulips.jpg	Skills Review
	Unit E folder: dme_3.htm **Unit E/assets folder:** fish_1.jpg fish_2.jpg fish_3.jpg over_logo.gif	Independent Challenge 2
	Unit E folder: dme_4.htm	Independent Challenge 3

Unit	File supplied on Project Disk	Location file is used in unit
	Unit E/assets folder: buster_tricks.jpg rapids_logo.gif	
	Unit E folder: dme_5.htm **Unit E/assets folder:** jacobs_logo.gif oranges.jpg poached_pear.jpg triple_cheesecake.jpg	Visual Workshop
Unit F	**Unit F folder:** dmf_1.htm **Unit F/assets folder:** nav_home_down.gif nav_home_up.gif nav_newsletter_down.gif nav_newsletter_up.gif nav_products_down.gif nav_products_up.gif nav_services_down.gif nav_services_up.gif nav_tours_down.gif nav_tours_up.gif tripsmart.gif	Lessons
	Unit F folder: dmf_2.htm **Unit F/assets folder:** blooms_logo.gif nav_ask_down.gif nav_ask_up.gif nav_bhome_down.gif nav_bhome_up.gif nav_events_down.gif nav_events_up.gif nav_plants_down.gif nav_plants_up.gif nav_tips_down.gif nav_tips_up.gif	Skills Review
	Unit F folder: dmf_3.htm **Unit F/assets folder:** jacobs_logo.gif	Independent Challenge 1
	Unit F folder: dmf_4.htm **Unit F/assets folder:** buffalo_fall.gif rapids_logo.gif	Independent Challenge 2
Unit G	**Unit G folder:** headphones.htm passport_holder.htm packing_cube.htm	Lessons

Unit	File supplied on Project Disk	Location file is used in unit
	Unit G/assets folder: headphones.jpg passport_holder.jpg packing_cubes.jpg tripsmart.gif	
	Unit G folder: agenda.htm exhibition.htm nursery.htm tearoom.htm **Unit G/assets folder:** blooms_logo.gif tearoom.jpg texas_rose.jpg yellow_rose.jpg	Skills Review
	Unit G folder: dinner.htm **Unit G/assets folder:** grapes.jpg jacobs_logo.gif	Independent Challenge 1
	Unit G/assets folder: over_logo.gif	Independent Challenge 2
	Unit G/assets folder: cd_sale.jpg offnote_logo.gif	Independent Challenge 3
	Unit G/assets folder: kayak.jpg	Visual Workshop
Unit H	**Unit H folder** clothing.htm dmh_1.htm dmh_2.htm **Unit H/assets folder:** hat.jpg nav_home_down.gif nav_home_up.gif nav_newsletter_down.gif nav_newsletter_up.gif nav_products_down.gif nav_products_up.gif nav_services_down.gif nav_services_up.gif nav_tours_down.gif nav_tours_up.gif pants.jpg tripsmart.gif vest.jpg	Lessons
	Unit H folder: annuals.htm dmh_3.htm dmh_4.htm perennials.htm water_plants.htm	Skills Review

Unit	File supplied on Project Disk	Location file is used in unit
	Unit H/assets folder: blooms_logo.gif fuchsia.jpg iris2.jpg nav_ask_down.gif nav_ask_up.gif nav_bhome_down.gif nav_bhome_up.gif nav_events_down.gif nav_events_up.gif nav_plants_down.gif nav_plants_up.gif nav_tips_down.gif nav_tips_up.gif water_hyacinth.jpg	
	Unit H folder: dmh_5.htm **Unit H/assets folder:** jacobs_logo.gif	Independent Challenge 2
	Unit H/assets folder: fruit_basket.jpg	Independent Challenge 3
	Unit H/assets folder: mask_fins.jpg night_coral.jpg	Visual Workshop

Dreamweaver 4

Glossary

Absolute paths Paths containing external links that reference links on Web pages outside of the current Web site.

Aligning an image Positioning an image on a Web page in relationship to other elements on the page.

Alternative text Descriptive text that can be set to display in place of an image while the image is downloading or when a mouse is placed over an image.

Assets folder A subfolder in which you store most of the files that are not HTML files, such as images and video clips.

Assets panel A panel that contains nine categories of assets, such as images, used in a Web site. Clicking a category icon will display a list of those assets.

Background color The color that fills an entire Web page, a frame, a table, or a cell.

Background image A graphic file used in place of a background color.

Bobby A free service provided by CAST to test Web sites for accessibility for handicapped people.

Body The part of a Web page that is seen when the page is viewed in a browser window.

Borders Outlines that surround an image, a cell, a table, or a frame.

Broken links Links that cannot find the intended destination file for the link.

Bullet A small raised dot or similar icon that is used to make lists easier to read than unformatted lists.

Cascading Style Sheet A file used to assign common formatting specifications to page elements such as text, objects, and tables.

CAST Center for Applied Special Technology.

Cell padding The distance between the cell content and the cell walls.

Cell spacing The distance between cells.

Cells Small boxes, within a table, that are used to hold text or graphics. Cells are arranged horizontally in rows and vertically in columns.

Check In/Check Out A Dreamweaver organizational feature that keeps track of which files in a Web site are currently "checked out" by other team members.

Clean up HTML and Clean up Word HTML Dreamweaver commands used to remove undesirable or unnecessary code, such as proprietary remarks or extra spaces.

Clip art collections Groups of graphic files collected on disks.

Code and Design View A Dreamweaver view which is a combination of the Code View and the Design View.

Code Inspector A panel that displays HTML code for editing purposes.

Code Navigation A toolbar icon that allows you to navigate through the source code.

Code View A Dreamweaver view that displays the HTML code for the page.

Comments Helpful text describing portions of the HTML code, such as a JavaScript function.

Debug To correct HTML errors.

Default base font Size 3, the size that is applied to text if no other size is assigned.

Default font The font used by a browser to display a Web page if a specific font is not specified.

Defining a Web site Creating a mirror image, or copy, of the root folder.

Definition lists Lists comprised of terms with indented descriptions or definitions.

Delimiter A comma, tab, colon, semicolon, or similar character that separates tabular data.

Description A short description of the Web site, usually two or three sentences, that resides in the head content.

Design Notes A Dreamweaver feature that helps you keep track of the various tasks you need to complete while working on a Web site.

Design View A Dreamweaver view that shows a full screen layout of a Web page, and is primarily used for designing and editing purposes.

Docked panels Panels that have been joined or docked together to form one panel.

Document-relative paths Paths that are referenced in relation to the Web page that is currently displayed.

Domain name An IP address expressed in letters rather than numbers.

Dreamweaver Support Center A Web site hosted by Macromedia with an extensive amount of help information about Dreamweaver.

Edit a page To insert, delete, or change page content, such as inserting a new image, adding a link, or correcting spelling errors.

Enable Cache A setting to direct the computer system to use temporary memory on the hard drive, or cache, while you are working in Dreamweaver.

Enhancing an image Improving the appearance of an image.

Exporting To save data that was created in Dreamweaver as a special file format.

External links Links that connect to Web pages in other Web sites.

Favorites Assets that you expect to use repeatedly while you work on the site and are categorized separately in the Assets panel.

File Management A toolbar icon that is used to display file management options.

Flash A Macromedia software program used for creating animation for Web pages.

Format a page To make adjustments in the appearance of page elements, such as resizing an image or changing the color of text.

Frames Multiple Web pages that appear in one window.

Frames panel A panel that contains a graphic layout of a frameset and helps you identify and modify the frameset structure as you work with frames pages.

Frameset A Web page that is used to tie frame pages together. A frameset page is never seen and contains no content

FTP The acronym for File Transfer Protocol, or the process of uploading and downloading files from a remote site.

Get To retrieve files from the remote server

GIF files Graphics Interchange Format file. A GIF is a type of file format used for images placed on Web pages.

Head content The part of a Web page that is not viewed in the browser window. It includes meta tags, which are HTML codes that include information about the page, such as keywords and descriptions.

Headings Six different text styles that can be applied to paragraphs: Heading 1 (the largest size) through Heading 6 (the smallest size)

Hexadecimal value A value that represents the amount of red, green, and blue in a color.

History panel A panel that lists the steps that have been performed while editing and formatting a document in Dreamweaver.

Home page The page that first opens when you go to a Web site and is usually named index.htm.

Horizontal and vertical space Blank space above, below, and on the sides of an image that separate the image from the text or other elements on the page.

Hotspot A clickable area on a graphic that, when clicked, links to a different location on the page or to another Web page.

htm The default filename extension that is added to a filename when you save a Dreamweaver file in Windows.

html The default filename extension that is added to a filename when you save a Dreamweaver file using Macintosh or Unix.

HTML The acronym for Hyper Text Markup Language, the language used to create Web pages.

HTML Reference panel A panel that gives descriptions of HTML tags.

Image map A graphic that has one or more hotspots placed on it.

Inspectors Panels that display the properties of the currently selected object.

Interlaced graphics A graphic characteristic of JPEG files that allow graphics to appear on a Web page before the browser has fully downloaded them, giving the viewer something to look at while they are waiting for images to finish downloading.

Internal links Links to Web pages within the same Web site.

Invisible Element Icons that only appear on a Web page being edited in Dreamweaver such as alignment tag icons. Invisible Elements is a menu command that must be chosen to activate the feature.

IP address An assigned series of numbers, separated by periods, that designates an address on the Internet.

JavaScript HTML code that adds dynamic content, such as rollovers or interactive forms, to a Web page.

JPEG Joint Photographic Experts Group file. A JPEG is a type of file format used for images that appear on Web pages.

Keywords Words that relate to the content of the Web site and reside in the head content.

Launcher bar A bar that contains icons that open Dreamweaver panels, inspectors, and windows.

Layout View A view in Dreamweaver that is used when you draw your own table.

Links or hyperlinks Text or graphics that, when clicked, direct a viewer to another location.

Local Web server A server that has local access to a computer with a Web site.

---

mailto: link An e-mail address that is formatted as a link that will open the default mail program with a blank, addressed message.

Menu bar A bar located at the top of the document window that lists the names of the menus that contain Dreamweaver commands.

Merge a cell To combine multiple cells into one cell.

Meta tags HTML codes that include information about the page such as keywords and descriptions and reside in the head content.

Named anchors Specific locations on a Web page that are used to link to those portions of the Web page.

Navigation bar A set of text or graphic links that viewers can use to navigate between pages of a Web site.

Nested table A table within a table.

Noframes option An option that allows viewers to be able to view a Web page without using frames.

Non-breaking space A space that will be left on the page by a browser.

Non-Websafe colors Colors that may not display uniformly across platforms.

Objects panel A Dreamweaver panel that contains icons for creating or inserting many types of objects on a Web page, such as tables, images, forms, frames, and layers.

Ordered lists Lists of items that have a specific order that they need to be placed in and are preceded by numbers or letters.

Orphaned files Files that are not linked to any pages in the Web site.

Panels Floating palettes that contain icons for activating Dreamweaver features and commands.

Path The location of an open file in relation to any folders in the Web site.

PNG Portable Network Graphics file. A PNG is a file format used for images placed on Web pages.

Point of contact A place on a Web page that provides viewers with a means of contacting the company.

Predefined framesets Templates of frameset designs.

Preview in Browser A toolbar icon that is used to display the current Dreamweaver page in a browser window.

Primary browser A Dreamweaver preference setting in which you can indicate which browser should be used first when testing your Web page in a browser window.

Progressive JPEG A JPEG image that begins displaying immediately as the browser downloads the file.

Property Inspector A Dreamweaver panel that displays the properties of the currently selected object in Dreamweaver

Publishing a Web site Making a Web site available for viewing on the Internet.

Put To send files to a remote server.

Ransom note effect A description used to imply that many fonts have been randomly used in a document without regard to style.

Reference A toolbar icon that activates the Reference panel.

Refresh Design View A toolbar icon that will force the browser to reload the page to view changes made while editing the page in Dreamweaver.

Refresh Local File List Automatically A setting that directs Dreamweaver to automatically reflect changes made in your file listings.

Relative paths Paths used with internal links to reference Web pages and graphic files within one Web site.

Remote server A server that does not have local access to a computer with a Web site.

Root folder A folder on your hard drive, zip disk or floppy disk that holds all the files and folders for the Web site.

Root-relative paths Paths that are referenced from a Web site's root folder.

Roundtrip HTML A Dreamweaver feature that means that HTML files created in other programs, such as Microsoft FrontPage, can be opened in Dreamweaver without additional code added.

Royalty free Graphics that are free to be copied and published after being purchased without having to pay a royalty to the company that created them.

Sans serif fonts No-nonsense, block style characters used frequently for headings and sub-headings.

Screen reader A device used by the visually impaired to convert written text on a computer monitor to spoken words.

Seamless image A tiled image that is blurred at the edges so it appears to be one image.

Serif fonts Ornate fonts with small extra strokes at the beginning and end of the characters used frequently for paragraph text.

Shockwave A player that must be installed on a computer in order to view movies created with Macromedia software.

Shortcuts and aliases Graphic icons that represent a software program stored on your computer system.

Show Site icon An icon on the status bar and the Launcher bar which is used to open the Site window.

Site Map A graphical representation of how Web pages relate to each other within a Web site.

Site window A window used when storing and managing Dreamweaver Web site files and folders.

Soft return A shortcut key which forces text to a new line without creating a new paragraph.

Split a cell To divide a cell into multiple rows or columns.

Standard View A Dreamweaver view that is used when you insert a table using the Insert Table icon.

Status bar A bar that is displayed at the bottom of the Dreamweaver window and displays the Window Size pop-up menu, the Launcher Bar and HTML tags.

Storyboard A small sketch that represents each page in a Web site and shows the relationship of each page in the Web site.

Tables Placeholders made up of small boxes called cells which text and graphics are inserted into.

Tabular data Data that is arranged in columns and rows and separated by a delimiter.

Tag selector A location on the status bar that displays HTML tags for the various page components, including tables and cells.

Target The location on a Web page that the browser will display in full view when an internal link is clicked or the frame that will open when a link is clicked.

Templates Web pages that contain the basic layout for similar pages in the site.

Theme Common design elements in a Web site.

Tiled image A small graphic that repeats across and down a Web page, appearing as individual squares or rectangles.

Title bar The bar at the top of a Dreamweaver window that displays the name of the program, the name of the file, and the title of the open page enclosed in parentheses.

Toolbar A bar that contains icons for changing the current work mode of Dreamweaver, previewing Web pages, debugging Web pages, and options for file management.

Transparent backgrounds A background comprised of transparent pixels, rather than pixels of a color, resulting in images that blend easily on a Web page background.

Unordered lists Lists of items that do not need to be placed in a specific order and are usually preceded by bullets.

Vector-based graphics Graphics based on mathematical formulas rather than pixels.

View Options A toolbar icon that activates the Options menu.

Visited links Links that have been previously clicked, or visited. The default color for visited links is purple.

Web design program A program that allows you to create dynamic interactive Web pages incorporating many types of components, such as text, images, hyperlinks, animation, sounds, and video.

Web safe colors Colors that will display consistently in all browsers, and on Macintosh, Windows, and Unix platforms.

Web server A computer that is connected to the Internet with a static (permanent) IP (Internet Protocol) address

Web site A group of related Web pages that are linked together and share a common interface and design.

White space An area on a Web page that is not filled with text or graphics

Work area The document window, the menu bar, the toolbar, inspectors and panels.

WYSIWYG An acronym for What You See Is What You Get, meaning that the way a page appears in the Dreamweaver window will be the same as in the browser window.

Index

Index

Index